PRISONERS OF THE MAHDI

Books by Byron Farwell

PRISONERS OF THE MAHDI

BURTON
A Biography of Sir Richard Francis Burton

THE MAN WHO PRESUMED
A Biography of Stanley

PRISONERS
OF THE MAHDI

*The story of the Mahdist Revolt which frustrated
Queen Victoria's designs on the Sudan, humbled Egypt, and led to
the fall of Khartoum, the death of Gordon, and Kitchener's
victory at Omdurman fourteen years later*

BYRON FARWELL

HARPER & ROW, PUBLISHERS
NEW YORK AND EVANSTON

TO RUTH
my wife

Contents

Acknowledgements

The author wishes to thank the following for their help and co-operation:

Imam El Hadi Abdel Rahman El Mahdi; Lt.-Col. H. S. Francis, O.B.E., Curator of the Royal Engineers Museum, Brompton Barracks, Chatham; Faisal Mohammed Abdel Rahman; A. R. Nasri, Librarian of the University of Khartoum; Richard Hill, School of Oriental Studies, University of Durham; Dr. Robert T. Hatt, P. M. Holt, David Dwynne Jones and Alexander Skinner.

Also, Mrs George Bambridge, Methuen & Co. Ltd, the Macmillan Co. of Canada Ltd and Doubleday & Co. Inc. for permission to reproduce one stanza from 'Fuzzy Wuzzy' by Rudyard Kipling, from *Barrack Room Ballads*.

Foreword

This is a history in biographical form; or rather, it is the story of several men's lives in terms of one important event: that fragment of history called the Mahdiya. The main course of events during the Mahdiya is outlined, but the campaigns in the eastern Sudan, the Mahdist war against Abyssinia, the pressures on Emin Pasha in Equatoria, interesting though they are, were on the fringes of the Mahdist Empire and each is a story unto itself, unrelated in most ways to the main action in the central Sudan. I have therefore made no attempt to deal with them fully. The story of the conquest of Darfur is told at some length, not only because it concerns one of the most interesting characters involved but because it also illustrates in a general way the pattern in other border areas.

In its broad outlines, the political history of the Sudan in the final quarter of the last century follows a familiar pattern; hardly a year now passes in which, to our astonishment, this pattern is not being repeated in some part of the world: political administration creates a situation disliked by those being administered and a bold man arises to exploit the discontent; when successful, as in the Sudan, the bold man or his successors create their own brand of discontent and are themselves overthrown, usually with violence, by internal or external forces.

The circumstances surrounding each repetition of the pattern vary, of course, with the time and place, and the drama that unrolled in the Sudan during the Mahdiya and the events leading up to it had some peculiar features. It was rare, for example, in the last century for barbarism to triumph over civilization, because civilization had more destructive weapons and did not hesitate to use them. In the Sudan less than one hundred years ago, spears triumphed over Remington rifles and even machine guns, at least for a while.

Today the civilized portion of the world is fast shrinking, despite the contrary impression fostered by new nations. Triumphs of barbarians over civilized men are no longer rare. Educated politicians in primitive countries can easily convince their western counterparts that they speak for their illiterate countrymen. As few Europeans or Americans have ever seen a barbarian, they tend to think of them only as simple folk who have not had the advantages

of schooling. Victorian Britons were firmly convinced that barbarous people must be ruled by Europeans, preferably Britons,
just as Americans today are convinced that barbarians can be
made civilized, i.e. made like Americans, through charity, medicine, political independence and schools, provided by, and preferably administered by, Americans.

In the last quarter of the last century events in the Sudan were
of intense interest to Englishmen; of less interest in the United
States, whose citizens were preoccupied with killing Indians,
settling the west and solving the problems involved in recovering
from their civil war. In Europe, and particularly in England, much
was written about the Sudan when popular attention was focused
on it, but after the reconquest of the Sudan Britain's attention
quickly shifted to the Boer War, which began the following year,
then to the Boxer Rebellion and World War I. Memories of the
Sudan and interest in it waned. Today most Englishmen know
about Gordon at Khartoum; they know something, too, of
Kitchener's reconquest of the Sudan. But between the fall of
Khartoum in 1885 and the reconquest of 1898 few Britons know
more than Americans about the events in the Sudan: at most,
Kipling's 'Fuzzy-Wuzzy' and perhaps the motion picture based on
A. E. W. Mason's novel, *The Four Feathers*. If more is remembered,
it is of actions around Suakin, not of the events in Omdurman,
capital and heart of the Mahdist state. Yet it was at Omdurman
that life under the Mahdi and the Khalifa was both most dramatic
and most historically interesting. Most of this book is concerned
with this place at this time.

The European prisoners of the Mahdi and the Khalifa who survived their ordeal did so because they learned to be patient in the
face of frustrations. It is apparently a virtue which all who deal
with the Sudan, however remotely, must acquire. Eight years ago
I first set foot in the Sudan. A foot was about all. I disembarked
at the Khartoum airport in the middle of the night, excited by the
prospect of seeing Khartoum and Omdurman in the morning.
While passing through customs it was discovered that a certain
stamp was missing in my passport and I was calmly told that I
could not enter the country. I argued and pleaded with officials
who were completely unconcerned. When asked where I could get
the stamp, a Sudanese customs official shrugged and blandly
suggested I go back to Cairo for it. Cairo was 1,200 miles away! I
did not get into the country and was forced to fly on to Nairobi.
From that time until the last two chapters of the completed manu-

script were mislaid in New York for several months and assorted portions of it were lost in the Channel Islands (improbable as that sounds) I have learned to live with frustration if not quite to accept it.

Not the least of the exasperating problems faced in writing this book has been the attempt to secure accurate information about the people, places and events I wanted to describe. All the facts and figures given here are as exact as it is possible for me to give them, but the statistics belie a part of the very essence of the Sudan: its vagueness. Facts about the Sudan always appear a bit blurred, figures not quite exact. There is a great indefiniteness about every aspect of the country. Its very name is ambiguous. In one sense the name applies to the entire region south of the Sahara and the Libyan Desert, stretching the width of Africa. Until recently there was a French Sudan and an Anglo-Egyptian Sudan. Now the French Sudan no longer exists and the Anglo-Egyptian Sudan is the Republic of the Sudan. Seventy years ago the name was spelled 'Soudan' in English, as it is still in French; now, for no known reason, it is spelled differently. Names of people, places and tribes change or disappear. Sometimes there are many different names for the same person, place or thing: the Suri tribe on the Abyssinian border is also called Churi, Shuri, Dhuri, Dhuäk and Kapoeta. To add to the confusion, the people of the Nuba hills (sometimes called mountains) are not Nubians but Nubas, although Nubians from Nubia (also called Kosh and Cush) are also Sudanese; people from Dongola are not Dongolas, but Donagla (singular: Dongolawi); the people from Berber are not Berbers, of course (these live in the Atlas mountains), but Berberines or Barabara. Of the events that took place in the Sudan less than a hundred years ago during the Turkiya and Mahdiya, vastly different estimates exist for the size of armies, numbers of guns, population of towns and the distance between any two points. There is scarcely a date given in this book, from the birth of the Mahdi to the death of Hicks Pasha, that could not be disputed. Today there is even disagreement over the colour of the flags carried by the Mahdi's khalifas, although these must have been seen and well known to tens of thousands of people.

This vagueness about the Sudan affects not only the Sudanese, but Europeans and Americans as well; the only difference being that while the Sudanese accept indefiniteness, Europeans and Americans confuse by pretending to be exact. Sir George Arthur in his two-volume biography of Kitchener says very precisely that

Kitchener received his orders to march into the Sudan 'at 3 o'clock' on the morning of 13 March; Winston Churchill in *The River War* says Kitchener received his orders 'shortly before midnight' on 12 March. In seven authoritative sources consulted regarding the size of the country five different numbers were found, ranging from 950,950 square miles to 1,000,000 square miles – Switzerland and Portugal would both fit into the difference between these estimates.

In writing about any part of the Arab world in English there is always the difficulty of transliteration of Arabic words with their elusive vowels into Roman characters. Scholars have developed several systems for accomplishing this which appear to be useful if one is familiar with Arabic sounds or wishes to transcribe the word back into exact Arabic, but these seem to be of little value to the average reader who is unfamiliar with the language. The Victorians spelled the words as they sounded to them. As no two people heard quite the same sounds there were usually a number of variant spellings, but at least they had a name or word that an Englishman could pronounce and perhaps remember. I have followed this system, preferring, for example, Abdullahi to 'Abd Allāhi. It has been necessary to use a certain number of Sudanese and Turkish words for which no exact translation exists. These are explained on their first use, but a glossary is also included in the back of the book.

I have again followed Victorian practice in referring to the people from the southern Sudan as Blacks and to the followers of the Mahdi as Dervishes, as they were called by all Europeans and as they called themselves until forbidden by the Mahdi, who preferred to call them 'ansar'. There were, and are, a number of orders of dervishes and the followers of the Mahdi were not, strictly speaking, dervishes. Where the term is used to denote the followers of the Mahdi, as is usually the case here, the word is capitalized.

This book can lay no great claim to original scholarship; there is little here that has not been printed in some form, somewhere, before. Most of the story is told through the eyes of three Europeans who all wrote accounts of their experiences on which I have relied heavily. There is a certain amount of material in Arabic from this period in the form of letters and proclamations, but not being an Arabic scholar I have made little use of this material except where it has been translated into English. My greatest use of it has been in describing the fate of Hicks Pasha and his army, where I have used the unpublished diary of Abbas Bey, secretary to the governor-general of the Sudan, who accompanied the expedition. This diary has a curious history. It was obviously taken from the body or the belongings of Abbas Bey after the battle of Shaykan. It was found fourteen years later on the body of a Dervish after the battle of Omdurman. There is no explanation of why or how it was preserved or why a Dervish should carry it into battle with him.

I have reported a number of conversations and, as imagined conversations are the favourite device of the historical novelist, my use of conversations requires some explanation. None of the speeches quoted were invented by me; all were reported by one of the speakers. Nevertheless, it is doubtful if the exact words quoted were used. I have repeated them, however, whenever it seemed to me that they accurately reported the subject and tenor of a conversation and because the person who recorded them was often able to convey much about the character of the person speaking and sometimes, unwittingly, about himself. Where quotations have been made from writings or reported conversations in English, no word has been changed. But in cases where other languages have been involved, such as a conversation held in Arabic and reported ten years later in German and then translated into English, I have taken the liberty of altering the syntax in an attempt to make the conversation read more easily without, however, in any way altering the sense of the speech. Even here I have made as few changes as possible.

Les Courtils
Petit Saconnex
Geneva, Switzerland

8 September 1966

Introduction

The Sudan is the largest country in Africa. It is larger than France, Germany, Austria, Italy, Spain, Portugal, Switzerland, Greece, Great Britain and the Benelux countries combined. Yet for all its size and strategic location, bracketing both the Arab world and black Africa, it is a neglected land, a political and economic backwater, protected by its swamps and deserts from world history. Only once was the attention of the civilized world focused upon it. This book is about that brief period, less than a hundred years ago, when the Sudan was aflame with such violence that Europe watched it with astonishment and alarm. It is called the Mahdiya.

The Sudan's peculiar topography has had the greatest influence on its history. For most Europeans and Americans the Nile is associated with Egypt, yet the Nile belongs to the Sudan. Three-fourths of its great length is in the Sudan, as are all its important tributaries: the Blue Nile, the Atbara, the Bahr el Ghazal and the Sobat. Most of the cataracts of the Nile are in northern Sudan, and in the south is the sudd, a dense mass of papyrus stems and aquatic grass that chokes the river for more than 300 miles. Were it not for these two great barriers to navigation, the history of the Sudan would be vastly different. Given the resources, the energy and the will, the Sudanese could choke Egypt to death by depriving her of the Nile's life-giving water. But the Sudan needs that stream of water running into Egypt, for it is her cultural and economic lifeline. As Winston Churchill said: 'The Soudan is joined to Egypt by the Nile, as a diver is connected with the surface by his air-pipe.'

The Nile's barriers are not the only obstacles to contact with the outside world. Other aspects of the Sudan's physical geography combine to isolate this vast land: a waterless waste to the north, swamps and morasses in the south; to the east desert, then a mountain barrier and to the west the entire length of the Sahara. North and south the land is hot. Nearly all the drama described in this book took place under a burning sun, for the northern Sudan has an exceptionally high proportion of cloudless days. At Khartoum, the capital, the mean daily temperature in June is 93·4° F, and even in January, the coolest month, the mean temperature is 74·7° F. The average monthly high is never below 90° F.

There is a sharp division, both geographical and cultural, between the north and the south in the Sudan. The band of savannah around the twelfth parallel which separates the desert reaches of the northern two-thirds of the country and the swamps and jungles of the south is very narrow, making a striking contrast between the two parts of the country. The south is wet and green; the north dry and yellow. The south has a heavy tropical rainfall; in the north it seldom rains and most of the people must depend on the rising and falling of the Nile to cultivate such crops as can be raised along the narrow strips of land by the river. There are, then, two Sudans, and two general types of Sudanese: the northern Sudanese who is part of Arabic and Islamic Africa, and the southern Sudanese who is part of negroid and pagan Africa. The northerner and the southerner are now, and have always been, in different stages of cultural, economic and political development. The two types of culture have always clashed. Perhaps they always will, for the realities of physical geography have separated them too long and the meetings of the two peoples in the past have not been happy.

The Arabic name for the country, Bilad-es-Sudan, means 'land of the Blacks'. The people referred to are the southern Sudanese: the Dinka, Nuer, Shilluk and other Nilotes who live in the provinces of Equatoria, Upper Nile and Bahr el Ghazal. These are the Blacks, people with a strong Hamitic element mixed with the Negro blood who are quite unlike the West African Negroes and their descendants in America; they are tall with clear-cut features, thin lips, high foreheads and high-bridged, but generally unflared, noses. They are proud tribes with their own complex social structure who resent outside influences and want only to be left alone with their cattle, the most important spiritual, psychological and economic factor in their lives. Unfortunately, from at least as far back as 2900 B.C. until a few years ago, they were preyed upon by slave raiders, for in captivity these Blacks made fine workers and excellent soldiers.

Through intercourse with their slaves the northern Sudanese long ago acquired a dark colouring, and most are brown or black. There are 115 languages spoken in the Sudan, but most of the northern people speak various Arabic dialects. Except for the family, the basic social unit is the tribe, and even the settled communities of the north are organized into the tribal hierarchies of nomadic Arabs with sheikhs, omdas and mazirs. During the period of Egyptian rule, the Turkiya (1821–85), an artificial governmental structure was imposed on the country, with a governor-general as the ruler and under him governors of provinces and then mudirs, governors of districts or towns, but for the Sudanese the tribe was still the most important political unit. Today there are fifty-six 'tribal groups' in the Sudan which include 597 separate tribes. In the last century there were probably not less, although their numbers were undoubtedly smaller, for in spite of all that has happened to the Sudan in the last 150 years the tribal structure has changed remarkably little. There are the tribes that live along the banks of the Nile, non-nomadic and living from planted crops or in the towns and villages along the river's banks, Khartoum, Dongola, Berber, Kosti; there are the cattle-owning tribes, the Baggara, from western Kordofan and Darfur who ride bulls, not as a sport but as a means of transportation; there are camel-owning tribes, nomads who wander the wastes of northern Kordofan searching for water and pasturage for their camels; and in the north-east are the three Beja tribes, a distinct race of unknown origin, and including the Hadendowa, the 'Fuzzy-Wuzzies' of Kipling's poem. Such early history of the Sudan as exists concerns these northern Sudanese tribes and those who invaded them – always from the north.

The first known Sudanese kingdom was that of Meroe, with its capital at Napata, near present-day Merowe. It began around 750 B.C. and lasted almost a hundred years. There have been a number since then. In Darfur ('land of the Furs'), the westernmost province of the Sudan, the Fur sultanate lasted, except for comparatively brief periods during the Turkiya and Mahdiya, for 300 years: from 1596 until 1916. The Fung kingdom, with its capital in Sennar, once extended from Abyssinia to Dongola and from the Red Sea to the borders of Darfur. It, too, lasted for 300 years until it fell to the invading armies of Mohammed Ali, commanded by his son Ismail Pasha, in 1820, marking the beginning of the Turkiya.

No one knows when Christianity first came to the Sudan, but Christians, seeking escape from Roman persecution in Egypt, often fled here, and for centuries the northern Sudan – at least in the more populous areas along the banks of the Nile – was Christian. But in A.D. 640 the Arabs conquered Egypt and the influence of Islam seeped southwards up the Nile and across the Red Sea to the Sudan's eastern border. For most Africans, Islam has always been a more appealing religion than Christianity, and in the Sudan Christianity disappeared until the end of the nineteenth century. But Islam in the Sudan has always been complicated by local customs and beliefs and prone to sire heresies. Fanatical movements have often swept the country, splitting Islam into militant sects (called tarikas) filled with holy men of all sorts, fikis, dervishes and ulema. Although in Islamic countries religion has always played a more important part in the daily lives of the people than in Christian countries, at least since the Middle Ages, it appears to have always been the dominant interest in the lives of many, perhaps most, Sudanese. Even today, in the government of the Republic of the Sudan there is a minister for religious affairs.

After religion, animals are the most important element in the life of the Sudanese, perhaps more so in the last century than now when one per cent of the land is planted with crops. The official *Sudan Almanac* lists 2,000,000 camels, 9,100,000 cattle, 8,660,000 sheep and (exactly?) 6,854 goats. All the cattle are in the south; all the camels in the north. The average Sudanese is indifferent to animals which do not supply him with food or transport, but the country is rich in wild life. In addition to elephants, lions, giraffes, crocodiles, hippopotami and other common central African animals, a number of rare animals are found in the Sudan: the giant derby elan, the handsome Nile lechwe, the sitatunga, whose long, divergent hoofs fit it for swamp life, and the white rhinoceros.

There are no statistics on the population of the Sudan during the Mahdiya (1885–98), but it has been estimated at between two and three million, although perhaps there were more. Today the population is between eleven and thirteen million, about 5 per cent of whom are literate. All but a small handful of Sudanese are poor, for their land has little to offer the outside world. During the last century its chief exports were slaves, ivory, ostrich feathers and gum arabic. Today slavery is forbidden, there are not enough elephants left, and there is no market for ostrich feathers. The Sudan still supplies four-fifths of the world's needs for gum arabic and now cotton is grown extensively, particularly in the Gezira district between the Blue and White Niles, but the *per capita* income is only $74 (less than £27). Such fertile land as exists is subject to droughts and plagues of locusts (two varieties: desert locust and the curiously named hairy-chested locust) which create famine. Cattle are afflicted by tsetse fly, rinderpest, foot-and-mouth disease, rabies, mange, worms and strangler. The people themselves are attacked by sleeping sickness, guinea worm, malaria, yellow fever, leprosy, bilharziasis and kwashiorkor. Even today, the life expectancy of a Sudanese at birth is only thirty-three years; it must have been considerably less seventy years ago. The Sudan is, and has always been, a harsh and primitive land.

Many Europeans who have visited this grim land have been appalled by what they saw. G. W. Steevens, who went there in 1898, thus described the northern Sudan:

Nothing grows green. Only yellow halfa grass to make you stumble, and sapless mimosa to tear your eyes; dompalms that mock with wooden fruit, and Sodom apples that lure with flatulent poison. For beasts it has tarantulas and scorpions and serpents, devouring white ants, and every kind of loathsome bug that flies or crawls. Its people are naked and dirty, ignorant and besotted. It is a quarter of a continent of sheer squalor. Overhead the pitiless furnace of the sun, under foot the never-easing treadmill of the sand, dust in the throat, tuneless singing in the ears, searing flame in the eye – the Sudan is a God-accursed wilderness, and empty limbo of torment for ever and ever.

The southern Sudan was even worse, if we believe Ewart S. Grogan, the first man to go through Africa from the Cape to Cairo:

In the course of a chequered career I have seen many unwholesome spots; but for God-forsaken, dry-sucked, fly-blown wilderness, commend me to the Upper Nile; a desolation of desolations, an infernal region, a howling waste of weed, mosquitoes, flies, and fever, backed by a groaning waste of thorns and stones – waterless and waterlogged. I have passed through it, and have now no fear for the hereafter.

General Charles Gordon, who lived in both the north and the south and who played such an important role in the history of the Sudan, said:

No one who has ever lived in the Sudan can escape the reflection 'what a useless possession is this land'. Few men also can stand its fearful monotony and deadly climate.

All these views, of course, are by Europeans of another age. For a modern Sudanese view, here is a quotation from the official *Directory of the Republic of the Sudan* under the section 'Tourist Attractions':

The Sudan offers many and varied attractions to the tourist. . . . A motor car tour (preferably with two vehicles) along the roads of the Sudan will provide a holiday of never-to-be-forgotten thrills . . . it becomes a test of motoring ability without parallel anywhere. The traveller must keep to the main road unless he wishes to encounter animals for whose presence he may be unprepared, and in some places it is necessary to keep to the beaten track in order to avoid risk of exposure to sleeping sickness or other diseases. Spare parts, spare tyres and tubes are essential, and petrol consumption has to be reliably gauged, since petrol filling stations do not exist in large numbers. . . .

When Egypt ruled the Sudan, Egyptian soldiers and officials usually regarded an assignment there as a punishment post. The Sudanese Arabs themselves have a saying that when Allah made the Sudan, he laughed. Yet, there were Europeans who went to the Sudan and found their life's work there; Europeans who loved the land could not resist returning, even after the most harrowing experiences there, for in spite of everything, it is a fascinating country.

Whatever one's sentiments on colonialism in general or about Egyptian rule in the Sudan, it is impossible not to admire the spirit, enterprise and sheer endurance of those individual Europeans who came to rule, teach, preach or explore the Sudan. A few, of course, were running away from something or someone, but most came with an honest spirit of adventure and a sincere desire to create something good out of a crude and barbarous land. The Europeans of the last century who went to live in the Sudan had diverse personalities, but they were nearly all individualists; not eccentrics necessarily, but men whose characters were somehow attuned to Sudanese life and who usually found there, even under the most trying of circumstances, that which they went to seek.

Part 1

The Rise of the Mahdi

The Sudan in the latter half of the nineteenth century.

I

The Mahdi of Islam

He sprang from the mud of the Nile and, although he never strayed more than 200 miles from its banks, he successfully defied the might of Great Britain, then the most powerful nation on earth, carving for himself a million square miles from the sprawling Ottoman Empire and establishing the first and only African nation ever to win independence from a foreign power by virtue of its own force of arms, courage and abilities. He angered Queen Victoria, nearly toppled a British government, made Europeans his slaves, defeated the Egyptian army, and founded a religious cult. In an age of repeating rifles, artillery and machine guns, his warriors held back the forces of the civilized world for fourteen years with spears, swords and a determined barbaric fanaticism. His name was Mohammed Ahmed, but he was called El Mahdi – the messiah.

On 10 November 1845 the saviour was born, the son of a carpenter, on Darar (or Labab), an island in the Nile near Dongola, between the third and fourth cataracts. Later the family moved to Karreri, twelve miles north of Khartoum. His father's name was Abdullah, or rather Sayid Abdullah, it being the family vanity that they were descendants of the Prophet Mohammed. As is common among the Danagla, he was probably of Nubian and Arabic ancestry, with perhaps an admixture of Egyptian, Turkish and other blood. Sayid Abdullah was a deeply religious man, well versed in the Koran, who never missed one of the five daily prayers. He fathered four sons: Mohammed, Ahmed, Mohammed Ahmed and Abdullah, in that order, and died before the last was born. After his death the children and their mother were taken by their uncle, Ahmed Sharif, to Abba, another island in the Nile opposite El Kawa, 125 miles south of Khartoum. All four boys were raised to be boat-builders like their uncle, but Mohammed Ahmed was the studious one, the religious one, the family prodigy.

At an early age he began to sit at the feet of the *fikih*, the religious teachers, learning suras (chapters) from the Koran. It is said that by the age of nine he had memorized the entire book. He had also learned his family genealogy and could recite, 'I am the Sayid Mohammed Ahmed, son of the Sayid Abdullah, son of Fahl, who was the son of Abdullah, son of Mohammed . . .'. As the list went back into antiquity, distinguished names began to appear: Yunes, Othman, Abdel Kader, the Khalifa Ali and Hassan the Martyr. Included, too, was that other Hassan, called El Askari, from whom, it was believed, the twelfth Imam of Islam, the Expected One, the Mahdi, would descend.

As a boy Mohammed Ahmed must have seen a fair cross-section of his countrymen and listened to much discussion of social and political events, for Abba was, quite literally, in the main current of Sudanese life; the Nile was the highway, and on it travelled ivory merchants, slavers, government officials, rich and poor, the op-pressed and the oppressors. El Kawa, across the way on the eastern bank, was a river port and the boat-builders on Abba were fre-quently called upon to repair nuggars, feluccas, dahabeahs and other Nile craft. The wooded island was also a refuge for those hiding from the hated 'Turk'.

There was constant talk of the 'Turk', not only among refugees, but among merchants, peasants, tribesmen and others, for few were unaffected by his tyranny. The term 'Turk' applied to anyone with light skin who wore a fez, whether he was a genuine Turk, a Syrian, an Albanian, a European or, as was generally the case, an Egyptian. For it was Egypt which ruled the Sudan, and she did not rule it well. It was the Egyptian who gave the evil repute to the word 'Turk'. He took much and gave little; he regarded the Sudan as a land to plunder rather than to administer. He came with soldiers to collect the taxes, taking enough for the government, enough for his superiors and much for himself. Sometimes he took only for himself: money, slaves, women, whatever was of value or gave him pleasure. The hippopotamus hide whip, the curbash, was always in his hand and the rifles of his soldiers were always behind him. If a village failed to pay its taxes, he took its women and used them as concubines for his soldiers until the money was found.

Since the armies of Mohammed Ali conquered the Sudan in 1820–2, Egyptian rule had blighted the land. Sir Samuel Baker, writing of the Sudan in 1870, noted its continuing deterioration:

> I observe with dismay a frightful change in the features of the country between Berber and the capital since my former visit. The rich soil on the banks of the river which had a few years since been highly culti-vated, was abandoned. . . . There was not a dog to howl for a lost

master. Industry had vanished; oppression had driven the inhabitants from the soil.

But as a boy, Mohammed Ahmed was more interested in the spiritual life than in the social and political conditions of the Sudan. In 1861, when only sixteen years old, he became a dervish and a student of the mystical Sufi doctrine. There were – and are still – many orders of dervishes; they correspond, very roughly, to the Christian monastic orders, but are more informal and without the sexual taboos. To occidentals, the best known are probably the *Muradiya*, who crowd the bazaars of India, and the *Maulawiyah*, or whirling dervishes of Egypt. In the Sudan, where Black Africa meets Arab Africa and where African fetishism, magic and superstition often became entangled with Islam, there were perhaps more dervish orders than in any other Muslim country.

Mohammed Ahmed was a disciple of a number of religious sheikhs before he joined himself to a tarika, or sect, known as the Summaniya Tarika. The leader of this tarika, the 'Master of the Prayer Rug', was Sheikh Mohammed Sherif wad Nur al-Dayim, who resided in Khartoum, a holy man of great local fame who possessed the prayer rug of the founder of the order and was a member of a family noted for its many holy men. The Summaniya Tarika was a strict order, but, as it developed, it was not puritanical enough for Mohammed Ahmed.

When Sheikh Mohammed Sherif's son came of age, the Sheikh declared that a feast would be held in connection with the circumcision ceremony. All the members of the order were invited, and the Sheikh announced that for the glory of the occasion the usual rules against worldly pleasures would be relaxed. There would be music and song, dancing girls and dancing boys, and good, rich food. Mohammed Ahmed alone objected. He protested so vigorously and at such length that Sheikh Mohammed Sherif turned upon him and expelled him from the order, accusing him of the sin of rebelling against his spiritual master and violating his oath of obedience. This was a staggering blow to the devout young dervish.

On the day of the circumcision feast, while Sheikh Mohammed Sherif and his disciples were making the final preparations for the celebration, Mohammed Ahmed was in the home of his cousin; a stout, elderly man who hired out camels for a living. The cousin must have been perplexed by what Mohammed Ahmed asked him to do; being a worldly, realistic man, he doubtless protested. But in the end he did what his young cousin asked, and he helped to fasten on Mohammed Ahmed's neck and arm the grotesque and painful shebba. This was a heavy wooden pole with a fork at one end that was often used on slaves whom the slave driver feared might try to escape. The fork was wedged against the throat and held fast by thongs tied behind the neck. Then the pole was raised to shoulder height and the victim's extended arm was bound to it. Properly positioned, the Adam's apple was so compressed into the crotch of the pole that if the arm was lowered the man would choke. There was also a refinement to this torture which Mohammed Ahmed insisted be added: his bare arm was bound to the pole with thongs of fresh antelope hide; as the thongs dried and shrank, they would cut into the flesh of his wrist and arm. Thus bound to the shebba, the penitent set off, an uninvited guest to the feast, for the house of his former master, chanting as he went the ninety-nine names of Allah: er Rahman, er Rahim, el Kerim – the Compassionate, the Merciful, the Generous, the Clement, the All-Seeing, the All-Hearing, the All-Powerful, the Avenger, the Forgiver. . . .

When Sheikh Mohammed Sherif came riding home from the mosque at the head of a procession of friends, disciples, musicians and dancers, all in the highest of spirits and ready for the feast, he found stretched out in the dust before his doorstep the yoked and repentant Dongolawi. The holy leader of the Sammaniya Tarika held up his hand, the musicians stopped, the crowd fell silent. Now was the moment for forgiveness. But the Sheikh was furious. No one heard what Mohammed Ahmed said, or if he spoke at all, but everyone heard the Sheikh. 'Miserable Dongolawi!' he shouted. 'Traitor!' Turning to the crowd in his rage, he cried, 'How true is the saying "A man from Dongola is a devil in human shape!".' There was nothing more Mohammed Ahmed could do. Humiliated and rejected, he went back to the island of Abba.

The date of his ignominious dismissal from the Summaniya Tarika and his return to Abba is unknown, but already he had two wives, both named Fatima, one of whom was the daughter of his uncle. They kept his clothes clean – for he had a horror of un-cleanliness – and sewed neat patches on his robe when it was torn It must have been difficult to keep his clothes clean on Abba, for he did not live in a house but in a cave-like hole on the bank of the Nile. There his wives brought him his meals, durra porridge or fish in his wooden dervish begging-bowl. In front of the cave he built a crude shelter, four stakes supporting a thatch of palm leaves. In its shade he placed the only piece of furniture he allowed himself: his angareb, a low bed consisting of a wood frame with interlacing hide thongs such as even the poorest possess in the Sudan.

He was described at this period as being a tall, broad-shouldered but lean man with a light-coloured, birthmarked face framed by a deep black beard. He had large, sparkling eyes, full lips and a V-shaped aperture between his front teeth (a good luck sign called a *falja*). His dress was usually a simple dervish robe of coarse cotton cloth with a belt and skull-cap of palm straw. Those who knew him spoke of his peculiar smile, which he often wore even when displeased. Sometimes he worked in his uncle's fields or with his brothers in the boat-yard, but most of the time he remained in his cave, praying and mortifying his flesh. As frequently happens among the religious, petulance was mistaken for penitence and Mohammed Ahmed began to gain a reputation as a holy man. As his fame grew, the story reached the ears of the aged Sheikh El Korashi (or Al Qurashi), head of a rival order of dervishes who, while following the rules of the Summaniya Tarika, did not acknowledge the leadership of Mohammed Sherif. Sheikh El Korashi sent one of his dervishes to Mohammed Ahmed, inviting him to become a follower and promising him honours and dignities. Mohammed Ahmed accepted, but before leaving Abba to give his allegiance to Sheikh El Korashi, another messenger arrived from Sheikh Mohammed Sherif. The messenger presented him with a beautifully written diploma and informed him that he had been re-instated in the order; he was even given the privilege of enrolling novices. Mohammed Ahmed replied that 'The wretched Dongolawi does not wish to discredit his former master'. He set off for the Blue Nile to kiss the hand of El Korashi at El Messellemiya.

Mohammed Ahmed now began the life of a wandering dervish, begging-bowl and iron-tipped staff in hand and quills and inkstand tied to his belt. To occidental eyes such men appear to be simply beggars, but in primitive societies they serve a purpose, fill a need. They are priest and scribe and doctor to the poor, and it is usually the poor who fill their wooden bowls with food. Mohammed Ahmed wandered through the towns and villages of the Sudan, no one knows exactly where, but he appears to have become well known in the Gezira district between the Blue Nile and the White, east as far as the Abyssinian border, and west into parts of the province of Kordofan.

It was apparently during this period that he first formulated and preached the doctrine that was to become famous throughout the Sudan. It is difficult to say how much, if any, inspiration

Mohammed Ahmed derived from the other religious reform movements of the nineteenth-century Islamic world – certainly he knew of the Senussi in Cyrenaica – but his teachings, like those of many of the other religious reformers, were based on a return to the basic tenets of the Koran and a clearing away from it of the moss of myth, superstition and legend which over the centuries had come to obscure the words of the Prophet. Religious reformation usually begins this way, of course, and usually ends by simply substituting new dogma for old, with political considerations and local situations shaping the dogma into patterns acceptable to the potential adherents.

Mohammed Ahmed preached a double doctrine, positive and negative, based upon the rejection of aliens and their ways, and upon the improvement of self. It had the virtue of simplicity and the appeal of the topical. In brief, he told his listeners to hate the Turk, and to follow Mohammed Ahmed's own path to heaven, which he called simply 'The Way'. There was a slight difficulty in condemning the country's rulers, for the Egyptians and most of the 'Turks' were Muslims, and even many wealthy Sudanese, particularly in Khartoum, had adopted 'Turkish ways'. But Mohammed Ahmed made it easy to hate the Turk and to distinguish him from the true believer: the Turk, although professing to be a Muslim, was a glutton, he drank wine, he oppressed other Muslims; therefore, he was not a true believer. He who dressed like a Turk and lived like a Turk, he was a Turk! Mohammed Ahmed told his followers: 'Put aside everything which has the slightest resemblance to the manners and customs of Turks and infidels.'

It is doubtful if Mohammed Ahmed realized at first the political implications of this half of his doctrine. After all, slavery and tyranny were a way of life. The Sudanese had known centuries of oppression; the idea of revolt did not come easily. But the dervish was, consciously or unconsciously, exploiting the natural antipathy between native and foreigner, rich and poor, peasant and city-dweller, ruled and rulers. Not only did he preach hatred of those already hated but he gave his hearers something rare and precious, hope, by showing them the road to salvation, 'The Way.'

The second half of Mohammed Ahmed's doctrine in turn had two parts, one positive and one negative. There were three easily avoided vices: envy, pride and neglect of the five daily prayers. There were six virtues, easily adhered to by a downtrodden, poor but hardy people: humility, meekness of spirit, endurance, eating little, drinking little and making visits to the tombs of holy men.

In this time and in this place, it was a powerful doctrine, as similarly framed doctrines have proved powerful in other times and other places. It was a clever creed for a strong man to preach to potential followers, and Mohammed Ahmed was both strong and clever; he was also sincere and devout. Perhaps the appeal of his doctrine surprised him; perhaps the slow realization of its potential frightened him, but his personal thoughts and feelings are unknown.

After a period of wandering and preaching, Mohammed Ahmed returned to Abba to meditate and pray. When Sheikh El Korashi died, Mohammed Ahmed, the most devout of his followers, succeeded him. He went to El Mesellimiya himself to join with the other disciples in building a tomb of mud bricks for their former master over the exact spot where he had died. It was there, by the half-finished wall of the mausoleum with a bucket of wet clay beside him, that Abdullahi Ibn Sayed Mohammed found him. Abdullahi was a Baggara (generic name for members of the cattle-owning tribes of the Sudan) of the Taaisha tribe from Darfur, a race of herdsmen and slave traders quite different from the settled Sudanese who lived along the banks of the two Niles. He was of medium height with a light brown complexion, an aquiline nose, a pockmarked face, well-shaped mouth and a slight moustache and beard, about two years older than Mohammed Ahmed, who was then in his early thirties. Although his father had been a religious man noted in his tribe for his ability to read omens in the desert sands, Abdullahi himself was not particularly interested in religion. He could not even read the Koran. Yet Abdullahi had been searching for some time for Mohammed Ahmed. His father, on his death-bed, had urged him to seek the holy man who lived on an island in the Nile. Abdullahi had been disappointed when he had failed to find Mohammed Ahmed on Abba, but he had continued in his search, and now had found him.

Abdullahi wanted to become Mohammed Ahmed's disciple and servant. The dervish first sent him to fetch water and a prayer rug. When he returned, Mohammed Ahmed took Abdullahi's hands between his own and interlaced them in a manner used in the engagement ceremony between a Sudanese man and woman. Then he made him recite a prayer and asked him if he sincerely turned to Allah with repentance. Abdullahi vowed that he did, and kissed the hand of his new master. Then he swore a great oath: 'In the name of Allah, the great, and of the noble Prophet, on whom be the prayer and the blessing, and as a guide to Allah, praised be his name, I do choose my lord, the Sayid Mohammed Ahmed Ibn

Sayid Abdullah, resolving never to swerve or separate from him. May Allah be my witness!' Three times Abdullahi repeated this oath. Then together the two men recited the *fatiha*, the short opening sura of the Koran often used as a prayer. Their lives were bound together for ever.

When the tomb was finished, Mohammed Ahmed mounted a donkey and started back to Abba. Behind him followed a small retinue of disciples and admirers, including Abdullahi the Baggara, marching in the dust, carrying a huge black flag on which were written verses from the Koran. Mohammed Ahmed did not at first associate with his new Arab disciple, whose dialect and bedouin manners were so different from those of his other followers, but Abdullahi was soon to achieve a position of power second only to Mohammed Ahmed, and eventually even greater.

It was not long after Mohammed Ahmed and his disciples reached Abba that it was announced that Mohammed Ahmed the dervish was the promised mahdi, the 'Expected One', the messiah. Islam, like several other religions, has for centuries carried the legend of a promised messiah, one who would cleanse and restore the faith, redeem its followers and destroy its enemies. It is not mentioned in the Koran, but is based upon a Hadith, one of the traditional sayings of the Prophet. Mohammed Ahmed was not the first to believe that he was that man. In the eighth century there had been a Mohammed el Mahdi, one of the Abbasid caliphs; in the tenth century there had been Obaidallah el Mahdi, first caliph of the Fatimite dynasty in North Africa, for whom was named the once important city of Mahdi in Tunisia; in the twelfth century there was Mohammed Ibn Abdallah ibn Tumart, a Berber who called himself El Mahdi and who founded the Almohades (or Muwahhadis) dynasty; later there was a host of lesser men who had claimed to be the hidden deliverer. Even in Mohammed Ahmed's time the head of the Senussi, a powerful North African Muslim fraternity, was called El Mahdi. Today, the Shi'ah sect believe in a mahdi to come, and this belief forms one of the principal differences between the Shi'ite and Sunnite sects of Islam. There had always been magic in the name of mahdi. Now, among the Sudanese of Mohammed Ahmed's time, there was a need. Mohammed Ahmed possessed all the looked-for attributes: the birthmark on the right cheek, the V-shaped aperture between the teeth, his ancestry – all were regarded as favourable signs that this man was indeed the promised deliverer, the true mahdi.

According to one version of the story, it was Abdullahi who first made the discovery that his master was the Expected One. Today, however, when the memory of the Mahdi is revered and that of Abdullahi is cursed as the author of all the evils of the Mahdiya, mahdists deny Abdullahi this honour. According to Imam El Hadi Abdelrahman el Mahdi, grandson of the Mahdi and now leader of the religious sect he founded, 'The Khalifa Abdullahi had no role in the announcement of Mahdism because this was done by the Mahdi himself through letters and personal messengers.' Imam El Hadi gives this version:

It is said that in 1860, the Mahdi disclosed to his devoted tutor Sheikh Mohammed Kheir his inner feelings that he was the expected Mahdi. 'Promise me on the Koran', he said, 'that this shall be a secret between us until the ordained time.' After leaving the Khalwa [centre of religious teaching] of Sheikh Mohammed Kheir, the Mahdi has [sic] toured round the important Khalwas of the Sudan and is known to have conversed in religious matters with all the learned religious teachers and Tariga Sheikhs [leaders of religious sects] of the time. During these tours the Mahdi is said to have spoken of Mahdism to those he fully trusted. Some of his famous friends and tutors such as Sheikh Mohammed Sherif Nur El Dayim and Sheikh El Korashi, and close members of his family has [sic] known and recognized his claim to Mahdism: this was as early as 1878. The open declaration of Mahdism was not until 29 June 1881. In August 1881, however, he declared the matter to the Government by telegram sent from El Kawa.[1]

Imam El Hadi's account appears a probable and natural sequence of events. The public announcement was a bold step, and it captured the imagination of Muslims throughout the Sudan.

The Mahdi invited all the important sheikhs in the Sudan to come to Abba. Some came from as far as Darfur, westernmost province of the Sudan, and Kordofan, and there were a few from the Hadendowa tribe by the Red Sea. At this assembly, on 29 June 1881, Mohammed Ahmed first openly proclaimed himself the Mahdi of Islam. Here, for the first time, the new creed was recited by Abdullahi. It added a line to the old creed, and some repeated it after him: 'There is no god but Allah. And Mohammed is the Prophet of Allah. And Mohammed el Mahdi is the successor of Allah's Prophet!'

The word spread that a dervish on the island of Abba was calling himself the Mahdi, it floated down the Nile, from boat to boat, from boat to bank; the news was carried along the caravan routes through the breadth of northern and central Sudan, to each

[1] Letter to the author.

tribesman and villager. It was discussed by the women at the wells and the men in the coffee houses, and finally the government in Khartoum was forced to recognize the disturbance. It is said that Sheikh Mohammed Sherif, who had cast Mohammed Ahmed from the Summaniya Tarika, first brought the matter to the attention of Rauf Pasha, the Governor-General, pointing out to him that such a man could be dangerous to both government and orthodox religion.

Rauf Pasha first sent a telegram to the kadi (religious judge) at El Kawa asking him to look into the matter. The kadi took two religious notables with him to visit Mohammed Ahmed on the island. He then reported to Rauf Pasha that the dervish did indeed claim to be the mahdi and he sent Rauf Pasha copies of some of the letters Mohammed Ahmed was sending out in all directions. Rauf Pasha next sent a mission to the Mahdi to convince him of the error of his ways and of the danger of continuing to preach such a false doctrine. Included on the mission were relatives of the Mahdi and several ulema (learned religious leaders) from Khartoum. The mission was headed by Mohammed Bey Abu Saud, Rauf Pasha's principal assistant.

Abu Saud was a typical Egyptian government official. When General Charles Gordon had first come to the Sudan as governor of the southern province of Equatoria, he had put Abu Saud in charge of abolishing the slave trade, but had dismissed him when he learned that instead Abu Saud was using his position to carry on a thriving business in slaves for his own account. But Gordon was gone now, and Abu Saud was again a trusted official of the government. It was rumoured that he now did business with the southern slave traders on behalf of Rauf Pasha as well as himself.

Abu Saud's mission to the Mahdi was a failure. Not only did Mohammed Ahmed continue to assert that he was the true mahdi, but he told Abu Saud that he considered himself superior to the Governor-General and recognized no authority but his own divinely inspired precepts. When Abu Saud reported his failure to Rauf Pasha, the Governor-General decided to take more drastic action. The ulema all spoke out against the Dongolawi pretender, as those ensconced in the hierarchy of organized religion are always against those who threaten to disturb the *status quo*, but the peasants, bedouins and ordinary people reacted differently. The most incredible stories were being circulated and disturbing things were happening: women in several villages were reported to have found hen's eggs with the word 'Mahdi' on them; a young theology student publicly stated that the birthmark and the V-shaped opening between the teeth were the seals of the genuine mahdi; a pamphlet written by the Mahdi was being widely circulated, proclaiming that its author, descended through twenty-nine generations from the Prophet, was indeed the mahdi, and calling upon the faithful to follow him and his creed.

Rauf Pasha ordered Abu Saud back to Abba with a steamer and two companies of Egyptian soldiers to capture the impostor. On 12 August 1881, a hot sultry night in the rainy season, the steamer *Ismailia* dropped anchor in mid-stream off the island of Abba. Abu Saud, in command of the expedition, decided to stay on board. In military matters he favoured the free enterprise system: he had no plan of attack but inspired a competitive spirit in the two company commanders by promising promotion to the one who succeeded in capturing the Mahdi. In some confusion the troops went ashore – and walked into an ambush. With sticks, stones and spears the followers of the Mahdi slaughtered 120 Egyptian soldiers and six officers. A few managed to escape both the ambush and the crocodiles and swim back to the ship. Abu Saud immediately gave the order to hoist the anchor and steam for Khartoum, but the captain of the ship assured him they were safe in the river and should wait to pick up any further survivors. Although the *Ismailia* mounted a small cannon, not a shell was fired.

On Abba the work was soon done. Fires were lit, drums boomed, and the captured arms and equipment of the Turk were piled under the victorious black flag of the Mahdi. The small herd of frightened captives, brought before him, saved their lives by kissing his feet and reciting the new creed that ended with '. . . And Mohammed el Mahdi is the successor of Allah's Prophet!'

The *Ismailia* waited until morning, but no more survivors appeared. It steamed back down the river to carry the news of the defeat to Khartoum, and from Khartoum and Abba the news spread fast that a miracle had occurred. Egyptian authority had been successfully defied; a handful of unarmed dervishes had defeated the government's soldiers. The news created fear or hope or uncertainty depending upon the status, aspirations or convictions of the hearer.

The Mahdi had no intention of waiting on his island for the next attack. He immediately announced that he must, like the Prophet Mohammed before him, perform a hegira, or flight. He set out at once, mounted on a scrawny Abyssinian horse, Abdullahi beside him, and his followers, many with their families, trailing behind. They marched south along the western bank of the Nile, then

south-west into the desert towards the Dar Nuba highlands. It was
an ill-armed and poorly equipped band. They had the rifles they
had captured from the soldiers on Abba, but few knew how to use
them. For the most part they had to rely upon a few swords and
some light spears to protect themselves. But the Mahdi possessed
military assets which in this land counted for more than weapons:
he had followers who were brave and devoted to him, plus the
military reputation won at the battle of Abba. He alarmed the
Egyptian garrisons he approached, but none attempted to attack
him. As the Mahdi and his followers came near El Obeid, the
capital of Kordofan, the governor of the province dispatched four
companies of infantry, under Mohammed Pasha Said to attack
them. The Mahdi's camp, filled with his tired and half-starved
followers, was soon located. But Mohammed Pasha Said was an
elderly man; fighting was a dangerous business; he camped near by
for three days, and then marched his men back to El Obeid.

The Mahdi finally brought his followers safely to rest at Jebel
Gedir, a remote mountain in the south-eastern corner of the Dar
Nuba in southern Kordofan. There was an old legend that said the
expected mahdi would come from Mount Masa, in the Atlas
mountains of Morocco, but the Mahdi announced that he had been
told in a vision that Jebel Gedir was really Mount Masa. The fame
of the Mahdi swept the Sudan and men came to Jebel Gedir to join
him. Runaway slaves, malcontents, religious fanatics and those
seeking to evade the clutches of the police made their way to the
Mahdi, and his forces grew. Many of these were seasoned fighters,
members of slave-raiding bands broken up by the government in its
efforts to stamp out the slave trade. If some joined only out of
hatred of the Turk, they were all soon converted to the beliefs of
the Mahdi, for he had a power to inspire men with a faith that
overcame the fear of death.

The flight of the Mahdi and his ragged followers towards the hills
seems to have allayed the fears of Rauf Pasha and ten days after
the battle at Abba Island he reported to the Khedive in Cairo that
there was nothing to fear. Rauf attached little importance to the
religious aspect of the revolt and assured the Khedive that the
traditional tribal jealousies of the Sudanese would prevent the
tribes from uniting to wage a full-scale rebellion. He thought that
if left alone the revolt would soon collapse of its own accord.

When the rainy season ended, Rashid Bey Ayman, the Mudir
(local governor) of Fashoda, asked permission to send out an
expedition to attack the Mahdi in the hills. Permission was refused

and Rashid Bey was told to attend to business at Fashoda. Disobeying these instructions, Rashid collected a mixed force of about 400 soldiers and 1,000 Shilluk tribesmen and set off to find the Mahdi. Word of Rashid Bey's advance preceded him; it is popular legend in the Sudan that a woman of the Kenana tribe walked all night to warn the Mahdi of the expedition advancing against him. Rashid Bey had hoped to surprise the Mahdi, but instead, on 9 December 1881, he was himself ambushed and his force nearly annihilated. Only a few Shilluks managed to escape and carry news of the defeat back to Fashoda.

The government authorities in Khartoum now became worried, for the Mahdi was obviously a serious threat. Rauf asked Cairo for reinforcements, and though his request was at first refused, eventually he was allowed one Sudanese battalion. As Rauf Pasha did not consider this enough and continued to ask for more soldiers, but did nothing to check the growing power of the Mahdi, he was dismissed as incompetent by the government in Cairo. Instead of a new governor-general, a ministerial post was created in Cairo to look after Sudanese affairs, and Abdel Kadir Pasha Hilmi was appointed to it. But it was two months before it was decided that Abdel Kadir Pasha should go to the Sudan and direct affairs personally, and in the meantime, the man left in Khartoum as acting governor-general was Giegler Pasha, a German who had formerly been in charge of the telegraph system.

Giegler Pasha felt that immediate action should be taken against the Mahdi and he began to assemble as large a force as he could scrape together. About 3,500 regulars and irregulars, placed under the command of Yusuf el-Shallali Pasha, an experienced soldier, left Khartoum for El Kawa on 15 April, a considerable number of troops deserting before they arrived. At El Kawa, Shallali Pasha was joined by about 2,000 volunteers from Kordofan under the command of a brave and experienced warrior named Abdullah Dafallah. This combined force continued to march south along the banks of the Nile to Fashoda, then westward into the desert. Just as they were leaving the Nile, however, Abdullah fell from his horse. Word of this mere accident, in which Abdullah was not even injured, spread among the superstitious troops, who regarded it as a very bad omen.

By the middle of May the force had reached a place called Funkur, where a long halt was made. The rainy season was late that year and apparently Shallali Pasha wanted to be sure of a sufficient supply of water ahead. While at Funkur the local chief turned over to Shallali Pasha several of the Mahdi's spies. These men were executed in front of the assembled troops in an unnecessarily atrocious manner: their arms and legs were chopped off one at a time. Whatever good effect Shallali Pasha attempted to create by this performance was spoiled by the spies' bravery and their deep religious conviction in the Mahdi's teachings: as their limbs were being hacked off they shouted words of defiance until they died, considerably shaking the morale of the troops.

On 21 May Shallali Pasha's force moved from Funkur towards Jebel Gedir, and by the evening of 6 June 1882 they had reached the base of the mountain and constructed a zariba (a camp surrounded by thorn bushes). The troops were tired and probably did not construct the zariba as well as they should have. The sentries were obviously either insufficient or careless. By dawn the next morning the Mahdi's men had removed enough of the zariba to create holes for the rebels to pour through and fall upon Shallali Pasha's army. The badly frightened troops, stunned by the suddenness of the attack, offered slight resistance. Abdullah fought bravely and the wife of one of the irregular leaders beat a war drum to rally her husband's tribesmen, but all were overwhelmed in the massacre.

After three successive victories in the space of a few months by the Mahdi's followers over government troops, there was no longer any doubt in the minds of most Sudanese as to which was to be the winning side in this conflict. From all parts of the country the Mahdi received messages of support. From a poor, unknown dervish, Mohammed Ahmed had become, in less than a year, the most talked of personage in the Sudan. Moreover, his limited religious influence over a handful of disciples had developed into an important and dangerous political as well as religious power; from a fugitive leading a tiny band of followers armed with swords and spears, he had become a military power that could defeat armies. This dramatic increase in power came about solely as the result of his own personality, intellect and sincerity, his conviction of the importance of his cause and personal destiny, his great force of persuasion, his energy and his firm, single-minded determination to see his cause prevail.

The armies sent against the Mahdi grew larger and larger, but his own followers increased at a far faster rate than the government anticipated or could imagine possible. Having defeated all the forces sent to capture him, he now rested on Jebel Gedir in comparative safety, content to wait a bit for his reputation to spread. Doubtless the magnitude of his victories grew in the telling. In many parts of the Sudan there were local revolts. Some of these were quickly crushed, but others, particularly in Kordofan, where the Mahdi's influence was strongest, succeeded in overwhelming several Egyptian garrisons. Giegler Pasha himself took the field to break up some of the more serious local rebellions in the Gezira. Meanwhile Abdel Kadir Pasha Hilmi had arrived in Khartoum and was making vigorous efforts to create a strong army. His request to Cairo for more troops was refused but he scraped up what he could in the Sudan. He withdrew some of the garrisons from the Abyssinian frontier and Equatoria; he formed two new battalions of Sudanese Blacks from the south who, when properly trained, made the finest soldiers in the Egyptian army; and he raised a substantial force of irregulars. By the end of July he had collected an army of 12,000 men. He sent 1,000 of these to El Obeid and began to fortify Khartoum itself.

Abdel Kadir Pasha was a resourceful man who knew of other weapons besides soldiers. He opened a correspondence with the Mahdi, promising him forgiveness if he would give up his divine pretensions. He commissioned two men to murder the Mahdi. He sent the Mahdi a present of poisoned dates. He requested Cairo to send him some 'dynamite envelopes'. None of Abdel Kadir Pasha's schemes worked.

To many Sudanese the Mahdi appeared all-powerful. Tough, savage Baggara warriors from the tribe of Abdullahi joined his army, including three of Abdullahi's brothers. It was said that in the battle with Shallali Pasha the bullets of the Turks had turned to water and that the blessings of the Mahdi would prevent any true believer from harm in battle. The Mahdi proclaimed a jihad, a holy war against the infidel. It was not enough to believe in Allah and his Prophet; a true believer must also believe in the Mahdi, and all who did not were infidels. Mohammed Ahmed would have been less than human if his spectacular successes and his rapid acceptance by the people had not wiped away any lingering doubts he might have had that he was the true mahdi, destined to restore the faith and conquer the world.

The Mahdi was without any knowledge of organization or administration, but it was obvious to him that something had to be done to organize the masses of people who now crowded Jebel Gedir. He took the only guide he knew: the Koran. Following the example of Mohammed, he announced the appointment of four khalifas (literally, successors). As first khalifa he named the faithful Abdullahi; the second was a relative, Mohammed esh-Sherif bin

Hamid, a young man still in his teens; the fourth, Ali bin Mohammed Helu, was one of the faithful from Abba. The third khalifa was
to have been the head of the Senussi, and a letter offering the post
was sent off to him in Cyrenaica. This sect, which still exists, placed
great emphasis upon peace, temperance, self-restraint and piety.
The head of the sect at this time called himself Al-Senussi al Mahdi,
and he was the father of Mohammed Idris, the present king of
Libya.

Each khalifa was given a flag, a special war drum and command
of a part of the Mahdi's army; the Khalifa Abdullahi was, in addition, given an ombaÿa, a horn made by hollowing out an elephant's
tusk. Abdullahi was allowed to keep the black flag and was put in
charge of the cattle-owning tribes, the Baggara; Sherif was given a
red flag and, being a Dongolawi, was put in charge of the riverside
Donagla; Ali Helu was given a white flag and the command of
the people from the Gezira. Under each khalifa, emirs and lesser
officers were appointed so that the rabble became a manageable
military and civil organization.

The Mahdi created a uniform for his followers to distinguish
them from the Turk. Called a jibba, it was like a dervish dress, a
shirt-like garment with wide sleeves patched with squares of black,
white, red and yellow cloth, such as the Mahdi himself wore. His
followers at once sewed on coloured patches, whether their clothes
needed them or not, and this garment of poverty and humility
became the military uniform of the Mahdi's army.

It was at Jebel Gedir also that the Mahdi first gave the name
'ansar' to his followers. Before this they had called themselves
Dervishes, the name by which they continued to be called by the
British, but the Mahdi now forbade the use of this name, saying that
anyone who called them Dervishes 'deserves to be beaten seven
times and receive many stripes'. The name 'ansar' comes from the
Koran – the word literally means 'helpers' or 'partisans' – and was
the name the Prophet Mohammed applied to the people of Medina
who received and supported him after his flight from Mecca. It was
a proud title, a promise of paradise.

It is important, if sometimes difficult in the light of his astonishing
political success, to remember that the Mahdi was first and fore-
most a religious reformer. His conception of himself and his
rebellion was in theological rather than political terms. He condemned the 'Turks' for their failure to follow the tenets of their
religion rather than their failure to make just laws and fairly
administer them, for their immoral life rather than their oppres-

sions. The Egyptians were simply ready examples of those who debased the true faith. The Mahdi was less hostile to complete infidels, such as he regarded the Europeans, than to the Egyptians – as Calvin doubtless would have felt more kindly towards a Hottentot than a cardinal. But the increasing political power of the Mahdi was necessary to enforce his own brand of religion.

As his power grew, the number of puritanical decrees multiplied. The Mahdi forbade smoking, drinking, fine clothes, jewellery, music, dancing, feasts, the use of abusive language and even the practice of buying brides. At first his enemies hoped that by forbidding so many pleasures dear to the Sudanese, the Mahdi's popularity would decline, not realizing that new religions are made by demanding abstinence, austerities and moral effort, rather than by allowing luxuries and giving indulgences. But the Mahdi was well aware of the impact of his creed on his followers. In a letter to the Sheikh el Islam in July 1882, he said: 'Belief in Mahdiism is a difficult task, and can only be embraced by those to whom Allah has decreed a share of true happiness.' The Mahdi demanded, and got, complete acceptance. There could be no half measures. He said:

> The Prophet, grace be upon him, several times said to me that he who doubts that I am the Mahdi is in the eyes of Allah and His Prophet a renegade, that he who opposes me is an infidel, and that he who wages war against me will neither succeed in this world nor in the world to come. His property and his children will become the property of the Muslims. Be it known to you that this is by the order of the Prophet. My war against the Turks is by His orders, and He told me many secret things, one of which is that all these countries shall be subdued by the holy religion and law.

The Mahdi now had an army that was purified, organized and fanatic. What they lacked in weapons and training they made up in bravery and devotion to their leader and his cause. The Mahdi was ready to take the offensive. In August 1882 he gave the signal and his uncounted hordes swarmed down the sides of Jebel Gedir, thousands of them, flags flying, drums beating, marching north to El Obeid, capital of Kordofan. As he marched, the sheikhs of Kordofan flocked to him, offering him their warriors, women and treasure. The Mahdi accepted them all. There also came to him a powerful sheikh from Darfur with two gifts of particular value. One was a woman called Aisha, daughter of a sheikh and descended from the ancient sultans of Darfur: she became the Mahdi's chief wife, her full title being Sittina Aisha Umm El Muminin,

'Our Lady Aisha, Mother of the believers'. The other gift was a remarkable sword that had been a family heirloom. It was very long, with a gold hilt decorated with stars and crescents, the sheath was similarly decorated and made of hammered gold. On the blade was inscribed in Arabic the names of Aisha's illustrious ancestors – and the double eagle of the Holy Roman Empire. Below the beautifully engraved eagle were the words VIVAT CAROLUS, and, further down, ROEMISCHE KAISER, all in gothic letters. It was, in fact, a two-handed sword of some sixteenth-century lansquenet. In the strange land of Darfur the people had a great liking for medieval weapons and armour, which were passed down from generation to generation, and even in these times Darfur tribesmen often went into battle wearing the polished armour of Christian crusaders. This beautiful ancient blade from Darfur became known as the 'sword of the Mahdi'.

By the end of July 1882 all the Egyptian garrisons in Kordofan had fallen except those at Bara and El Obeid. The Mahdi sent three messengers to Said Pasha, the Mudir of El Obeid, demanding that he surrender and acknowledge the Mahdi. Said Pasha called together the principal men of the town to hear the messengers. In spite of their humble, patched jibbas, the messengers behaved so arrogantly that Said Pasha, against the advice of a number of those present, ordered them to be instantly hanged. In a few minutes their lifeless bodies were dangling from the gallows.

El Obeid was the largest and most important town of the western Sudan. It was the commercial centre of Kordofan and the gateway to Darfur. Sitting in a slight hollow in a plain, it was able to collect enough water in its wells during the winter months to last the remainder of the year. Most of the houses were built of mud, except for the government buildings of sun-dried bricks. Its population was estimated at 100,000, although this seems high. It contained a number of wealthy merchants, dealers in camels, gum, ostrich feathers, cattle, skins and senna. There were also a number of foreigners, principally Egyptians, Syrians and Greeks, and, of course, many government officials.

On 4 September 1882 the Mahdi marched on El Obeid with a force estimated to be 30,000. As he approached, many of the towns-people as well as some of the irregular soldiers came out to join him. Of those who remained, many were in sympathy with the Mahdi and a number of the most prominent citizens were in direct communication with him.

Said Pasha had made energetic efforts to fortify the town. He had constructed a parapet with a deep ditch in front of it around the perimeter and an inner circle of fortifications that surrounded the government buildings, barracks and principal houses. But he had fewer than 4,000 men, including irregulars – insufficient strength to man adequately the outer ring. When the Dervishes, roused to a fighting pitch by the Mahdi's speeches, launched their attack, they quickly swarmed over ditch and parapet and poured into the town.

The garrison retreated to the inner fortifications and poured a steady, deadly fire into the masses of Dervishes that clogged the streets. Said Pasha's men were armed with American Remingtons, the best rifle produced since the Civil War and for many years the most modern rifle seen in the Sudan. Although at one point the inner ring of fortifications was pierced and a fierce fight raged around the magazine, the hole in the line was plugged and the Dervishes caught within the ring were killed. Late in the afternoon it became apparent, even to the Mahdi, that his forces could not penetrate the inner fortifications, nor could his men long withstand the deadly musketry of the Remingtons. He retreated, and the Dervishes fell back in such confusion that had Said Pasha set out in pursuit, he doubtless would have won a complete victory. But Said Pasha felt, probably rightly, that his force was too small and that his men were too exhausted for the effort.

The Mahdi had learned his lesson. Never again would he order a direct assault upon a fortified city defended by a fresh and well-armed garrison. He had lost nearly 10,000 men, including two of his brothers and a brother of Abdullahi. There were no prisoners taken on either side. Having known only victory, the Mahdi was badly shaken by this setback and at first wanted to retreat to the mountains. The more experienced fighters among his advisers dissuaded him, however, and he sat down to wait until the defenders starved or surrendered.

The Dervishes who had so boldly and disastrously attacked El Obeid were armed only with swords and spears. Until now, the Mahdi had scorned to use the weapons of the Turk. However, the slaughter of his ansar in the streets of El Obeid by the Remingtons of the government's forces had been convincing proof of the need for more potent arms, and he now sent back to the Nuba hills for the rifles and ammunition he had captured in previous battles.

El Obeid was completely surrounded; nothing could come in or go out. In Khartoum, Abdel Kadir Pasha hastily put together a relief column to go to the aid of the besieged garrisons. On 24 September a force consisting of two regular battalions and 750 irregulars,

3,000 men in all, set out across the desert for El Obeid. The Dervishes watched them all the way, picking off stragglers and destroying the wells ahead of them. Tortured by thirst, the wretched soldiers plodded on. At last they found a water-hole in a patch of woods that had not been filled in or contaminated. The troops broke ranks and ran for it. As they did so, the Dervishes fell upon them. Nearly half were killed. The remainder fought their way to Bara and joined the besieged garrison there.

Abdel Kadir Pasha had no more troops to spare for the relief of El Obeid and conditions in the besieged town rapidly deteriorated. When all the camels and cattle had been eaten, the people turned to donkeys, dogs and mice; next came crickets, white ants and cockroaches. Hundreds died of starvation and hundreds more of scurvy and dysentery. The dead were left unburied in the streets and scores of carrion-kites feasted on them. Some of the birds, too gorged with human flesh to fly, were quickly killed and eaten by the soldiers. Eventually, there was only gum and leather to eat. Some provisions were smuggled into the city and sold for fantastic sums, but the smugglers were caught by the Dervishes who, on the Mahdi's orders, cut off their right hands, tied their bloody arms to their necks and marched them around the Dervish camp as a warning to others.

The end came at last when Bara fell, and on or about 19 January 1883, El Obeid surrendered. The horrors of the siege were followed by even greater horrors as the Dervishes invested the town. In a frenzy of joy, and greedy for loot, they pounced upon the starved and helpless citizens. Children, servants and slaves were flogged until they revealed the hidden family valuables, Said Pasha was tortured until he divulged the location of the state treasure. He was later chopped to death with axes. The soldiers, mostly Blacks from the southern Sudan, were simply enrolled in the Mahdi's army. Eventually, when another government force was raised to march into Kordofan, it was attacked by the very men it was sent to relieve. The brave and disciplined Blacks fought as well for the Mahdi as they did for the Egyptians.

It was about this time that a representative of the head of the great Senussi fraternity arrived in El Obeid. He had been sent to see in person if this man who claimed to be the Mahdi was indeed what he pretended to be. He had travelled hard and far from Kufra in Cyrenaica on a white camel. What he saw in the streets of El Obeid convinced him that the leader of this barbaric horde could not possibly be a holy man of peace. He did not even try to see the

Mahdi, but turned his camel around and started back to report to his master. There would be no third khalifa for the Mahdi.

Unaware of Al-Senussi's emissary, the Mahdi wrote to Cyrenaica a second time, saying that 'Mahdiism is like time. No one understands its true nature but Allah the Almighty.' He ordered Al-Senussi either to 'fight for the cause of Allah in your own provinces, marching down on Egypt and its neighbourhood ... or you are to set forth to us'. Al-Senussi did neither.

With the sack of El Obeid, many emirs became suddenly rich; they took over the best houses in El Obeid and vied with each other in the number of cattle, slaves, wives and camels they possessed. Although they continued to wear the jibba, the coloured patches were artistically arranged to make an attractive dress. In short, they began to live like the despised Turk. The Mahdi was furious. One emir was forced to give up twenty of his wives, and the Mahdi sent a proclamation to all his men:

> I have heard that after looting, many of you deserted from the fight and refused to obey your khalifas and emirs. Beware lest Allah punish you. If you persist in doing this you will be destroyed. Allah will burn you up with fire, and the earth will open her mouth and swallow you. I have warned you so that you may have no excuse. Repent, obey my orders, and return all the loot you have taken, for the Prophet, grace be upon him, has told me that any man that still keeps loot in his possession will be destroyed, and our Prophet keeps his word. Again I say, repent, for He who has destroyed the Turks will find it no difficult matter to bring you into subjection. The Prophet, grace be upon him, has told me that after I have killed the infidels and captured this province I must return and punish those who refuse to obey me. Such punishment will be death. Take heed, therefore, and obey the orders of the Prophet.

The Mahdi tightened the rules. His spies were everywhere and justice was harsh. The mildest punishment a man caught drinking could expect was to have his drinking bowl tied about his neck and be driven with whips about the market place, enduring the insults of the people. Sometimes a man caught taking a nip had his drinking bowl broken over his head, children threw mud and filth at him, and he was dragged before the kadi (religious judge) to be awarded eighty lashes, the first of which usually brought blood. Smoking was regarded as an even greater offence than drinking and was punished by a hundred blows. Blasphemers and murderers were instantly put to death, no extenuating circumstances being allowed. A thief had one hand and one foot cut off. Fornication was punished by eighty lashes; adultery called for beheading the man and stoning the woman. If the decrees of the Mahdi seem strict and the punishments cruel, they did not seem unduly harsh to the primitive people over whom he ruled, who had known Egyptian overlords. The Mahdi's laws were, in fact, well designed to control the half-wild tribes and races of the Sudan. But the Mahdi delegated the administration of justice to his khalifas and relatives, and often a culprit could escape punishment by the payment of a sufficiently large bribe.

All that was connected with the old order of government or the old practice of religion was destroyed: books of theology, government records, papers of all kinds. Slaves freed by the Egyptian government again became slaves; debts contracted with the government were cancelled; the wearing of the fez was prohibited and even shoes were banned, the Mahdi's followers being forced to go barefoot or wear only sandals. Power, of course, corrupts, and luxury, when readily available, is a powerful temptation. It is not so difficult to be an ascetic when luxuries are unknown and seemingly unattainable, but it is more difficult when pleasure is at hand, easier to take than to resist. Such was the Mahdi's case, and he began to change his way of life. As he had found it a wise policy to accept the presents of wives and concubines from powerful sheikhs whose support he wanted, his harem grew to be immense and he began to take inordinate pleasure in the sensual delights it offered. Although he never drank wine, he became addicted to a popular Sudanese drink made of date syrup mixed with ginger, which he drank from silver cups looted from the Roman Catholic mission church in El Obeid.

The Mahdi, with his unruffled smile and pleasant, equable manners, was an able diplomat, as he proved by his success in persuading mutually antagonistic tribes and races to work together for him in a common cause. His popularity among all races and classes was tremendous. All oaths and statements began with the phrase: 'By the Victorious Mahdi . . .'. Beggars learned laudatory verses that praised his wisdom, appearance and victories over the Turks; these they recited from door to door for alms. The most popular song was one that began, 'The Mahdi is the light of our eyes . . .'. Women thought him the handsomest of men and worshipped him.

In a dispute between two men as to which would have the highest seat in heaven, the Mahdi or the Prophet, the matter was finally taken before the kadi. Deciding that 'the living was better than the dead', he ordered that the man who had championed the Prophet's claims should be thrown into prison, the reason being that the tone in which he had argued the matter was insulting to the Mahdi.

To make a distinction between religious and political matters seems not to have occurréd to the Madhi. His was a rule by dreams and visions. Still, there were certain administrative matters that were absolutely necessary and he and his khalifas attempted to cope with them as best they could. There was, for example, the treasure that was almost daily pouring in. Besides gold, silver and jewels, there were cattle, camels, slaves, captured arms and equipment, and merchandise of all sorts. Some method had to be devised for keeping control. The solution to this problem came to the Mahdi in a dream. He created a treasury, called the Beit el Mal, in which were deposited all booty, presents and fines, animate and inanimate, and he placed one of his most trusted followers in charge.

Prisoners were also a problem. All foreigners except Egyptians – and this included a number of European missionaries – were placed in the charge of a trusted Greek, who was, or pretended to be, a Mahdist. Many of the Egyptian soldiers were incorporated into the Dervish army, but they were not at first allowed to have fire-arms. The Black prisoners constituted a separate category. They were, or had been, the best troops in the Egyptian army except that, being Sudanese, they had no particular loyalty to Egypt. These men were now formed into a special force of the Dervish army, called the jihadiya, and were issued captured rifles. They were the only trained regular troops, familiar with the use of rifles, in the Dervish army. The jihadiya were placed under the command of Hamdan Abu Anga, a man devoted to the Khalifa Abdullahi, who became one of the best of the Dervish generals.

The timing of the Mahdi's revolt was, quite accidentally, perfect. While the Sudanese were trying to throw out the foreigners, meaning the Egyptians, the Egyptians themselves were also trying to throw out the foreigners, meaning the French and British. In 1879 when Ismail, the Khedive of Egypt, was replaced by the young and inexperienced Tewfik, the country was bankrupt, officials and soldiers were unpaid, and the morale of the country as a whole was low. In debt to England and France, the Khedive had to submit to two controllers-general, one from each country, whose task was to reform the administration and establish financial stability. Their struggle against apathy, inefficiency and corruption was hopeless, and they created great resentment among all classes of people, but particularly among government officials and army officers.

Early in 1881 two colonels, one of whom was named Ahmed

Arabi, presented a petition to the government on behalf of the army. To appease them, the minister of war was dismissed. A few months later Arabi was back in Cairo with demands that the entire ministry be dismissed and the size of the army be increased. Again his demands were granted. The controllers-general began to lose their influence and the British and French governments were disturbed. On 8 January 1882 they sent a joint note to the Khedive formally pledging to support him against the militant officers. The effect of this note was to gain popular support for Arabi, for he was now viewed as a nationalist struggling to throw off the yoke of the foreigners. As the Khedive was nominally the vassal of the Sultan of Turkey the Sultan sent a commissioner with instructions to maintain the Khedive's authority and arrest Arabi. Without any force other than his papers, the commissioner was helpless and his task hopeless. The British and the French governments, being more practical, sent squadrons of ships to Alexandria. Nevertheless, the Khedive was forced to appoint Arabi Minister of War.

On 11 June fifty Europeans were killed in Alexandria and the rest of the foreign colony was seized with panic and tried to flee. When the Egyptian army began to fortify Alexandria and erect batteries of guns pointed towards the squadrons in the harbour, the British admiral sent an ultimatum saying that the work must cease. The ultimatum was ignored. The French refused to take any action, but on 11 July the British bombarded the town and landed a force to occupy Alexandria. The Khedive dismissed Arabi and accepted British assistance; an army of 5,000 men under Sir Garnet (later Lord) Wolseley was sent from India to put down what was now a full-scale rebellion of the Egyptian army under Ahmed Arabi. On 13 September 1882 the British army defeated Arabi's forces at Tel el Kebir, near Zagazig, and the rebellion was crushed. Arabi was exiled to Ceylon and the mutinous soldiers were disarmed. As France had refused to take part in these operations, Britain now found herself master of Egypt. Not long after, Evelyn Baring (later Lord Cromer) was appointed British Agent and Consul-General, and he became virtual viceroy of Egypt.

It was during the course of this uproar in Egypt that the Mahdi succeeded with his rebellion in the south. But with the defeat of Arabi the attention of the Egyptian government turned to the alarming state of affairs in the Sudan. When, shortly after the battle of Tel el Kebir, Abdel Kadir Pasha again appealed to Cairo for help, the government was prepared to support him and an army was put together to crush the Mahdi.

2

A Small Punitive Expedition

Although Britain had conquered Egypt, and now maintained an army of occupation there, and her diplomatic agents exercised control over the administration and finances of the Egyptian government, she tried to maintain the illusion that Egypt was still master of its own affairs. Britain felt that she must rule, but she wanted to do as little ruling as possible: she simply felt that it was necessary, for the good of European civilization, to preserve order and to protect British financial interests. This was not hypocrisy, merely an attempt to avoid responsibility. In particular, this reluctant ruler wanted to avoid responsibility for those elements of Egyptian affairs which she wished did not exist. The mess in the Sudan was one such element.

Britain had no interest in the Sudan. It was a nuisance. Still, she was unwilling to force Egypt to abandon this huge province with its revenues, soldiers, administrators and subjects; she was also unwilling to undertake a military expedition for the suppression of the rebellion. An expedition would be costly in both money and soldiers. On the other hand, there were sentimental but powerful reasons for not forgetting the Sudan. To abandon it would be to throw large numbers of people who were loyal to the government, and some of whom were civilized, to the rude mercy of fanatic barbarians. One of England's most colourful soldiers, Colonel Charles 'Chinese' Gordon, had recently ruled this area as governor-general and had made the Sudan well known to Britons. The influential Anti-Slavery Society had taken a keen interest in Gordon's efforts to stamp out the thriving slave trade. So, as is usual with most governments when faced with such a problem, Britain compromised. Egypt would be allowed on its own initiative to put down the rebellion, and a handful of British officers would be permitted to take service under the Khedive to lead the expedition, but there would not be any direct participation by Britain.

In January 1883 William Hicks, a retired Indian Army colonel, was selected to be chief of staff of the Egyptian army in the Sudan and was given a rank equivalent to major-general. Hicks Pasha was fifty-three years old, of medium height and build, with fierce eyes, a thick moustache and a goatee beard. He was an impatient man, undiplomatic, obstinate and somewhat vain; he wanted things done his own way, or at least in the way he himself had been taught. He was accustomed to commanding well-disciplined troops, and certainly men of his temperament in command of good troops can win battles. Unfortunately the Egyptian soldiers were not of the quality to which he was accustomed, and his chain of command was unclear.

As this was a religious rebellion, it was thought wise to have a Muslim rather than a Christian as titular head of the expedition. Sir Edward Malet, British Agent and Consul-General in Cairo told Hicks that 'nomination of a Christian would fan fanaticism'. Therefore, Sulayman Pasha Niyazi, a Circassian described by one British officer as 'a miserable-looking old man of seventy-four or seventy-five', was given the title of commander-in-chief, although it was understood – at least by Hicks – that the actual command of the army would be completely in his own hands. It did not take long for the unsatisfactory aspects of this situation to become apparent.

The bulk of the Egyptian army had itself, only a few weeks previously, been in open rebellion. After the battle of Tel el Kebir the British had decided to completely remodel it and had disbanded Arabi's rebellious, demoralized and ill-trained soldiers. As a new army was just in the process of being formed and could not yet take the field, it was decided to gather up the remnants of Arabi's troops, reconscript them, and send them off to Hicks Pasha in the Sudan. There were two major advantages to be gained by this scheme: a large number of potentially dangerous malcontents would be removed from Egypt proper, and the soldiers, once they were in the hostile surroundings of the Sudan, would be less likely to desert. These troops were reinforced (if that is the word) by the physical rejects of the new Egyptian army. So terrified were these conscripts of being sent to fight the Dervishes that they did everything possible to escape: two men even threw lime in their own eyes to blind themselves rather than go to the Sudan. All in all, the prospects of accomplishing anything of military value with such unpromising material did not appear great. Those who saw the army being pieced together in Egypt predicted defeat. When Colonel J. Colborne, one of Hicks Pasha's British staff officers, dined one night in Cairo with messmates of his old corps, the King's Royal

Rifles, his fellow officers cheerily advised him to procure a good fast horse as his men would probably bolt or mutiny.

In February 1883 this rabble of an army was shipped off up the Nile to the Sudan. It was decided, perhaps wisely, to send the troops disarmed and ship the guns and ammunition separately. As there were mass desertions before the men were shipped off, many were put in chains and not released until they reached their destination. When the soldiers actually arrived in Khartoum, some of them cried openly. Nevertheless, they were arranged into military units and began a training programme. They were, after all, not much worse than the Egyptian soldiers already in the Sudan.

Colonel J. D. H. Stewart of the 11th Hussars, a man whom Kitchener thought 'the finest soldier I have ever met', had been sent ahead by the British government the previous November to report on conditions, but he had been told: 'under no circumstances presume to act in any military capacity'. On 5 January 1883 he sent back a report on the Egyptian troops stationed in the Sudan:

> Besides the gross ignorance of the Egyptian officers, nothing is more striking than their want of initiative and their unwillingness to assume any responsibility. Not one of the officers in any of the out-stations will think of attacking unless they have previously sent into Khartoum to ask for leave, the result being an enormous loss of valuable time, and of many favourable opportunities. It is owing to this cause that the enemy, although there are several strong garrisons along the White and Blue Niles, can move unmolested about the immediate country and pass almost within gun-fire of the forts. . . . The troops in garrison here are working at elementary drill and tactics and are making some progress. It is, however, very uphill work; the officers are so ignorant, and so incapable of grasping the meaning of the simplest movement. Quite one-third of the troops are also ignorant of the use of the rifle, and they would be more formidable adversaries were they simply armed with sticks. Many have also superstitious ideas of the power of the Mahdi and others think the Khedive has simply sent them here to get rid of them.

Hicks Pasha and his staff did not travel with their troops but made their way leisurely by the overland route across the desert from Suakin to Berber. While resting in Berber, they read in *The Times* that Khartoum itself was threatened by the Mahdi, but that it was believed Colonel Stewart would be able to hold out with the assistance of the British officers who were on their way. According to Colonel Colborne: 'We all laughed heartily at this, Colonel Stewart being on a purely civil mission and Khartoum not being threatened in the least.' Ridiculous, of course, to think of Khartoum, the capital of the country, being in any danger. Then Hicks Pasha received a letter from Colonel Stewart, reporting the fall of El Obeid and Bara and announcing that the whole of Kordofan was in the hands of the Mahdi. As Stewart strongly advised him to come as quickly as he could, Hicks Pasha and his staff proceeded up the Nile at once.

They reached Khartoum on 4 March and Hicks Pasha at once inspected the army he was expected to command. On the first day of parade he stood in the centre of a square facing inwards and addressed his men through his interpreter:

> I am desired by His Highness the Khedive to inform you that if you perform your duty faithfully and gallantly, so far from being left here in the Sudan – as it is reported you seem to expect – you will, at the expiration of the campaign, be allowed to return to your homes in Egypt. I myself will take you back, and present you to the Khedive. I promise you this in His Highness's name. With the weapons in your hands, if you only use them properly, you cannot fail to be victorious over the enemy.... All that is required of you is firmness and steadiness, and you must always win the day.

The soldiers now began three weeks of practice with their rifles in the desert outside Khartoum under the direct supervision of the British staff officers. In general, the troops were well armed. Besides the modern Remingtons, Hicks had rockets, Krupp howitzers, brass mountain guns and even some Nordenfeldt machine guns. Maxim's recoil-action machine gun was not introduced to the military world until the following year and the Nordenfeldts, like the Gatlings, were operated by a crank. But they were very efficient weapons, capable, as long as the operator's arm lasted, of firing 1,000 rounds a minute. A group of Egyptian soldiers under Captain Forestier Walker had been left behind in Cairo to take special training in this weapon. When they arrived in Khartoum, about a month after Hicks Pasha, they gave a demonstration. Sulayman Pasha, Hicks Pasha and the staff were all on hand. Colonel Colborne gave the following account of their proficiency:

> During their passage from Cairo, men and officers had completely forgotten their drill. When the guns were attempted to be brought into action, dire confusion reigned. Men ran against each other; the ground was strewn with cartridges; hoppers were placed anywhere but where they ought to have been. No one appeared to have the slightest knowledge of how to feed, aim, or discharge the pieces. In the

midst of all this, poor Walker – not knowing anything of the language beyond the words of command – stood aghast.

Hicks Pasha was furious. 'I have never seen such a disgraceful thing in my life!' he thundered. He ordered Captain Walker to remain in the scorching desert camp with his men for three days of continual drill. As a result, Captain Walker was felled by sunstroke and had to be invalided back to Cairo.

Colonel Stewart continued his criticism of the Egyptian soldiery:

It is impossible for me to criticize too severely the conduct of the Egyptian troops, both officers and men, towards the natives. Their general conduct and overbearing manner is almost sufficient to cause a rebellion. When to this conduct cowardice is added, it is impossible for me to avoid expressing my contempt and disgust.

In addition to the Egyptian soldiers, Hicks Pasha also had a force of bashi-bazouks, irregular cavalry of Balkan extraction. The custom of employing these mercenaries was Turkish. The nineteenth-century Turkish bashi-bazouks were generally noted for their wildness and cruelty, but those in the army of Hicks Pasha appear to have been even more turbulent than the average. Most of those employed in the Sudan had been born there, descendants of the bashi-bazouks who, after helping Mohammed Ali conquer the Sudan, had stayed on and settled there. Colonel Stewart described them as 'swaggering bullies, robbing, plundering, and ill-treating the people with impunity'. At first they were stationed in Khartoum, where they fired their weapons in all directions inside the town, picked quarrels and wounded a number of citizens. They took what they wanted from the shops, and if a shopkeeper asked for his money, they put a pistol to his head and cried, 'Am I not a bashi-bazouk?' Hicks Pasha finally had to move them out of town to a separate camp on the other side of the Blue Nile.

A body of 100 cuirassiers added another bizarre element in Hicks's army. These were mounted warriors, probably from Darfur, who were armed and costumed like knights and men-at-arms in the days of Saladin and Richard Coeur de Lion. After the crusades, some medieval war surplus merchants found a ready market for their wares in the Sudan. So here were Sudanese tribesmen covered from head to foot in suits of chain- or ring-mail. A long, two-handed sword was carried between the right leg and the saddle, and some carried lances. Sometimes their horses' heads were encased in steel as well, and their bodies covered with a quilt thick enough to turn a spear. A British staff officer, on first encountering one of these

Sudanese knights by moonlight, thought he was seeing a ghost.

It was indeed a queer sort of army: soldiers who landed crying and in chains, lawless bashi-bazouks, and Arabs dressed like King Arthur. Frank Power, the twenty-five-year-old correspondent of *The Times*, who arrived in Khartoum on 1 August 1883, called the army 'a cowardly, beggarly mob'. A Dutch adventurer, Johann Maria Schüver, who owned three Nile boats from which he flew the Dutch flag, and who was suspected of supplying arms to the Mahdi, viewed Hicks Pasha's expeditionary force with amusement and unconcealed contempt. Speaking of the Dervishes to Colonel Colborne, he said, 'Do you think you are going to overcome them with the forces at your disposal? Never! Your army will never return!'

In April Hicks Pasha moved the bulk of his force, about 5,000 men, to El Kawa to put down the rebellion in the Sennar district. Because of the intense heat, many of the officers preferred to live in native mud huts rather than their tents. One hot day at El Kawa Colonel Colborne wrote: 'I see from the opening of my beehive hut the poor sentries huddling under shelter. They are placed nearly as thickly as by night. This seems to be the Egyptian military idea, and it is hopeless to interfere with them at this point. Without a swarm of sentinels about every two yards they do not feel secure.' Until the British officers insisted upon it, no outlaying pickets were used at all. The reason for this neglect was – as Hussein Pasha Muzhar, the Egyptian second-in-command, explained – because 'the men might get killed'. However, once instituted, the practice gave efficient results. The soldiers detailed to such duty were so frightened that they took care to stay on the alert.

After three weeks at El Kawa, the army moved further south along the Nile towards El Jebelein. The troops were still far from being fully trained, and they were not yet acclimatized to the harsh environment of the Sudan, but they had learned some elementary drill and simple tactics and Hicks Pasha was impatient to begin work. As they were now marching through hostile country, Hicks Pasha ordered the troops to march in open column, but Sulayman Pasha protested that this was a ridiculous order as in case of attack the men would never be able to form square quickly enough. He was right. The men had to be put into a square and marched in this position over the scorched, cracking ground and through the mimosa scrub.

On 26 April 1883, eighteen miles south of El Kawa, the enemy was sighted in force for the first time. About 1,000 mounted warriors rode towards them through a mirage on the horizon, giving the appearance of a phantom army. The soldiers stood uneasily but ready in their square awaiting the attack. When the horsemen had ridden to within a thousand yards, Hicks Pasha opened fire with his howitzers. The shells burst in the midst of the enemy and scattered them. It was probably the first time most of the Dervishes had encountered artillery. They quickly drew off and did not attack again, although they stayed in the vicinity of the army and watched it.

Three days later, near the village of Al-Marabi, two of the British staff officers, who had been reconnoitring in front, rode quickly back to the marching square with the news that the enemy was advancing rapidly in force. Fortunately, there was sufficient time to arrange the square in good order on a level plain. The baggage, camels and camp followers were placed in the centre of the square. The rocket tubes and howitzers were positioned inside the square and the Nordenfeldts were put outside in front of the files. The white-helmeted English officers made themselves conspicuous to give encouragement to the troops.

They did not have long to wait. Soon about 5,000 Dervishes, part mounted and part on foot, rushed from a small wood about 800 yards away in a confused mass, shouting wildly under their huge banners inscribed with texts from the Koran. Hicks Pasha opened fire at once with his rockets and howitzers, but the rockets burst among his own men and the shells failed to discourage the attackers. The files of Egyptian infantry on the side nearest the enemy now opened fire, followed by the Nordenfeldt machine guns that laid the massed Dervishes in rows. Still they came on, spreading out to sweep around the corner of the square.

The British officers found it impossible not to admire the bravery of these men who, armed only with sword and spear, charged without cover the well-armed Egyptians. Colonel Colborne became almost lyrical when he described the conduct of the sheikhs who led them: 'And what gallant men were they! Right up to the cannon's mouth, right up to the rifle muzzle they rode, encouraging their followers with the promise of paradise, to break our square. But Nordenfeldts and Remingtons are no respecters of creeds or fanatical idiosyncrasies.'

Without the element of surprise and without adequate cover, the Dervishes did not have a chance against the superior weapons of the Egyptians. Twelve of the leading sheikhs fell and Colonel Arthur Farquhar estimated that between 500 and 600 of the enemy were killed. The remaining Dervishes retreated. The troops were ordered to hold their places in the square in case of a second attack. While they waited, a tall, gaunt Bagarra, armed with a spear, strode out of the woods towards them, chanting the creed: 'There is no god but Allah . . .'. Hicks Pasha, thinking he intended to surrender, told his interpreter to order the man to throw down his spear. Instead, the Bagarra waved it defiantly over his head and came on. He was shot.

Within six yards of the square were two Dervishes lying on the ground, apparently dead; beside them was a Mahdist banner. An Egyptian captain was sent out to get it, but the moment he took hold of the flag the Dervish who lay beside it quickly sat up and sank a spear into his left hand. The officer drew his sword and cut him down with a blow on the neck, but then found himself engaged with the second 'dead man'. The Dervish was finally shot and the flag captured, but none was willing to trust the dead after that.

Except for these incidents, all was quiet around the square. Several Dervishes, apparently ignorant of the Remington's range, calmly walked about, turning over corpses looking for the bodies of friends or relations. These were coolly shot. Some of the English officers rode out to look for the enemy, but they had vanished. There would not be a second attack. When the soldiers learned that they had routed the much-feared rebels, that they had actually defeated the undefeatable, they shouted and yelled; the band struck up a wild triumphant air, the bashi-bazouks raced around on their camels, waving their rifles and shouting; and all gave three cheers each for the Khedive, for Hicks Pasha and for Sulayman Pasha. Then the order was given to resume the march, leaving the battle-field to the vultures and hyenas, who had already begun their feast. As they marched, the soldiers came across many wounded Dervishes who had fallen in their flight. Sometimes the entire army would pass a wounded man by, but usually someone would put a bullet through his head. It was a great victory for Hicks Pasha.

The success of this expedition raised the hopes of the government and improved the morale of the troops, but there was friction among the senior officers. Sulayman Pasha was not content to be a figurehead and Hicks Pasha resented his interference with his command. On 13 May, from the island of Abba, Hicks wrote to the Earl of Dufferin, the British Commissioner in Cairo, asking that he be put in 'indisputable command' of the army. Sir Edward Malet, the British Agent in Cairo, politely suggested that perhaps the request of Hicks Pasha should be granted, but the British government seemed more concerned by Hicks's persistence in writing to

British rather than Egyptian authorities. Lord Granville, the Foreign Secretary, fearful that Britain would become involved, telegraphed to Sir Edward that 'Her Majesty's Government are in no way responsible for the operations in the Sudan, which have been undertaken under the authority of the Egyptian Government, or for the appointment or actions of General Hicks'.

Hicks Pasha returned to Khartoum, leaving his army to follow him, and began making plans for the major campaign in Kordofan, the object of which was to recapture El Obeid and defeat the Mahdi's main army. The difficulties were at once apparent. On 3 June he telegraphed to Sir Edward Malet:

> The force we have is not nearly sufficient to undertake the Kordofan campaign. Every ounce of food must be taken from here. We march through a hostile country, inhabited by powerful tribes. The line of communication must be kept open, and depots must be formed which must be sufficiently garrisoned. Each convoy will require escort. Our available strength will be under 6,000; of these, many will most likely be sick after the fever season. I cannot withdraw a man from the Blue Nile station. Khartoum is full of rebels, and a sufficient garrison must be left there. The garrison on White Nile will be reduced as much as possible. I shall have available for the campaign about 5,000 infantry. Of these, at least 2,000 will be necessary on the line of communication, thus leaving only 3,000 infantry for the attacking force. I consider this number quite inadequate. It should be 10,000 men. . . .

More troublesome to Hicks than lack of money, supplies and soldiers was the blurred line of command and, in particular, his relations with Sulayman Pasha. After writing a series of complaints to which little attention was paid, he finally, on 16 July, telegraphed to Malet: 'My orders and arrangements here are quite disregarded; promises are made that they shall be carried out, but nothing whatever is done. Sulayman Pasha disregards them altogether. It is useless to keep me here under these conditions, and it is a position which I cannot hold. I beg you will have me recalled.' A week later he actually sent in his resignation. This brought matters to a head and Sulayman Pasha was recalled and given a new post as Governor of the Red Sea provinces. Hicks Pasha withdrew his resignation, but his position was not much improved as it was decided that, for the sake of Egyptian prestige, Ala al-Din Pasha Siddik, who had replaced Abdel Kadir Pasha as Governor-General of the Sudan, should accompany the army on its expedition into Kordofan.

In spite of the victories in Sennar on the Blue Nile – which Evelyn Baring referred to as 'trifling successes' – the conditions within the army had improved very little. Colonel Stewart, speaking of the 'utter worthlessness of the Egyptian infantry', said: 'It is almost impossible for me to convey an idea of the contempt with which all classes of people here regard them. The Negro troops will not associate with them, nor will, curiously enough, the Egyptian officers in command of those troops.' On 5 August, Hicks Pasha reported that 'the men at Kerkoj are twenty-five months in arrear of pay, and Fazoglu nine months, and neither have clothes nor food . . . troops insubordinate . . . all means of transport wanting . . .'. He finally concluded that the proposed expedition to El Obeid was impossible and that Egypt should 'wait for Kordofan to settle itself'. Colonel Stewart also wrote: 'I am strongly of the opinion that to advance on Kordofan would be exceedingly injudicious . . .'. Lord Dufferin had already reached the same conclusion and told Ibrahim Bey, the head of the Sudan Department in Cairo, that 'if the Egyptian Government were wise, it would confine its present efforts to the re-establishment of its authority in Sennar'.

The British government did not, however, attempt to enforce its views. In fact, following the instructions of Lord Granville, it continued to maintain an arms-length attitude towards the Sudan and its problems. Hicks Pasha, being a proud man, did not want to press his view that the undertaking was too dangerous. So the Egyptian government, unwilling to lose such vast territory, gave Hicks some additional reinforcements, and all the money it could spare, and, although both troops and money were inadequate, the army for the reconquest of Kordofan assembled in Omdurman.[1] Frank Power wrote to his brother Arnold a month after his arrival in Khartoum:

> In three days we march on a campaign that even the most sanguine look forward to with the greatest gloom. We have here 9,000 infantry that fifty good men could rout in ten minutes, and 1,000 cavalry (bashi-bazouks) that have never learnt even to ride, and these, with a few Nordenfeldt guns, are to beat the 69,000 men the Mahdi has got together. . . . That Egyptian officers and men are not worth the ammunition they throw away is well known.

[1] One of the most curious aspects of the expedition is the fact that the exact number and composition of the force is still unknown. Even more curiously, historians of the era appear not to have noticed, or to have ignored, the discrepancies. Three excellent authorities who were on the spot when the army was assembled variously estimated the number of bashi-bazouks as 400, 1,000 and 3,000. Perhaps their wildness and ubiquitousness led observers to overestimate their numbers. It would appear, too, that some writers counted the 2,000 camp followers as infantry; it may well have been difficult to tell camp followers from soldiers in this army.

When the force paraded at Omdurman on 8 September, it consisted of 7,000 infantry (plus or minus two or three thousand), an unknown number of which were Sudanese; from 400 to 3,000 cavalry, some of which may or may not have been regular Egyptian or Turkish troops; and about 100 cuirassiers. Transport was provided by 5,500 camels, better counted than the soldiers and apparently more valuable. The army carried ten brass mountain guns, four Krupp mortars, and six or seven Nordenfeldt machine guns.

In addition to Hicks Pasha and eight European staff officers, there were a number of other Europeans who intended to accompany the expedition: Edmund O'Donovan, the correspondent of the *Daily News*; Frank Vizetelly, the artist for the *Illustrated London News* and *Graphic*; a surgeon and at least two German orderlies, one of whom was named Gustav Klootz. Frank Power, with a crew-cut and a van Dyke beard, started with the expedition, but in spite of his parasol and blue vest to protect him from the sun and his crimson cummerbund to guard against dysentery, he fell sick and went back to Khartoum. Young Power shared with Gladstone a sympathy for the political aims of the Dervishes. He wrote his brother:

> I am not ashamed to say I feel the greatest sympathy for them, and every race that fights against the rule of Pachas [*sic*], backsheesh, bribery, robbery and corruption. I pity Hicks; he is an able, good, and energetic man, but he has to do with wretched Egyptians, who take a pleasure in being incompetent, thwarting one, delaying, and lying.

Power never changed his attitude. Even several months later, when his own neck was in danger, he wrote his mother:

> I will, indeed, forgive the fellow who puts his lance into me, if that is to be my fate, because I will feel he is right as long as I am of the same colour as the scoundrels who have robbed him and his for so many years. . . . The rebels are in the right, and God and chance seem to be fighting for them. . . . Better a thousand times the barbarities of slavery than the detestable barbarities and crimes of the Egyptian rulers.

Hicks Pasha and his army marched south, hugging the Nile, to Ed Dueim, 130 miles from Khartoum. From here it is 150 miles in a straight line to El Obeid, but the land between is desert, broken in parts by scrub and woodland, and a rare stream or water-hole. The distance was normally covered in twelve caravan marches or five post marches, but Hicks was to be on the road for forty-three days, twenty of them marching days, without ever reaching El Obeid.

At Ed Dueim the army was joined by the Governor-General, Ala al-Din Pasha, and his staff. As Ala al-Din spoke no European language and Hicks spoke no Arabic, close rapport between the two men was handicapped from the start. Incredibly, Hicks Pasha and Ala al-Din now sat down to discuss for the first time the route to be taken. Ala al-Din had hired guides whom he believed to be trustworthy and from the information they were able to supply a route was finally selected. The following day, 24 September 1883, a detachment sent out to look for water on the line of march reported that there were fifty wells at Shat, one day's march away, and a small brook halfway there. Three days later the army formed itself into a huge square and, leaving behind the security of the Nile, lumbered into the desert. The arrival of the army at Shat was chaos. They did not get there until midnight and the units failed to maintain their proper positions, some being 4,000 yards away from the square. Hussein Pasha, the second in command, complained to the Governor-General of the great danger of this disorder and attributed the fault to Hicks Pasha. Ala al-Din tried to send him to Hicks, but Hussein swore he would not talk to Hicks Pasha and argued that he himself should be given command of the army. When Hicks heard of this he tried to have Hussein dismissed. All the next day was spent bickering. Hicks said either he or Hussein Pasha would have to return to Khartoum. Abbas Bey Afandi Hilmi, the secretary to the Governor-General, tried to patch up the matter by blaming the entire difficulty on the translators of Hicks Pasha's orders. The news that their commanders were quarrelling spread among the soldiers and did nothing to raise morale. An ombashi (corporal) who was attached to the staff of the Governor-General deserted, and Abbas Bey recorded in his diary that 'we are sorry that he has beheld the anger that has arisen between Hicks Pasha and Hussein Pasha and the discontent it has caused to all.' So, news of the quarrel was carried to the enemy.

For a force as large and as slow as this one, thirst was a nightmare more dreaded than the enemy. The army moved from one watering place to the next, never really knowing more than one day's march ahead if water would be available. Hicks Pasha, in an undated dispatch to Khartoum, wrote: 'We have depended upon pools of rain water for supply, which we have fortunately found. . . . Water not to be obtained by digging wells. I have no information regarding water between Serakna and Norabi, nor reliable information of the supply there. This causes me great anxiety. . . . The heat is intense.'

In nearly all published accounts of this march, the Dervishes are said to have filled in or otherwise spoiled the wells ahead of the advancing army. In fact, this only happened once, and then it is uncertain if it was by accident or design. On 2 October Captain Arthur Herlth, an Austrian staff officer, rode out in the morning with a hundred horsemen to look for water. He returned after sunset with the report that Arabs had watered cattle at the ponds, leaving them muddy and foul.

That evening a council of war was held to review their situation and decide on future plans. Present at the meeting were the Governor-General, Hicks Pasha, Hussein Pasha, Colonel Farquhar, Abbas Bey and the commanding officers of the 1st and 4th battalions. The main discussion concerned not the present situation but a matter of policy that ought to have been decided before the march began – the question of whether or not garrisons should be left at the wells along the way to establish a line of communications or retreat. It had been hoped that the tribes inhabiting the area through which they marched would come in and swear their allegiance to the government, offer them aid and provide reinforcements. So far this had not happened. On the contrary, it was evident that the inhabitants were hostile: all the villages they encountered were deserted and any soldier who strayed from the square was cut down by the enemy scouts who were constantly watching them. Garrisons left at watering places would have to be strong and would still be in danger; to leave a string of garrisons along the route would weaken the attacking force. On the other hand, not to protect their line of communication would mean that they would be cut off and at the mercy of the uncertain water supply ahead of them. Hussein Pasha wanted to send back to Khartoum and call up the troops left on guard there to man the proposed garrisons. Hicks Pasha thought this was out of the question, and again the two engaged in a violent argument. According to Abbas Bey, no decision was reached; according to Hicks Pasha, it was decided to march on without leaving garrisons on their line of communications. Hicks sent back to Khartoum a dispatch which reported this decision. It was the last message received from him.

The next day, 4 October, Colonel Farquhar went out with a cavalry patrol and found water two hours away – one day's march for the infantry. Hicks Pasha's cook, Mohammed Nur al Barudi, later described what happened. After finding the water and starting back, the guide remembered that he had left his rifle behind and returned to fetch it. He did not return to the patrol. The next day, when the army reached the water, they found the guide sitting under a tree with both hands cut off.

For the army, each day's primary problem was the same: water. On 10 October the army set out for Akila where water was said to be plentiful. Although only one day's march away, they did not get there in so short a time. Abbas Bey wrote in his diary: 'The guides did not know the direct route, but led us very crookedly, and finally we were worn out and in a pitiful state of thirst, so bad that I am afraid to describe it lest we should grieve the authorities.' But he did describe the confusion in the army. As the men's water-bottles became empty, they started dropping out of the ranks, some to search on their own for water and others to fall behind, prey for the Dervishes that followed them. Hicks Pasha, Ala al-Din Pasha and the staff officers rode around and around the square, urging the officers to keep their men in hand. Hicks Pasha was in a frenzy and swore that if a hundred Arabs attacked them now there would be a general massacre. A few melons were found and this helped to relieve the thirst of some. When Captain Herlth found a small stream, the army lunged towards it.

Anxious for the safety of his men, Hicks Pasha tried frantically to make them set up camp and build a zariba, but they would not leave the water and gathered in confused masses beside it. Hicks Pasha sent orders by Abbas Bey to Hussein Pasha to get the men back to build the camp, but Hussein Pasha pointed to Hicks and snapped, 'There is their commander, let him keep order if he can because I am not able to do so.' When this speech was reported to Hicks Pasha, he flew into a rage. 'Hussein Pasha quite forgets that this disorder is entirely due to his own mismanagement. I shall refuse to keep him as my second in command. He does nothing but disobey my orders, and thinks that I should be junior to him!'

The following day, 11 October, the army reached Akila with its excellent water supply. They were now about halfway to El Obeid, but still not a single tribe had come to support them, no garrisons had been established in their rear and it had been eight days since any word had been sent back to Khartoum: no messenger could be found willing to make the trip, even though a large reward was offered.

As the first night in Akila was the evening before the Muslim feast of Bairam, the Governor-General permitted the band to play; then, thinking they might be attacked while the soldiers were listening to the music, he ordered it stopped. An hour later a few Dervishes were seen near the camp and everyone began firing.

Abbas Bey was almost killed by the erratic musketry of his own men. After about seven minutes, the Arabs disappeared and the firing ceased. Ala al-Din Pasha complimented the men on their gallantry and assured them that if they continued to act so well they would certainly defeat the enemy.

The next day, 12 October and the Feast of Bairam, the Governor-General held a reception for all the officers, guns were fired in a salute and everyone gave cheers for the Khedive. Water was plentiful and the spirits of the troops were good – until a group of men wandered 2,000 yards from the zariba without their guns and were slaughtered.

Later that day, a proclamation was framed by the Governor-General; an Arab woman had been found who was willing to deliver copies to the local tribes. The proclamation read:

> No doubt you have heard of the victorious army that has come to destroy the rebels and is now in the midst of your country. For your well-being we offer you this advice: be obedient and loyal to the government and, for the welfare of your country, hasten to meet us with all your followers. Then the Aman of Allah and his Prophet be upon you. The disobedient and rebellious among you shall reap the fruit of his doings and no blame rest on us.

This was signed by Ala al-Din Pasha and by Hicks Pasha, who wrote 'I the Englishman, Commandant and leader of the Egyptian Army'.

On 14 October the army left Akila. Just before starting, an officer's orderly was found disembowelled; he had gone alone to get water the evening before. It was not until the next day that it was discovered that less than 30 per cent of the water jars had been filled at Akila. Consequently, four soldiers, 101 camels, eleven horses and a mule died of thirst. Everyone blamed someone else for the neglect.

The following day Ala al-Din and Hicks Pasha quarrelled violently over the positioning of the irregular cavalry. Hicks Pasha thought the cavalry unreliable and wanted to keep it inside the square; Ala al-Din Pasha insisted it be put on the flanks. The Governor-General began a running quarrel with Hicks Pasha over the treatment of the camels. Hicks Pasha tried to dismiss several officers who were popular in the army, but was unable to do so as the other officers turned rebellious.

On 18 October there was an alarm when some of the Dervishes who were following them came too close to the square. The Governor-General ordered two of the Krupp guns to open fire.

Abbas Bey wrote: 'But it grieves me to say that the Krupps could not fire because of some harm that had befallen their machines, and so they were compelled to use other guns.' Blame for this state of affairs fell upon the officer commanding the artillery, whom Abbas Bey called 'a burden and a source of trouble to the army'. The next day the only water they could find was in two muddy brooks, and that evening, Abbas Bey wrote: 'Praise Allah that this day will end at last. Tomorrow we shall have to set out carrying filthy water for a journey of eight hours.'

Now a new source of disagreement arose among the leaders of the army. The European officers were losing faith in the guides. The Governor-General, who had selected them, felt obliged to defend his choice and to look upon the distrust of the guides as a personal affront. On 20 October Colonel Farquhar, relying on his compass rather than the guides, led the army into thick bush. Men and units lost their way and the army dropped all semblance of a military formation. The soldiers began to say that Hicks Pasha intended to have them annihilated; otherwise, why did he lead them into the bush. Abbas Bey wrote: 'Is this what they call the skill of the English, to lead us blindly against the advice of our guides into a dense bush? . . . I praise Allah the enemy did not fire the grass or the result would have been terrible.'

That night Hicks Pasha ordered a guard to be set over the guides to keep them from leaving the camp, thus enraging Ala al-Din Pasha, who told Hicks: 'I have obtained the guides, and am quite satisfied as to their loyalty. I do not wish you to interfere with my people.'

The next day there was a skirmish with a band of Dervishes. Small actions then continued daily until, on 26 October, the army reached Er Rahad, forty miles (six days' march) from El Obeid. Here they stopped for four days and erected a small fort; there was water to be had from a shallow lake. While the Dervishes were obviously following every move of the Egyptian army, Hicks Pasha had no information at all as to the movements, size or disposition of the enemy. To obtain information, it was decided that Hussein Pasha should take a strong detachment out to capture a neighbouring village, but Hicks Pasha and the Governor-General quarrelled over the best way to do this, as Hicks Pasha doubted the Egyptian troops were capable of fighting in any formation other than a square and an attack on a village required a more open formation. In any case, Hussein Pasha set out with a patrol to see what he could do, but the village was deserted when he arrived.

It was apparent, however, that the number of hostile Arabs around them was increasing, and from their costumes it could be seen that some came from distant tribes. On 28 October two Arabs were captured who reported that the Mahdi was summoning all the tribes to come to him and that most were answering his call.

Within the army, the number of quarrels among the officers multiplied and the artillery officers complained to the Governor-General that the European staff officers were interfering with them. Ala al-Din Pasha complained to Colonel Farquhar; Farquhar, in turn, was disillusioned with Hicks Pasha, and his diary reflected his bitterness over what he regarded as the military mistakes of his superior. A civilian merchant travelling with the army was caught writing a letter to his father, who was with the Mahdi: Hicks Pasha called a council of officers at which it was decided to disarm all the civilians.

At Er Rehad, Gustav Klootz, a blond, blue-eyed young German who had been an orderly, first for Baron Freiherr von Seckendorff, one of the staff officers, and then for Edmund O'Donovan of the *Daily News*, concluded that the army was headed for disaster. Frank Power said that Klootz had been a sergeant of Uhlans and 'had the iron cross for bravery', but if he had any courage, it left him now. He talked over the situation of the army with another German youth and the two of them decided to desert to the Mahdi. Pretending that they were going out to gather wood, they left the camp. Beyond the lines they heard firing and the other German boy grew frightened and turned back, but Klootz ran on.

When night came, Klootz found a tree and went to sleep beneath it. The next morning he debated whether or not he should return, but decided that as his countryman had probably told of his desertion it would be better if he went on. He started out again, but was soon stopped by three Arabs who challenged him with pointed rifles. Klootz quickly threw down his own rifle and revolver and held up his hands. Not speaking a word of Arabic, he called out in German, 'Dervish – where is the Dervish?' (meaning the Mahdi). The Arabs took his money, weapons, watch and boots and pointed in the direction of the Dervish camp.

Barefoot, he plodded on until he found himself surrounded by horsemen who led him into the large camp of Abu Girga, a Mahdist emir. Thinking he had captured an English officer, Abu Girga loaded him with chains, put a rope around his neck and had him taken to the Mahdi in El Obeid.

O'Donovan was annoyed by Klootz's flight and mentioned it in his diary as an instance of the general feeling of despair that pervaded the army: 'What must be the condition of an army when even a European servant deserts to the enemy?' O'Donovan himself probably contributed to Klootz's state of mind, for he was growing more and more pessimistic: 'I make my notes and write my reports, but who is going to take them home?' Colonel Farquhar recorded a conversation he had with the journalist: 'I spoke to Mr O'Donovan today and asked him where he thought we should be eight days hence? "In Kingdom-come", was his reply.'

On 30 October the army, without hope or faith, left Er Rehad and continued the march towards El Obeid. By 1 November they had reached a place called Aloba, skirmishing all the way and enduring almost continual sniping. On 3 November a letter arrived for Hicks Pasha from the Mahdi, which said in part:

> Every intelligent person must know that Allah rules, and his authority cannot be shared by muskets, cannons, or bombs, and no one has any strength except he whom Allah the Almighty strengthen. . . .If you have light, you will believe in Allah, in His Prophet, and in the next world, and will accept the truth of our mission as Mahdi, and will come out to us, surrendering yourselves. He who surrenders shall be saved. But if you refuse and persist in denying my divine calling, and trust in guns and powder, you are to be killed, even as the Prophet foretold many others before you.

The warning was ignored.

On 4 November Captain Herlth wrote in his diary:

> These are very bad times; we are in a forest and everyone very depressed. The general orders the band to play, hoping that the music may enliven us a little; but the bands soon stop, for the bullets are flying from all directions, and camels, mules and men keep dropping down; we are all cramped up together, so the bullets cannot fail to strike. We are faint and weary, and have no idea what to do. The general gives the order to halt and make a zariba. It is Sunday and my dear brother's birthday. Would to God I could sit down and talk to him for an hour! The bullets are falling thicker.

There are no further eye-witness accounts of Hicks Pasha's expedition to Kordofan. By the end of the following day all the diary writers were dead.

3

Mahdism Grows

While Hicks Pasha marched blindly towards El Obeid, knowing nothing of the enemy's strength or position, the Mahdi knew all about the movements of the Egyptian army. He followed its progress step by step and made his preparations to meet it. He sent messengers to all of the tribes, near and far, to send their fighting men. It was said, and generally believed, that the Mahdi had promised 40,000 angels from paradise to fight at their sides. Tribe after tribe answered his call until it seemed that the entire population of the Sudan was massing at El Obeid. Daily the Mahdi preached, affirming his divine mission and calling on his people to follow his way. He gave his followers something to believe in and something to hate: the Mahdi and the Turk. Just how many warriors he mustered can never be known, but it has been estimated that there were 100,000 people with him when, on 1 November 1883, he marched out of El Obeid. The Mahdi had inspired in all of them the wildest enthusiasm, and they were eager to kill.

The information he had received from Klootz regarding the demoralized condition of Hicks Pasha's army elated the Mahdi. He scattered hundreds of papers in the path of the advancing army calling on Hicks and his soldiers to surrender. The Mahdi was incensed when he learned that the Egyptian soldiers used these divine words for toilet paper.

On 3 November Abu Anga, one of the Mahdi's most capable generals, with his jihadiya, the trained Black riflemen, concealed themselves in the woods of Shaykan, near Kashgeil, about fifteen miles from El Obeid, in front of the advancing Egyptians. Other forces of the Mahdi moved to positions on the flanks and rear. The following day, when the thirsty army reached the woods, the jihadiya began the attack with a deadly fire into the front ranks. Caught by surprise, the Egyptians panicked: horses, camels and men fell before the deadly fire. When the Egyptians tried to fall back, the Dervishes attacked from the flanks. Many of the soldiers shot their own comrades in the confusion. All afternoon the fighting continued, with the Dervishes drawing a tighter and tighter noose around the Egyptians and Hicks Pasha trying vainly to form his demoralized men into a proper square. When night fell, the Dervishes crept close and continued to pour bullets into the huddled masses of men and animals.

The next morning, Hicks Pasha tried to advance, for he had to have water, but he was able to move less than a mile. The Dervishes fell upon him in overwhelming numbers. The square broke and the massacre began. The terrified soldiers tried to flee but were cut down as they ran. It took a long time to kill so many men, and the work was not finished until the following day. Hicks Pasha with some European officers made a heroic stand under a baobab tree and were among the last to fall. When his white horse was wounded in the back, Hicks Pasha dismounted and fought on foot with his sword until at last he fell, his body pierced with spears. It is said that the spear that killed him was thrown by Khalifa Mohammed Sherif.

Except for about a hundred soldiers, some of whom escaped by hiding under the piles of dead bodies, the entire army of 10,000 was annihilated. Incredibly, only about 350 Dervishes were killed. The heads of Hicks Pasha and Baron Seckendorf were cut off and sent to the Mahdi. Gustav Klootz identified them for him.

Most of the survivors of the battle of Shaykan were eventually executed. The only man known by name to have escaped was Mohammed Nur el Barudi, Hicks Pasha's cook: he convinced Wad Nejumi that he was a doctor and served in this capacity with the Dervishes for five years before making his escape to Egypt just before the battle of Toski in August 1889.

After the battle, several emirs were left behind with their men to gather the plunder and deposit it in the Beit el Mal, the Mahdi's treasury. They took everything, even the clothing from the corpses. Klootz, who claimed to understand doctoring, was permitted to search for medicine on the battlefield. The dead of the Egyptian army were left to rot on the ground; there was too much meat for even the vultures and hyenas. Klootz wandered about, turning over the naked, mutilated bodies of those whom only a few days before had been his friends. After Klootz, it was twenty-two years before another European saw this battlefield.

The Mahdi's return to El Obeid in triumph was a scene of dusty, barbaric splendour. First came tribesmen carrying the huge, many-coloured flags, followed by massed thousands of Dervishes murmuring 'La Ilaha il'lallah' – There is no god but Allah. Now and then, men would leap outside the dusty ranks, waving blood-stained spears and yelling. The three khalifas came next, and then the cavalry, carrying swords and lances. Behind them the prisoners, naked and wretched, were dragged by ropes through the dust. They were followed by the captured mountain guns, Krupps and Nordenfeldts, pulled by wounded mules. Last of all came the Mahdi, mounted on a magnificent white camel and surrounded by his most devoted followers chanting 'La Ilaha il'lallah'. As he passed, the spectators threw themselves on the ground and kissed the dust. Women screamed and called 'Mahdi Allah – The Mahdi of God!'

As news of this great victory spread throughout the Sudan, there were few indeed who could deny that the Expected One had arrived with all the divine powers he himself claimed. There were ansar who swore they had seen the promised angels fighting beside them in the battle at Shaykan. The prestige of the Mahdi was enormous and the magic of his name united all in his cause. He was worshipped almost as a god, and even the water he used to wash himself was passed out to the faithful who drank it as an antidote for every ill.

Considering his fantastic accomplishments, it is not surprising that he inspired awe, provoked wonder. In the summer of 1881 he had been a poor, insignificant fanatic with a handful of followers; only two and a half years later he had conquered most of the Sudan, shattered the Egyptian army, and captured 20,000 rifles and nineteen guns.

No Egyptian official, and certainly no Christian European could believe anything but that the Mahdi was an impostor, his divine mission a fiction to serve his own political ambitions. But so incredible was his swift success, even before the disaster to Hicks, that Europeans themselves found it hard to think of the man in terms that were not supernatural. Colonel Stewart, that cool professional soldier, expressed an almost unthinkable thought in an official report: 'Here is a Government well supplied with arms, ammunition, money and soldiers utterly defeated and paralysed by a poor simple Fakih. How can such a result happen except by the direct interposition of God?' How indeed.

With the destruction of Hicks Pasha's army, there were few Sudanese who were not convinced by the Mahdi's military victories, if not by his religious dogma, that he was the true Mahdi of Islam. Among Egyptian officials and others for whom belief in the Mahdi was impossible, terror spread in ever-widening circles:

to the capital of the Sudan in Khartoum and to the remote provinces of Darfur, Bahr el Ghazal and Equatoria which were still controlled by European governors. There was consternation in Cairo, where the danger to Egypt of a Sudan ruled by a militant and hostile religious fanatic was all too apparent.

England, too, was stunned by the news of Hicks Pasha's fate. It seemed incredible that an army of 10,000 men led by an English officer could so completely disappear. Lord Edmund Fitzmaurice, speaking in the House of Lords, said: 'Probably since Pharaoh's host perished in the Red Sea, there has been no disaster so sudden and so overwhelming, no such complete destruction of a host, as the destruction and disappearance, we might almost say, of General Hicks' Army in the wastes of Kordofan.'

It was not only in Kordofan that the Mahdi was triumphant. His ideas spread quickly, and men and tribes who had never seen him took up arms in his cause. On the very day of Hicks Pasha's defeat, in the Red Sea littoral on the opposite side of the Sudan, a small band of ansar, less than 200 men armed only with clubs and spears, attacked in the Mahdi's name a well-armed force of 500 Egyptians at a place called El Teb. The Egyptians lost eleven officers and 148 men, 300 rifles, a cannon and 50,000 rounds of ammunition. Also killed was Captain Lynedoch Moncrieff, a British naval officer who was the British Consul for the Red Sea area.

The leader of the Dervishes in this attack was a remarkable man named Uthman Ben Abu Bakr Digna, who was to become known throughout Europe and the British Empire as Osman Digna. Born about the year 1840 at the Red Sea port of Suakin, he was a member of a large and prosperous family which had been in the eastern Sudan for more than three centuries. His first cousin was the chief merchant of Suakin. Osman with his brothers and two cousins developed a thriving trade in cotton, ostrich feathers and slaves with the merchants of the Arabian coast. Slave trading, though illegal, was openly conducted on a large scale. However, in the late 1870s the British took active steps to curb the slave trade in the Red Sea area and in 1877 H.M.S. *Wild Swan* caught a Digna ship loaded with ninety-six slaves near what is today Port Sudan. Next the Digna shop and compound at Jedda was raided and the family firm was ruined. Osman Digna then worked for a time as a water contractor in Suakin and later as a broker and merchant in Berber. During Arabi's rebellion in Egypt he tried to cause trouble for the government in Suakin, but he was not successful and, though his

activities were reported to the authorities, no action was taken
against him.

Just when Osman Digna was converted to Mahdism is not
known, but one of his brothers had been an early convert and
Osman himself made his way to Khartoum and then to El Obeid,
arriving shortly after the fall of the town in January 1883. His
brother had died of disease during the siege and, as he had been
well liked by the Mahdi, Osman Digna was warmly welcomed. He
was made emir of the Eastern Provinces and sent back loaded with
proclamations and letters to the Red Sea littoral with instruction
to raise the tribes against the Turk. One of the proclamations was
addressed 'From Mohammed el Mahdi to all his beloved, the
believers in Allah and His book' and said in part: 'I send you
Sheikh Osman Digna of Suakin as your emir in order to revive the
true religion. On his arrival, join him and obey his orders. Advance
against the Turks and drive them out of your country.'

There is a low, scorched coastal shelf where the Sudan meets the
Red Sea. The coastline is guarded by coral reefs, and when the
water is highest the land is only a few inches above it. This narrow
plain stretches for more than a thousand miles along the north-east
African shore, seldom extending further than forty miles inland.
In the Sudan, the plain gives way to foothills and then to mountains
that form a massif with peaks four to five thousand feet high. In the
foothills and mountains live a number of wild tribes collectively
called Beja, of which the principal are the Hadendowa, Amara
Beni Amir and Bisharin. They are a Hamitic people with some
mixture of Nubian and Arab blood. Although Muslims, they have
their own distinctive customs and costumes. Their wild, frizzy hair
style, picturesque if unhygienic, gave them the name of Fuzzy-
Wuzzies among British soldiers and it is by this name that they are
known to British and American readers of Kipling:

'E rushes at the smoke when we let drive,
    An', before we know, 'e's 'ackin' at our 'ead;
'E's all 'ot sand an' ginger when alive,
    An' 'e's generally shammin' when 'e's dead.
'E's a daisy, 'e's a ducky, 'e's a lamb!
    'E's a injia-rubber idiot on the spree,
'E's the on'y thing that doesn't care a damn
    For the Regiment o' British Infantree!
So 'ere's *to* you, Fuzzy-Wuzzy, at your 'ome in the Sowdan;
You're a pore benighted 'eathen but a first-class fightin' man;
An' 'ere's *to* you, Fuzzy-Wuzzy, with your 'ayrick 'ead of 'air –
You big black boundin' beggar – for you bruk a British square.

H. C. Jackson, who spent twenty-four years as a British civil servant in the Sudan, described them as 'truculent, fearless, independent, proud, vindictive. A wrong, real or imaginary, is never forgotten or forgiven unless it has been wiped out with money or washed away with blood.'

It was among these wild hillmen that Osman Digna, the city merchant, found his followers. But it was not easy. The Mahdi was far away and the Hadendowa and other Beja tribes, never having been subdued, had not suffered under Egyptian administration. Moreover, both Arab and Beja were greatly influenced by their religious leaders, and here, as in the central Sudan, entrenched orthodox religion was reluctant to change to the strict ways of the Mahdi and the established leaders were not eager to submit to his authority.

Osman Digna had little success with his letters and proclamations from the distant Mahdi until his dramatic interview with Sheikh Tahir el Majzub, who at this time was the acknowledged spiritual leader of the Hadendowa and the most influential religious leader in the Red Sea hills. He was so venerated that all who came into his presence humbled themselves before him. He sat in a chair while his followers and guests sat on the ground. Sheikh Tahir was the leader of the religious fraternity to which Osman Digna had belonged and the new Mahdist emir brought with him a letter from the Mahdi. Osman Digna found the Sheikh dressed in beautiful silk and satin clothes seated on his chair and surrounded by devotees. Instead of making the customary obeisance, Osman Digna walked boldly to him and presented the letter. Sheikh Tahir took the letter, read it, raised it to his head and eyes and kissed it; then he retired to an inner room of his house. In a few minutes he returned dressed in the coarse white garment of a herdsman. To the astonishment of his devotees, he motioned for Osman Digna to sit in his chair, then crouched before him. The merchant turned Mahdist emir now had the kind of moral support he required and some of the tribesmen gave him their allegiance and assistance. As soon as he had collected a handful of followers, Osman Digna launched his first attack.

Along a thousand miles of coastline, Suakin was then the only important harbour. It was a very ancient port. More than a thousand years ago Chinese merchants came here to trade their silk and pottery for ivory and shark fins. Its white coral buildings spread over a small island in a bay connected by a causeway to the mainland, and the oldest part of the town. It was dirty and cramped but picturesque, and the Sudan's only seaport of any importance. From Suakin two caravan routes led into the African interior: one wound its way to Kassala and on into Abyssinia; the other went to Berber and thus connected the central Sudan with the Red Sea and the outside world. Forty miles inland from Suakin, in the foothills on the Berber caravan route, was Sinkat, small but important, the gateway to the Sudanese interior.

On 5 August 1883 Osman Digna, with 300 of his new ansar, attacked Sinkat. It was defended by seventy Black soldiers commanded by Tewfik Bey, a Cretan Jew who was governor of the district. It was a small fight, few history books mention it. But, like many small engagements, it was important. If Sinkat had fallen at this time, Osman Digna would soon have occupied Suakin, then virtually defenceless. But Sinkat did not fall. Tewfik and his Blacks fought heroically in hastily loopholed barracks. Osman Digna was beaten off with a loss of seventy-five men, including two of his brothers and a nephew, and he himself was wounded on his head, hand and side. Tewfik lost only seven men, although at the end of the battle there were only twelve rounds of ammunition per man left.

Osman Digna lost more than men in this first fight. Those tribes that were uncertain and wavering in their loyalty – which was most of them – now refused to join him. Had strong government forces followed up this victory and launched a vigorous campaign against the rebels, the Red Sea littoral might well have been saved from all Mahdist influence.

Tewfik Bey tried to pursue Osman Digna, and he did succeed in winning another small victory and further reducing Osman Digna's forces and his prestige, but his resources were too meagre and it was at this time that Sulayman Pasha Niyazi arrived on the scene, after Hicks Pasha had succeeded in removing him from the main theatre of action in the central Sudan. Sulayman Pasha preferred diplomacy to war and reproached the gallant Tewfik for firing upon poor ignorant tribesmen who had been deceived by the words of the false mahdi. He offered Osman Digna a pardon and even compensation for the loss of his slaves captured by the British six years earlier, but Osman Digna correctly interpreted this as a sign of weakness and refused, saying simply, 'I am setting out in the religion of Allah'.

As the Egyptian forces remained inactive, many of the tribes came to realize that the government was feeble and that much might be gained by siding with Osman Digna and the Mahdi. Soon

Osman was able to take the field again with a larger force. Tewfik Bey was besieged at Sinkat and a relieving force was cut to pieces. Tokar, on the caravan route to Abyssinia, was also besieged. An Egyptian force then made an abortive attempt to relieve Tokar and was disgracefully defeated at El Teb.

Osman Digna's prestige now rose rapidly. With each victory over the Egyptian forces, with each sign of weakness on the part of the government, more tribesmen joined him. After the defeat of the Egyptian force at El Teb, on the same day as the defeat of Hicks Pasha, many of the larger and most warlike tribes swore their allegiance to the Mahdi and fought under Osman Digna for Allah and loot. The government was left with only Suakin, a precarious toe-hold on the Red Sea, and the besieged towns of Sinkat and Tokar. Osman Digna's forces grew until he had an estimated 11,000 warriors in his army.

Sulayman Pasha, having failed to win over Osman by diplomacy and finding his garrisons besieged and his columns attacked, determined to gain some quick victory to offset the effect created in Cairo by the news of defeats and sieges in his province. He therefore took his only remaining regular troops, a splendid battalion of Blacks and some Egyptian units, and sent them to the relief of Sinkat. This force had reached a place called Tamai when it was attacked by 3,000 Dervishes. The Egyptians bolted at the first sign of an attack, leaving the Blacks to fight alone. Whether fighting for the Mahdi or the Egyptians, the disciplined Blacks always fought well, but at Tamai they were overwhelmed. An exhausted Black sergeant made his way back to Suakin to report. An Egyptian cursed him and called him the son of a dog, while an Egyptian staff officer who had run away from the fight spat at him. Only two officers and thirty-three men returned from this fight. Now there was no force available in the eastern Sudan to go to the relief of the beleaguered inland garrisons.

In December 1883 only six weeks after the defeat of Hicks Pasha, there arrived at Suakin the last remnant of a military force Egypt could spare: the Gendarmerie. It was commanded by that most extraordinary character, Valentine Baker Pasha, younger brother of Sir Samuel Baker, the explorer. Until the age of forty-eight he had been considered a gallant and able British officer. An expert on cavalry tactics, he had distinguished himself in a Kaffir war and in the Crimea; for thirteen years he commanded the 10th Hussars; he was in France as an observer during the Franco-German war, being imprisoned briefly by the French as a German spy; and he had travelled in the wilder parts of Persia and Russia. His brilliant career as a British officer came to a sudden end on 2 August 1875, when he was found guilty in the Croydon assizes of having indecently assaulted a young lady in a railway carriage. Dismissed from the British army, he went to Turkey, where he served as a major-general in the Turkish army and fought the Russians. At the battle of Tashkessan he is said to have fought 'one of the most successful rearguard actions on record'. In 1882 he accepted an offer to take command of the new Egyptian army, but when he arrived in Cairo the offer was withdrawn as it was believed that British officers would be unwilling to serve under one who had been ignominiously dismissed from the British army. Instead, he was given command of the police. Now, it seemed, he would see action after all.

Although the constabulary force Baker commanded was organized along military lines, it contained poor fighting material and he had had little time to make it into a semblance of an army. His troops – those who did not desert the moment they learned they were to be sent to the dreaded Sudan – left Egypt amid the loud lamentations of their relations. Leg irons had been placed on the most cowardly to prevent their desertion. Even the officers at first refused to go. Moberly Bell, *The Times* correspondent in Cairo, sympathized with Baker's position and spoke of the 'hopelessness of his mission' as he described the tearful departure of the Gendarmerie. Once in Suakin, Baker was instructed by the Khedive to 'act with the greatest prudence on account of the insufficiency of the forces placed under your command'. But he did not. He had every reason for wishing to distinguish himself in action. For the first time since his dismissal from the British army he was fighting for England, more or less. This must have seemed an opportunity to redeem himself in the eyes of his former comrades in the only way he knew, for he was aware of how much courage, even reckless daring, was respected in the British officer corps. Perhaps, too, there was something else on Valentine Baker's conscience: it was he who had recommended Hicks Pasha to the Egyptian government.

After only a few weeks, Baker took his force by boat to the harbour of Trinkitat, about sixty miles south of Suakin, and, on 5 February 1884 he started inland for Tokar, twenty miles away. After a few hours' march he reached the wells of El Teb, where the Egyptians had been routed exactly three months earlier. The Dervishes of Osman Digna were waiting for him. They attacked. There were less than a thousand Dervishes, armed only with clubs and spears, against 3,500 well-armed Egyptians. An almost incredible drama now took place. The Egyptian officers and men were panic-stricken; many were completely paralysed with terror. Some fled, throwing away their weapons and accoutrements. Others knelt in the sand and begged for mercy. The Dervishes simply seized them by the head and cut their throats. One Dervish picked up a rifle and, not knowing how to fire it, used it to smash the skull of its cowering owner. An Egyptian officer buried his head in his horse's neck while his terrified men huddled around him. A single tribesman with a sword rode in among them, hacked away the soldiers and cut down the officer, who was too frightened to defend himself. Only the European staff officers and a handful of Blacks tried to fight, but the confusion created by the terrified Egyptians made it nearly impossible for them to do so.

Osman Digna's men killed ninety-six officers and 2,225 men. They captured four Krupp guns, two Gatling machine guns, 3,000 rifles and carbines, and half a million rounds of ammunition. Among the dead was Captain Forestier Walker, the unfortunate machine-gun officer whose attack of sunstroke had saved him from marching with Hicks Pasha.

A few days later, the gallant Tewfik Bey attempted to break out of Sinkat and fight his way to Suakin. The garrison and its loyal inhabitants had held out for six months. They had eaten all the available food, including the dogs and rats, and were reduced to boiling boots and thongs from the angarebs. Realizing that relief was impossible, Tewfik Bey tried to fight his way through the besiegers, carrying the women and children with him in the centre of his square, about 600 people in all. Osman Digna's men cut them down. Only six men and about thirty women and some children were spared, the women to become concubines and the children to be sold into slavery. With the death of Tewfik Bey, the government lost the bravest and most sensible man in the Red Sea littoral. Even Osman Digna praised him: in a report to the Mahdi he referred to Tewfik as 'one of the ablest of the God-forsaken Ala al-Din's men, well known for his bravery and good administration'. Queen Victoria wrote Gladstone: 'The fall of Sinkat is terrible.'

The massacre of Hicks Pasha, the defeat of Baker Pasha, and the fall of Sinkat, combined to create panic in Suakin and Khartoum, consternation in Cairo, and indignation and cries of alarm in London. In England, politicians, humanitarians and a large section of the English public were so shaken by the state of affairs in the Sudan that they clamoured for the government to take action against the rebels. Evelyn Baring, the British Agent in Cairo, was instructed by the Foreign Office to inform the Egyptian government that 'in the event of an attack on Suakin on the part of the rebels, the town would be defended by a British force', and a detachment of British marines was landed there. But this was not enough to satisfy public opinion and at last, against the advice of Evelyn Baring, a cabinet council at No. 10 Downing Street decided to mount an expedition for the relief of Tokar.

By 28 February 1884 a force of more than 3,000 British troops under the command of Major-General Sir Gerald Graham, V.C., with General Redvers Buller as second in command, landed at Trinkitat. There they learned that Tokar had fallen a few days before, but it was decided to march there anyway. The following day Graham's force started inland. Again Osman Digna's forces attacked at El Teb. This time, however, the fanatic tribesmen were met by the steady fire of disciplined British troops. The result was predictable: out of 6,000 Dervishes who took part in the attack, more than a third were left dead on the field; British losses were 189 officers and men killed and wounded.

The expeditionary force marched on and, having reached Tokar without further opposition, turned round and marched back. Osman Digna reported to the Mahdi: 'The English did not stay long. God struck fear into their hearts, and they went back the next morning.'

On 14 March the expeditionary force set out for Tamai, on the Sinkat road, scene of another Egyptian defeat, and slaughtered an additional 2,000 tribesmen with a loss of 221 British killed and wounded. It was here that the Fuzzy-Wuzzy 'bruk a British square'. On the following day Osman Digna's camp was burned, and on 17 March General Graham telegraphed to the War Office: 'The present position of affairs is that two heavy blows have been dealt at the rebels and followers of the Mahdi, who are profoundly discouraged. They say, however, that the English troops can do no more, and must re-embark and leave the country to them.' And so they did. Gladstone spoke of this campaign as a 'frightful slaughter of most gallant Arabs in two bloody battles'.

The British withdrew, contenting themselves with leaving a garrison at Suakin. Osman Digna's followers were indeed discouraged, but as no further action was taken, Osman Digna was again able to rally them. He was soon back in control of most of the Red Sea littoral in the Sudan, where he continued to harass the British and Egyptian forces for a decade. Evelyn Baring aptly summed up the results of Britain's first military effort in the Sudan: 'Many valuable lives were lost. A great slaughter of fanatical savages took place. But no political or military result was obtained commensurate with the amount of life and treasure which was expended.'

The facts of the situation were now obvious. There was no longer an organized army in the Sudan, and only about 24,000 soldiers in scattered garrisons. Besides, with British troops in occupation, Egypt was not even sure it was free to act. Added to other difficulties, there was a serious outbreak of cholera. The forces of the Mahdi were sweeping the Sudan, and Egypt had neither the men nor the money to reconquer it, or even to continue to hold the ground it still held. Britain had the men and money but was unwilling to expend them to obtain an unwanted addition to the Empire. The Sudan must be abandoned. Evelyn Baring saw this clearly, but the British and Egyptian governments and the British public did not want to see it; they did not want to face the unpleasant truth. When all the politicians had spoken, when all the newspapers had expressed their indignation, when all the high civil servants had exchanged their telegrams and letters, the bitter fact still remained that Egypt was unable to hold the Sudan. If the Sudan had to be abandoned, it would be by a decision of reason, not of sentiment. It had to be done, but no one, Baring excepted, could bring himself to do it. And it was at this point that the great British public found their own mahdi, a saviour who would take the situation in hand, sweeping away all doubts and confusion. The British messiah was 'Chinese' Gordon.

4

The Mandarin who turned Messiah

Charles George Gordon was born on 28 January 1833, at Woolwich, the fourth of eleven children. There was never any doubt as to his career: he would become a soldier, like his father, his grandfather and his great-grandfather. After a boyhood spent in Ireland, Scotland, Corfu and England, young Gordon entered the Royal Military Academy at Woolwich at the age of fifteen. Impatient of restraint and quick to anger, he did not take well to discipline; his career was twice endangered by rash and intemperate acts while at the military school. He did get through, however, and was posted to the great military base at Chatham as a sub-lieutenant in the Royal Engineers.

The Crimean War broke out in March 1854, but Gordon was not sent to the Crimea until January 1855, and then he was put to work building huts. Officers assigned to building winter quarters seldom find glory, but Gordon managed to spend a considerable amount of time in the trenches and to bring himself to the notice of his superiors. Colonel C. C. Chesney later said of him that he had 'a special aptitude for war, developing itself amid the trench work before Sebastopol in a personal knowledge of the enemy's movements such as no other officer attained'. In a letter home Gordon wrote that he found war to be 'indescribably exciting'.

For a year following the Crimean War Gordon was assigned to boundary delimitation work, first in Bessarabia and later in Armenia, and then back to Chatham for a dull interlude as field-work instructor. In July 1860 he was posted to China, and there the twenty-seven-year-old captain found the action and excitement he craved. He was at this time a handsome young man, five feet five inches tall with a trim, wiry figure, small hands and feet, light-blue eyes, and a small but well-shaped head topped with tight brown curls. All who knew of him spoke of his great energy. He often gesticulated when he talked, and when excited he would speak too rapidly and stammer. He was exceptionally religious for a young officer, very ambitious, still quick-tempered, still not amenable to discipline, and he had a monumental pride.

The so-called Second Foreign War had been in progress, fitfully, since 1856, and Gordon arrived in time to participate in its final discreditable stages. He was in Peking at the end and took part in the destruction of the Summer Palace, one of the most extraordinary examples of official vandalism in modern times. The Summer Palace was in fact a collection of more than two hundred buildings crammed with artistic and historical treasures. In a letter home, Gordon described the destruction: 'You can scarcely imagine the beauty and magnificence of the palaces we burned. It made one's heart sore to burn them; in fact, these palaces were so large, and we were so pressed for time, that we could not plunder them carefully.' The palace was destroyed in retaliation for the ill-treatment of British prisoners and to 'teach the Chinese a lesson', but the moral was lost on the Chinese who simply thought the barbarian European troops had run amuck.

For Gordon, the excitement of war was too soon finished and he was detailed to construction work in Tientsin. He found China dull and uninteresting: 'If you have seen one village you have seen the whole country', he wrote. In March 1862 he came down with a mild case of smallpox and when he recovered he was sent to Shanghai. It was there, in the most bizarre circumstances, that he found fame.

Religions always change their forms when they change cultures, but perhaps the strangest transformation of Christianity occurred in China when it passed through the mind of a man named Hsiu Chüan. He was a schoolteacher who fell under the influence of an American Baptist missionary, becoming at first one of his most devout followers, assiduously distributing Bibles and religious tracts. Then he began to have visions. At first he saw himself called upon by God to convert his countrymen. He found followers and soon they were being organized into societies that had definite political overtones. There were more visions and eventually he was calling himself the son of God and demanding that his followers call him Tien Wang, or Heavenly King. He renounced his allegiance to the Manchu régime, raised an army and proclaimed the restoration of the Ming dynasty. His followers then donned Ming clothing and wore their hair long, as had been the fashion under the Mings. He proclaimed the Tai Ping, or Great Peace, for all China, and his followers were from then on called Taipings. His fame spread, his army grew, and within three years he was in control of all the southern provinces, had captured Soochow, centre of the silk industry, and had installed himself with a number of wives in the ancient capital of Nanking – another Chinese warlord.

The Taipings moved north and east and soon were lapping at the gates of Shanghai. In England and America considerable hope was seen for a warlord who distributed thousands of Bibles, built churches and so rapidly converted his countrymen. Little was heard of the luxury and sensuality of his court or the barbarities of his officers. Few of the foreign merchants, soldiers and officials in Shanghai were deceived. They saw the Taipings as a threat, and prepared to defend themselves. They hired an American soldier of fortune to raise a private army, recruiting Chinese soldiers and using otherwise unemployed Europeans as officers. Christened the Ever Victorious Army, it began its career with a series of defeats. The commander was killed in one of the early engagements and was replaced by another American adventurer named Henry A. Burgevine. When Burgevine used his troops to steal from the merchants he was supposed to protect, he was dismissed and decamped with some of his officers to join the Taipings. At this point the merchants prevailed upon the British military authorities to give them a commander. Although the official British policy was one of non-intervention in the struggle between the Imperialist government of the Manchus and the Taiping rebels, it was obvious that the Manchu government was unable to protect Shanghai, so General Charles Stavely, in charge of British forces in Shanghai, allowed Gordon, now a major, to be appointed general of the Ever Victorious Army.

The 3,000-man army Gordon took over left much to be desired as a fighting force. The average Chinese soldier occupied a place in the social structure only slightly above a brigand, and the men of the Ever Victorious were probably somewhat worse. The officers were renegades, adventurers and fugitives from the United States and Europe. They had no sympathy for the people, nor for the ideals and aspirations of either side in the civil war. Officers and men alike fought only for money and loot. Burgevine had been popular with the officers and they did not take kindly to the trim little regular army major from the Royal Engineers who now came to command them.

One of Gordon's first acts was to give his army a uniform. He designed it himself: green jackets and knickerbockers, black boots, and bright green turbans. As a personal bodyguard, he selected three hundred of the best men and dressed them in bright blue

uniforms with red facings. He then began a quarrel with Li Hung
Chang, Governor of Kiangsu province, of which Shangai was the
principal city. Li had his own troops in the field commanded by a
General Ching. Of the Manchu army two French observers of the
war reported that the soldiers treated 'friend and enemies with
most perfect impartiality, plundering all alike' – a statement that
helps explain the desire of the Shanghai merchants for their own
army. Gordon flatly refused to serve under General Ching. He
would report to Li and to the Shanghai merchants who paid his
soldiers, but he made it quite clear from the start that he would
brook no interference from anyone.

Gordon next turned his attention to the enemy. The merchants
were content if the Taipings could be kept thirty miles from
Shanghai, but Gordon saw his mission as being the destruction
of the enemy forces. He at once took the offensive. In his first
action he marched his army eighty miles and captured a Taiping
town without the loss of a single man. His plan of attack was
simple but effective, and he was to repeat it over and over. He
carefully surveyed the town to be attacked, which was usually
protected by a mud wall, brought up his artillery in the night and
opened a bombardment at dawn. When a breach had been made
in the wall, he led his men through it, a cigar in his mouth and a
cane in his hand. The Taiping defenders usually fled or changed
sides, swelling the ranks of the Ever Victorious Army.

Town after town was captured as Gordon struck at the Taiping
supply route. Soon he was able to write to his mother: 'I am now a
Tsung Ping Mandarin (which is the second highest grade) and have
acquired a good deal of influence.' He had his portrait painted in
full mandarin regalia, looking very stiff and Chinese, except for his
blue eyes set in his incongruous British face. He was very pleased
with himself. Although when he first took command he had
astonished Li by refusing to take any money from the Imperialist
government, not even a 'shoe latchet', he now accepted a salary
of £260.

In spite of his military victories, Gordon had his troubles as a
commander of a Chinese army. Although his troops respected his
professional competence, they were dismayed by their commander's indifference to loot and appalled by his desire to fight
almost continuously; there was barely enough time between
battles to dispose of the booty, and scarcely any time at all to
enjoy the proceeds. At one point all the officers sent him their
resignations. Gordon ignored them. He simply marched his army

out and sent word to his officers that he expected them to join their men by the next afternoon. They did. When his artillery mutinied and threatened to blow up his camp, he marched up with his bodyguard and pulled a corporal out of the ranks with his own hands. He was shot on the spot. Gordon then threatened to shoot every fifth non-commissioned officer unless the mutineers returned to their duties. They did.

Gordon got into a violent quarrel with General Ching over who had actually captured the town of Kunshan. Both wrote violent letters to Li, denouncing each other in extravagant terms. Ching fired on the Ever Victorious and Gordon threatened to kill Ching. Li in a masterly understatement noted that 'reports from each of them regarding the other indicate an ill-feeling'. Li supported Gordon in this argument, but then Gordon turned on Li, accusing him of plotting to turn the Ever Victorious over to Ching. Li, thinking that Gordon simply wanted money for himself, promised him a rich reward when Soochow was taken. Gordon was insulted and resigned. He was finally persuaded to resume his command, but his relations with Ching and Li remained strained.

The important city of Soochow was captured in December 1863 through an arrangement with the Taiping generals charged with its defence. Gordon handled the negotiations and it was agreed that a gate to the city would be left open and unguarded so that the Imperialist forces could enter unopposed. In return, Gordon and Ching agreed that the city would not be looted and that the lives and property of the generals would be spared. All went according to plan except that Ching's men looted the city and Li ordered the execution of the generals. Gordon was furious. It was not simply that he regarded the killing of prisoners as barbarous, he felt that his own honour had been violated; he had personally promised the Taiping generals good treatment. He returned to Shanghai, resigned and sulked in his quarters for two months. Li carefully avoided Gordon, but he gave him full credit for the capture of Soochow, awarded him an important decoration and tried to press a small fortune upon him. Gordon would have none of this; he refused the treasure and he wrote indignant letters to everyone, including the local and English papers.

In the end Gordon did return to his command, but not until he had convinced himself that it was his duty. It was not the flattery, the gold or the weak excuses of Li, but his own peculiar logic that brought him to renounce what he himself had declared to be his moral principles. He reasoned that without him the Taiping revolt would drag on and thousands of people would be needlessly killed; that without his leadership the Ever Victorious would break up; that if he did not return, Burgevine, who had again returned to the Imperialist side, would go back to the Taipings. He gave all his reasoning in a letter to Sir Frederick Bruce, the British minister to China, adding that if he followed his own desires he would not go back, 'as I have escaped unscathed and been wonderfully success-ful'. As for Li, he thought that perhaps there were 'some extenu-ating circumstances in his favour' for 'although I feel deeply on the subject, I think we can scarcely expect the same discernment that we should from a European Governor'. It is probable that the real reasons, unstated because not to be believed, was that the thought of being without the intoxicating excitement of war was unbearable.

On 19 February 1864 Gordon went back to his command of the Ever Victorious Army and was soon busy plotting his campaign to finish off the war. The next few months were a repetition of his former successes – and of his difficulties with his own troops. When his troops grew mutinous because he would not allow them to sack a city they had captured, he again pulled out one man at random and had him shot on parade. His forces suffered two reverses, while Gordon was disabled by a wound in the leg – the only wound he ever received – but for the most part his army proceeded methodically to capture town after town on the road to Nanking, the Taiping capital. There were no more troubles with Ching, for Ching was killed in battle; Gordon cried when he heard of the death of his old enemy.

On 10 May 1864 Gordon wrote to his mother about the war and his part in it:

> The losses I have sustained in this campaign have been no joke: out of 100 officers I have had 48 killed and wounded; and out of 3,500 men nearly 1,000 killed and wounded; but I have the satisfaction of know-ing that as far as mortal can see, six months will see the end of this rebellion, while if I had continued inactive it might have lingered on for six years. Do not think I am ill-tempered, but I do not care one jot about my promotion, or what people may say. I know I shall leave China as poor as I entered it, but with the knowledge that through my weak instrumentality upwards of eighty to one hundred thousand lives have been spared. I want no further satisfaction than this.

He was right about the campaign being soon over. The day after writing this letter he fought his last battle in China. His fifteen months as a Chinese mandarin were ended by an order from the British government withdrawing permission for its officers to serve in Chinese armies. The Imperialist forces, without the aid of either Gordon or Ching, stormed Nanking and forced their way into the palace. There they found the Heavenly King dangling by the neck from a silk cord. He had hanged all his wives and then himself.

Gordon, feeling that only he could command such an unruly army as the Ever Victorious, disbanded it against the advice of the British minister and the wishes of the Shanghai merchants. He was not reprimanded, however, for he was now an acknowledged hero. In the English press he was called 'Chinese Gordon' and he was the idol of the moment for the British public. The Chinese made him a Ti Tu, highest rank in the Chinese army, and gave him the high reward of a yellow jacket and permission to wear a peacock's feather in his hat; they also requested the British government to honour him, but Gordon's own government was not so lavish with its honours. He was advanced one grade in rank and, later, was made a Companion of the Bath. Gordon had ambivalent feelings about honours. He protested that he despised them and once said: 'I had rather be dead than praised.' But he protested more vehemently when he felt that his efforts were unappreciated.

In January 1865 Gordon, now a thirty-three-year-old lieutenant-colonel, returned to England – not to greater glory, but to six years of oblivion.

Gordon found the boredom of home leave and particularly the adoration of his family harder on his nerves than all the battles in China. He could be cruel in his rejection of the admiration of his family. He once entered a room when his mother was proudly exhibiting to a group of her friends a beautifully executed map he had made as a young man at Woolwich. He tore the map from her hands and threw it into the fire.

In 1865, after a restless home leave, Gordon was appointed Commanding Engineer at Gravesend. It was a dull post after the excitement and romance of China, but he was to remain there for nearly six years. With his passion for war and violent action, this post might have been unbearable had he not had a second, equally strong, passion: religion. It was his sister, Augusta, who had first aroused his religious instincts while he was in the military academy at Woolwich. Augusta was twelve years older than her brother, and a spinster; religion was her life. She convinced Gordon of the need to turn to the light of God and away from the darkness of the world, and he became a religious fanatic. For him, as for his sister, the body was an evil thing in which the soul was forced to dwell until finally liberated at the appointed time to make its way to heaven or hell. It was an unusual doctrine for a young, high-spirited officer to hold so strongly. Perhaps it was fortunate that women had no appeal for him.

Religion absorbed his energies during the years at Gravesend – religion and an interest in boys. His hundreds of letters to Augusta are filled with these two topics. He developed a fatalism akin to that of a devout Muslim. As the Arab is accustomed to carefully punctuate his speech and writing with 'Inshallah' – God willing – when referring to anything that will take place in the future, so Gordon's letters are punctuated with '(D.V.)', for *Deo volente*. In battle there was no need to fear, for he would die when his creator wanted to take him, and if not he would 'be home by Christmas (D.V.)'.

There was nothing inhibiting about his religion. He could kill in war without a qualm and, although he saw the evils of the world as being the evils of the flesh, he never denied himself brandy or cigars (at least not for long) and he saw no evil in his love of young boys, whom he called 'kings'. He always had boys around him and he never tried to apply to them the discipline he demanded of men. The first of his 'kings' had been Ivan, a handsome, devoted boy he had found in Armenia. Gordon read the Bible with him and protected him. When Ivan threatened to fall in love with a housemaid, Gordon took steps to prevent it. He wrote to Augusta about the budding love affair and told her: 'I do not mean to allow it, as he belongs to me.'

In reorganizing the Ever Victorious Army, he had chosen six handsome young boys as his personal attendants and he added more as he went along, including dozens of lost or orphaned Chinese boys. With them he had romped and played; he had fed and clothed them, gave them pet names and showered them with affection, to the astonishment of his officers and men, to whom he was ever a strict, unbending disciplinarian.

Now at Gravesend, he surrounded himself with boys again. He turned his home into a school, hospital and church. He sheltered waterfront youths, mothered them, nursed them, talked to them about God and found jobs for them. Over his mantel was a map of the world covered with pins that marked the cruises of his former 'kings' for whom he had found berths on ships. On a visit to the Midlands he found 'there were boys running about worth millions'. In Scotland he was angered by a relative who tried to prevent him from talking with young boys. To Augusta he wrote: 'I believe there

are many Kings (red-haired) about, but I cannot get at them.'
When he fell into periods of depression, the arrival of a new boy
would wipe away the gloom and he would thankfully write
Augusta to tell her about him: 'A country lad of our Lord, a Hebrew,
fourteen years old, has fallen to me.'

He prayed a great deal and kept a special book in which he
wrote the names of those for whom he prayed most earnestly: it
included all his enemies. He read the Bible daily, and his favourite
part was the Book of Isaiah, although he had no thought of beating
his own sword into a ploughshare. He began distributing religious
tracts, hiding them where people might come upon them by surprise: under stones, in boats, by paths and in bushes. Travelling
in trains, he would open the window and throw out his tracts to
people along the way. From time to time Augusta came to visit him
– 'My sister comes (D.V.) next Monday, and the place is to become
a hermitage.' The two of them read the Bible together and discussed vile flesh and the glory that would be theirs when God
released them from their bodies.

The Abyssinian Expedition of 1868 marched to the conquest of
Magdala, but Gordon remained at Gravesend. Occasionally there
were articles in the press that urged more active employment for
Chinese Gordon, but the government was cool. In October 1871
he accepted a post as a member of the Danube Commission which
had been established under the terms of the Treaty of Paris to study
ways and means of improving the mouth of the Danube. At
Galati, in eastern Rumania, he found that his work was more
diplomatic than technical and that his most arduous task was to
keep up with the continual social round. To Augusta he complained
that 'it is impossible to hear God's voice in a whirl of visits'. It was
not a post for a soldier-saint.

In Constantinople in the summer of 1872, Gordon met Nubar
Pasha, the shrewd Egyptian politician and diplomat who was three
times to become Prime Minister of Egypt. Nubar Pasha asked him
to recommend someone to replace Sir Samuel Baker as governor of
the Equatorial Provinces of the Sudan. Gordon recommended
himself. A year later the British government gave its approval and
in September 1873 the Khedive made a formal offer. On 28 January 1874, his forty-first birthday, just at the time when the death of
Livingstone became known in London, Gordon set off for Central
Africa.

Although he had been offered £10,000 a year by the Khedive, he
refused to accept more than £2,000. This unusual decision created

much comment. Even more publicity was aroused by his next decision: he arranged while passing through Cairo for Abu Saud, an ex-slaver and a confirmed rascal, to be released from prison and made a member of his staff. It was Abu Saud who later failed so miserably to capture the Mahdi on Abba Island. Sir Samuel Baker, who had had endless trouble with the man and had put him in prison, sent off an angry letter to *The Times* and hastily scribbled his disapproval of the appointment in an appendix to *Ismailia*, the book on his Central African experiences he had just completed. But Gordon contentedly made his way to the Sudan, writing to Augusta: 'I am happy and peaceful, and feel more and more that, get into what trouble I may, God will take me out of it.' He reached Suakin on 25 February, and with an escort of 220 Egyptian soldiers set out across the desert to Berber; on 12 March he arrived in Khartoum.

He paused in the capital only eight days and from here issued his first decree, proclaiming that henceforth the ivory trade was to be a government monopoly and that it was forbidden to recruit or organize armed bands or to import gunpowder in the Equatorial Provinces. Then he made his way up the White Nile and into the wild, sweltering swampland he was supposed to govern. He was shocked by the wretchedness of the natives in this preserve of the slave hunters. 'What a mystery, is it not,' he wrote, 'why they are created! – a life of fear and misery night and day! One does not wonder at their not fearing death. No one can conceive the utter misery of these lands – heat and mosquitoes day and night all the year round. But I like the work, for I believe I can do a great deal to ameliorate the lot of the people.'

To assist him in his lofty schemes, Gordon brought with him, in addition to Abu Saud, an assortment of white men that included Charles Chaillé-Long, a former American army officer who had served in the Civil War and for the past five years had been an officer in the Egyptian army; Romolo Gessi, an Italian, who had fought in the Garibaldi campaigns and whom Gordon had known as an interpreter in the Crimea; and E. Linant de Bellefonds, son of a distinguished French engineer who had worked for Mohammed Ali in Egypt and the Sudan.

Chaillé-Long later described how he first met Gordon. He was dining late one night after the theatre in Cairo when a note was brought to him: 'Will you come with me to Central Africa? Come and see me at once. Very truly, C. C. Gordon.' Chaillé-Long left his dinner and went to Gordon's quarters. The interview was hurried. Gordon offered him a brandy and soda and Chaillé-Long noted that the bottle stood on the table beside an open Bible. 'You are to go with me as Chief of Staff,' Gordon told him. 'You will command the soldiery. I don't want the bother.' He answered Chaillé-Long's questions briefly, and then put an end to them by stating that they would leave the following night. Chaillé-Long protested that he could not possibly leave so soon – he did not even have proper clothes. Gordon threw him a pair of shoes, insisted that he try them on and declared them a perfect fit. He seemed to feel that with this the problem of equipment had been solved, but Chaillé-Long, who felt that a journey to Central Africa and an indefinite stay there called for more supplies than a pair of shoes that pinched, held out for at least one more day to make his preparations. His insistence made Gordon angry, but he finally agreed and hustled his guest off with instructions to hurry.

Gordon saw his mission as being the suppression of the slave trade, and he was terribly anxious to get on with it. On the steamer from Khartoum he bawled for more speed and slapped the captain's face when he did not get it. The captain complained to Chaillé-Long, who went in search of Gordon in order to remonstrate. He expected to find him angry and violent, but already Gordon was in quite a different mood. 'I've been very low, old fellow,' he said. 'Don't be hard on me. This is a terrible country.' When, on 16 April, he reached his squalid equatorial capital at Gondokoro, no one there had even heard of his appointment.

Now began three years of torment for Gordon. He energetically dashed about and sent his officers flying to remote portions of his barbarous province to carry out good works, but little was accomplished. There were established interests in Equatoria and the Bahr el Ghazal – slave traders, tribal chiefs, Egyptian government officials, witch doctors – and Gordon managed to alienate them all. This would have been unimportant to him had he been able to suppress the slave trade, but he could not. When he captured a gang of slaves or bought them himself, as he sometimes did, he did not know what to do with them. They were too far from their homes in the interior and could not make their way back, so they simply became, in effect, his slaves. The ablest people in the land were the slave raiders themselves; after imprisoning them, Gordon would often enlist them, like the slaves, into his service, arousing the distrust of the tribes whose confidence he wanted to cultivate.

The slave raiders and traders he tried to reform were rarely impressed; most soon leagued with other slavers against him.

Abu Saud had to be thrown in prison. He was pardoned – 'One wants some forgiveness one's self,' Gordon said, 'and it is not a dear article' – but later he had to be imprisoned again, for he was unchangeably corrupt. Gordon's decisions and actions seemed bizarre to everyone, even to his own staff, and Chaillé-Long was glad enough to go off on an independent assignment.

In this slow land where only violence and sickness were swift, terror ruled: for the inhabitants there was fear of other men, of the climate, of the animals and insects, of the nameless diseases. Egyptians and Europeans usually shared the terror. For those who, like Gordon, could not be frightened, despair replaced terror. Gordon found support in his Bible and brandy, but he was subject to wild fluctuations of mood. When not busily attacking slavers, issuing proclamations and building forts, he would often shut himself in his tent or hut, sticking an axe with a flag on it outside as a sign that he was not to be disturbed. Faced with problems he could not solve, he would open his Bible at random and find his solution in what he read there. One day he would snarl at his officers and the next he was the amiable gentleman begging their forgiveness for his rudeness. He quarrelled constantly, with those around him and, by letter, with those in authority in Khartoum, Cairo and London. He threatened to resign, but did not; he resigned, but withdrew his resignation. He was unwilling to admit failure, yet he found it impossible to go on. After three frustrating years he reached a decision: to do his work he must be Governor-General of the entire Sudan. Having arrived at this conclusion, he left Equatoria. Behind him were his meagre accomplishments: a bit more of the land explored, a few miserable forts, several thousand bewildered, homeless, free slaves – and the thriving slave trade he had found when he arrived.

On Christmas Eve 1876 Gordon returned home to England. Again he was the subject of a considerable amount of publicity; his anti-slavery ideas being popular, his accomplishments were somewhat magnified. Two months later he was back in Cairo to convince the Khedive Ismail that he should dismiss Ismail Ayub Pasha, the Governor-General of the Sudan, and appoint him. When the British government gave Gordon its support, the Khedive consented. It was specifically set forth that Gordon's objectives would be to improve communications, suppress the slave trade and negotiate with King John of Abyssinia to settle existing disputes between Egypt and Abyssinia.

The government was not yet aware of the existence of the

Dongolawi religious named Mohammed Ahmed, nevertheless the Sudan was in its usual state of ferment. Prior to the nineteenth century, the Sudan had been only a geographical concept, not a political entity with well-defined frontiers. Egypt attempted not only to control this vague area but to establish firm and ever-wider boundaries. Sir Samuel Baker and Gordon, with the help of Romolo Gessi, had pushed the southern boundaries to Lake Albert and Lake Kyogo. On the east, the Egyptians, with Turkish permission, had taken over a strip of the Somaliland coast and pushed inland until they were defeated in battle by the alarmed Abyssinians. In the west, Egypt had always coveted the lands of Darfur, but had been too weak to trust her soldiers against the vast, harsh geography and the warlike peoples of those areas. In 1874, however, a powerful Arab slaver named Zubair Rahman, who controlled a strong private army in the Bahr el Ghazal, offered to combine with the Egyptians to launch a two-pronged attack on Darfur. Egypt accepted.

In the campaign that followed, all the honours went to Zubair, who did most of the fighting, killed the sultan and marched into the capital of El Fasher before the Egyptian forces arrived from Kordofan. Zubair now found himself in effective control of an area larger than France and the Benelux combined. The Governor-General of the Sudan was jealous and the Khedive was afraid. Zubair was made a pasha, and invited to Cairo. He unwisely accepted, taking with him as presents for the Khedive 100 fine Arab horses, four lions, four leopards, sixteen parrots and more than eight tons of ivory. He was received with great honour – and kept there. Although not imprisoned, he was forbidden to leave Cairo and was constantly under surveillance. A man of great ability and in the prime of life thus found himself suddenly deprived of all power and authority. And so Egypt acquired Darfur and the Bahr el Ghazal, in name if not in fact. Zubair's forces, with his son Suleiman in charge, were still intact when Gordon became Governor-General.

Instead of going straight to Khartoum, Gordon went first to tackle the problems with Abyssinia. He was glad to be active again and to leave the court of Cairo: 'I am so glad to get away, for I am very weary. I go up alone, with Almighty God to direct and guide me; and I am glad to so trust in Him as to fear nothing, and, indeed, to feel sure of success.' His orders were vague and without guidelines, saying simply: 'Il y a sur la frontière d'Abyssinie des disputes; je vous charge de les arranger.' His arrangements were hardly those of a diplomat, even a nineteenth-century diplomat, but they suited the purposes of the Khedive. He did not see King John, although he sent messengers to him, but he helped Walad el Michael, a contender for the Abyssinian throne, to set up a separate government, an arrangement which was sure to keep King John and Walad el Michael concerned with each other and not with the affairs of Egypt; this was not Gordon's intention, but it served the interest of the Khedive as effectively as a treaty. Tired of Abyssinian politics, which held little interest for him, Gordon set off for Khartoum. There, on 5 May 1877, he was formally installed as Governor-General of the Sudan.

A. Egmont Hake, a nineteenth-century biographer of Gordon, made an excellent summary of the work now confronting the new Governor-General:

> It was a stupendous task: to give peace to a country quick with war; to suppress slavery among a people to whom the trade in human flesh was life and honour and fortune; to make an army out of perhaps the worst material ever seen; to grow a flourishing trade and a fair revenue in the wildest anarchy in the world. The immensity of the undertaking; the infinity of details involved in a single step towards the end; the countless odds to be faced; the many pests – the deadly climate, the horrible vermin, the ghastly itch, the nightly and daily alternation of overpowering heat and bitter cold – to be endured and overcome; the environment of bestial savagery and ruthless fanaticism – all these combine to make the achievement unique in human history.

Hake's assumption that Gordon succeeded in conquering all difficulties and accomplishing his many objectives is certainly an overstatement of the case, but this was a fair statement of the difficulties the new Governor-General faced.

Gordon was a dreamer and an eccentric, but he was not a fool. His approach to many of the problems he faced was realistic, and he used great vigour in his attempts to master them. He recognized the obvious fact that slavery was the keystone of the economic and social structure of the country, and he recognized that any tampering with it must be done in such a way that the socio-economic structure of the country did not come tumbling down in the process. He made no attempt to interfere with domestic slavery; he knew it would be futile to try. Learning that the Catholic missionaries were in the habit of giving asylum to runaway slaves, he ordered them to stop it. When they refused, he wrote a letter to the Pope, asking him to keep his priests from interfering with his government. The missionaries were not pleased, but they obeyed.

Unlike previous holders of his office, Gordon had no intention of sitting in his capital and issuing edicts. He went out to see the country and handle local problems on the spot. After only a few days in Khartoum, he set out on a camel for Kordofan and Darfur with an escort of 200 men, whom he often left miles behind him in his haste. He found that he could not march directly to El Fasher, however, for the situation in Darfur was much too unfriendly. The pretender to the sultanate was raising the standard of revolt and Suleiman Zubair was there with 6,000 armed slaves. He was forced to sit and wait, and waiting was depressing. 'It is lamentable work,' he wrote, 'and over and over again, in the fearful heat, I wish I was in the other world . . . this inaction, with so much to do elsewhere, is very trying indeed to my body. It is such a country, so worthless, and I see nothing to be gained by its occupation.'

Gordon now became involved in local disputes and tribal revolts. Some tribes sided with him and some against him. Fortunately, there were enough friendly tribes with sufficient fighting spirit to suppress those who rose against his government, for he found his Egyptian troops worthless. He dashed about from place to place, raiding the camps of slavers, worrying about what to do with the slaves he released, searching for supplies of grain, sending out expeditions against hostile tribes, spying and attempting to avoid being spied upon, and vainly trying to control the only government force that was willing to fight: the bashi-bazouks. Still he had not faced his greatest danger, the forces of Suleiman Zubair, who raided and plundered with impunity.

Gordon at last reached the point where he felt that a direct face-to-face encounter with Suleiman Zubair was the only solution. His direct, unorthodox approach was perhaps the bravest act in his career. In a letter, dated 2 September, to Augusta Gordon described his arrival at Dara, then the principal town in southern Darfur:

I got to Dara about 4 p.m., long before my escort, having ridden eighty-five miles in a day and a half. About seven miles from Dara I got into a swarm of flies, and they annoyed me and my camel so much, that we jolted along as fast as we could. Upward of 300 were on the camel's head, and I was covered with them. I suppose that the queen fly was among them. If I had no escort of men, I had a large escort of these flies. I came upon my people like a thunderbolt. As soon as they had recovered, the salute was fired. My poor escort! where is it? Imagine to yourself a single, dirty, red-faced man on a camel, ornamented with flies, arriving in the divan all of a sudden. The people were paralysed, and could not believe their eyes.

Such, doubtless, was the origin of the tale that Gordon rode entirely alone into the camp of Suleiman Zubair and demanded his surrender. The actual meeting with Zubair was daring enough and took place the following day. Gordon described the encounter in the same letter to Augusta:

At dawn I got up, and putting on the golden armour the Khedive gave me, went out to see my troops, and then mounted my horse, and with an escort of *my* robbers of Bashi-Bazouks, rode out to the camp of the other robbers three miles off. I was met by the son of Sebehr [Zubair] – a nice-looking lad of twenty-two years – and rode through the robber-bands. There were about 3,000 of them – men and boys. I rode to the tent in the camp; the whole body of chiefs were dumbfounded at my coming among them. After a glass of water, I went back, telling the son of Sebehr to come with his family to my divan. They all came, and sitting there in a circle, I gave them in choice Arabic my ideas: That they meditated revolt; that I knew it, and that they should now have my ultimatum, viz.: that I would disarm them and break them up. They listened in silence, and then went off to consider what I had said. They have just now sent in a letter stating their submission, and I thank God for it.

Gordon continued his mad dashes about the country. He went to Shakka where the only other foreigner before him had been a lone American; back to Khartoum for a brief spell; a whirlwind tour of inspection in Dongola, a land sunk in misery through a crop failure; then off to the Abyssinian frontier where Walad el Michael was causing trouble and where again Gordon walked into the enemy's camp with a handful of men, trusting to God and his own bravery. He was on his way back to Khartoum via Suakin and Berber and thinking of again going to Darfur when a strange message reached him from the Khedive.

Always plagued by debts, it occurred to the Khedive that the man who was doing so much to sort out affairs in the Sudan might also succeed in helping him with his number one problem: the tangled, complex Egyptian financial situation. Besides, his creditors were British and French, and Gordon was an Englishman. He summoned Gordon to Cairo. Although he knew nothing of finance, had no interest in money and could not even keep his personal accounts straight, Gordon did not hesitate to go to the Khedive's assistance. He had no fear of the financial problems, only of the life of society and, as one who never willingly spent more than ten minutes feeding his flesh, of those long dinners. He who fearlessly and frequently risked his life in the Khedive's service now wrote:

'The idea of dinners in Cairo makes me quail.' No sooner had he arrived in the capital than he was whisked from the railroad station to the palace, where the Khedive was waiting at dinner for him.

The Khedive lost no time in asking Gordon to accept the presidency of a Commission of Inquiry that was to be formed to look into Egyptian finances. Gordon quickly accepted and found himself caught up in a spider's web of intrigue, diplomacy and high finance. The villains in the piece, as far as Gordon and the Khedive were concerned, were the four European Debt Commissioners who were responsible to the holders of Egyptian bonds for the collection of the annual seven per cent interest. Egypt was so sunk in debt, and the Egyptian government bureaucracy so hopelessly corrupt, that she could never hope to pay off the principal and it was an annual struggle to pay the interest. Gordon's simple course of recommended action was to suspend the payment of the next instalment of interest by imperial decree and to do away with the meddlesome Debt Commissioners.

As most finance ministers today would agree, Gordon's soldier's solution was the correct one, but repudiation of debt, even temporary suspension of interest, was an unheard of action among nations. No one then would have believed that both Britain and France would within sixty years fail to meet their own financial obligations to a nation that had assisted them in time of need. The Khedive could not resist the great pressures put upon him, particularly by the British government; Gordon returned to the Sudan and the Egyptian fellaheen were again forced by the lash of the curbash to pay the taxes for Egypt's interest on its debts.

It was during this experience as a financial expert that Gordon first encountered Evelyn Baring, whose rise to fame as 'the maker of modern Egypt' resulted from his handling of the financial difficulties of that country. They were opposite types of men. Gordon thought Baring 'pretentious, grand and patronizing' and said that 'when oil mixes with water, we will mix together.' Baring had an equally low opinion of Gordon: 'The sole reason why the negotiation broke down was that it was evident to everyone concerned, including General Gordon himself, that he was not fitted to conduct any financial inquiry.' When on 4 April 1878 a commission was finally formed, Ferdinand de Lesseps was appointed president, but he wisely refrained from taking any active part in the commission's work and left the country a month later.

Back in the Sudan again Gordon soon found enough to do. There was trouble in the west, where Suleiman Zubair had revolted again in the Bahr el Ghazal. Gordon gave the command of an expedition against Suleiman to Romolo Gessi, and from July 1878 until March 1879 Gessi waged a series of successful campaigns in the Bahr el Ghazal. Although he destroyed Suleiman's stronghold, he was not able to catch Suleiman himself. Gordon decided to set out on a supporting campaign in Darfur. In July he conferred with Gessi at Taweisha and authorized him to kill Suleiman if he had the chance.

On returning to Khartoum, Gordon learned that Khedive Ismail had been deposed and Khedive Tewfik had replaced him. He also learned of Gessi Pasha's final campaign against Suleiman, which ended in the slaver being killed, allegedly while attempting to escape. By this time, Gordon's over-vigorous life was beginning to take its toll. He had ridden more than 7,500 miles by camel in the preceding three years and he was suffering from a disease which he himself diagnosed as angina pectoris. Sick, exhausted and discouraged, he now set out for Cairo with the intention of resigning. He arrived on 23 August and had several interviews with the new khedive. To his surprise, he liked Tewfik, who persuaded him to accept another mission to Abyssinia. It was an arduous trip. Gordon suffered from boils, prickly heat and 'palpitations of the heart'. The terrain over which he had to travel was difficult in the extreme, and he slept many nights in the open in all sorts of weather. He had to endure insults, arrest and long interviews with Abyssinian generals. King Johannis of Abyssinia was, like Gordon, a religious fanatic; he cut off the noses of subjects caught taking snuff and the lips of those caught smoking. Gordon described him as being 'of the strictest sect of Pharisees – drunk every night, at dawn he is up reading the Psalms'. At the beginning of an interview, Gordon found his chair placed at some distance from that of the King's and on his left. Picking up the chair, he placed it close to the King on his right. 'Do you know that I may kill you for this?' Johannis asked. 'I do not fear death,' Gordon replied.

The mission to Abyssinia was a futile one; nothing was accomplished. On 2 January 1880 Gordon was back in Cairo. He stayed less than a week, during which he quarrelled with Baring, refused Khedive Tewfik's offer to return to the Sudan, embarrassed Sir Edward Malet, the British Consul who had succeeded H. C. Vivian, by appearing unexpectedly as the thirteenth guest for dinner, and threatened to fight a duel with Nubar Pasha because he had made disparaging remarks about Vivian. 'Vivian,' Gordon explained, is a C.B. and I am a C.B. too. I will not permit anyone to speak in

Hicks Pasha and his staff. Hicks is seated, second from right. *(From J. Colborne's* With Hicks Pasha in the Sudan, *published by Smith, Elder, 1884)*

Sudanese warriors dancing.

A painting of Gordon in mandarin dress. (*Royal Engineers Museum*)

Charles Gordon. Two sides of Gordon's character may be seen in this remarkable photograph by covering the right half of his face and then the left. (*Royal Engineers Museum*)

Lieutenant Colonel J. D. H. Stewart, 11th Hussars.
(*Royal Engineers Museum*)

Valentine Baker Pasha. (*Royal Engineers Museum*)

The House of the Khalifa Abdullahi.

The Khalifa's harem, the only two-storied building in Omdurman.

such a way of a man who belongs to the same order of knighthood as I do. Nubar Pasha shall apologize to me or fight.' Malet tried to talk him out of it. After all, Vivian was a public official and thus a natural target for criticism, but Gordon would not be moved. In the end, Malet succeeded in persuading Nubar Pasha to apologize and Gordon sailed for England from Alexandria on 10 January. The officials in Cairo, British and Egyptian, were not sorry to see the back of this soldier with medieval concepts of religion and knighthood. As for Gordon, he left with bitter thoughts of how all his work would soon be ruined by his successor as Governor-General of the Sudan, Raouf Pasha, a man he had twice dismissed from lesser posts.

Gordon, the man of boundless energy, was now idle. He visited his family, quarrelled with government officials, took his nephew to Switzerland and at last accepted a post for which he was completely unsuited: private secretary to Lord Ripon, the new Viceroy of India. He resigned five days after his arrival in Bombay. Then, against the express orders of the War Office, he set out for China. There he tried to resign his commission in the British army, prevent Li Hung Chang from starting a rebellion and the Manchu authorities from starting a war with Russia.

On his way back to England he thought of going to Australia, or Borneo or Zanzibar, but he did not. In London he sat for the famous *Vanity Fair* cartoonist and in the character sketch that accompanied it he is characterized as 'the most conscientious simple-minded and honest of men'. He visited Ireland and wrote a long letter, published in *The Times*, in which he outlined his views on solving the problem of the Irish famine. He irritated the War Office with an article in the *Army and Navy Gazette* on irregular warfare. He further annoyed his military superiors by a letter to *The Times* advocating the evacuation of Kandahar. And there were more than the usual number of letters to newspapers and friends on religious themes. At last he took a job which promised to satisfy neither his military nor his religious aspirations: the command of the Royal Engineers in Mauritius, a small island in the southern Indian Ocean. There in his loneliness he fought the battle against the flesh, struggling to give up smoking and liquor and sending progress reports to Augusta.

After a year in Mauritius he was promoted to Major-General and in the spring of 1882 he accepted a command in South Africa to put down a budding Basuto rebellion. He immediately started off on the wrong foot. In a letter to Augusta he ruefully told of his first dinner with the governor on the day after his arrival in Cape Town: 'I dined with Sir Hercules Robinson, trod on Lady Robinson's train going in to dinner, called her *Lady Barker* on going away – a person she hates – and spoke evil of several people in Hong Kong and elsewhere who had been kind to me.' Three weeks later he drew up a memorandum which accused the British government of breaking its treaty with the Basutos and demanded that the tribesmen be allowed to assemble and voice their grievances. As these views were not very popular, he was soon on his way back to England. He stayed in England only from 7 November to 28 December, when he left to go to Jerusalem.

Gordon spent a year in the Holy Land. It was to be a period of withdrawal from the world and worldly things, a time for religious meditation, but meditation by itself he found too passive an occupation; he had to be doing something. Being an excellent topographer, he combined his civil engineering skill with his religious interests and set about the task of finding the exact location of famous biblical sites. When he had located to his satisfaction the sites of Golgotha, Tophet and Zion, he went on to fix the exact geographical location of places in a more complex and strictly personal cosmogony. For example, when the voice of God was first heard on earth the devil fled to the furthermost spot on the globe from the throne of God, viz. 'over 31° 41′ S long. 144° 45′ W, close to Bass Isle, south of Otaheite, not far from Pitcairn's Isle, where the mutineers of the *Bounty* settled'. In other words, the antipode of Palestine.

During his stay in the Holy Land he wrote long and frequent letters to Augusta, to his brother Henry and to a host of friends. One of his chief correspondents was the Reverend R. H. Barns whom he had met in 1880 in Lausanne, Switzerland. Most of his letters were filled with theological talk – 'I had the heresy of no free will and no eternal punishment. I have come back to the fold and wish I had never said or written a word against either' – but there were also revealing bits of autobiography: 'I wished I was a eunuch at 14. I went to Crimea, hoping, without having a hand in it to be killed.' To General Sir John Donnelly he wrote: 'I like all men, even *cats*. Women are fearful, yet most valuable. I dare say they think us ditto. I fear susceptibilities or I would say more.'

His year of comparative quiet was broken by another acceptance of an unsuitable position. Off and on during the past few years King Leopold II of Belgium had been attempting to enlist his services to help Henry M. Stanley in the Congo. Finally, he accepted. He telegraphed the War Office for permission and received the follow-

ing reply: 'Secretary of State decided to sangdon [*sic*] your employment of Congo.' It was several weeks later before he learned that
some clerk had erred; the message should have read 'declines'
instead of 'decided'. Gordon went to Brussels to talk with Leopold
and then to London where, on 7 January 1884, he sent in his
resignation from the British army. The next day he was interviewed
by W. T. Stead, the crusading journalist who was then editor of the
Pall Mall Gazette. Stead told Gordon that Gladstone's government
had decided to abandon the Sudan and asked his opinion. Gordon
poured out a torrent of facts, figures, opinions and theories: 'I
have laid the egg which the Mahdi has hatched. I taught the people
that they had rights. Everything has sprung from that.' He refused
to believe that the Mahdi was in any sense a religious leader. He
described the Sudanese as 'very nice people' who only needed good
government to be happy. 'You cannot evacuate,' he told Stead.
'You must either surrender absolutely to the Mahdi or defend
Khartoum at all hazards.' He was certain that if Khartoum were
properly fortified the rebellion would fall to pieces of itself. The
next day the *Pall Mall Gazette* published the interview under the
heading: GORDON ON THE SUDAN. It also ran an editorial by Stead
headlined: GORDON FOR THE SUDAN, advocating Gordon as the man
to be sent to straighten out the mess there.

This was not the first time Gordon's name had been suggested for
the Sudan. As early as 17 November 1882 – even before the destruction of the army of Hicks Pasha was known – Sir Harry Verney
suggested to Lord Granville that Gordon be employed in the
Sudan: 'He has always exercised a very remarkable influence over
wild, uncontrollable, uncivilized peoples,' Verney said. On the
same day, incidentally, Granville had talked with Gordon about the
situation in the Sudan. Gordon told him that he thought the
rebellion had been 'immensely exaggerated'.

In his interview with Stead, Gordon had said he was opposed to
the policy of abandoning the Sudan; ten days later, in a meeting
with Granville and other cabinet members, he agreed with the
policy. Such was Gordon's nature. He had considered himself a
forgotten man whose own government had no good use for his
services. He had resigned his commission to serve the King of the
Belgians in the Congo. Ten days later, thanks to Stead and his
paper, he was the most talked about man in England and hailed
on all sides as the man of the hour.

For a long time Gordon's name had been a household word and
his romantic career was well known throughout Britain: he was the

soldier saint whom government inexplicably refused properly to employ. Following Stead's lead and quoting his article, *The Times* and every other important newspaper in the kingdom took up the cry that Gordon should be sent to Khartoum. Few could be found to disagree that Gordon was exactly the man to redeem British prestige, rectify the errors of government and punish those savages who had humiliated Britain. Queen Victoria agreed with her people and only wondered why he had not been sent 'long ago'. Gladstone and his ministers were forced to yield to public pressure. Gordon resigned as second-in-command to Stanley in the Congo before he had even begun and, yielding to the pressure of his own theories, conceit and to public opinion, he set off for Khartoum to save the Sudan.

5

Khartoum

'During the course of an official career which extended over a period of nearly fifty years, I at times had some hard work. But I never had such hard work, neither was I ever in a position of such difficulty, or in one involving such a continuous strain on the mind, the nerves, and, I may add, the temper, as during the first three months of the year 1884.' So wrote the Earl of Cromer eighteen years later of the time when he was Sir Evelyn Baring, the British representative in Egypt and the most influential man in the country, the Khedive not excepted. It was at this time that a policy had to be adopted concerning Egypt's continued relations with the Sudan and an able man had to be selected to carry out the policy.

Great pressure was brought to bear upon good civil servant Baring, the pressure of his superiors in London who were in turn being pressed by newspapers, politicians, the Queen and the great mass of the British public. If Gordon was to go to the Sudan he would have to work with and for Baring. Baring was doing a brilliant job in a difficult position; his equal could not be found to replace him. Therefore, his consent to Gordon's appointment was essential. On 1 December 1883 Baring received the following telegram from Lord Granville, Gladstone's Foreign Secretary: 'If General Charles Gordon were willing to go to Egypt, could he be of any use to you or to the Egyptian Government, and, if so, in what capacity?' Baring replied that he did not think it would be wise to send Gordon as the revolt in the Sudan was religious and the appointment of a Christian to a high command at this time would probably alienate the tribes still faithful to the government.

The distasteful idea of telling Egypt to abandon the Sudan was forming in the minds of British officials. Baring had proposed the idea and Granville agreed with him. In a private letter to Baring, Granville said: 'It takes away somewhat of the position of a man if he has to sell his racers and hunters, but if he cannot afford to keep them, the sooner they go to Tattersalls the better.' There was concern, though, that if the policy of abandonment were forced on

Egypt, Mohammed Sherif, the Egyptian Prime Minister, would resign, but Granville thought that 'some plausible Egyptian' could be found to replace him and, with British help, the policy could be implemented. A passing thought was given to the attitude of the Egyptian masses, but Viscount Cross (Richard Cross), who had stopped off in Egypt on his return from a visit to India, gave it as his opinion that as far as Egyptian fellaheen were concerned, 'their first prayer is for water, and their second to be saved from being sent to the Sudan'. In actual fact, some Egyptians were themselves pro-Mahdist, particularly in Upper Egypt. The greatest difficulty, however, was to devise some way to withdraw the Egyptian garrisons now in the Sudan, as well as all the Egyptian officials with their families, and those Sudanese who had exhibited their loyal support of the Egyptian government. This would be a formidable task, for Khartoum was then, as now, separated from such civilization as existed on the African periphery by nearly a thousand miles of desert. However, if the policy was adopted someone would have to be appointed to carry out the work. On 10 January 1884 Granville telegraphed: 'Could General Charles Gordon or Sir Charles Wilson be of assistance under altered circumstances in Egypt?' Baring thought that if the Sudan should be evacuated, and he believed this was the only solution, the job should be done by an Egyptian. He was against sending an Englishman to the Sudan. He again turned down Lord Granville's suggestion. Writing of these times in later years, Baring wrote: 'I had thus twice rejected the proposal to send General Gordon to Khartoum. Would that I had done so a third time!'

But the pressure from London was too great. On 14 January, Granville wrote to Gladstone saying, 'If Gordon says he believes he could, by his personal influence, excite the tribes to escort the Khartoum garrison and inhabitants to Suakin, a little pressure on Baring might be advisable.' The pressure was exerted, Baring gave in, and four days later Gordon left London for the Sudan.

The decision to send Gordon to Khartoum was extremely popular in Britain, and, as the *Pall Mall Gazette* truthfully said, it 'was applauded enthusiastically by the press all over the country without distinction of party'. Gordon was the hero and saviour of the day. When Lord Cairns extolled his virtues in the House of Lords and called him 'one of our national treasures', he was greeted with cheers from all sides. Gladstone in the House of Commons said, 'It is no exaggeration in speaking of General Gordon to say that he is a hero . . . and that in his dealings with Oriental peoples he has a genius.' Long after the Sudan affair was over, with the wisdom of hindsight and the protection of retirement and honours, Baring, now Lord Cromer, wrote:

> Mr Gladstone's Government made two great mistakes in dealing with Soudan affairs in their early stages. One of these was a sin of omission, and the other a sin of commission. The sin of omission was that the Government did nothing to stop the departure of the Hicks expedition. The sin of commission was the dispatch of Gordon to Khartoum.

The original concept of Gordon's mission was simply to report on the situation in the Sudan and to recommend measures for the evacuation of Egyptians, foreigners and loyal Sudanese from Khartoum. Such was the government's original view; Gordon appeared to understand his orders; this was what the British public was told to expect. But so great was the enthusiasm, so wild were the hopes, so firm was the faith in the soldier-saint that this understanding of the work to be done became blurred and coloured by what the people really wanted and soon came to expect: that Gordon would save the Sudan; that he would avenge the defeat of Hicks Pasha and the Anglo-Egyptian humiliations; that he would punish the rebels, quell the rebellion and restore order. All this was to be done without troops, without financial aid, simply by the magnetism of his personality. What the British public expected came to be what the government at least hoped for, although this was never officially admitted, and what Gordon himself thought he could do. Of course, no one had any real conception of the true situation in the Sudan. Baring knew more than most, but not enough to argue convincingly against Gordon's appointment. Even had he known the full extent of the Mahdi's influence and the deterioration of the Egyptian government in the Sudan, it is doubtful if he could have persuaded his superiors in London or the British public to recall the man they now regarded as the British saviour of the Sudan. Queen Victoria knew no more than her subjects about the Sudan, but, like them, she felt that something must be done, and she wrote Gladstone on 9 February 1884, saying, 'We must not let this fine and fruitful country, with its peaceful inhabitants, be left a prey to murder and rapine and utter confusion. It would be a *disgrace* to the British name, and the country will *not* stand it.' The Queen is probably the only person ever to call the Sudan fruitful or, in that era, to call its inhabitants peaceful.

Although Gordon had readily agreed to put himself under Baring's orders, the idol of England found it difficult in practice to obey or even consider the wishes of a man he personally disliked and who represented a class of officials he regarded as 'arrant humbugs'. Baring, though he always tried to be fair and to put duty and love of country above his personal feelings, had great difficulty in disguising his contempt for Gordon. He knew soldiers were useful, but believed they should obey orders, and Baring had his doubts about Gordon's sense of discipline. On 21 January 1884 he wrote to Lord Granville: 'It is as well that Gordon should be under my orders, but a man who habitually consults the Prophet Isaiah when he is in difficulty is not apt to obey the order of any man.' He was right. It never occurred to Gordon, for example, to consult Baring before proceeding to the Sudan. He planned to go directed to Suakin, cross the desert to Berber, then down the Nile to Khartoum.

Although never profitable, it is often irresistible to speculate on what might have been had one historical event not taken place. It seems certain that history, particularly British history, would have lost one of its most dramatic and tragic episodes had Baring not interfered with Gordon's travel plans and diverted him from Suakin to Cairo. Baring himself in later years speculated on this: 'General Gordon would possibly never have got to Khartoum, and it would not, therefore, have been necessary to send any British expedition to the Soudan. It is probable, indeed almost certain, that in a few weeks he would have returned to England without having effected anything of importance towards the accomplishment of his mission.' Had this happened, it is doubtful if there would have been a reconquest or a condominium and the history of north-east Africa and perhaps of Islam itself would be radically different today. But the change in Gordon's travel plans was made and history proceeded to unroll its awful story.

Gordon arrived in Cairo on the evening of 24 January full of ideas and plans. He at once took up with Baring the question of what he was supposed to do and what he intended to do. His orders and his intentions were not quite the same thing. While on his way to Cairo Gordon had drafted a memorandum outlining his plan of action. While admitting that the Sudan should be abandoned and the soldiers, officials, foreigners and others loyal to the government should be withdrawn, Gordon was concerned that the withdrawal of officialdom would leave the Sudanese without any form of stable government. He believed that this political vacuum could be filled by restoring the country to the petty sultans who had been in control of various parts of the country before the conquest of Mohammed Ali more than sixty years earlier.

On the morning following his arrival in Cairo, a meeting was held with Gordon, Baring, Nubar Pasha, Colonel Stewart and Sir Evelyn Wood. Gordon presented his plan; Colonel Stewart concurred and Baring raised no objection. Thus the nature of Gordon's mission was shifted from one of reporting, advising and simply evacuating refugees to an attempt to carry out a scheme for establishing a new form of government for the Sudan. It did not seem to have occurred to any of these men that if Egypt had the power to set up a new government it would not need to abandon the Sudan at all. But Gordon could be a charming and powerful persuader and, for the moment, even Baring fell under his spell and wrote Granville: 'What a curious creature he is! He is certainly half-cracked, but it is impossible not to be charmed by the simplicity and honesty of his character.'

Of course, the real difficulty, and the source of future problems, controversies and tragedies, was that none of these wise and experienced men was aware of the true nature of the situation in the Sudan. And, it must be said in all fairness, neither was anyone else in Egypt. The spectacular rise of the Mahdi and the extent of his power and influence were such revolutionary and astonishing developments that even had those in power in Cairo been told, it is doubtful if they would have believed, so incredible would the truth seem, even – perhaps especially – to those who thought they knew the Sudan and the Sudanese. There was no chance at all that Gordon's plan could succeed. Except in Darfur, the old families which had once been influential were now powerless. Gordon need not have feared a political vacuum; the Mahdi's government would quickly take up any slack left by the retreating Egyptians – and even before they could retreat if they did not hurry. As if there were not problems enough, Gordon was concerned with a problem that did not exist. Even the plan to evacuate the refugees could only be partially successful, for it was impossible to move the people out of the Sudan fast enough. Gordon, in spite of his long residence in the Sudan and his reputed understanding of its people, appeared to regard the Mahdi as simply another Heavenly King and to believe the ansar were as venial as the Taipings. It was always difficult for Gordon to realize that the religious convictions of non-Christians could be as firmly held as those of his own faith.

Gordon, Baring and their advisers in Cairo proceeded in their ignorance to plan for Gordon's entry into the Sudan. How far Gordon's mission was changed from a see-and-report trip to one attempting positive political action is shown by the reappointment of Gordon as Governor-General of the Sudan. He was armed with khedival proclamations and given the widest discretionary powers to act as he saw fit to carry out his mission.

As part of Gordon's plan to reinstate local sultans, a member of the former ruling family of Darfur was found in Cairo and persuaded to return to the Sudan with Gordon. Until the Sultan of Darfur had been deposed and exiled to Cairo, his family had ruled Darfur for more than four hundred years. From a number of potential sultans at Cairo, Gordon first selected an eighteen-year-old boy who had already acquired forty-two wives and a confirmed taste for gin. He was talked out of this and settled for Emir Abdul Shakour, son of Abdul Rahman, the last reigning sultan, who was a few years older and had slightly fewer wives. He had been living the slothful life of a king in exile on a fairly generous dole from the Egyptian government and was described by Colonel Stewart as a 'common-looking, unintelligent, and badly dressed native'. Common-looking and unintelligent he remained, but his appearance was improved by an impressive uniform and the largest decoration that could be found.

Also in exile in Cairo at this time was Zubair Pasha, the energetic slaver who had conquered the Bahr el Ghazal and Darfur. Gordon had reason to beware of Zubair. Acting under Gordon's orders, Gessi Pasha had killed Zubair's son, Suleiman. Gordon had first asked Baring to have the man watched and then had recommended that he be deported to Cyprus. During his brief stay in Cairo, however, Gordon accidently met Zubair, had a brief conversation with him, and took an immediate liking to the slaver. He had a 'mystic feeling' that he could be helpful. In a memorandum to Baring he said: 'Zobeir is the most able man in the Soudan, he is a capital general, and . . . has a capacity of government far beyond any other man in the Soudan.' Gordon wanted to take him back to the Sudan and establish him as a power in the western provinces. His assessment of Zubair's abilities was correct, and had the state of affairs in the Sudan been as Gordon imagined it Zubair might very well have been useful. Baring, although more sensitive to the political situation in England and aware of the anomaly of having Gordon, the darling and standard-bearer of the anti-slavery movement, setting up in power one of the world's most notorious slavers, nevertheless reluctantly recommended it to the Foreign Office. Granville became so alarmed by this suggestion that he wanted to recall Gordon. The cabinet discussed the matter, but decided Zubair should be kept out of the Sudan. The Queen sided with

Gordon and telegraphed to Granville (14 March 1884): 'Having placed entire confidence in Gordon, have you now decided to throw over his advice and that of Baring and risk loss of all the garrisons?'

Without Zubair, but with a credit at the Finance Department of £100,000, a title, two proclamations from the Khedive, the newly crowned Sultan of Darfur in tow and boundless confidence in his own ability, Gordon set out on the night of 26 January for Khartoum. Colonel Stewart, who accompanied him,[1] described the departure from Cairo: 'Some delay was caused at starting by the numerous retinue of the Darfour Sultan. Extra carriages had to be put on for the accommodation of his twenty-three wives and a quantity of baggage. At the last moment, his gala uniform was almost forgotten, and there was some commotion until it was found.' In spite of this delay and confusion, Gordon was in high spirits. His last words to Nubar Pasha were, 'I shall save the honour of Egypt.' Baring's feelings were quite different: 'My own heart was heavy within me. I knew the difficulties of the task which had to be accomplished. I had seen General Gordon.'

No sooner had Gordon left Cairo than he began a stream of communications to a wide variety of people which alarmed good civil servant Baring. From Korosko on 1 February, Colonel Stewart wrote, 'Gordon is so full of energy and action that he cannot get along without doing something, and at present he revenges himself for his enforced inactivity by writing letters, dispatches, etc., and sending telegrams.' Baring began complaining of the 'large number of very bewildering and contradictory messages from General Gordon'.

To C. D. Clifford Lloyd, then an inspector-general in the khedival service, Gordon wrote of his intention of going directly to the Mahdi's camp and confronting him. When Baring learned of this he quickly ordered Gordon to do no such thing. Gordon wrote to King Leopold of Belgium telling him of his intention of taking possession of the Bahr el Ghazal and Equatorial provinces and handing them over to Leopold. Baring ordered him not to go south of Khartoum. Once Gordon even announced his intention of resigning his commission in the British army. As Baring felt that he must communicate Gordon's many plans to his own superiors, there was a flurry of telegrams between Cairo and London. Once, when the telegraph line temporarily broke down, Gordon's correspondents sighed with relief and Lord Granville told Baring: 'I am not sure that the

[1] Gordon's comment: 'They sent Stewart with me to be my wet-nurse.'

stoppage of communication with Gordon for a time is the greatest of misfortunates either for himself or us.'

On 29 January Gordon telegraphed: 'The Emir Abdul Shakour has taken to drinking.' The following day, at Aswan, the new Sultan of Darfur decided he had gone far enough. He was eventually urged on as far as Dongola, where he stayed a few uncomfortable months before returning to Cairo.

Gordon and Colonel Stewart went on, reaching Berber on 11 February. Here Gordon decided to show the local sheikhs one of his secret firmans from the Khedive proclaiming the intention of the Egyptian government to abandon the Sudan. Both Stewart and Baring thought this a mistake. In telling Baring about this step, Stewart wrote: 'Gordon has taken his leap in the dark and shown his secret Firman. How it will act, and what will be the result, goodness only knows.' Sir Reginald Wingate referred to this document as the 'fatal Proclamation which gave the Soudan away'. By this act Gordon lost the support of those sheikhs and tribes who intended to remain in the Sudan but whose support and help he needed now to accomplish his mission; he certainly gave encouragement to his enemies; and he threw all those who might still be wavering in their allegiance into the arms of the Mahdi. The most curious aspect of this affair was that Gordon revealed the proclamation, written in Arabic, without fully understanding what it said! In his journal he wrote: 'I showed it, not knowing well its contents.'

A second decision taken at Berber was a practical one in the circumstances, but it created a furore in England. One of the natural results of abandoning the Sudan was that the slave trade would be stimulated and encouraged. As one of the most objectionable aspects of Egyptian rule for the Sudanese had been the attempt to abolish slavery, Gordon, seeing that he had no power to control the trade, now tried to turn his, or rather Egypt's, weakness to advantage by issuing a proclamation that said 'whoever has slaves shall have full right to their services and full control over them. This Proclamation is a proof of my clemency towards you.' Baring supported Gordon in this measure, but there was a terrible outcry in the British press. Gordon ignored the uproar and Baring parried the indignant questions of press and government as best he could.

On 18 February 1884 Gordon arrived in Khartoum. He was received with great enthusiasm, but perhaps the general sentiment was best summed up in a comment of an Arab as reported by Frank Power in *The Times*: 'Gordon Pasha will be received as a friend of the Arabs and blacks. His coming means no more Turks with their backsheesh and kourbash. But he should have come a year ago: it is now too late.'

In Gordon's first proclamation he announced that there would be no more taxes for two years and he burned all public records of tax debts; that there would be no more attempts to suppress the slave trade; and that Egypt would no longer rule the Sudan but would return it to its former 'sultans'. He publicly burned the hippopotamus hide whips and other instruments of torture used by the Egyptians to maintain their government. To the inhabitants of Khartoum he announced: 'I come without soldiers, but with God on my side, to redress the evils of the Soudan. I will not fight with any weapons but justice.'

Grossly underestimating the power, influence and piety of the Mahdi, Gordon sent him a red robe of honour, a fez and a letter offering to make him Sultan of Kordofan. To this the Mahdi gave a dignified reply, addressing his letter to 'the dear one of Britain and of the Khedive, Gordon Pasha':

> Know that I am the Expected Mahdi, the Successor of the Apostle of Allah. Thus, I have no need of the sultanate, nor of the kingdom of Kordofan or elsewhere, nor of the wealth of this world and its vanity. I am but the slave of Allah . . . and Allah has succoured me with the prophets and the apostles and the cherubim and all the saints and pious men to revive His faith. . . . As for the gift which you sent Us, may Allah reward you well for your good-will and guide you to the right. . . . It is returned to you herewith with the clothing We wish for Ourself and Our Companions who desire the world to come.

The Mahdi sent Gordon a patched jibba. Several letters were exchanged: The Mahdi tried to convert Gordon to Islam; Gordon, in reply, spoke of the virtues of Christianity. In one letter the Mahdi offered Gordon a safe conduct to Egypt, but Gordon refused it. Soon both men realized that the correspondence was profitless: neither could convert or frighten or bribe the other.

As confident of his own powers and of his mission as was the Mahdi, Gordon telegraphed to Sir Evelyn Baring that 'at present it would be comparatively easy to destroy Mahdi'. But to do so would require more troops than were readily available. After the destruction of Hicks's army there were only 2,000 soldiers (unpaid for eight months) guarding Khartoum. Later, 6,000 additional troops were gathered in from outlying garrisons. Still, there were not enough to think of attacking the Mahdi. Gordon suggested a solution: an appeal should be made to British and American millionaires for £300,000; the money would purchase the services of 3,000 troops from the Sultan of Turkey. This bizarre proposal was vetoed.

Colonel Stewart saw matters very clearly quite soon after his arrival and he made a more practical recommendation. Following a trip up the White Nile he wrote a private letter to Baring on 1 March 1884, in which he said that in his opinion the Mahdi was simply waiting to see if British troops were following Gordon; if none came, the Mahdi would advance on Khartoum. 'The prestige of the Government has greatly declined,' he wrote, 'confidence in it is everywhere shaken, people see that we have no force at our command and that we are inclined to give up the Soudan. I heartily approve giving up this useless and unprofitable country, but I think we are in honour bound to withdraw the garrisons and others in safety . . .' Stewart recommended that British troops be sent, although he regretted the necessity: 'The country is only intended by nature for nomad tribes and a few settled Arabs along the banks of the Nile. It annoys me greatly to see blood and treasure wasted on it.'

Not only was there an actual need for British troops but there was an equal and more immediate need to convince the population of Khartoum that soldiers would come. On 27 February 1884 Gordon first proclaimed that 'troops of the British Government are now on their way and in a few days will be at Khartoum'. It was a lie he was to repeat many times in the next eleven months. Gladstone was worried when he learned of this announcement: 'Gordon assumes a licence of language to which we can hardly make ourselves parties.'

On 12 March a force of 4,000 Dervishes under the command of one of the Mahdi's fathers-in-law captured Halfaya, a village on the White Nile just north of Khartoum, and severed all communications between Khartoum and Egypt. Three days later Gordon's soldiers attempted to recapture the village and were driven back. Before the end of the month the Dervishes were established on the north bank of the Blue Nile and were shooting into the palace in Khartoum, Gordon's headquarters. Meanwhile, small Egyptian garrisons scattered throughout the Sudan fell one by one. On 27 April the garrison at Fedasi, halfway between Khartoum and Sennar, surrendered to the Dervishes, who captured 2,000 rifles and fifty sailing boats loaded with grain. On 26 May Berber fell and Gordon was completely cut off from either escape or hope of quick relief. With him in Khartoum were about 25,000 civilians and 8,000 soldiers.

Gordon's mission had not been entirely fruitless: he did manage to evacuate some 600 sick and wounded soldiers and about 2,000 civilians down the Nile to Egypt before the escape route was cut. But the cold facts of history regarding the fate of the hopes and optimism of Gordon, the British people and government were succinctly recorded by Baring:

> Everything of political importance connected with General Gordon's Mission took place within a few weeks of his arrival at Khartoum. The essential facts connected with the history of those eventful weeks can be summed up in a few words. General Gordon proposed that Zubir Pasha should govern the Soudan as a feudatory of the Egyptian Government. Colonel Stewart and myself at first hesitated as to the desirability of sending Zubir Pasha to the Soudan, but after a brief interval we came round to General Gordon's opinion. The British Government would not agree to the employment of Zubir Pasha. Subsequently, the tribes round Khartoum rose. General Gordon and Colonel Stewart were besieged. It was clear that General Gordon's political mission had failed, and from that moment there only remained an important military question to decide, viz., whether a British military force should or should not be sent to the relief of Khartoum.

On 24 March 1884, in a private letter to Granville, Baring said, 'Certainly of all the difficult positions the English Government – not to speak of their perplexed representative – has ever been in, I do not think it would be easy to find anything in the past to equal the difficulty of this Egyptian–Soudan situation.' In the same letter he blamed himself for consenting to Gordon's mission, adding, 'I do not think we can leave him stranded at Khartoum if from the military point of view it is at all possible to help him.'

In England there was much talk of a relief expedition, but Gladstone's government refused to act; Gladstone himself was violently opposed to a relief expedition and had convinced himself that it was unnecessary. On 12 May 1884 a vote of censure was proposed in the House of Commons on the grounds that the government had failed to assist Gordon or provide for his safety. Replying to the charge, Gladstone argued that if the government took 'severe measures' it would mean war, 'a war of conquest against a people struggling to be free'. At this there were cries of 'Oh! Oh!' but Gladstone continued: 'Yes, these are people struggling to be free, and they are struggling rightly to be free!' The government majority on the division was only twenty-eight.

While in the British press and in government circles the discussion raged over the question of whether or not to send a relief expedition,

Gordon smuggled out to a perplexed Baring a series of plans and ideas, usually contradictory, regarding what should be done in the difficult circumstances that faced him. Meanwhile he was concerned with the day-to-day problems of the siege: problems of food supplies, communication, morale, troops and ammunition.

The Mahdi sent one of his best fighting emirs, Abd al-Rahman Wad Nejumi, to take charge of the siege while he spent the month of Ramadan fasting at Er Rahad. On 23 February Gordon had telegraphed Baring: 'No chance of Mahdi's advance personally from Obeid.' But in August the Mahdi did set out for Khartoum, taking with him an estimated 60,000 followers. Gordon tried to keep control of as much territory as possible around Khartoum, but on 5 September Mohammed Ali Bey, his best general, was ambushed and killed along with a thousand of his best troops. This was a terrible loss to Gordon, and he was now forced to keep his remaining troops close to Khartoum. Bahr al Ghazal and the Equatorial provinces were still holding out, as were the garrisons at Sennar and Kassala, but except for Khartoum all the rest of the Sudan was in the hands of the Mahdi.

No one was more aware of the desperate plight of Khartoum than Gordon, yet, curiously enough, he seemed to be enjoying himself. His messages to the outside world, and even his journals kept during the last months of the siege, cannot conceal his delight in the drama of the situation and his pleasure in conducting the daily operations involved in defending the city. He confessed fear, he sent alarming messages on the deteriorating situation and he complained violently of the failure of his government to support him and of the worthlessness of the people he was trying to save. Yet there were no black moods, no sinking into sloughs of despair, none of those feelings of helplessness most other men would have felt under similar circumstances. In fact, the more hopeless the situation, the more cheerful Gordon became. 'Somehow this advance of the Mahdi has raised my spirit,' he wrote in his journal. Above all, he never swerved an inch from his bedrock principles. He had many flighty ideas, but when it came to basic ethical or religious questions, Gordon was steady and firm in his faith.

Many of the Europeans who had fallen into the hands of the Mahdi had renounced, or pretended to renounce, their Christian faith. Rudolf Slatin, Gordon's former Governor of Darfur, was one who had done so. When these people attempted to communicate with Gordon, he rejected them out of hand. He maintained an interest in the fate of Slatin, but, except in a general offer to ransom all the Europeans, he did not lift a hand to assist him in any way. In his journal he wrote that

> it is not a small thing for a European to deny our faith; it was not always so in old times, and it should not be regarded as if it was taking off one coat and putting on another. . . . Politically and morally . . . it is better for us not to have anything to do with the apostate Europeans in the Arab camp. Treachery never succeeds, and, however matters may end, it is better to fall with clean hands than to be mixed up with dubious acts and dubious men.

Gordon was impressed by reports that some of the Catholic priests and nuns in the Mahdi's hands had refused to deny their faith, but he did no more for them than for Slatin.

As always, Gordon took pleasure in the children he found around him, particularly the boys. He was touched by the accidental death of a small Arab boy and wrote in his journal: 'One is drawn towards the children of this country, both browns and blacks – the former are of a perfect bronze colour.' When it came to boys, it did not matter to Gordon whether they were the sons of friends or enemies: 'Report in town says the Mahdi is at his Isle of Abba, 160 miles up White Nile, attending to the circumcision of his son (poor little fellow).'

Gordon spent much of his time on the roof of his palace with his telescope. Through the glass he could watch the movements of the Dervishes, check on the alertness of his own men and look down the river for the relief force. The telescope was both useful and fun; he thought every well-fortified place ought to be equipped with a hundred.

With the arrival of the Mahdi and his ansar from Kordofan, the pressure on the Khartoum garrison increased. Gordon thus began his account of the first encounter with what he described as 'the Mahdi's personal troops':

> One tumbles at 3 a.m. into a troubled sleep; a drum beats – tup! tup! tup! It comes into a dream, but after a few moments one becomes more awake, and it is revealed to the brain that *one is in Khartoum*. The next query is, where is this tup, tupping going on. A hope arises it will die away. No, it goes on, and increases in intensity. . . . One exerts one's self. At last it is no use, up one must get, and go on to the roof of the palace; then telegram, orders, swearing, and cursing goes on till about 9 a.m. Men may say what they like about glorious war, but to me it is a horrid nuisance.

Although the range was long, the Mahdi's artillery sometimes opened fire on the palace. Gordon's sense of fair play was outraged: 'This always irritates me, for it is so personal,' he said.

It was even more galling to think that the guns were manned by former Egyptian troops, perhaps even by the splendid Blacks. Like other professional British officers with the Egyptian army, Gordon was proud of his Black troops from the southern Sudan, comparing their bravery and fortitude with the cowardice and timidity of the Egyptians. It enraged him to think that his orders were to take out the worthless Egyptians and it distressed him to think that if he were rescued he would 'lose all my beautiful black soldiers'.

Gordon's pride and hope were his little Nile steamers. They were able to go, in a sense, behind the enemy lines and to bring in food. They offered a means of escape, too. Gordon never considered leaving Khartoum himself, but on 9 September he sent off one of the steamers, the *Abbas*, loaded with dispatches and official papers and carrying Colonel Stewart, Frank Power, the French Consul, and nineteen Greeks as a bodyguard down the Nile to Egypt. Two additional steamers provided an escort until the *Abbas* had passed Berber. Gordon hoped that Colonel Stewart, even better than his dispatches, would be able to enlighten the Egyptian and British governments on the situation at Khartoum. The *Abbas* got off to a bad start. The first day it ran into the bank of the Nile and damaged a wheel. The second day it ran on a mud-bank and was four hours getting off. Although they were occasionally fired on, they were able to find enough friendly natives to keep them supplied with wood for the boilers and cleared Berber. Just below Abu Hamad, nine days after leaving Khartoum, the *Abbas* again ran aground. Stewart and Power were lured on shore by seemingly friendly tribesmen. There they were murdered. The steamer was captured and all on board were killed or taken prisoner.

It was weeks before Gordon heard of the disaster and even when he heard the news he could not believe it. Meanwhile, the British government had, in great anguish and under pressure from the British press and public, decided to send off a relief expedition. Parliament voted £300,000 for the expedition on 5 August and Lord Wolseley was finally selected to command it, but there was further debate on how the campaign should be conducted and the best route to be taken. In a letter to Lord Hartington, the Secretary for War, Gladstone referred to the Sudan problem as 'this most perplexing and distressing affair'. Gordon did not hear of the expedition until 20 September and even then the arrangements were not complete. It was not until 5 October that the army actually started its long, 1,600-mile march south towards Khartoum.

PUNCH, OR THE LONDON CHARIVARI—FEBRUARY 2, 1884.

GETTING A LIFT!

OR, "THE GRAND OLD MAN OF THE (RED) SEA."

Gordon's reaction to the news that a relief expedition was on the way was typical: His main concern was that it should not be thought the expedition was undertaken on his account. In his journal he wrote: 'I hope I am not going down to History as being the cause of this expedition, for I decline the imputation. *The expedition comes up to deliver the garrisons.*' He sent back word to those in Egypt: '*I will not allow that you come for ME. You come for the garrisons of the Soudan.*' And when he read in an old newspaper that reached him that Lord Wolseley was seen off at Victoria Station on his way to Egypt to command the 'Gordon relief expedition' he was incensed and poured out his rage in his journal.

Whether he was relieved or not, Gordon had already made up his mind that he would never return to England. He made this remarkable statement in his journal: 'It is one of my joys that I never have to see Great Britain again. . . . I say this in order that those who may have to do with me may know how very determined a man's will must be who does not wish (and indeed *will not ever*) go back to England.' He added that 'no persuasion will induce me to change my views'. Several weeks later he wrote: 'I dwell on the joy of never seeing Great Britain again, with its horrid, wearisome *dinner* parties. . . . I would sooner live like a Dervish with the Mahdi than go out to dinner every night in London. I hope, if any English general comes to Khartoum, he will not ask me to dinner. Why men cannot be friends without bringing the wretched stomachs in, is astounding.'

Gordon entertained vague plans for going to the Congo if he survived the siege, but as time dragged on he doubted more and more that he would get out. As early as 1 March 1884 he had said in a telegram to Baring that he was 'convinced I shall be caught in Khartoum'. Even when he knew the relief expedition was on its way, he did not believe it would arrive in time. In his journal on 13 October he wrote: 'It is, of course, on the cards that Khartoum is taken under the nose of the expeditionary force, which will be *just too late.*' And so it was. On 27 October he wrote: 'We must either be relieved, or fall, before the end of November.' By 3 November Wolseley had reached Dongola. But December came and Khartoum was still defending itself, although a furious Dervish attack in early November had isolated the fort at Omdurman, across the river from Khartoum, and cut it off from food and supplies. On 13 December he wrote: '*If some effort is not made before ten days time the town will fall.*' The following day he wrote a letter to Lt.-Col. Charles Watson, an old friend in Cairo, in which he said that he could hold out for ten days more, but added, 'the game is up'. This was the last letter anyone ever received from Gordon, though the ten days passed and the siege went on. The Omdurman fort was forced to surrender on 15 January, but in Khartoum Gordon still had ammunition and a little food left, and the relief expedition under the command of Lord Wolseley was cautiously making its way up the Nile.

On 17 January 1885 the advance guard of Wolseley's expedition, commanded by General Sir Herbert Stewart, was attacked at a caravan station and wells called Abu Klea (true name: Abu Tuleih), sixty-three miles south-west of Ed Damer and twenty-five miles west of the Nile, by a large Dervish army under Musa Wad Helu, one of the Mahdi's best generals. So furious and fearless was their assault that they actually broke the square. The force of their charge was broken, however, by the camels crowded together on the rear face of the square where the breach had been made. The British were soon able to reform their square and to kill all those who had penetrated it. The bodies of 1,100 Dervishes were counted in the immediate proximity after the battle. Out of a force of 1,500, forty-four British officers and men were killed, including the tall (6 ft. 4 in.) and colourful Colonel F. G. Burnaby who, among other exploits, had crossed the English Channel alone in a balloon less than three years before. Burnaby had requested permission to join the relief expedition and his request had been refused, but he came anyway, and Wolseley was glad to have him. It had been agreed that if anything happened to General Stewart, Burnaby would assume command of the advance column.

A forced march by night brought the advance guard closer to the Nile, but they were again attacked before they could reach it. Although the Dervishes were beaten off, General Stewart was struck in the groin and died a few days later. The command of the column now fell upon Colonel Sir Charles Wilson, an excellent staff officer but not a fighting soldier.

The column reached the Nile at last and made an abortive attempt to capture El Metemma, opposite present-day Shendi. On 21 January four steamers arrived at the British camp on the Nile, sent by Gordon from Khartoum. Had Burnaby been alive and in command, he would undoubtedly have seized this opportunity to load the steamers with British troops and rush them to Khartoum, now only a hundred miles away. But the dashing Colonel Burnaby was dead and Wilson was more cautious.

The men on the steamers must have told Wilson that conditions inside Khartoum were frightful. Most of the soldiers were sick with diarrhoea from eating gum, strips of hide from angarebs and the crushed cores of palm trees. Certainly the Mahdi knew how weakened the garrison was, for on 16 January 1885 a merchant and two officers with some of their men deserted to the Dervishes and described in detail the conditions they had left behind them.

On 25 January Gordon summoned the principal people of the town to the palace. He himself did not talk to them but deputed Giriagis Bey, his chief clerk, to speak for him. Looking through his telescope mounted on the palace roof, he had noticed increased activity in the Dervish camp; he wanted all males over eight years old to man the fortifications. Giriagis Bey said that Gordon appealed to them for the last time to make a determined stand, for in twenty-four hours the English would arrive.

After the meeting, Bordeini Bey, a prominent merchant in Khartoum and one of Gordon's principal supporters, asked to see Gordon. He found him sitting disconsolately on a divan, smoking. In front of him were two boxes of cigarettes. When he saw Bordeini Bey, Gordon pulled off his fez and threw it across the room. 'What more can I say?' Gordon exclaimed. "I have nothing more to say. The people will no longer believe me. I have told them over and over again that help would be here, but it has never come, and now they must see that I tell them lies. If this, my last promise, fails, I can do nothing more. Go and collect all the people you can on the lines and make a good stand. Now leave me to smoke these cigarettes."

Bordeini Bey, who survived the fall of the city and eventually succeeded in escaping to Egypt to tell his tale, said: 'I could see he was in despair, and he spoke in a tone I had never heard before.' He went on to describe the appalling conditions existing that last day in Khartoum: 'Hundreds lay dead and dying in the streets from starvation, and there were none to bury them.' On the fortifications around Khartoum, the sick and starving men complained, 'The Pasha has deceived us.'

The falling river left a stretch of muddy ground on the side of the defences that faced the White Nile. It is said that a deserter pointed this out to the Mahdist emirs, but it was probably visible to them from the start. Along this strip of land, unprotected by a wall or a ditch, the Dervish army passed just before dawn on 26 January, pouring into Khartoum. A wild flurry of gunfire, cries of alarm and excitement, and in two hours it was all over. Gordon was killed on the steps of the palace.

The steamer *Ismailia* was lying only 300 yards from the palace gate and the captain saw Dervishes making for the palace. He got up steam and waited as long as he dared for Gordon to come. When the Dervishes started moving towards his steamer, he cast off and moved into midstream. He cruised up and down in front of the town until, later in the day, he was offered the Mahdi's pardon. Because his family was still in Khartoum, he accepted the offer, landed and ran to his home. He found his ten-year-old son dead on his doorstep; inside, his wife lay pierced with several spears.

Fathalla Gehami, a wealthy Syrian married to the daughter of a French merchant in Khartoum, had buried all his money in a corner of his house. His most trustworthy servant, a Dongola boy whom he had raised from a child, helped him. When the situation grew desperate in Khartoum, Gehami sent the young man to relatives in the Mahdist camp, telling him that if the government was victorious he could return to him and if the Mahdi was successful, he would then be able to repay the merchant for his kindness to him. On the day of the Dervish attack, the servant rushed to his master's house. 'Open! Open!' he cried. 'It is your servant, Mohammed.' Fathalla Gehami quickly unbolted the great iron gate he had erected. Instantly the young man plunged a spear into his body and leaped into the house, followed by his Dervish friends. They dug up the money and started out with it. On the way out, Mohammed tried to kill the wife as well, but she threw herself on the body of her dying husband and the boy's Dervish friends pulled him away.

Martin Hansal, the Austrian consul, was killed by one of his own kavasses, who dragged his body out of the house, poured spirits on it and burned it to a cinder. Nicholaos Leonticles, the Greek consul, had his hands cut off first and was then beheaded. An Austrian tailor named Klein was so indiscreet as to make the sign of the cross. His throat was slit from ear to ear before the eyes of his wife and children. His eldest son, eighteen years old, was speared to death and thrown at the feet of his mother. In a state of mad despair, the mother held her baby to her breast and with a five-year-old son clinging to her, she fought like a tigress and saved her babies, but her young daughter was seized and carried off to be a concubine.

For the most part, the women were not killed. Instead, they were herded into pens, like cattle, until they could be divided among the conquerors, the Mahdi taking first choice, then the khalifas and the emirs in order of rank. The robes of many of the women were still bespattered with the blood of their husbands and children when they were handed over to their Dervish masters. The old and the ugly were left to wander naked about the market-place begging for food. Unweaned babies were left to die in the streets.

Two days after Khartoum had fallen, Rudolf Slatin, a prisoner in the Mahdi's camp, heard the booming of guns and the sharp crack of rifle fire. From the Dervish camp he could see that the fire was directed towards two small steamers on the Nile before the town. Sir Charles Wilson had waited three days after the arrival of the steamers at the camp of the advance column near El Metemma, and it was not until 24 January that he started up the river with twenty British soldiers and about 200 Blacks in two of the small steamers. Khartoum had held out for 317 days, but Sir Charles was just two days too late. He arrived within sight of Khartoum at eleven o'clock in the morning; then, seeing that the Egyptian flag was no longer flying from the palace and being fired on from the shore, he turned his steamers about and made his way back downstream. The date was 28 January 1885. It was – or would have been – Gordon's birthday: his fifty-second.

'Too late!' The words were passed slowly back out of the Sudan, then by telegraph to Cairo and on 5 February 1885, by cable to London. The shock, grief and anger of the British people was tremendous. 'Too late!' The words were a caption on a cartoon in *Punch* (14 February 1885) showing Britannia at Khartoum, her arm covering her eyes as the Dervish hordes swarmed into the palace. The *Pall Mall Gazette*, which had been so influential in sending Gordon to Khartoum, ran an Extra with the headline: 'Too Late!' And the words were repeated over and over again in press, parliament and pub. Tennyson used them in his poem on Gordon:

> By those for whom he lived he died. His land
> Awoke too late, and crowned dead brows with praise.

Baring said: 'Rarely has public opinion in England been so deeply moved. . . . When General Gordon's fate was known, a wail of sorrow and disappointment was heard throughout the land.'

Queen Victoria sent a telegram to her Prime Minister: 'These news from Khartoum are frightful, and to think that all this might have been prevented and many precious lives saved by earlier action is too frightful.' She did not code the telegram but, to Gladstone's dismay, sent it *en clair*. Gladstone refused to admit that his government's decisions – and indecisions – had caused the tragedy, but he confided to his diary and family his fears that the circumstances might put an end to the government. He was hissed

PUNCH, OR THE LONDON CHARIVARI.—FEBRUARY 14, 1885.

"TOO LATE!"

Telegram, Thursday Morning, Feb. 5.—'Khartoum taken by Mahdi. General Gordon's fate is uncertain.'

when he went to the theatre; for three weeks crowds in Downing Street hooted and jeered him; in the music halls the initials of the 'Grand Old Man', as Gladstone was called, were reversed to M.O.G. – Murderer Of Gordon – and a music hall song predicted that when he died he would 'sit in state on a red-hot plate between Pilate and Judas Iscariot'. Not long after, some of his closest colleagues turned against him in the House of Commons on the issue of reducing armaments, and his government fell.

There was talk of converting the relief expedition into a punitive expedition and reconquering Khartoum, but in the end the project was abandoned and the British army withdrew.

On 22 June 1885 the Mahdi died of natural causes in Omdurman. Reginald Wingate, the British Intelligence Officer, who knew more of Mahdism than any other man outside the Sudan, wrote of him: 'There is no doubt that, until he was ruined by unbridled sensuality, this man had the strongest head and the clearest mental vision of any man in the two million square miles [*sic*] of which he more or less made himself master before he died.'

Suddenly the principal actors were gone from the scene: Gladstone and his government, including Lord Granville, the Mahdi, Gordon and Stewart. Only Baring remained. New actors appeared on history's stage and the character of the drama changed. The remaining centres of resistance in the Sudan soon vanished: Kassala fell in July and Sennar the following month. There was scattered fighting along the fringes – on the Egyptian border, along the Red Sea coast, on the frontiers of Abyssinia – but the central Sudan remained isolated, cut off from the rest of the world, and firmly in the hands of the Mahdi's successor, Abdullahi Ibn Mohammed, the first Khalifa. And so it remained for thirteen years.

Part 2

The Prisoners

The Prisoners

The Sudan now belonged to the Sudanese. Things Egyptian, Turkish, European were destroyed or allowed to rust, rot and disintegrate. Foreign manners and ways of doing things largely disappeared. History, past and future, became only what men could or would remember. Today it would be impossible to reconstruct life during the Mahdiya were it not for the recorded memories of three European men – a priest, a soldier and a merchant – who lived in the Sudan throughout much of this era.

Their characters were as different as their professions, and each reacted differently to the ordeal of captivity. The outstanding traits of character revealed were not those which would be expected from them. The shrewdest of the three was not the merchant, but the soldier, Rudolf Slatin. Although brave, Slatin was not as courageous as the priest, Joseph Ohrwalder, while the man who suffered most by clinging to his religion was the merchant, Charles Neufeld, the most stubborn and stout-hearted of all. The circumstances of their captivity were also quite different: Father Ohrwalder was never actually in prison; Neufeld spent almost all of his time in chains; Slatin, the only one of the three who had actually fought against the Mahdi, spent only a few months in prison and was for much of the time almost a confidant of the Khalifa.

Although all three men lived in Omdurman for years and had much in common – the same desire to escape, the same mother tongue (German), the same alien religion and the same hatred of their captors – they rarely saw each other and when they did they rarely discussed those aspects of their lives which most concerned them. Consequently, they saw the Mahdiya from three different points of view, although all agreed, naturally, in their detestation of Mahdism, for no prisoner loves his gaoler.

In telling the story of these captives, it has been necessary to present their own view of the Mahdiya, which, quite naturally, was not the view of the Sudanese man on the street of Omdurman. Unfortunately, no known personal history of an ansar of the Mahdiya exists to balance the picture.

While these chapters will tell the story of three individual men, they will also tell the story of Abdullahi, the humble Baggara who inherited the Mahdi's Empire after his death and had the wit and ability to hold it. Although a primitive, uneducated, uncultured man – ruthless, cruel, unjust, often childish and wary of innovations – he was also loyal, devout, politically wise, immensely shrewd and attentive to the task of holding together both the new religion and the new state. Again, it is unfortunate that we do not possess the memoirs of Sudanese who knew him to check the facts of his character here presented, but modern Sudanese opinion, which in a sense is the synthesis of handed-down reminiscences, supports the generally unfavourable estimate of his character. Today the Sudanese tend to blame the Khalifa Abdullahi, who ruled through most of the period here covered, for the ruin of the Mahdist cause, but this may only be because he led them to defeat, and followers are seldom kind to leaders who lose.

Thus, the best picture that can be pieced together of those thirteen years when the Sudan was united under one Sudanese ruler with its unique state religion is best – or at least most completely – shown through the eyes of three Europeans, and the chapters in this section are primarily from material found in their own published accounts of their experiences.

6

Rudolf Slatin: Governor of Darfur

Rudolf Anton Slatin was born on 27 June 1857 at Ober Sankt Veit, then just outside Vienna and now a part of the city, the fourth of six children. His great-grandfather had been a Jew, but had been converted to the Catholic faith as a young man. None of the Slatins appears to have taken religion very seriously; Catholicism was the principal Austrian sect, the most acceptable, and the Slatins accepted it. However, the family was always regarded as Jewish and, although Slatin's father was a prosperous merchant in Vienna and Rudolf's elder brother Heinrich became a senior civil servant in the Imperial Household, the Slatins were subject to the racial discriminations embodied in the laws and customs of the Austro-Hungarian Empire.

Rudolf did not start school until he was nine and he left at sixteen, his last three years being spent in the Vienna Commercial School. He made bad marks both in his studies and in conduct. Through the secretary of the commercial school he learned of a position available as a clerk to a bookseller in Cairo. With his poor academic record Rudolf could not hope for a better position in Austria and he wanted to travel. He took the job. While in Cairo he met Theodor von Heuglin, the Austrian traveller and ornithologist who had once been the Austrian Consul in Khartoum and was at this time planning an exploration trip to the Red Sea provinces. It was von Heuglin, apparently, who inspired the young man to visit the Sudan. Originally, Slatin planned to go to the Sudan with him, but when the expedition was cancelled Slatin decided to go anyway; he gave up his job at the bookstore and made his way up the Nile to Khartoum.

After spending a month or two in Khartoum, he set off for Kordofan, visiting the Austrian Catholic Mission at Dilling in the Dar Nuba mountains. It was interesting country. Unlike most of the Sudan, the Dar Nuba area was one of heavy vegetation, rich soil, and colossal trees; deer, giraffe, wild boar and even elephant were to be found. Young Slatin wanted to see more of the country and perhaps even go on to visit newly conquered Darfur, but a revolt of the Hawazma Arabs against the payment of Egyptian taxes made the area unsafe and he was ordered back to El Obeid, out of the danger zone.

Slatin returned to Khartoum, where he met that astonishing fellow countryman with the Turkish name, Dr Mohammed Emin, later to achieve fame as Emin Pasha. Both Slatin and Emin wrote to Gordon, then Governor of the province of Equatoria, offering him their services. It was two months before they received an answer inviting them to come to Lado. Emin accepted and was at once hired. Slatin wanted to go but he had been in the Sudan for more than a year already and his family was urging him to return: he was suffering from fever and he still had not completed his military service in the Austrian army. Reluctantly, he started home, but he begged Emin to recommend him to Gordon for employment later. Going to the Sudan was an extraordinary adventure for such a young man. Neither the dangers nor the hardships of the life discouraged him; the country cast its spell over him, and he wanted passionately to return.

Slatin joined the Austrian army on his nineteenth birthday and passed his examination to become an officer of the reserve. Austrian armies had started to occupy, not without difficulty, Bosnia and Herzegovina when, in July 1878, young Slatin, then serving as a sub-lieutenant in Archduke Rudolf's 19th Hungarian Infantry on the Bosnian frontier, at last received a letter from Gordon, now Governor-General of the entire Sudan, offering him service with the Egyptian government. He longed to accept, but it was not until December, when the Balkan campaign ended and his battalion went into winter quarters at Pressburg, that he obtained the necessary permission to go.

After his release from the Austrian army, he spent eight days in Vienna getting ready and saying good-bye to his family. His mother, naturally, was pained to see him leave. Just before he left she made a prophetic speech which he was long to remember: 'My son! My Rudolf! Your restless spirit drives you into the world. You are going to distant, almost unknown, lands. But a time will come, perhaps, when you will long for us and for a quiet life.' Rudolf Slatin left Vienna for Trieste on 21 December 1878. He never saw his mother again, and it was nearly seventeen years before he again saw Vienna and the rest of his family.

He sailed for Suez and then to Suakin, crossing the desert to Berber and then sailing up the Nile to Khartoum, arriving there his back upon civilization to live and work in a land where climate, flora (or lack of it), fauna and the bulk of the inhabitants were against him. A. B. Theobald, in his biography of Ali Dinar, has described Darfur, the land Slatin was now to rule, as 'a harsh, hot land, where most of the people live on the edge of hunger, and where the bare necessities of life for man and beast must be wrung from an inhospitable soil'. The country has not changed much in the past hundred years, but in Slatin's day, when tropical diseases were terrifying mysteries, Sudanese and Europeans were killed or maimed by malaria, bilharzia, leprosy, tuberculosis, guinea worm, tropical ulcers, sleeping sickness, yellow fever and terrible eye infections such as granular blepharitis, trachoma and 'Sudan blindness' (Onchocerciasis). Darfur is particularly rich in insect life, and there under the burning sun millions upon millions of flies, in dozens of varieties, converge upon all exposed flesh, living or dead, boldly exploring nostrils, eyes and ears. Even today, conditions in this harsh environment are alleviated only by inadequate supplies of sprays, vaccines and medicines. It is a hard land.

When Slatin left the banks of the Nile that morning to ride towards Dara, he doubtless thought he knew something of the dangers and difficulties he faced. But he could neither know nor imagine the strange and terrible circumstances which were to make his life one of the most bizarre and fantastic ever recorded.

All started smoothly enough. When he reached El Obeid, he found a Dr J. Zurbuchen, a Swiss employed as a sanitary inspector, who was also going to Darfur and agreed to accompany him. The Governor of Kordofan provided them with baggage camels and, just as they were about to leave, he handed Slatin a telegram from Gessi announcing that he had defeated the forces of Suleiman Zubair.

Slatin and Dr Zurbuchen left El Obeid early in July 1879 and travelled to Foga, the end of the telegraph line, and then on to El Fasher, capital of Darfur, where they received a warm welcome from the Governor, an Italian named Giacomo Bartolomeo Messedaglia. From here they moved south to Dara. As they reached the boundaries of Slatin's mudiria, he took a boyish delight in riding ahead and pretending to be only an aide. When the villagers asked questions about the new governor, Slatin replied, 'Oh, I think he will do his best, and I believe he is inclined to be easy-going.'

'But is he brave and kind-hearted?' they asked.

'He does not look as if he were afraid,' Slatin replied guardedly, in mid-January 1879. His first assignment was as Financial Inspector, and he travelled about the Sennar and Gizera districts listening to the complaints of taxpayers. In his report to Gordon he expressed his opinion that the system of taxation was unjust, taxes falling more heavily on the poor than the rich, and that the methods by which the taxes were collected, using soldiers and bashi-bazouks, was tyrannical and oppressive. The twenty-one-year-old Financial Inspector had encountered problems which his limited knowledge of finance and his meagre experience in life made impossible for him to solve:

> I found an immense collection of young women, the property of the wealthiest and most respected merchants, who had procured them and sold them for immoral purposes, at high prices. This was evidently a most lucrative trade; but how were the establishments of these merchants to be taxed and what action was I to take?

He resigned.

Gordon then appointed him Mudir of Dara. A mudir is the governor of a district, or mudiria, and Slatin's mudiria consisted of the south-western part of Darfur, which was divided into three districts, with Dara (near present-day Nyala) as the capital. By telegraph, Gordon ordered Slatin to meet him somewhere between El Obeid and Tura el Hadra, on the White Nile. Slatin went by steamer up the Nile to Tura el Hadra, and on board Gordon's steamer they discussed in detail the situation in Darfur. As Slatin knew little English, they spoke in French. Gordon predicted, correctly, that the campaign being waged by Gessi Pasha against Zubair's son Suleiman would soon be concluded. In Darfur, Sultan Harun Dudbenga, son of the former ruler of the country, was trying to regain control from Egypt and for several years he had been keeping the country in a state of ferment. Slatin was ordered to wage a vigorous campaign against Sultan Harun to force his submission.

Their discussion ended about ten o'clock that night, and when Gordon saw Slatin over the side of the steamer he said, 'Good-bye, my dear Slatin, and God bless you; I am sure you will do your best under any circumstances. Perhaps I am going back to England, and if so, I hope we may meet there.' Slatin stood on shore for an hour until he heard the steamer's whistle and the sounds of the anchor being weighed. Gordon steamed off down the Nile for Khartoum and Slatin never saw him alive again. The next morning Slatin set off on his long ride to Dara.

Back in Austria Slatin could have found an outlet for his energies in sport, soldiering and travel. Instead he had voluntarily turned 'but I haven't yet heard much about his courage. He has a manly appearance, and I believe he is kind-hearted, but of course it is impossible for him to satisfy everyone.'

Such deception was easy, for Slatin was still trying, unsuccessfully, to grow a moustache, while Dr Zurbuchen, an older man with a long black beard and spectacles, looked much more like a governor than young Slatin. But the Sanitary Inspector, who spoke little Arabic, was more confused than amused by the trick.

Slatin had scarcely arrived at his mud village capital when an opportunity for action presented itself. He was dining with the principal personages of the town on roast mutton, fowls and rice covered with butter and honey when he heard a disturbance among the servants who were trying to prevent two men from approaching them. He asked Zogal Bey, his chief government official and, as afterwards became known, a nephew of Mohammed Ahmed, to find out what was happening. Zogal Bey got up, licking the grease from his fingers, and went out to investigate. He returned shortly to say that messengers had arrived with news that Sultan Harun was preparing to attack Bir Gowi, a small outpost garrisoned by 120 irregulars three days' march south-west of Dara. That very night Slatin set off, taking 200 regular Black infantry and twenty horsemen. Writing years later, he recalled his youthful enthusiasm:

> I was young, strong, and keen to have some fighting experience, and I well remember my delight at the thought of a brush with Sultan Harun. The idea of difficulties and fatigue never crossed my mind; all I longed for was a chance of showing my men that I could lead them.

Both in Dara and in the villages where they stopped along the way, Slatin was offered presents of horses or women by the local headmen. His refusal to accept these gifts and his insistence on giving a receipt for food taken were viewed with astonishment. Then as now, in all countries where dishonest practices are hallowed by custom, the honest man was viewed as a freak and was often suspect.

Arriving at Bir Gowi, Slatin was told that Sultan Harun was gathering his forces, but had not yet moved to attack. He waited impatiently for four days until spies came in to report that Sultan Harun had learned of his arrival in Bir Gowi and had disbanded his men. Thoroughly disappointed, Slatin returned to Dara.

Back at headquarters he found that his Arab clerk, who had been with him when he was financial inspector and whom he had brought with him to Dara, had gone mad. Slatin went to see him and found him raving: 'Zogal Bey is a traitor! Beware of him. I have ordered the fires in the engine to be lighted in order that the train may take you to Europe. . . . I will come with you, but we must be careful about Zogal.' The poor clerk died five days later, but, as Slatin was to learn, mad men often tell the truth.

He had been back at Dara for about a month when a letter came from Messedaglia Bey ordering him to move towards Jebel Marra to attack Sultan Harun in his own den at Niurnia. Other government troops were being sent to join with him in the attack. Slatin left Dara with 220 regular infantry and sixty bazingers for Jebel Marra. It was February and the soldiers suffered much from the cold in the mountains. Several died. Not much was accomplished, for Niurnia and the villages around it were deserted when Slatin and his troops arrived there. After waiting ten days and only capturing some women, they turned back. On the way he learned that the wily Harun had attacked Dara itself. Being repulsed, he had turned aside to ravage other villages in the area. Slatin found his tracks and after several days' hard marching, caught up with him. Although greatly outnumbered, Slatin made a swift bold attack from front and flank and completed routed the enemy. Had Slatin had cavalry he could have captured the entire rebel force. As it was, Harun himself barely escaped, and Slatin captured 160 rifles, four large copper war-drums, two flags, two horses and all the women Harun had taken in his raids.

A month later Sultan Harun reorganized his forces and started raiding in the Kulkul district. Gordon's district governor, Nur Bey Angara, surprised Harun's band in camp and dispersed them, killing Sultan Harun, whose head was cut off and sent to El Fasher.

Slatin now started out on an inspection tour of his province and the remainder of the year was taken up with administrative problems which involved him in the numerous petty disputes between tribes and officials. At the end of January 1881 he left Dara to go to Khartoum and there called upon Rauf Pasha, a swarthy, handsome man who had replaced Gordon as Governor-General. Rauf Pasha greeted Slatin coolly and told him with evident irritation that the leave of absence he had requested to visit Cairo had been granted.

'But I never wrote to Cairo for leave of absence,' said Slatin, astonished.

'Then what does this telegram mean?' asked Rauf Pasha.

Marcopoli Bey, the Governor-General's secretary, read out the telegram from Cairo: 'To the Governor-General of the Sudan:

Three months leave on full pay has been granted to R. Slatin, Mudir of western Darfur.'

'I think that you, as a soldier, should have known better than to have acted in this irregular manner,' Rauf Pasha said. 'You should have applied for your leave through me, and not direct to Cairo. And now you say you never asked for any!'

Slatin could only protest that he had never attempted to go over the head of his superior and that he had not asked for leave, but it was obvious that Rauf Pasha did not believe him. The next day letters from his family cleared up the mystery. Some time earlier Slatin had written to his mother telling her that he was suffering from fever. Frau Slatin, fearing that her son was seriously ill, wrote to the authorities in Cairo asking that he be sent there for medical treatment. Slatin hastened to explain the matter to Rauf Pasha who apologized for his accusations. Although his own mother, he said, was but a poor Abyssinian ex-slave, he understood a mother's affection and concern for her son.

While staying in Khartoum Slatin was appealed to by a Darfuri named Hassen Wad Saad en Nur who was being held in custody by Rauf Pasha. Slatin interceded on his behalf and Rauf Pasha reluctantly agreed to release him if Slatin would agree in writing that he would be responsible for Nur's good behaviour. Slatin did so – and lived to regret it.

In Khartoum Slatin naturally found friends among his fellow countrymen at the Austrian Roman Catholic Mission. Bishop Daniele Comboni and Fathers Ohrwalder and Dichtl had recently arrived from Cairo and the two priests shared Slatin's quarters. On 29 March, when he left Khartoum, he took Bishop Comboni and Father Ohrwalder with him as far as El Obeid. At Foga he found a telegram waiting for him from the Khedive. Messedaglia Bey had clapped one of his senior officers in irons and sent him to Khartoum on charges of cruelty. For his pains, Messedaglia Bey was himself relieved as Governor of Darfur and Slatin was appointed to his place and given the title of Bey. Rudolf Slatin, not quite twenty-four years old, was now the ruler of a territory two and a half times larger than England.

Arriving in El Fasher, his new capital, he discovered a mass of suits, petitions, charges and countercharges awaiting him; everyone was intriguing, from the mudir to the lowest clerk. Some of the disputes he attempted to settle, but most he ignored. One was a case against the former mudir and commander of troops, Said Bey Guma. Slatin reinstated him. Justifying his action, he wrote:

There was no doubt he was an intriguer; besides being excessively parsimonious, he was not liked by the other officers, and was famed for his vocabulary of bad language; but at the same time he was a brave soldier in the field, and this quality – especially amongst Egyptians – was excessively rare in these distant regions. I therefore re-employed him.

About the middle of December 1881 Slatin left El Fasher with 200 infantry and some irregular cavalry to settle a tribal dispute in the northern part of his domain. On the way a messenger caught up with him and gave him a telegram in French cypher:

A dervish named Mohammed Ahmed has, without just cause, attacked Rashid Bey near Gedir. Rashid Bey and his troops have been annihilated. This revolt is very serious. Take the necessary steps to prevent malcontents in your province from joining this dervish.

Except for some vague rumours that a religious sheikh was causing trouble, this was the first news Slatin had heard of the Mahdi.

He settled the tribal dispute as quickly as possible and hurried back to El Fasher. On 7 June, when Yusef Pasha esh Shellali's army was defeated by the Dervishes, all southern Kordofan fell into the Mahdi's hands, giving him much-needed money, arms, horses and food. The swiftly rising tide of Mahdism was soon felt in southern Darfur, particularly in Slatin's former mudiria where Zogal Bey was now acting-governor. A discharged government official named Ali Madibbo had raised the standard of revolt among a section of his own Rizighat tribe.

Early in 1882 Slatin himself left El Fasher for Dara with 350 mounted men. There he wrote letters to the various Arab tribes, sent off an expedition to Shakka to restore order there, court-martialled and shot a man caught distributing Madhist proclamations, and had an earnest talk with Zogal Bey, who admitted he had received several letters from his uncle the Mahdi, but protested that he was loyal to the government. Leaving the mounted troops at Dara, Slatin hurried back to El Fasher. The first news that greeted him was that the telegraph station at Foga had been destroyed by Homr Arabs and that the entire countryside in the neighbourhood of Om Shanga was, to use the current expression, 'unsettled'. This was followed by a complete disruption of the postal system. Messages to El Obeid or Khartoum now had to be sent in hollowed-out lance staves, in the soles of boots or sandals, or sewn in clothing.

The extra ammunition he had ordered had reached El Obeid, but now could not be sent on. Of the additional 400 cavalry he had requested, only 100 reached him and the rest were held at El Obeid. Stray soldiers or government officials were often murdered; trusted sheikhs deserted with their tribes to the Mahdi. With the situation worst in southern Darfur, Slatin decided to make his headquarters at Dara. Taking 200 infantry and seventy-five of the newly arrived cavalry, he started back. On the way he learned of a defeat inflicted by Madibbo on one of his officers, Mansur Helmi, near Shakka. Mansur was now cowering in his zariba and begging for help. Slatin sent off reinforcements, leaving himself only 110 men. Madibbo then switched his attack from Mansur to Slatin, who had formed a zariba near Deain.

About sunset one evening the advance guard of Madibbo's forces approached on horseback and dismounted in a clump of trees not far from Slatin's zariba. Fifty men were sent out and drove them off, killing three. He then set his men to work digging a trench inside the zariba.

At dawn the next morning an Arab approached with a white flag. Slatin went out to meet him. It was a sheikh named Ishak el Abd, whom Slatin knew well, and he brought a message from Madibbo. The letter gave an account of the massacre of Yusef Pasha esh Shellali in which Madibbo himself had taken part; he declared that Mohammed Ahmed was indeed the true Mahdi; and he called upon Slatin to surrender, urging him as a former official and friend to submit to the inevitable. Slatin laughed and asked his old friend Sheikh Ishak what he thought of it.

'Master,' said Ishak, 'I have eaten bread and salt with you, and therefore I will not deceive you. The whole country is in revolt, and everyone says he is the true Mahdi. If you intend to submit to Madibbo, I can guarantee that you need have nothing to fear.'

'Never!' Slatin replied. 'I shall never lay down my arms to an Arab. Go tell Madibbo, and tell him that battle must decide between us!'

'Master, I will not deceive you. Every word I have said is true. I, personally, shall not fight against you, but my tribe is no longer under control.'

'It is all the same to me whether you fight against me or not. One man alone cannot make much difference one way or the other.'

As they shook hands Ishak said, 'If one day I am forced to fight you, I will let you know.' He then mounted his horse and rode quickly away.

Slatin returned to the zariba and positioned his men. They did not have long to wait. Two hours later the Dervishes attacked. They advanced rapidly from the north-west, where a small wood gave considerable cover. Slatin stationed himself in a chair on a small mound in the centre of the zariba where he had a good view of the advancing enemy and could keep an eye on his own troops. As the Dervishes advanced to within rifle range, their bullets began to whistle through the zariba. Slatin stood up to shout an order and a bullet shivered his chair to pieces. He wisely moved to a less exposed position. His men were fairly well protected by the trenches, but he was losing many of his camels and horses. He decided to make a sortie. Selecting fifty men, he led them out the southern end of the zariba, turned west and came up on the enemy flank. Caught in a deadly cross-fire, the enemy retreated with considerable loss; Slatin lost twelve men.

Although the enemy had withdrawn from view, Slatin knew that they had not gone far and that they would undoubtedly renew their attack the next day. With him in the zariba was Sheikh Afifi Wad Ahmed of the friendly Habbania tribe. That night he sent Sheikh Afifi and some of his men out to scout the enemy positions. Two hours later they reported back: Madibbo was with his bazingers in a village and the hostile Arabs were camped just to the south and west. Afifi reported that, although it was a large force, they had taken no precautions for defence and the scouts had been able to creep up quite close to their camp-fires.

Taking seventy men, Slatin led them out for a night attack. In an hour they were in position within 600 yards of the enemy and Slatin ordered his bugler to sound 'Commence firing'. Madibbo's men were caught completely off guard. Never dreaming that Slatin's small force would dare to attack, they could only assume that he had been reinforced by fresh government troops. The bazingers fled, leaving their arms behind them. Horses broke their ropes and were pursued in the dark by frightened Arabs. The enemy were completely routed. Slatin fired the huts of Madibbo's village and threw the captured saddles and matchlocks into the flames. Taking only the forty Remington rifles left by the bazingers, he marched back to an enthusiastic reception in his zariba. Only two soldiers were wounded by thrown spears. The next morning at sunrise, Slatin gave the order to march, and in a few days they were at Dara.

While at Dara Slatin did all he could to increase his fighting force: He managed to obtain a number of bazingers; some friendly Arab horsemen joined him; and 100 regulars arrived from El Fasher. The bazingers were mostly obtained from gellabas (or jellaba), travelling merchants, usually dealing in slaves, who kept private armies of armed men. Zogal Bey and his brother provided 200. But Slatin was worried about his low stock of ammunition. Although he had ordered more from El Fasher, Said Bey Guma had not sent it on, saying he did not have enough camels to transport it. Slatin sent a curt note ordering his officials to give up their own camels as his need was urgent, but he did not wait. He set off with all of the men he could muster for Hashaba where he had arranged to meet friendly tribesmen. When all had assembled, Slatin counted his forces. He had:

Regulars		550
Gellabas		200
Bazingers		1,300
Various		100
Arab spearmen	about	6,000
Arab horsemen		400
Total number of men		8,550

He had 2,150 small arms, of which only 600 were Remingtons; most of his men were armed only with swords and spears. He also had a muzzle-loading Krupp mountain gun (a survivor of the Franco-Prussian War of 1870-1) with thirteen artillerymen to man it. With this force he planned to march to Shakka, build a fort and then make excursions into the Rizighat country, where Madibbo had been raising tribes in revolt. The only other troops in southern Darfur were those he had left as a garrison with Zogal Bey at Dara: 400 regulars, seven guns and their gunners, thirty horsemen and 250 bazingers.

At the end of October 1882 Slatin moved south towards Shakka with his mixed force, the largest he had ever commanded at one time. The country through which he advanced was covered with thick bush and scattered forests. Fearing attack while on the march, he took elaborate pains to arrange his men so as to prevent their being surprised. As the rearguard position was the most dangerous, dusty and troublesome – they had to take care of faltering men and animals – he arranged that the men on this duty should be rotated each day with the men on the flanks.

Reaching Deain, he camped on the site of his old zariba and discovered that Madibbo had rebuilt his village and had stored a quantity of grain there. The guards he had left made little resistance and were soon overpowered; Slatin distributed the grain to his troops. He remained here for several days while his horsemen scouted the route to Shakka to be certain there was sufficient water to be found on the way. Receiving a favourable report, he set out with all his forces. 'I had little fear as to the eventual result of our operations,' he said, 'but at the same time I was anxious to get to Shakka before being attacked.'

Unfortunately, just at this time Slatin came down with a 'heavy bout of fever'. The second day after leaving Deain, there was an alarm: Madibbo's Arab horsemen were attacking the flank. In spite of his fever, Slatin joined the rearguard. Although it was difficult to estimate the size of the enemy force, he signalled to his flank guards to join him and he moved quickly to engage the enemy. After a brisk skirmish the Arabs were driven off and Slatin's men captured six horses; his own losses were two men missing, seven horses killed and a number of wounded. That night they camped at a place called Om Waragat.

The next morning, still suffering from fever, he turned his troops over to his second-in-command, Sharaf ed Din. They reached some more or less open but boggy ground and the men were soon struggling to extricate the animals that sank into the mire. Then the alarm sounded from the rear, followed immediately by rifle shots. Slatin started at once for the fighting by way of the left flank, signalling for his reserve of ninety regulars to join him. When he reached the rear he saw that he was too late.

Sharaf ed Din had forgotten to arrange for the rotation of the rearguard. The regulars, annoyed by being on this duty when it was not their turn, had gone back to their companies; the irregulars had drifted off to join their tribesmen on the flanks. Consequently, when the attack came there were only about 250 bazingers guarding the rear. They had time to fire only one volley before they were overwhelmed. Those that could fell back in disorder on the rear face of the square. With friend and foe rushing in upon them together, the men on the rear face of the square were unable to stop the rush, and by the time Slatin arrived some enemy tribesmen were already inside the square.

Slatin ordered his bugler to signal 'lie down' to his own men in the square. He then moved in with his reserves who, armed with Remingtons, checked the rush. The attackers peeled off on either side of the square and engaged the guards on the flanks. These men were already fighting with other hostile Arabs who had attacked their front. Although the rush of Madibbo's wild Rizighat into the rear of the square had been halted, those who had already penetrated it created a frightful havoc among the bazingers who, armed only with muzzle-loaders, were almost defenceless.

So swift had been the attack and so great the confusion that many had not even had time to draw their bayonets. Slatin with his party of regulars eventually managed to cut down the intruders, but their losses were frightful.

During the confusion of the battle Slatin saw an Arab running off with the red bag containing the fuses for the mountain gun. It is doubtful if the man knew what was in the bag; he was probably attracted by its colour and assumed it was valuable loot of some sort. It was indeed, for without the fuses the only artillery piece was useless. Slatin jumped from his horse and gave it to his orderly, a young Black, telling him to bring back the fuse bag. Armed with only a spear, the young man leaped on the horse and sped away. He returned shortly with the red bag and a dripping, red-tipped spear.

While Slatin was clearing and re-forming the square, his men on the flanks, caught between enemy forces on their front and rear, suffered worse than those in the square itself. They broke up entirely and fled in all directions, to be ridden down and killed by the Rizighat horsemen. Hundreds were massacred.

Slatin managed to hold a portion of his force together until the Arabs, loaded with loot or hot in pursuit of fleeing soldiers, had left the battlefield. When the last of the enemy had disappeared, Slatin ordered the bugler to sound 'Assembly'. Only a few hundred answered the call. He divided his men into two parties, detailing one group as guards and the other to collect the arms and ammunition of those who had fallen and load all on the remaining camels. Near by was a small village standing on a sandy plain. Slatin, fearing a second attack, moved the remains of his army there and hastily constructed a zariba of thorn bushes. Only when this had been done was attention given to the wounded. Those able to walk or crawl made their own way to the zariba; the seriously wounded were now carried in. Looking over the battlefield, Slatin saw the ground strewn with dead bodies. Beyond his view were still more bodies of men cut down by the wild Rizighat.

He ordered a roll-call. Less than 900 men were there to answer. Only thirty horsemen were left. Out of fourteen infantry officers, only four were alive and one of these was wounded. Of the thirteen artillerymen, one was left. Among the missing was an orderly, Morgan Hosan, a quiet, brave, intelligent boy about sixteen years old. It had been his duty to guard one of Slatin's horses. From Isa, another orderly boy, he learned the fate of Morgan Hosan.

'Master, I did not want to make you more sorry than you are,' Isa began. 'I found him not far from here, lying on the ground with a spear wound in his chest. When he saw me he smiled and whispered, "I knew you would come and look for me. Say good-bye to my master, and tell him I was not a coward. I did not let go his horse, and it was only when I fell down stabbed in the chest that they cut the bridle to which I clung, and took him. Show my master the bit of bridle that is still in my hand, and tell him Morgan was faithful. Take the knife out of my pocket – it belongs to my master. Give it to him, and say many salaams to him from me." '

For Slatin there was much to do still and he had little time to mourn. He put all his men to work strengthening the zariba and preparing for the next attack, which he knew must sooner or later be made by Madibbo's men. Just before sunset the Rizighat Arabs returned from their bloody pursuit and were surprised to find Slatin and the remainder of his army well entrenched in the village. Madibbo sent his bazingers to attack the zariba, but after a short fight they were driven back. Darkness fell and all firing ceased.

That night Slatin talked with his remaining officers and chiefs. It was proposed that they should attempt to retreat under cover of darkness, but Slatin argued against this as it would mean leaving the wounded behind: 'We have now nothing to fear but hunger,' he told them. 'The wounded and tired camels can be killed for food for the soldiers. Besides, we can exist somehow or other for a few days. We shall most certainly be attacked . . . but we shall equally surely drive off the enemy. In this way the men will regain confidence after the terrible shock we have all suffered. I know the Rizighat; they will not stay here and watch us. . . . Our wounded comrades will have time to recover their strength a little; those only suffering slightly will be able to march in a few days and the others we can mount on our horses.'

He won over the chiefs to his view that they should remain where they were for a few days and lick their wounds. Late that night when he was left alone with his own thoughts, he lay awake thinking of their position and of the consequences of their defeat. It was probable that he would be able to retreat with his forces on Dara, but he dreaded the effect which the news of their disaster would have on the garrison and inhabitants, particularly if brought to them by fleeing deserters or by the enemy. He woke up his clerk and ordered him to write to Zogal Bey, telling him that in spite of heavy losses all was well and they would return to Dara in about a fortnight. He told him that if any deserters or fugitives came in with alarming news about their situation they were to be arrested and kept under close guard.

Slatin also wrote a personal letter in German to Gottfried Rott, a Swiss who had been appointed Inspector for the Suppression of the Slave Trade and had only recently arrived at Dara. He was supposed to have made his headquarters at Shakka, but Slatin had kept him at Dara and had begged him not to attempt any anti-slavery activities at this time. To Rott, Slatin described his situation and told him not to be down-hearted. At the same time he enclosed letters to his mother, brothers and sisters which he asked Rott to forward in case he was killed.

These letters were entrusted to one of his Arab horsemen who set out that night to ride through the enemy to Dara. The next day Slatin wrote to Frank Lupton, a former Red Sea captain who had succeeded Gessi as Governor of Bahr el Ghazal, asking him, if he could, to attack the Rizighat from the south and relieve the pressure on Darfur. This letter he concealed in a dry pumpkin gourd and sent out with two bazingers who knew their way to Lupton's headquarters. But Lupton was unable to help. He was having a difficult time himself, for the population was preparing to revolt. In the markets of Bahr el Ghazal in August 1883 they were trading slaves for ammunition and rifles: a boy for three packets of cartridges, a girl for five packets, and two girls for a Remington.

Slatin and his men remained six days in the zariba and were attacked at least once every day. On the third day one of Madibbo's best commanders was killed, and after this the attacks were not pushed so vigorously. The real enemy now was famine. Their regular food supply was exhausted and, as it was obvious they could not remain in the zariba any longer, they prepared to leave. Shells for the mountain gun as well as the hammers from the percussion guns belonging to those who had been killed were thrown into a rain pool; the stocks of the percussion guns were burned and the lead for the cartridges was placed in the bottom of graves in which were buried the bodies of several men who had recently died of wounds.

On the seventh day after the disaster, just after sunrise, Slatin marched his men out of the zariba and formed a marching square with flank and rearguards. Each able-bodied man carried about 200 rounds of ammunition. The only two remaining camels pulled the loaded mountain gun. There were 160 wounded inside the square, the most serious cases being carried on the backs of the few remaining horses. The retreat began.

They marched towards the north-east, where the ground was more open and favourable for defensive action. Unfortunately, all the guides had either deserted or been killed, and they did not know where, or if, they would find water. They had only been on the march for an hour when the first attack came – as usual, from the rear. Slatin instantly halted his men, marshalled the flank guards closer to the square, ran out the mountain gun to the rear face of the square, and with an escort of fifty men went himself to take command. On reaching the scene of action, Slatin jumped off his horse; in the Sudan this meant the commander had no intention of running away but would win or die with his troops.

The first charge was from spearmen, holding long lances in their right hands and bundles of small throwing spears in their left. A few well-directed volleys from the rearguard seemed to check the advance momentarily, but the place of those who had been cut down was quickly taken by other spearmen and they rushed the square. They came so close that several of Slatin's men were wounded by their spears, but the Remingtons and the mountain gun forced them back.

The next attack followed soon after, the spearmen giving way to Madibbo's bazingers. Slatin summoned reinforcements from the other sides of the square and after a brisk exchange of fire for about twenty minutes the bazingers were also driven off.

While Slatin was fighting with the rearguard, the left flank was also engaged. The enemy was driven off, but Slatin lost his best remaining officer, a Nubian who had been promoted from the ranks for conspicuous gallantry in action. He now lay dying with a bullet through his right lung. Slatin took him by the hand and asked how he was. The officer murmured, 'Now that we have conquered, we are all right.' He died a few minutes later.

Slatin's men were elated by their success in beating off the attack and they formed up to continue the march with renewed confidence. But Slatin had lost, in addition to the valuable officer, twenty men killed. There were also a number of seriously wounded who would have to be carried.

About three o'clock in the afternoon there was another attack. The enemy were soon beaten off, but Slatin decided to stop for the night and construct a zariba. There were no more alarms that day and they were able to pass an undisturbed night. The following day they drank the last of their water and marched on. They easily beat off one small attack, but by midday they still had found no water. They came across a few *fayo*, a kind of juicy radish, and the troops sucked these avidly, but it was imperative that they find water and food soon or they would all perish.

That afternoon they came upon a Rizighat shepherd with a large flock of sheep. Sheep and shepherd were quickly seized. Slatin promised the shepherd that he would spare his life and give him a reward if he would guide them to a rain pool. The shepherd agreed, but Slatin did not trust him and kept him tied and guarded. They passed a thirsty night in a zariba and marched at dawn the next morning. It was not until noon that their reluctant guide pointed out to them a rain pool in a clump of trees. Reasoning that the enemy would probably be lying in wait for them there, Slatin tried to keep his men in good order, but except for his personal escort of forty men and about another forty men from the rearguard, all the rest of his army ran in a mob for the rain pool, plunging up to their waists in the water. Again and again the bugler sounded assembly, but the men were completely out of hand and in a frenzy of delight with the luxury of water.

The enemy was indeed waiting for them and opened a general attack on all sides. Fortunately, they had been forced to go some distance away in order to find concealment. Slatin's men at the rain pool returned at once when the shooting started and fell in their places. After a few minutes of heavy firing, the enemy retired. Slatin lost one horse.

With plenty of water and food, the troops constructed a zariba, built fires and roasted the sheep they had confiscated – their first full meal in many days. Slatin had already decided to remain here for a day to rest his men when an enemy messenger from Madibbo approached. He announced that the Mahdi was camped before El Obeid and would soon capture it. Madibbo called on Slatin to surrender and promised to treat him respectfully and send him with a safe escort to the Mahdi. Slatin had the letter read to the troops, who greeted it with jeers. The messenger was told to tell Madibbo that if he wanted to enjoy the pleasures of Paradise which the Mahdi had promised him he should come and attack them. 'We shall wait for him,' Slatin said, 'and for his sake we shall not march tomorrow.'

Madibbo did not attack the next day, however. The only sign of the enemy was a Rizighat horseman who rode into their camp by mistake. When he realized what he had done he cried out, 'Allah is great! I have killed myself!' The man was bound and his horse taken from him. Slatin gave orders that he was not to be harmed and a guard was set over him, but the next morning when he called for the prisoner to question him he found that one of the soldiers had split his skull with an axe. Slatin later said that 'knowing in what condition my men were, I thought it better to let this incident of brutality pass'. The retreat continued.

There was one more attack, but it was the last. Madibbo withdrew his forces and Slatin made Dara in safety. He himself needed rest and attention. Suffering from fever, weighted with responsibilities and worries, he had also been wounded three times in the various fights: a bullet had shattered the ring finger on his right hand and it had to be amputated at the root; another bullet had hit him in the leg and flattened against the bone; and a thrown lance had hit him in the right knee. Of his return to Dara he said, 'I felt weak and overdone, and was very glad of a few days' rest.'

It was little enough rest that he got. The day after his return he ordered all the durra he could find to be bought up and stored against the day when Dara itself would be attacked and perhaps besieged. He now had to contend with plots, rumours and dispiriting news. Gottfried Rott took sick and died. More and more tribes deserted to the Mahdi's cause. Sheikh Afifi sent word that his tribe had revolted, although he himself, true to his promise, would not fight against Slatin but would come and join him. He was murdered on the way. Slatin sent men to El Fasher for ammunition and reinforcements. They came back with the ammunition, but the officials there refused to send reinforcements in spite of his direct order. His own officers and officials in his capital were hostile to him; there were rumours that he had really been removed by the government but that official word had not arrived or that he was concealing the order. He uncovered a plot among his noncommissioned officers in Dara and was forced to court-martial and execute six of them. But the worst disaster for Slatin occurred in Kordofan. When El Obeid fell this was the deciding argument for most of the tribes in Darfur and nearly all hastened to swear allegiance to the Mahdi.

Among those who remained loyal to the government there was a feeling of despair. Even among Slatin's own troops, those who had fought and suffered beside him, there was a belief that he would never win a victory because of his religion. In other times it had made little difference to the soldiers what religion their commander adhered to, but this was a religious war and the Mahdi's agents made much of the fact that Slatin was a Christian.

One night Slatin talked over this situation with Mohammed Farag, an Egyptian and one of his best-educated officers. At the end of a long talk Slatin asked, 'Suppose that I now turn Mohammedan. Would my men believe in me and hope for victory? And would that give them more confidence in me?'

'Of course the men would believe you,' Mohammed Farag told him. 'At least the majority of them. They trust you implicitly. But will you change your faith from conviction?'

'Mohammed Effendi, you are an intelligent and well-educated man. Here conviction has nothing to do with the case. In this life one has often to do things which are contrary to one's persuasions, either by compulsion or from some other cause. I shall be quite content if the soldiers believe me and abandon their silly superstitions. Whether others believe me or not is a matter of indifference to me. I thank you most sincerely. Keep our conversation entirely to yourself. Good night!'

When Mohammed Farag left him that evening, Slatin considered the matter for a few minutes and decided to announce to his troops the following morning that he had embraced Islam, a step which, in Gordon's estimation, put him beyond the pale. Many years later he wrote that he took the step in order to have a better chance of saving the province with which he has been entrusted by the Egyptian government. 'In my early youth my religious ideas were somewhat lax; but at the same time I believed myself to be by conviction as well as by education a good Christian, though I was always inclined to let people take their own way to salvation. The simple fact was that I had not been sent to the Sudan as a missionary but as an official of the Egyptian Government.' Again, in another place, he said, 'I had no pretentions of holding very strict religious views on the expedience or otherwise of the step I had taken, nevertheless, at heart I was, I believe, as good a Christian as the majority of young men of my acquaintance.'

The next morning Slatin assembled all his troops and announced: 'I am not an unbeliever. I am as much a believer as you.' Then he recited the creed, bearing witness that 'there is no God but Allah and Mohammed is His prophet!' His men raised their rifles and shouted congratulations; the officers advanced to shake his hand. When order was restored, Slatin told them that from now on he would openly attend prayers with them and that as an Islamic name he had chosen Abdel Kader. He then ordered the men to march back to their quarters and invited the officers to have food and coffee with him. Slatin ordered Mohammed Farag to distribute twenty of the best oxen to the men as a sacrificial offering and from his own stock to give an ox to each officer.

The effect on his men of Slatin's change in religion was even better than he expected. Although the enemy was daily increasing in numbers, there was no longer any reluctance on the part of the troops to go out against them. He also received what seemed at the time to be good news from Khartoum: the government was raising a large force for the reconquest of Kordofan. This was the army of Hicks Pasha.

Although Zogal Bey had done nothing disloyal, Slatin had always been suspicious of him because of his relationship to the Mahdi. When Slatin embarked on his ill-fated expedition to Shakka he had confided his suspicions to Rott and had asked him to keep an eye on Zogal. Now that the Mahdi seemed certain of success, Slatin thought he detected a subtle change in Zogal Bey's attitude, although outwardly he still appeared loyal and submissive. Slatin had a talk with him and gave him permission to go to Kordofan and pretend to change sides, with instructions to secretly pass on letters to the government in Khartoum and to do all in his power to prevent Darfur from being attacked from Kordofan. Zogal said he would carry out his instructions faithfully and thus prove his loyalty. He left his wife and children in Dara as a pledge and went straight to El Obeid, arriving just before the battle of Shaykan. The defeat of Hicks Pasha convinced him that the Mahdi's cause was the right one – or at least that the Mahdi was leading the winning side. His promise to Slatin was ignored and he applied his talents to Mahdism.

Slatin, not content to wait for an attack, set off with 250 regulars, 100 bazingers and twenty-five horsemen on a small punitive expedition against hostile Arabs who had recently plundered two friendly tribes. He was successful in defeating the hostile tribe, forcing them to return the women and children they had taken and to pay a fine of 100 horses and 1,000 oxen. His men attributed their success to his conversion to Islam.

His old enemy, Madibbo, had now collected a force of horsemen and bazingers and was marching on Dara. When he was only one day's march away, Slatin moved out at night with 150 regulars and fifty horsemen and attacked his camp at sunrise. Surprised by this sudden attack, the enemy fled and Madibbo himself narrowly escaped capture by jumping on his horse barebacked and fleeing with his men. Losses were slight on both sides, but Slatin captured Madibbo's copper war-drums, the loss of which, in the Sudan, was considered a disgrace.

Madibbo had fled, but he was not finished. These small successes could not bolster the crumbling Egyptian government in the Sudan, and Slatin's little expeditions were like chasing off flies who only returned in greater swarms. He could not keep this up much longer. He was still short of rifle ammunition and Said Bey Guma, his governor in El Fasher, swore he could not send any because of the defection of the tribes in northern Darfur. All Slatin's hopes were at this time centred on the expedition of Hicks Pasha. If Hicks was successful in Kordofan the entire situation would at once take a turn for the better in Darfur. He struggled to hold on. He made bullets for empty Remington cartridge cases by melting down the bullets for the muskets and percussion guns. He made bullets from the small supply of copper he had in store and from the melted down copper bracelets and anklets he bought from Sudanese women.

More Arabs were raiding in the neighbourhood and he was forced to send out a part of his force to drive them off. He was at this time so ill with fever that he could not sit on a horse, so he sent out eighty men under the command of a brave Black officer guided by Wad Kabbashi, a friendly Arab. The following evening Wad Kabbashi was back with only ten men. Slatin, in great agitation, demanded to know where his troops were. 'Scattered or killed,' said Wad Kabbashi, and seating himself carefully on the edge of Slatin's carpet so as not to soil it with his blood, he told how the party had been ambushed at dawn. Slatin could ill afford the loss of seventy men and their rifles. Besides, this defeat caused more tribes to revolt and there were few now on whose loyalty he could depend.

Hassan Wad Saad Nur, the man whose pardon Slatin had obtained in Khartoum, had been brought to Dara and given a house just outside the fort. When his horse had died of disease, Slatin had given him another. But Nur now decided that the time had come to desert his benefactor. Taking the horse Slatin had given him, he rode off to El Obeid, to become one of the Mahdi's faithful followers.

Communication with the government outside Darfur had become almost impossible; it was even difficult to get messages to and from his capital at El Fasher. All the devices Slatin had previously used to conceal his messages had been discovered. One day, seeing some of his soldiers performing an operation on a donkey that was lame in the foreleg, it occurred to him that a donkey might well serve as the unwilling bearer of a message. Taking a large donkey into the privacy of his house, he tied it and threw it on its side. Making a careful incision in the skin near the shoulder, he inserted a small note, folded to the size of a postage stamp and wrapped in a piece of goat's bladder. He sewed up the cut with silk thread and when he released the donkey he was pleased to see that the animal could walk without difficulty. Entrusting the donkey to a loyal Arab, he sent him off to deliver the message to Ala al-Din Pasha, the Governor-General. Slatin could have saved himself the trouble. The Arab and donkey found Ala al-Din Pasha at Shatt and delivered the message just before the Governor-General set out with Hicks Pasha into Kordofan.

Madibbo, smarting under the humiliating loss of his war-drums, now attempted an all-out effort to crush Slatin. Calling on all the rebel tribes in the area to join him, he assembled a large force just one day's march from Dara. Slatin, with only twelve rounds of rifle ammunition per man, knowing that even if the expedition of Hicks Pasha was successful relief was still far off, tried to gain time. He sent one of his men to the enemy camp to investigate the possibility of capitulation. The man returned with a report that Madibbo was encamped with a large force and called on him to surrender. Slatin sent his man back to arrange for a meeting with the Arab chiefs.

At sunrise one morning the meeting took place under a large Adamsonia tree not far from the fort. He entertained them with dates to show that although times might be hard he could still afford such luxuries. All the Arab chiefs were present except Madibbo, who wanted simply to press the siege and not waste time talking. Slatin was not displeased by this division of opinion among his enemies and he tried to enlarge it. Knowing how jealous each tribe was of the others, he asked, 'To which of you do I turn over my arms and horses?' Naturally there could be no agreement on this matter and they were all the more inclined to agree with Slatin's proposal that he should surrender to a personal representative of the Mahdi.

After much talk it was at last settled that Slatin should write a letter to the Mahdi at El Obeid and send it with one of his own men:

In the name of the Most Merciful Allah. From the slave of his God, Abdel Kader Slatin to Sayed Mohammed el Mahdi. May Allah protect him and confound his enemies! Amen! For a long time I have been defending the province which the Government confided to my care, but Allah's will cannot be fought against. I therefore hereby declare that I submit to it and to you, under the condition that you send one of your relatives, with the necessary authority to rule this country, and to whom I shall hand it over. I demand a pledge from you that all men, women and children within the fort shall be spared. Everything else I leave to your generosity.

With this the Arabs were content and they packed up their tents and left. Madibbo, unable to carry on the siege without the support of the tribesmen, also decamped. Slatin, satisfied that he had gained the time he needed until Hicks Pasha could defeat the Mahdi's forces, returned to Dara and attempted to reopen communications with Khartoum. In the meantime there was nothing to do but gather in supplies and listen to rumours. Everyone knew of the army marching towards El Obeid, but it was not until the end of November that rumours began to circulate that Hicks Pasha had been defeated. Slatin tried not to believe, but, as he said, the stories 'sounded suspiciously near the truth'. The bad news could no longer be doubted when it was learned that Zogal Bey, now a Dervish emir, had arrived in Darfur as Governor-General of the West and that the garrison at Om Shanga had surrendered to him.

On 20 December 1883 the Egyptian whom Slatin had sent with his letter to the Mahdi, appeared at the gate of the fort dressed in a jibba. He told Slatin in detail of the massacre of the army of Hicks Pasha which he had personally witnessed, and he brought with him a letter from Zogal Bey calling on him to surrender and arranging for a meeting on 23 December. Knowing the futility of attempting to keep this news secret, Slatin at once informed the kadi, the principal merchants and his officers. The officers discussed the situation among themselves, and that evening Farag Effendi and the commandant of artillery came to him and said they had all decided that the only thing to do was to surrender. Slatin told them he would consider the matter and give them his decision in the morning.

All that night he lay awake turning over the discouraging aspects of his present position and struggling with the emotions that welled within him. Everyone around him, military and civilian, was convinced that there was no hope of relief; his troops were dispirited; his total force of regulars at Dara consisted of only 510 men; he had scarcely enough ammunition to withstand one attack; there was not another free European within 600 miles. There seemed no other course but to submit. It seemed a hard fate after fighting so hard for so long. For four years he had held his province, fighting thirty-eight battles against rebellious tribes and struggling with intrigues from within and without. Were all his efforts to end in failure? And what of his own position?

As an officer, the idea of surrender to such an enemy was repulsive in the extreme. I had no fear of my own life; I had risked it sufficiently during the past four years to effectually dispose of any notion that my surrender was occasioned by any want of personal courage . . . but the very word 'surrender' was repellent to me, and doubly so when I thought over the consequences which must follow to me – a European and a Christian – alone amongst thousands and thousands of fanatical Sudanese and others, the meanest among whom would consider himself superior to me.

Yet Slatin was young; life was dear to him. He wanted to live and was unwilling to sacrifice his life in a lost cause. He was not much disturbed by the religious aspect of the surrender: he was willing to don the jibba and pretend to be a convert.

The next morning when the two officers came to him to learn his decision, he showed them Zogal's letter which promised that Slatin and all of the men, women and children living in the fort would be spared and protected. While he was talking with his officers, a report came in that the town's chief merchant and all the bazingers had deserted during the night. Any remaining doubts about the advisability of fighting vanished with this piece of news. Slatin at once dictated a letter to Zogal, who had now taken the name of Sayed Mohammed Ibn Khaled, agreeing to his terms and offering to meet him at a place called Hilla Shieria.

Slatin left at midnight that night with four kavasses. 'During my service in Darfur I had had many disagreeable experiences, but this journey was quite the hardest,' he said later. The next day they reached Hilla Shieria where Sayed Mohammed Ibn Khaled was waiting. He greeted Slatin warmly, pressed him to his bosom and begged him to sit down on his carpet. He showed him his letter from the Mahdi giving him his appointment and he told Slatin that it was entirely due to his good offices that the Mahdi had decided to pardon him. Slatin thanked him and was then introduced to the Mahdist emirs who had accompanied him. Food was served and they began to discuss Khaled's trip to Dara. While they were talking, one of Slatin's officers arrived. Ignoring Slatin, he went straight to Mohammed Khaled and greeted him effusively; he had been one of Khaled's spies, a 'Black Zogal'.

Although well treated, Slatin was now the prisoner of his former lieutenant. As he lay down to try vainly to sleep that night the realization of his position came to him with its full force. It had been five years since he had left his home, and now it seemed impossible he would ever see it again. They would be holding church services in Vienna this night. It was Christmas Eve.

7

Slatin: Prisoner of the Mahdi

When Slatin was brought back to Dara by Mohammed Ibn Khaled (Zogal) he was allowed to live in his house and to keep his servants. Madibbo, who had come to pay his respects to Khaled, came to see him there. They shook hands politely and Slatin asked him to sit down. Madibbo seated himself with dignity and after a moment's hesitation he said: 'We have fought each other, each seeking his own advantage. I fought against the government, but not against you personally. Allah knows, I have never forgotten that you were once friendly to me. Therefore, let anger depart from your heart and be a brother to me.'

'I am not at all angry at what you have done,' Slatin told him. 'You are but one among many, and if I had been annoyed with you, your words have quite reconciled me.'

'May Allah strengthen you and, as He has protected you so far, may He continue to protect you!'

'In truth,' said Slatin, 'I put my trust in Him. Still, it is hard to have to bear all that has now happened. But I suppose it must be.'

'Not so. I am only an Arab, but listen to me. Be obedient and patient. Practise this virtue, for it is written: Allah is with the patient. However, I have come to ask you something, and my request is this: if you are really a brother to me, then in token of our friendship, I wish you to accept my favourite horse.'

Before Slatin could reply, Madibbo rose and went out, and in a few minutes came back leading his own horse, the finest in his tribe. He handed the leading-rope to Slatin.

'I do not wish to insult you by refusing to accept your present,' Slatin said, 'but I do not need it. I will not want to ride much now.'

'Who knows,' Madibbo said, 'he who lives long sees much. You are still young and may often ride yet – if not on this horse, then on another.'

Such a princely gift called for another, and Slatin had one close at hand: the war-drums of Madibbo captured in the night attack on Kershu. His servants placed them before the pleased old warrior and Slatin laid on top of them a handsome sword. 'Today they are mine and I can offer them to you,' he said. 'Tomorrow they may be another's.'

'I thank you and accept them gladly,' said the Sheikh.

When Madibbo had left, Slatin sat thinking of his words: Allah is with the patient. He who lives long sees much. They were only well-worn Arab sayings, but they spoke so directly to the prisoner that their wisdom struck him afresh. To live long, or even for a short time, in his present circumstances required certain traits of character and talents not generally regarded as admirable in the European social milieu with which he identified himself. To stay alive, or at least to increase the odds for staying alive, would require humility to the point of humiliation, servility equal to any demand and a degree of shrewdness that prostituted intelligence. At this point in his captivity, Slatin probably did not fully realize all that would be required of him, but he embraced a philosophy that demanded this price, and he paid it. It was a philosophy he was to learn well and to practise for the next eleven and a half years.

The next morning, all the inhabitants of Dara except Slatin and his officers were ordered out of their houses and told to stand in front of the police station near the market. They were allowed to take with them only the clothes they wore and a few cooking utensils. All servants and slaves were divided among the Mahdists, and the prettiest girls were put aside for the Mahdi. Houses and other buildings were then systematically ransacked and everything carried off to the local Beit el Mal, which had been formed at the former government headquarters. As no money or jewellery was found, all those suspected of having any were brought before the emirs and beaten. Some were tied head down in wells. Among those who most cruelly used the prisoners was the man Slatin had freed from prison in Khartoum and befriended, Hassan Wad Saad en Nur. Slatin complained of him in his presence to Khaled.

'Do you think you are governor of Darfur and can say what you like?' Nur sneered.

Slatin warned him not to go too far and reminded him that he had once obtained his release from prison and that even the horse he was riding belonged to him.

'It was Allah who released me, and it is Allah, and not you, who has given me your horse to ride.'

Khaled turned on him angrily and ordered him out. 'Take no notice of him,' he said to Slatin, 'his father, Saad en Nur, was the Sultan's slave, and slave blood always shows itself.'

As they were now alone, Slatin took the chance to complain of the treatment being given the inhabitants of Dara, reminding Khaled that he had pledged himself to protect them. Khaled spoke sharply: 'I am not going to put anyone to death, but they have no right to the money they are concealing. It is contrary to the arrangement and it must be taken from them by force.'

On 3 January 1884 Khaled set out to lay siege to El Fasher, capital of Darfur. Said Bey Guma, who had agreed to surrender the city, now decided, after hearing of the way the people of Dara had been treated, to fight instead. Khaled moved out with his entire force, and Slatin was taken along, but being unwilling to fight against those he had so recently ruled, he pleaded illness and asked to be allowed to return to Dara. Khaled permitted him to go after demanding a pledge that Slatin would not attempt to commit any hostile act. To this Slatin agreed. Before he left, Khaled gave him some of his intercepted letters to read. One was from the Khedive, complimenting him on his service; another was from Nubar Pasha, the Prime Minister, who also wrote of his satisfaction with his work; the third was from Zubair Pasha asking him for news of the family of his son. Already these letters seemed to be from another age. When he had finished reading them, Khaled took them back; scoffing at the Khedive who thought he could defeat the 'Expected One'. There would be still harder times ahead for the 'deluded Turks', he predicted. Slatin remained silent, remembering the advice of Madibbo: 'Be obedient and patient'. He was convinced of the wisdom of the advice, however difficult it was to follow.

On 15 January El Fasher fell to Khaled's Dervishes and the inhabitants were subjected to even greater cruelties than those inflicted on the people at Dara. Again, all property was to be given up. One Egyptian officer, Major Hamada, stubbornly declared that he had no money, but one of his female slaves testified that he had a quantity of gold and silver hidden somewhere. Consequently, he was brought before Khaled, who tried to convince him that he should willingly give it up. As he still refused, Khaled called him an 'unbelieving dog'. Hamada, losing control of himself, called Khaled a 'wretched Dongolawi'. He paid a heavy price for his angry words. Khaled ordered him to be flogged until he confessed the hiding-place of his money. He received a thousand lashes a day for three days without yielding, his only answer a dogged, 'Yes, I have concealed money, but it will remain buried in the ground with me.' Khaled ordered the flogging stopped and turned Hamada over to the Mima Arabs who were told to guard him.

Early in February Slatin was summoned to El Fasher again. He was allowed his horses and servants, but all else he was required to turn over to the Beit el Mal as an 'act of renunciation'. This he did. Hearing the story of Major Hamada's resolution, Slatin visited him. He found him in a pitiable condition: there were gaping wounds from his shoulders to his knees that were now fast mortifying. Every day his tormentors poured over him buckets of salt water seasoned with Sudanese pepper, hoping to wring a confession from him in his agony, but he refused to utter a word.

Slatin went to Khaled and begged his permission to take Hamada home with him. 'He is dishonest,' Khaled said coldly. 'He has concealed money and has publicly insulted me. For this he must die a miserable death.'

'For the sake of our old friendship,' Slatin pleaded, 'I pray you to forgive him and hand him over to me.'

Khaled considered the matter carefully, then said he would if Slatin would prostrate himself before him. Slatin felt the blood rush to his face. In the Sudan this was considered a terrible humiliation. Yet, he thought of the tortures of Hamada, and with an effort knelt down and laid his hands on Khaled's bare feet. Khaled at once drew back his feet and raised him, apparently ashamed of having asked such a thing. 'It is only for your sake that I will liberate Hamada. But you must promise that if you find out where his treasure is, you will let me know.'

Slatin promised and then hurried off to get Hamada. His servants carried the tortured officer on an angareb to Slatin's house, where Slatin washed his wounds and spread fresh butter on them. He fed him some soup and made him as comfortable as possible, but it was obvious that the poor man could not live long. When he had been cared for in Slatin's house for four days, he called Slatin to him and motioned for the servants to leave. He was dying and he wanted to tell where he had buried his treasure, but Slatin stopped him. It would be of no use to him and he did not want to break his word to Khaled. Hamada held his hand and with an effort whispered, 'I thank you. May you become fortunate without my money. Allah is merciful!' Then, stretching his limbs and raising his forefinger, he slowly murmured the creed: 'There is no god but Allah and Mohammed is his prophet!' He closed his eyes and died.

It was about this time that a long letter reached Slatin from Cairo ordering him to concentrate his troops and all war material at El Fasher and to turn over his province to Sultan Abdul Shakour. This was the man Gordon had found in Cairo and had tried to carry with him to the Sudan as part of his scheme to return the country to its original rulers. The Sultan, it will be recalled, wisely took to drink and never attempted to go past Dongola.

From El Fasher Slatin managed to smuggle out a letter to his family, which eventually arrived in Vienna. Either to reassure his family or because he still had no inkling of the fate that awaited him, he said: 'The enemy has treated me with respect and I cannot complain. . . . In the near future I hope to go to Kordofan to learn what is going on there and to make the requisite plans for rejoining you. . . . You need have no anxiety about me. . . .'

In due course Slatin did go to Kordofan, but not to make plans for returning to Austria. He went because the Mahdi sent for him; and he went under guard with two other prisoners: Said Bey Guma and a Greek merchant named Dimitri Zigada. They were, how-ever, permitted to keep their horses and servants. When they reached Er Rahad, where the Mahdi was staying, they were kept for the night in some huts outside the town. Slatin had a servant who knew something of tailoring, and he had been instructed to make jibbas for the three prisoners. Slatin's jibba was made with large black patches sewn on with such evenness and regularity that he thought he looked 'exactly like a lady in a fancy bathing cos-tume'. Said Bey Guma and Zigada wore parti-coloured patches which made them look like harlequins. The next morning, dressed in their new jibbas, they prepared to meet the Mahdi. But no one met the Mahdi without passing through the hands of Abdullahi.

Slatin thought it prudent to send a servant to the much-feared Khalifa Abdullahi to tell him they were coming. The servant did not return. After waiting for some time, they decided to proceed into Er Rahad anyway. As they neared the market-place, they heard the loud baying of an ombeÿa, an elephant's tusk horn; this was the signal that the Khalifa had gone out on his horse, but at the time Slatin did not know what it meant. He came across a Darfuri and asked him why the ombeÿa was blowing. The man replied, 'Very probably Khalifa Abdullahi is giving orders for someone's head to be cut off and this is the summons for the people to witness the execution.' It hardly seemed a propitious time for the ex-governor of Darfur to meet the great man, but they rode on.

When they came in sight of a large open area Slatin's servant and another man came hurrying towards them calling to them to stay where they were. Slatin halted and his servant told him that the Khalifa had ridden out to meet him. The other man dashed off to inform the Khalifa of Slatin's presence. A few minutes later they saw several hundred horsemen approaching. At the far end of the open space they halted and the Khalifa now began to direct his men in a sort of cavalry drill: Four horsemen abreast would dash up to a point at a full gallop, pull short and shake their spears, then turn around and gallop back. Sometimes they would charge at Slatin, shaking their lances in his face and shouting, 'For Allah and his Prophet!' After half an hour of this the Khalifa sent word that Slatin should ride towards him. Slatin dashed at full speed towards the Khalifa, pulled short and cried, 'For Allah and his Prophet!' and then rode back. The formalities over, the Khalifa now prepared to return to the town and sent word that Slatin and his party should follow him.

When they reached the enclosure that was the Khalifa's quarters, the rest of his party stayed at a respectful distance while a special attendant helped him dismount and he went inside. In a few moments he sent out word that the captives should come in. Slatin found himself in a small square room with straw walls and a thatched roof containing several angarebs and some palm mats on which they were told to sit. Dates and a mixture of honey and water in a pumpkin gourd were served to them. When they had finished eating and drinking, the Khalifa himself came in, greeting them cordially and extending his hand to be kissed. 'Allah be praised, we are at last united!' he said. 'How do you feel after your long and tiring journey?'

'Yes, indeed, Allah be praised for having granted me to live to see this day!' Slatin answered. 'When I beheld your countenance my fatigue at once left me!'

Thus Slatin began the long course of flattery which was to win him a unique place among the prisoners of the Mahdi. A meal of asida and meat was brought in to them. The Khalifa sat cross-legged on an angareb, while his prisoner-guests sat on palm mats on the floor eating. Slatin studied him carefully. He was wearing a jibba covered with small square patches of many colours and wore a Mecca takia, or skull cap, with a cotton turban wound around it. He had come a long way from the days when, as the humble Abdullahi, he had marched in the dust carrying the Mahdi's flag. He was now a great power in the land and his orders were obeyed as those of the Mahdi himself. The Mahdi being more interested in spiritual pursuits, it was the Khalifa Abdullahi who executed the leader's wishes and ruled in the temporal sphere. He was a shrewd, suspicious, vain and ruthless man, and he was greatly feared.

After they had eaten, a slave came in to say that several people were outside asking permission to enter. The Khalifa, after politely asking if Slatin was not too tired, told the slave to show them in. In the group were some whom Slatin had known before under different circumstances, while others he met now for the first time; all were important personages in the Mahdi's court. Included were Ahmed Wad Ali, formerly one of Slatin's government officials in Darfur and now the Kadi of Islam, or chief judge; Ahmed wad Suleiman, the treasurer of the Beit el Mal; Sayed Abdel Kader, the Mahdi's uncle; and Abderrahman ben Naga, formerly deputy governor of Kordofan. When they left, Abderrahman gave Slatin a wink and as they walked a few steps together he muttered quickly, 'Be very careful. Hold your tongue and trust no one.'

When the Khalifa had left them, Slatin warned those with him to be most careful. Dimitri Zigada, however, took out a plug of tobacco and began to chew it. Slatin was alarmed, as he knew that all forms of tobacco were strictly forbidden by the Mahdi, but Zigada said, 'I am only a common merchant and have lost all my money, but you will have to keep a sharp lookout yourselves, for you are former government officials and military men, so he will watch you very carefully.'

About two o'clock in the afternoon the Khalifa returned and took them to the open-air mosque. This was a huge rectangle about 1,000 by 800 yards surrounded by a mud wall (later of brick); except for a few acacia trees at the western end and a mud-walled mirab protected by some trees at the opposite end of the yard, there was no shade and the worshippers were exposed to the burning sun. When they arrived Slatin saw that the entire area was crowded with devotees, ranged in packed lines. A path was soon made for the Khalifa and he proceeded to the front with Slatin, Said Bey Guma, and Zigada following him. A sheepskin was spread on the ground and the Khalifa kneeled on it, directing his charges to take places beside him. The Mahdi's quarters, consisting of several large straw huts surrounded by a thorn zariba, was located in a corner of the mosque. Near the front rank of worshippers was a small hut for the use of the Mahdi when he wished to talk with someone in private.

When the Mahdi emerged from his small hut, the Khalifa stood up and Slatin and his companions followed his example, although the rest of the crowd remained seated. The Mahdi advanced towards them and greeted them courteously. He was wearing a short, quilted jibba, spotlessly clean, and, as he drew near, Slatin could smell his special perfume of sandalwood, musk and attar of roses, which his disciples called Rihet el Mahdi (Odour of the

Mahdi) and was thought to be like that of the dwellers in Paradise. The Mahdi extended his hand to be kissed, which Slatin did several times, and then he asked, 'Are you satisfied?'

'Indeed I am,' Slatin replied readily. 'On coming so near to you I am most happy!'

'Allah bless you and your brethren!' said the Mahdi. 'When news reached us of your battles against my followers, I used to pray to Allah for your conversion. Allah and His Prophet have heard my prayers, and as you have faithfully served your former master for perishable money, so now you should serve me. For he who serves me and hears my words serves Allah and His religion, and shall have happiness in this world and joy in the world to come.'

Slatin thanked him and promised to be faithful. He then asked that they might have the honour of being given the *beia*, or oath of allegiance, having been previously advised to do so. The Mahdi seated himself on his sheepskin and had them kneel before him. Taking their hands in his, he told them to repeat after him: 'In the name of Allah the most compassionate and merciful, in the name of the unity of Allah, we pay Allah, His Prophet, and you our allegiance. We swear we shall not associate anything else with Allah, that we shall not steal, nor commit adultery, nor lead any one into deception, nor disobey you in your goodness. We swear to renounce this world and look to the world to come, and we shall not flee from the religious war.'

Slatin, Said Bey Guma and Zigada took the oath and then kissed his hands. They were now enrolled among the Mahdi's devoted adherents, being given, in theory at least, all the privileges, but subject, certainly, to all the punishments given for any infraction of the many strict rules.

This over, the muezzin gave the call to prayer. After the usual opening prayers, the people all raised their hands and asked Allah to grant victory to the faithful. Then the Mahdi began his long sermon. He spoke of the vanities of this world and urged his followers to renounce them. He told them to consider only their religious duties and the jihad. He spoke of the pleasures of Paradise and of the delights that awaited those who practised the principles he preached to them. Occasionally his speech was interrupted by the shouts of a fanatic in ecstasy. Slatin was struck by the fervent devotion of those who were around him, and he was convinced that except for Said Bey Guma, Zigada and himself, all those present firmly believed that Mohammed Ahmed was indeed the true mahdi of Allah.

All afternoon Slatin and his companions knelt in prayer at the mosque. The Khalifa left, the Mahdi came and went, but the new disciples stayed. After evening prayers, Slatin asked permission to leave as he was to have dinner with the Khalifa; the Mahdi gave his consent. Slatin's legs were so painfully cramped from kneeling for so long that he could hardly walk, but it was necessary to exhibit a smiling face to the Mahdi. Said Bey Guma, being more accustomed to the position, did not suffer, but Zigada limped along, muttering frightful imprecations in Greek. That evening they dined with the Khalifa and learned for certain that Berber had fallen; communications were now cut between the besieged Khartoum and Egypt. When the evening meal was finished and the Khalifa dismissed them, they were glad to stretch out on their angarebs and to be alone with their own thoughts after the nervous excitement of the day. In the dark Slatin heard Zigada chewing away in secret on his plug of tobacco.

The following day the Khalifa introduced Slatin to his younger half-brother Yakub, his most trusted and powerful adviser. He was an ugly little man with a round, pock-marked face, small, turned-up nose and slight moustache and beard. He had more education than his brother: he could read and write and recite the Koran by heart. An early convert to Mahdism, he had joined the Mahdi and his brother on the trek from Abba to the Nuba hills in 1881. Like the Mahdi, he smiled continuously; he also had a curiously sympathetic way of talking. Slatin knew him by reputation: 'Woe to the unfortunate man who differs in opinion with Yakub, or who is suspected of intriguing against him, he is infallibly lost!'

When the Khalifa summoned Slatin and his companions the next day and asked them if they wanted to return to Darfur, they knew this was but an attempt to test them, and they all replied that they did not want to leave as they would deeply regret leaving the Mahdi. The Khalifa commended their decision and then proceeded to assign them their new places. Dimitri Zigada was turned over to a Greek emir and Said Bey Guma to an Egyptian emir. Then, turning to Slatin he said, 'Abdel Kader, you are a stranger here and have no one else but me . . . therefore, in accordance with the Mahdi's orders, you are to remain with me as a mulazem.' A mulazem (plural: mulazemin) was a kind of servant-courtier-bodyguard.

Slatin answered: 'That is the very wish of my heart. I call myself fortunate to be able to serve you, and you can rely on my obedience and fidelity.'

'I knew that,' the Khalifa said. 'May Allah protect you and

strengthen your faith. You will no doubt be of much use to the Mahdi and me.' He then advised Slatin not to fail to attend noon and evening prayers. Slatin assured him that he would follow his advice and the Khalifa gave orders for a hut to be built for him near his own zariba.

At evening prayers, Slatin took a position in the second rank behind the Khalifa. The Mahdi, seeing him there, ordered him to take his place beside the Khalifa: 'Drink of my words, and that will be of inestimable benefit to you.' Slatin excused himself by saying that as the Khalifa's mulazem he did not think it proper to stand beside his master. The Mahdi praised him for his self-abnegation, but told him in the future he should sit in the front rank, 'for in the place of worship we are all alike'.

In the days that followed Slatin saw many other former government officials who, like himself, had been forced to surrender and were now taken before the Khalifa and the Mahdi to beg forgiveness. Many covered themselves with ashes and some even donned the shebba as they entered the Khalifa's presence to beg forgiveness and to proclaim themselves believers in the Mahdi. Slatin often talked with these men and from them learned the news of the Egyptian government's continuing defeats and the decline of its power in the Sudan. Combining past knowledge with present circumstances, he was perhaps the best-informed man in the world on the true position of the Sudan at this time. Unfortunately, he was not able to put his knowledge to much use.

A Greek named George Calamatino was sent to Khartoum with a message to Gordon demanding his surrender. Slatin risked his life by sending with him a few lines of his own to explain his pretended conversion and his surrender, but Gordon sent no reply.

After the fast of Ramadan, the Mahdi announced that the Prophet had commanded him to go personally and lay siege to Khartoum. Summoning all his followers, men, women and children, he left Er Rahad on 22 August on the greatest wholesale migration ever seen in the Sudan. Slatin, as mulazem of the Khalifa, naturally went along. It was while on the slow march to Khartoum that he first heard the strange rumour of a European wandering about alone in the Sudan. The rumours were of the wildest sort: that he was the Emperor of France or that he was a relative of the Queen of England. Whoever he was, all agreed he was on his way to see the Mahdi.

In October 1885 two nuns escaped from the Sudan and arrived at the outpost of the Frontier Field Force at Wadi Halfa. Sister

Rudolf Slatin (left) after his escape, with Colonel Wingate.

Hadendowa warriors, Kipling's "Fuzzy-Wuzzies."

Rudolf Slatin in Dervish jibba. *(From C. Rudolf Slatin's* Fire and Sword in the Sudan, *published by Edward Arnold, 1896)*

Father Joseph Ohrwalder with the two nuns and Adila the slave girl who escaped with him. *(From J. Ohrwalder's* Ten Years' Captivity in the Mahdi's Camp, *published by Sampson Low, 1893)*

Charles Neufeld in chains with Umm es Sholc.

Sister Teresa Gregolini with her Greek husband and baby.

A Nile steamer carrying 21st Lancers.

Cameron Highlanders, part of Kitchener's army, advancing towards Omdurman.

Looting the Dervish dead after the Battle of Omdurman.

Mahmoud in his bloodstained jibba, captured at the Battle of the Atbara, 8 April 1898.

A British officer on a camel inspects the remains of the Mahdi's tomb at Omdurman. The holes in the dome were made by British howitzers.

The gallows in the market place at Omdurman. The crowd is looking at the body of the last man to be hanged by the Khalifa.

The statue of Gordon, now at the Gordon Boys School in Surrey, which stood before the palace in Khartoum until Sudanese independence.

Raising the British and Egyptian flags over the ruins of the former palace at Khartoum, 4 September, 1898.

Lieutenant Winston Churchill (right) with Lieutenant R. Molyneux, wounded in the charge of the 21st Lancers at the Battle of Omdurman.

Maria Caprina, who had been five and a half years in the Sudan, and Sister Fortunata, described as a Negress, told the puzzled intelligence officer of the presence of a Frenchman in the Sudan. Gordon in Khartoum also heard of him, and speculated on who it might be. He thought it might be Ernest Renan who had recently published the first volume of *Vie de Jésus*. In his journals Gordon wrote: 'If he comes to the lines, and it is Renan, I shall go and see him, for, whatever one many think of his unbelief in our Lord, he certainly dared to say what he thought, and he has not changed his creed to save his life.'

There was a substantial amount of truth in the rumour. There was indeed a Frenchman who had come to the Sudan seeking the Mahdi. Although it was not Renan, the story was hardly less bizarre. One evening the Khalifa summoned Slatin to him and told him that a European had arrived at El Obeid.

'Do you belong to the French race?' he asked Slatin. 'Or are there different tribes in your country as there are here with us in the Sudan?'

Slatin told him as much about Europe as he thought the Khalifa would understand. 'But what would a Frenchman want with us that he should come all that long distance?' the Khalifa asked.

'Perhaps he is seeking your and the Mahdi's friendship,' Slatin said.

The Khalifa looked at him incredulously and said curtly, 'We shall see.'

A few days later, just after they had halted, the Khalifa sent for Slatin: 'Abdel Kader, the French traveller has arrived. I have now ordered him to be brought before me. You had better wait and listen to what he has to say.'

When the mysterious stranger entered the hut, Slatin saw a tall man, about forty-two years old, with a bronzed face, a fair beard and a moustache, wearing a jibba and turban. He greeted the Khalifa in halting Arabic, but the Khalifa did not rise from his angareb and merely motioned to him to be seated. His first words to him were: 'Why have you come here? What do you want from us?'

The Frenchman tried to reply in Arabic, but he spoke so badly that the Khalifa interrupted him. 'Speak in your own language with Abdel Kader, and he will explain to me what you want.'

The stranger looked at Slatin distrustfully and said in English, 'Good day, sir.'

Slatin replied in French: 'Do you speak French? My name is

Slatin. Stick to business entirely now. Later on we can speak privately.'

'What are you talking about together?' muttered the Khalifa peevishly. 'I wish to know what he wants.'

'I only told him my name and urged him to speak openly with you, as both you and the Mahdi are men to whom Allah has granted the power to read the thoughts of others.'

'Well, try and find out the truth,' snapped the Khalifa.

'My name is Oliver Pain,' said the man, 'and I am a Frenchman. Since I was quite a boy I was interested in the Sudan, and sympathized with its people. It is not only I but all my compatriots who feel the same. In Europe there are nations with whom we feud; one of these is the English nation which is now settled in Egypt, and one of whose generals, Gordon, is now commanding in Khartoum. I have therefore come to offer you my assistance and that of my nation.'

Slatin translated almost word by word. The Khalifa interrupted to demand, 'What assistance?'

'I can only offer you advice, but my nation, which is anxious to gain your friendship, is ready to help you practically with arms and money, under certain conditions.'

'Are you a Mohammedan?'

'Yes, certainly. I have been of this faith for a long time, and at El Obeid I openly acknowledged it.'

Oliver Pain did not make a good impression on either the Khalifa or Slatin, though for different reasons: Slatin believed him; the Khalifa did not. The Khalifa told Slatin to stay with the Frenchman while he went off to tell the Mahdi about this suspicious stranger who claimed to have travelled so far for the sake of friendship. While the Khalifa was gone, Slatin told Pain it would be more prudent to say that his motives were religious rather than political.

When the Khalifa returned he took them off to prayers. Pain sat in the second rank of worshippers. When the Mahdi entered the mosque, he smiled at the stranger, but did not shake hands with him. Using Slatin as an interpreter, he asked Pain why he had come and was told the same story as had been given to the Khalifa. When he had finished the Mahdi, raising his voice so that all could hear, said, 'I have heard your intentions and have understood them. But I do not count on human support. I rely on Allah and his Prophet. Your nation are unbelievers and I shall never ally myself with them. With Allah's help, I shall defeat my enemies through my brave ansar and the host of angels sent to me by the Prophet.'

This speech was greeted, as he had intended, by shouts of acclamation from the thousands of worshippers around him. The Mahdi gave Pain his hand to kiss, but he did not administer the oath of allegiance. After the sermon, Slatin was directed to take Pain to his tent and await further instructions.

Alone with Pain, Slatin questioned him closely about his curious mission. It would appear that Pain deliberately deceived Slatin in telling him about himself and his reason for coming to the Sudan; Slatin never learned the truth. Pain said that he worked for a Paris newspaper called *Indépendence*, but that his trip to the Sudan was strictly a private venture. It is possible that Slatin misunderstood – his French was not completely fluent – for Pain had at one time worked for the radical *L'Intransigeant*. He was a free-lance journalist who probably came to the Sudan hoping for an exclusive interview which he could sell to some newspaper in France, but undoubtedly he was influenced by his political views. He was violently anti-British, an attitude which was then, as so frequently in their history, common among the French. Since the Mahdi was a source of embarrassment to England, Pain was pro-mahdist and he apparently hoped in some vague way to assist the Mahdi by offering the friendship and assistance of his country.

Pain was born in Troyes, France, in 1843. For awhile he was on the staff of *Mot d'Ordre* and *L'Afffranchi*, both Socialist papers in Paris. He was deported to New Caledonia for his part in the defence of the Paris Commune, but escaped and returned to Europe, writing for radical newspapers in Geneva. He covered the Russo-Turkish War of 1877–8 as a war correspondent, and returned to France under the amnesty of 1879. He left a wife and two children to come to the Sudan. He had a difficult time getting there. When he reached Wadi Halfa, the British authorities had turned him back; on his way down-river, however, he had fallen in with some Alighat Arabs whom he bribed to take him into the Sudan by the desert route running west of Dongola through El Kaab to El Obeid.

By the time he actually reached the Mahdi much of the romance of the trip must have been gone, but he told Slatin, without revealing the real reasons for his journey, that he hoped the Mahdi could be induced to enter into friendly relations with France. Whether he succeeded or not, he hoped soon to be able to return to Paris. Slatin thought it quite unlikely that the Mahdi would allow him to leave and he told him so. Trusting to Pain's unintelligible Arabic, he also told him that he himself considered the Mahdi and his people as enemies and that he hoped Pain's proposals would not be accepted. He then ordered his servants to prepare some food and sent for Gustav Klootz (now called Mustafa) to join them. They had scarcely sat down to eat when two mulazemin of the Khalifa entered and told Pain to follow them. A few minutes later Slatin himself was summoned to the Khalifa's hut. He found him alone.

'Abdel Kader, I look on you as one of us,' the Khalifa began. 'Tell me, what do you think of this Frenchman?'

'I believe he is sincere and means well,' Slatin replied, 'but he did not know the Mahdi or you. He did not understand that you trusted only to Allah and sought no support from other powers, and that this was the reason you are continually victorious. Allah is with those who put their trust in Him.'

'You heard the Mahdi's words when he told the Frenchman that he wished to have nothing to do with unbelievers, and that he could defeat his enemies without their help?'

'Most certainly I did. Therefore, the man is useless here and may as well return to his nation to tell them about the victories of the Mahdi and his commander-in-chief, the Khalifa.'

'Perhaps later,' said the Khalifa. 'For the present I have ordered him to stay with Zeki Tummal, who will take care of him.'

'But it will be very difficult for him to make himself understood in Arabic. He is by no means a good Arabic scholar yet.'

'He was able to get here without an interpreter,' snapped the Khalifa. 'However, you have my permission to visit him.'

When he had been dismissed, Slatin went to look for Pain. He found him sitting disconsolately under a tree, wondering why he had not been allowed to stay with Slatin. 'It is the Mahdi's nature,' Slatin told him. 'And the Khalifa is even worse in working his will in contrariety to every human being under the sun. You are going through a course of what they call "putting to the test one's patience, submission, and faith", but you need have no fear. However, the Khalifa suspects us both, and is anxious to keep us apart.'

Zeki Tummal came up and Slatin introduced him to Pain. Zeki Tummal, though now a Mahdist emir, was an old friend from Darfur and Slatin commended him to Pain, telling him: 'He was with me in many a fight.' Zeki greeted him warmly, but told him not to come often because the Khalifa had told him that Pain was to be kept away from other Europeans. 'These orders do not apply to me,' Slatin told him. 'Just this moment I left our master's hut, and he has given me permission to visit your guest.'

Slatin's concern for and aid to people like Pain and Klootz can only be explained in terms of his hunger to talk to and be with fellow Europeans. Doubtless, too, there was a feeling that any European, however wrong his views or debased his character, was the superior of any native. In any case, he did not forward his own reputation with the Mahdists by his attempts to help other Europeans.

The next morning the Khalifa's great war-drum (called El Mansura, 'The Victorious') boomed the signal for departure, and the huge camp moved another step towards Khartoum. As they only marched from early morning until noon, progress was slow. When they had made their midday halt, Slatin again looked up Pain and, when he found that he had not eaten any of the asida Zeki had sent him, ordered his servants to prepare something more to a European's taste. That night he told the Khalifa that as Pain was not accustomed to Sudanese food, he might become ill if forced to eat it. 'He should get used to it as soon as possible,' the Khalifa said. 'Incidentally, where is Mustafa (Klootz)? I have not seen him since we left Er Rehad.'

'He is staying with me,' Slatin told him. 'He helps my servants to look after the horses and camels.'

'Then send for him!'

Slatin sent for Klootz. When he came the Khalifa questioned him angrily: 'Where have you been? I have not seen you for weeks. Have you forgotten that I am your master?'

'With your permission I went to Abdel Kader, whom I help in his work. You do not care for me now and have left me alone,' he said in a sulky tone.

'Then I will take good care of you in the future,' cried the Khalifa. He called in a mulazem and ordered him to put Klootz in chains.

Turning to Slatin, he said, 'You have servants enough, and you can quite well do without Mustafa. I took him for myself, but he left me without any cause. I then ordered that he should serve my brother Yakub, but he complained and left him too. Now that he is with you he thinks he can dispense with us altogether.'

'Pardon him,' Slatin pleaded. 'He is merciful who forgives. Let him stay with your brother. Perhaps he will improve.'

'He must remain a few days in chains so that he will know I am his master. He is not the same as you, who come every day to my door.'

Five days later the Mahdi and his followers reached Shatt, where the Mahdi intended to stop for a few days. It was here that the

Mahdi had the satisfaction of receiving as a fearful penitent his former master and religious leader, Sheikh Mohammed Sherif, who had turned him out of his tarika. The Mahdi was now so powerful that he could afford to be generous. He not only forgave Sheikh Mohammed Sherif, but presented him with gifts, including several horses and two exceptionally pretty Abyssinian girls.

From Shatt the Dervishes advanced to Duem, where the Mahdi held an enormous review of his forces. In a speech to his assembled masses he pointed to the Nile and said, 'Allah has created this river. He will give you its waters to drink, and you shall become the possessors of all the land along its banks.' This promise, implying that he would conquer Egypt, had an exhilarating effect on his people, who cheered wildly.

The Mahdi and his huge mass of followers continued their march, moving like a great tortoise slowly along the bank of the river towards Khartoum, his ranks swelling daily by the thousands of new adherents from all parts of the Sudan, but particularly by the riverine peoples who had not ventured to follow him into the desert but who, now that he was among them, joined his ranks.

Throughout the march Slatin was much concerned for Pain, now despondent and sick with typhus. His condition grew so bad that Slatin found the courage to ask the Mahdi for help. The Mahdi at once sent to the Beit el Mal for about £5 to be given to Pain and added a message wishing him a safe recovery. On the other hand, the Khalifa, also appealed to, said simply: 'If he dies here he is a happy man. Allah in his goodness and omnipotence has converted him from an unbeliever to a believer.'

Early one morning during the first week in October, Pain sent for Slatin and told him that he thought he was dying. He thanked Slatin for his kindness and begged him, should he ever escape, to tell his wife and children in Paris that his last thoughts had been of them. Slatin tried to comfort him, but already the great drum was beating for the departure and he had to hurry away; he left one of his servants, Atrun, to look after him.

That evening, Slatin waited impatiently for Pain and his servant to arrive at camp. When at last Atrun came in, he was alone. 'Where is Yusef [Pain's Muslim name]?'

'My master is dead,' he replied. 'And that is the reason I am so late.'

'Dead!'

'Yes. Dead and buried.'

'Tell me at once what happened.'

'My master Yusef was so weak that he could not ride, but we had to go on marching. Every now and then he lost consciousness. Then he would come to again and speak words we could not understand. So we tied an angareb on to the saddle, and laid him on it, but he was too weak to hold on and he fell down suddenly and very heavily. After this he did not come to again, and he was soon dead. So we wrapped him up in his farda and buried him, and all his effects were taken to Zeki by his slaves.'

Slatin reported Pain's death to the Khalifa. 'He is a happy man,' was the Khalifa's curt reply.

On 14 October 1884, three days after Pain had died, they reached the neighbourhood of Khartoum. That evening the Mahdi sent for Slatin and directed him to write a letter to Gordon telling him that he, Mohammed Ahmed, was indeed the true mahdi and that Gordon ought therefore to surrender at once to save himself and his soul. 'Tell him also that if he refuses to obey we shall every one of us fight against him,' the Mahdi said. 'Say that you yourself will fight against him with your own hands. Say that victory will be ours and that you merely tell him this to avoid useless bloodshed.'

Slatin sat silent for so long that he had to be called upon to answer. Then he said: 'O Mahdi! Listen, I beg of you, to my words. I will be honest and faithful. I pray you to forgive me if what I say is not pleasing to you. If I write to Gordon that you are the true mahdi, he will not believe me. If I threaten to fight against him with my own hands, he will not be afraid of that. Now as you desire to avoid shedding blood, I shall simply summon him to surrender. I shall say that he is not strong enough to attempt to fight against you who are ever victorious as he has no hope of help from the outside. Finally, I shall say that I will be the intermediary between you and him.'

To this the Mahdi agreed and Slatin went back to his camp to write the letter. He no longer had a tent. It had been torn to shreds by wind, sand and hard usage during the march and he had given away the pieces. During the day he stretched strips of cloth on sticks to provide some protection from the fierce sun, and he slept at night under the stars. He now searched about for a lantern, found one and sat down on his angareb to write his letters. He wrote in German, prefacing his remarks with a few words in French to explain that his French dictionary had been burned by the Dervishes, who thought it was a prayer book, and that without it he did not feel capable of properly expressing himself in that language. He counted on Martin Hansal, the Austrian Consul and oldest

European resident in Khartoum, to translate his letters to Gordon.

Slatin's long letter in German revealed how little he knew of his former chief. He wrote a defence of his actions by telling how long and hard he had fought against the Dervishes and how he had surrendered only when he no longer had the means to defend himself further. He proclaimed himself a Christian, but told why he had pretended to become a Muslim and how, initially, this act of apparent conversion had been successful in helping him control his soldiers. He told Gordon how by his 'obedient and submissive behaviour' he had been able to gain in some measure the confidence of the Mahdi and the Khalifa. He then proposed that Gordon help him to escape and assured him that he would be willing to conquer or die by his side.

Slatin also wrote a letter to Hansal which Gordon characterized as being 'quite different in tone to the one he wrote me'. In this letter Slatin wanted to know the chances of Gordon surrendering as he was well aware of the fate that would await him if he deserted the Mahdi and was then recaptured in Khartoum. As he wrote later: 'It seemed to me that it was quite reasonable on my part to seek such assurance.'

Early the next morning, in the presence of the Mahdi, the letters were turned over to one of Slatin's servants, a youth of about fifteen, who was told to deliver them to General Gordon. On the evening of the following day the boy returned, but to Slatin's surprise and chagrin he brought back no answer. Slatin could not understand it.

What he failed to understand was that Gordon was as much of a fanatic as the Mahdi. All Slatin's bravery and ability in holding Darfur as long as he had was as nothing to Gordon compared to his defection, whether real or pretended, from the Christian faith. Gordon could no more accept his pretended change of faith than would the Mahdi if one of his followers had pretended to be a Christian. And Slatin's 'obedient and submissive behaviour' to gain the confidence of the Mahdi and the Khalifa was an act so foreign to Gordon's nature, so repugnant to him, that he could never have been expected to understand the motives which led Slatin to adopt such an attitude.

In Gordon's journal for 16 October he wrote: 'The letters of Slatin have arrived. I have no remarks to make on them, and cannot make out why he wrote them.' Consul Hansal also gave Gordon a translation of the letter he had received and Gordon did make a comment on this:

Slatin's letter to Austrian Consul contains the remark 'that if he comes over to me I must promise never to surrender the city, *as he would then suffer terrible tortures and death*'. He evidently is not a Spartan, he also says 'that he changed his religion because he had not had much attention paid to his religious beliefs when young'. If he gets away I shall take him to the Congo with me, he will want some *quarantine*; one feels sorry for him.

'Spartan' was the wrong word. Slatin was Spartan enough, he simply was not interested in adding his name to the roll of Christian martyrs. Slatin was brave and capable of enduring long suffering, but he was a young man who loved life and did not, like Gordon, look forward to death as an escape from the troubles of this world.

Only a few hours after the letters to Gordon and Consul Hansal had been sent off, horsemen arrived in the Mahdi's camp from Berber with the news of the capture of Gordon's steamer *Abbas* and the murder of Colonel Stewart and Frank Power. They brought with them all the papers and documents found on board, and Slatin was soon summoned to examine those written in European languages. There were several private letters as well as official documents and reports, including a military report describing day-to-day events in Khartoum. Before he had time to examine all the papers thoroughly, he was summoned by the Mahdi, who was eager to know their contents. Slatin told him they were mostly private papers and a military report which he did not understand. Unfortunately, there were a number of documents written in Arabic, enough to give the Mahdi and the Khalifa a good understanding of the situation in Khartoum. There was also an Arabic telegram from Gordon to the Khedive in code which was deciphered by a former government head clerk. Hoping to demoralize Gordon by telling him of the loss of his steamer, the Mahdi discussed with his chief advisers which papers should be sent to Gordon as proof. Slatin, who knew that Gordon would not be demoralized but that he ought to be told of the disaster, pointed out that the only document likely to convince Gordon was the military report. After a long discussion, it was decided to send it. Although Slatin was under the impression, even years later, that the report had been sent, in fact it was not and Gordon did not believe either the Mahdi or Slatin.

When Slatin's boy returned empty-handed from the government lines, Slatin was again instructed to write to Gordon and to tell him of the wreck of his steamer. Seated on his angareb, and by the flickering light of an old lantern, Slatin wrote once more to Gordon. He told him what he knew of the loss of the *Abbas* and repeated much of what he had written in his first letter, adding that if Gordon thought he had done anything contrary to the honour of an officer he hoped he would given him a chance to defend himself He begged earnestly that Said Bey Guma and he be allowed to join him in Khartoum: 'Pray, Excellency, do your best to give us permission, because we are always in fear of spies. I pray God that He may give you success in the Siege.'

Gordon wrote in his journal:

I shall have nothing to do with Slatin's coming in here to stay, unless he has the Mahdi's positive leave, which he is not likely to get: his doing so would be the breaking of his parole, which should be as sacred when given to the Mahdi as to any other power, and it would jeopardise the safety of all those Europeans, prisoners with the Mahdi.

This time Slatin did receive a reply, but it was perplexing. The letter, from Consul Hansal, was written in German with an Arabic translation:

DEAR FRIEND SLATIN BEY – Your letters have been duly received, and I request you will come to Tabia Ragheb Bey (Omdurman fort). I wish to speak to you about the steps to be taken for our rescue: you may then return unmolested to your friend.

Yours very truly,

Hansal

If the letter was meant to deceive the Mahdi, the Arabic would have been sufficient. Was Consul Hansal planning to desert to the Mahdi? What did he mean by referring to the Mahdi as Slatin's friend, even in the German? Could Gordon really have refused his request? Slatin did not know what to make of it. He took the letter to the Mahdi and read it to him. The Mahdi asked if he wanted to go and meet Hansal. Slatin said he was ready to comply with the Mahdi's orders.

'I am rather afraid,' said the Mahdi, 'that if you go to Omdurman to speak to your consul, Gordon may arrest or kill you. Why did he not write to you himself, if he thinks well of you?'

'I do not know why he is so silent,' Slatin replied truthfully. 'Perhaps it is contrary to his orders to enter into communication with us. However, when I meet Hansal I may be able to arrange matters.' He then hastened to assure the Mahdi that there was no danger of Gordon killing him and that even if he were taken prisoner he was certain the Mahdi would be able to release him.

'Get yourself ready to go then,' said the Mahdi, 'and I will let you know.'

While on his way to the Mahdi's hut with the letter, Slatin had heard that Lupton Bey had arrived from Bahr el Ghazal. Now Slatin went to look for him. He found Lupton outside the Khalifa's door waiting to be received. Although it was strictly forbidden to speak to a prisoner before he had received the Mahdi's pardon, Slatin could not resist greeting him.

Frank Lupton was the only English prisoner of the Mahdi. He was born in 1854 in the village of Ilford, in Essex, the son of a local merchant. He became a sailor and was first mate of a Red Sea steamer plying between Suakin and Jidda when, in 1879, he left his ship and joined a camel caravan for Berber. He made his way south to Khartoum and persuaded Gordon to employ him. Gordon sent him to Equatoria where he worked for a while as Emin's assistant in charge of the Latuka district. When Gordon was succeeded by Rauf Pasha, the latter appointed him Governor of Bahr el Ghazal. He was first attacked by the Mahdi's ansar in August 1882. Like Slatin, he was cut off; and like Slatin he announced his conversion to Islam to hold his soldiers; he fought as long as he could, and was at last forced to give in. On 20 April 1884 he wrote to Emin: 'Most of my people have joined the Mahdi's force. ... I don't know where it will end. ... I hardly know if I am Lupton Bey or the Emir Abdallah.' Six days later he wrote Emin again, saying, 'It's all up with me here. Everyone has joined the Mahdi, and his army takes charge of the mudiria the day after tomorrow. What I have passed through these last few days no one knows.' He surrendered to the Emir Karamallah on 28 April 1884. He was taken first to El Obeid and then to Omdurman, where he met Slatin outside the door of the Khalifa's house.

When Lupton was called into the Khalifa, Slatin went back to lie impatiently on his angareb until the Mahdi should tell him he could go to Omdurman fort and meet Hansal. He waited a long time. It was after dark before a mulazem of the Khalifa's came for him. Slatin jumped up, bound his turban around his head, put on his belt and sword, and was taken to Yakub's camp, where the mulazem said the Khalifa was waiting for him. At Yakub's camp they were told that the Khalifa was waiting for them at the zariba of Abu Anga. Slatin began to be uneasy; all this wandering about at night was most unusual.

Abu Anga was a tall, strong Black who had formerly been a slave of the Khalifa's, but who had risen by his exceptional ability and astuteness to become a leading emir and one of the Mahdi's best generals. His zariba was an immense enclosure filled with small shelters made of strips of cotton fixed on poles and separated from each other by small durra-stalk fences. When Slatin and the mulazem arrived, they were admitted into the zariba by a sentry and shown to one of the small shelters. There by the dim light of a small lantern he saw a group of Dervishes sitting in a circle talking earnestly. He recognized Yakub, Abu Anga, Fadl el Maula, Zeki Tummal and Hajji Zubeir; behind them stood several armed men. There was no sign of the Khalifa, and he now expected the worst. He was told to come in and sit between Hajji Zubeir and Fadl el Maula facing Abu Anga.

'Abdel Kader, you have promised to be faithful to the Mahdi, and it is your duty to keep your word,' Abu Anga began. 'It is also your duty to obey orders, even should you suffer thereby. Is this not so?'

'Certainly,' Slatin replied, 'and you, Abu Anga, if you give me any orders from the Mahdi or the Khalifa, you will see that I know how to obey them.'

'I received orders to make you a prisoner,' Abu Anga said, 'but I do not know the reason.'

As he said these words, Hajji Zubeir snatched Slatin's sword, which he had, as usual, laid across his knees, and handed it to Zeki Tummal. Hajji Zubeir then seized his right arm with both hands.

'I did not come here to fight. Why should you seize my arm?' Slatin said to Hajji Zubeir. Then, turning back to Abu Anga he said, 'But you, Abu Anga, of course you must do as you are bidden.'

Pointing to a shelter scarcely visible in the darkness, Abu Anga told him to go there and directed the others to go with him. Slatin did as he was told. Inside the other shelter he was ordered to sit on the ground with his legs outstretched. That which as Governor of Darfur he had often inflicted on others, he was now about to endure himself. His feet were placed in two large iron rings joined by a thick iron bar, then the rings were hammered closed. An iron ring was placed around his neck, and attached to it was a long chain with eighty-three large figure-of-eight links – he had ample time to count them later. The links were so arranged that he had the greatest difficulty in turning his head. All this he endured in silence.

Left alone with his two guards and his own thoughts, he remembered again the words of his old enemy Madibbo: 'Be obedient and patient, for he who lives long sees much.' He had been obedient; now he had to learn patience. But would he live long enough to see much?

When he had been lying sleepless on his palm mat for about an hour, he saw several mulazemin approaching with lanterns. In the middle of the group he could make out the Khalifa Abdullahi. Slatin made the effort and stood up.

'Abdel Kader, are you submitting with resignation to your fate?'

'Since my childhood,' Slatin replied quietly, 'I have been accustomed to being obedient. Now I must be obedient whether I like it or not.'

'Your friendship with Saleh Wad el Mek and your correspondence with Gordon have cast suspicion on you, and we doubt if your heart is inclined to us. That is the reason I have ordered you to be forcibly directed in the right way.'

Saleh Wad el Mek was, like Slatin, a 'converted' government official who had been captured shortly after Slatin himself and had been given the Mahdi's pardon. He had a brother who was still with Gordon's army in Khartoum. Slatin now attempted to defend both himself and his friend: 'I made no secret of my friendship with Saleh Wad el Mek,' he said. 'He is a friend of mine, and I believe he is loyal to you. As regards my correspondence with Gordon, the Mahdi ordered me to write the letters.'

'Did he also order you to write what you did?'

'I think I wrote what the Mahdi required, and no one knows the contents except myself and the person who received the letters. All I require is justice, and I beg you not to listen to lying intriguers.'

The Khalifa left him, and Slatin was alone again. The heavy iron around his feet and neck pained him a great deal. He was not by nature a worrier, but he would have been less than human had he not been anxious about his present position. He lay sleepless through the night, kept awake by his forebodings and the torment of his chains.

At dawn the next day, Abu Anga came to him, leading several servants with trays of food: chickens, rice, honey, roast meat and the ever present asida. It was quite a feast, but Slatin could not eat; he had no appetite. Abu Anga sat down on the palm mat beside him.

'I think, Abdel Kader, you are afraid, and that is why you do not eat,' Abu Anga said gently.

No, he was not afraid, Slatin insisted, and he managed to swallow a few mouthfuls of food to prove it while Abu Anga talked.

'The Khalifa was rather disappointed yesterday,' said Abu Anga, 'when he saw you were not humbled. He said you were strong-headed and that, he supposed, was the reason you were not afraid.'

'How could I throw myself at his feet and crave his pardon for a crime I never committed?' Slatin demanded. 'I am in his hands and he can do as he likes with me.'

'Tomorrow we shall advance,' Abu Anga told him, 'and draw nearer to Khartoum. We shall press the siege more closely, and then make a sudden attack. I shall ask the Khalifa to let you stay with me; that will be less hard for you than going to the common prison.'

Slatin thanked him for his kindness and Abu Anga left him.

The next day the war-drum sounded, tents were struck, baggage packed and loaded on camels, and the entire camp was in movement. A donkey was brought for Slatin. He wrapped the eighty-three-link iron chain around his body and was lifted on the donkey and held there by his two guards. On the march he saw several old friends, but not one dared to speak to him. In the afternoon they halted on some rising ground and Slatin saw in the distance the palm trees of Khartoum. It had been a long time and much had happened to him since he had last looked at the capital of the Sudan. Sitting on his donkey with his neck and feet in iron rings and his body wrapped in chains, he looked longingly at the doomed city, wishing he could be one of its defenders.

The Mahdi and his huge force now joined the Dervish army besieging Khartoum. Abu Anga had obtained permission for Slatin to be kept with him: a tattered tent was pitched for him around which thorn bushes were placed and guards were stationed at the entrance. His guards were changed every day and his welfare depended entirely on their nature as Abu Anga was occupied with the siege and could no longer give him his personal attention. If the guards were slaves, he was most carefully watched and allowed to speak to no one; if they were old soldiers who knew him, they were more lenient and often performed little services for him. Abu Anga's wives had been ordered to feed him, but he was given little food and the food he did receive was of the worst description. One day when one of his guards was a former soldier whom he had known before, he sent a message to Abu Anga's chief wife complaining that he had not been fed for two days. Her reply was: 'Does Abdel Kader think we are going to fatten him up here while his uncle, Gordon Pasha, does nothing but fire shells all day at our master, whose life is always in danger through his fault? If he had made his uncle submit, he would not now be in chains.'

Occasionally, some of the Greeks were allowed to visit him and from them he learned the latest news and heard the current rumours. From George Calamatino he learned of the advance up the Nile of the relief expedition under Lord Wolseley. The expedition was moving slowly; the advance guard was only at Dongola. No one knew if it would arrive in time to save Khartoum. Even if the expedition did arrive in time to save the city Slatin was not at all sure it would save him. Christmas and the sad anniversary of his first year in the hands of the Dervishes found him still in chains.

From other Greeks he learned that Lupton Bey had also been thrown in chains, being suspected of wanting to join Gordon. When Lupton's effects were searched, a document was found which cast considerable suspicion upon his 'conversion'. Signed by all of his former officers, the paper testified that he had been forced by circumstances to surrender his province.

Lupton had married an Abyssinian servant-girl named Zenuba who had formerly been a servant in the home of Frederick Rosset, the German Consul in Khartoum. When Lupton was put in chains, all his property was confiscated and his wife and five-year-old daughter were sent to live in the Beit el Mal.

Later, Slatin heard that Lupton had been forced to help work a cannon which had been placed in position opposite Tutti Island. No one knew what kind of force had been used, but Slatin knew he had been promised that his wife and child would be well taken care of if he did this. When Gordon's officers reported that a European was directing the Mahdi's artillery, Gordon speculated on who it might be, wondering if it was the Frenchman whom he had thought might be Renan.

Pressure was also brought to bear on Slatin. A man named Abdullah Wad Ibrahim was sent to tell him it was the Mahdi's earnest wish that he take charge of a gun, and that if he did he would be given his liberty. Slatin thought this too high a price to pay. He told Wad Ibrahim that his captivity in chains had made him too weak and ill; besides, he said, he had no idea of how cannon were worked.

'Perhaps,' said Wad Ibrahim, 'you are unwilling to fire on Gordon, who is said to be your uncle, and that is your reason for making excuses.'

'I have neither uncle nor any other relatives in Khartoum,' Slatin told him, 'and my shells alone would certainly not force Khartoum to surrender. However, my present state of health will not allow me to undertake the work.'

Wad Ibrahim left, and within a few hours some mulazemin came and forged on his ankles still another set of iron rings and a bar. Slatin stoically submitted. He was already so weighted by irons and chains that another iron more or less made little difference to him. However, the Greeks were now forbidden to visit him and he was cut off from all news.

One night, just as he was drifting off to sleep, his guard roused him and ordered him to stand. As he struggled to get to his feet, he saw one of the Khalifa's mulazemin who announced that his master was coming. Soon Slatin saw the Khalifa Abdullahi approaching, surrounded by men, some carrying lanterns. While his servants stretched out his sheepskin on the ground, the Khalifa greeted Slatin kindly, told him to sit down, and himself sat down beside him.

'I have here a piece of paper,' the Khalifa began, 'and I want you to tell me what is written on it and so prove to me your fidelity.'

'Certainly, if I can,' Slatin replied, taking the paper. It was a very small piece of paper, about half the size of a cigarette paper, and covered on both sides with fine writing in black ink. As Slatin held the paper close to a lantern to read it, he at once recognized the handwriting and signature. The message was in French:

> I have about 10,000 men; can hold Khartoum at the outside till end of January. Elias Pasha wrote to me; he was forced to do so. He is old and incapable; I forgive him. Try Haji Mohammed Abu Gira, or sing another song.
>
> Gordon

This was a curious message. Elias Pasha was formerly a prominent man at El Obeid; he deserted to the Mahdi before El Obeid was attacked. Abu Gira was the Dervish emir in charge of the Gezira district: in the reference to him here, it is not clear what Gordon meant. Gordon certainly did not have 10,000 men at this time. There was nothing to indicate for whom the note was intended. Slatin knew he was the only person in the Mahdi's camp who could read French; otherwise the Khalifa would not have brought him the note.

'Have you made out what it means?' the Khalifa asked impatiently.

'The note is from Gordon,' Slatin replied. 'It is written with his own hand in French cipher which I cannot understand.'

'What do you say?' asked the Khalifa impatiently. 'Explain yourself better.'

'There are some words written here the sense of which I cannot make out. Every word has its own special meaning and can only be understood by those accustomed to the use of ciphers. If you ask any of the old officials, they will confirm what I say.'

'I was told that the names of Elias Pasha and Haji Abu Gira are mentioned. Is this so?' shouted the Khalifa. He was now quite angry.

'The man who said that told you the truth, and I also can read their names, but it is impossible for me to understand the reference. Perhaps the man who told you their names were there can also make out the rest of the letter. Besides, I can also make out 10,000 in figures, but whether it means soldiers or something else, it is impossible for me to say.'

The Khalifa angrily snatched the paper from his hand and stood up.

'Pardon me,' said Slatin. 'I would gladly have proved my fidelity to you and regained your gracious favour, but it is out of my power. I think your clerks understand about ciphers better than I do.'

'Even if I do not know what this paper contains,' said the Khalifa, 'still Gordon shall fall and Khartoum will be ours!'

With this the Khalifa stalked out. Slatin, alone again, pondered the information he had just acquired. It was now the end of December; Gordon had said he could hold out until the end of January: one month left. Could the relief expedition arrive in time? The decisive moment was drawing very close. But even if the expedition arrived and Gordon was saved, his own position would be unchanged, if not worse. In any case, he was in chains and unable to alter the course of events.

On the morning following the visit of the Khalifa, Slatin received a surprise visit from a Greek who gave him the latest news and told him the story of what had happened to his friend Wad el Mek. Wad el Mek's brother had been killed while leading a sortie from Khartoum. His head had been cut off and sent to the Khalifa, who ordered that it be taken to the prison and shown to Wad el Mek. When his brother's bloody head was thrown at his feet, Wad el Mek made not the slightest change in his expression. Gazing at his brother's head, he said, 'This is his punishment. This is his fate.' Then, turning to the chief gaoler, he asked, 'Did you intend to startle me by this, or make me afraid?'

'What nerves and self-control the man must have had!' thought Slatin.

In mid-January, Slatin learned that the Omdurman fort, which had been cut off from Khartoum by the Dervishes, was at last forced by famine to surrender.

On 21 January, a loud wailing of many women was heard in the Mahdi's camp. It was a curious sound, for the Mahdi had forbidden the expression of any sort of grief for those of his ansar who had entered the gates of Paradise while fighting in his cause. What the Mahdi forbade was simply not done, but this time there were too many women grieving for the loss of husbands, brothers and sons. The news spread quickly through the huge Dervish camp: Musa Wad Helu, who had been sent with a force of nearly 10,000 men to attack the advancing British colomn, had been defeated and his force nearly annihilated at Abu Klea. Musa Wad Helu himself had fallen, along with most of his emirs. Of those who returned, many were wounded. It was the most serious defeat the Dervish forces had ever suffered in the central Sudan. The Mahdi ordered a 101-gun salute to be fired, as for a victory, in an attempt to deceive the garrison in Khartoum, but Gordon from the roof of his palace had seen the weeping women in the Dervish camp through his telescope.

When Slatin was told the reason for the wailing, he felt his heart pound harder. For the first time there seemed real hope that the relief force might arrive in time, and perhaps deliver a crushing blow to the Mahdi's army. In the next few days, news arrived of other British victories over the Dervishes at Abu Kru and Gubat (or Kubba), and of the erection of a fort on the Nile near El Metemmeh. Growing more agitated every day, Slatin listened for the sound of a steamer's whistle on the river or the boom of its guns announcing the arrival of the British army. In the Dervish camp there was considerable tension and anxiety. The Mahdi and his leaders knew that Khartoum must be taken soon or not at all.

On the evening of 25 January, the Dervish forces were gathered for the final attack. The Mahdi himself spoke to them, preaching the glories of the jihad and urging his followers to fight to the death. Slatin, aware of what was happening, thought this night 'the most excitingly anxious one in my life'. All night long he lay awake listening for the sounds of battle. There was not a sound. Just before dawn, exhausted from the strain, he drifted off to sleep. Then he was startled by the crash of thousands of muskets and rifles, the boom of cannon. It lasted only a few minutes. Then, except for an occasional rifle shot, he heard nothing. Could this be the great attack on Khartoum? He waited impatiently for news.

A bright, red sun was rising over the horizon when he heard shouts in the distance. His guards heard them too, and ran off to learn the news. Soon they returned in the greatest excitement – Khartoum had fallen. Slatin crawled out of his tattered tent and looked around him. The quarters of the Mahdi and the Khalifa were not far away, and he saw that a great crowd had collected there. As he watched, there was a movement in his direction and he saw the crowd come towards him. Three Black soldiers were in the lead, one of whom he recognized as a man named Shatta, a former slave in the bodyguard of an officer in Kordofan. Shatta was carrying something wrapped in a bloody cloth.

Slatin stood silent as they stopped in front of him, their faces triumphant. With a smile, Shatta undid the cloth while the crowd shouted. Slatin looked: It was Gordon's severed head.

Slatin felt the blood rush to his face, but he struggled to maintain his self-control. He gazed silently at the bloody head. The blue eyes were half open; the mouth was natural; the hair and short whiskers were almost white except where stained with blood.

Shatta held the head before him and demanded, 'Is not this the head of your uncle, the unbeliever?'

'What of it?' Slatin managed to answer. 'A brave soldier who fell at his post. Happy is he to have fallen; his sufferings are over.'

'Ha! So you still praise the unbeliever,' jeered Shatta, 'but you will soon see the result!' He turned and, taking the head with him, returned to the Mahdi's quarters, drawing the crowd after him.

Slatin crept with jangling chains back into his tent.

8

Slatin: Slave of the Khalifa

Khartoum had fallen, Gordon was dead, and the British relief expedition had turned back. Slatin was left without hope of deliverance. Without hope, many men die, for in exceptionally painful or unpleasant circumstances hope is a peculiarly essential quality. But Slatin was saved by four personal characteristics: however black and hopeless his situation appeared – and at this point his chances of ever leaving the Sudan alive seemed remote indeed – he never completely despaired of some day, somehow, regaining his freedom. Also, he was a shrewd man and a keen observer; he never lost interest in the people with whom he was forced to live, and he was conscious of the truly unique opportunity he had to learn the inner workings of the Mahdiya and to observe the historical events taking place at this time in the Sudan. Perhaps more than any other single factor, it was this lively curiosity regarding the Sudanese scene that kept his mind active, his wits nimble and his spirit resilient. Thirdly, he was endowed with a remarkably hardy constitution, without which he would most certainly never have survived. And lastly, Slatin, unlike Lupton, was capable of servility.

Of the virtues, that which Slatin needed most in the days immediately following the fall of Khartoum was patience. Five days after Gordon's head had been shown to him, a small band of soldiers came to his ragged tent and put him, still shackled and bound, on a donkey and led him off to the general prison in Omdurman. There an exceptionally heavy iron bar with rings was hammered on to his ankles. This particular form of irons was known as the Hajji Fatma; it weighed about 18 pounds and it was usually placed only on prisoners who were considered exceptionally dangerous or stubborn. Slatin did not know at this time why he had fallen still lower in the Khalifa's favour. Actually, information regarding the Dervish army which Slatin had sent to Gordon had been passed on by Gordon in letters to some of his senior officers. One of these was found after the fall of Khartoum. It is remarkable that Slatin was not executed.

The prison at this time was simply an immense zariba. Slatin was put in one corner and warned that he must talk with no one without permission; if he disobeyed, he would be instantly flogged. At sunset he was taken from his corner and chained with a group of slaves to the trunk of a tree; at sunrise he was unfastened and led back to his corner. In another corner of the zariba he could see Frank Lupton, who had been in prison for some time already. Lupton had permission to talk with most of the other prisoners, but not with Slatin.

For food Slatin received only uncooked durra in the same portion as the slaves. Fortunately, one of the gaoler's wives, a woman from Darfur, took pity on him and boiled the grain for him; she was not allowed to give him any other food, however, as her husband feared that Idris es Saier, the principal gaoler, would find out about it.

Gradually Slatin's lot improved somewhat. At first he lay on the bare ground with only a stone for a pillow; but one day while being driven to the river to wash, he picked up the discarded lining of a donkey saddle and hid the treasure under his arm. 'That night I slept like a king on his pillow of down,' he said later. Eventually he was allowed to talk with the other prisoners occasionally and his lightest foot irons were removed; but he was still burdened with the Hajji Fatma and the other heavy iron and chain.

One day Lupton's Abyssinian wife Zenoba came to the prison to see him, bringing with her their little daughter Fatma, whom Slatin called Fanny. Lupton sent them over to see Slatin, who remembered having seen Zenoba in the house of Frederick Rosset, the German Consul in Khartoum. She spoke of those happier days and broke down completely when she contrasted them with her present misery. Slatin tried to console her: she must be brave; everything might yet end well. 'Besides,' he added, 'it was never intended that human beings should always live well and comfortably.'

A few days later there was another visitor to the prisoners: the Khalifa Abdullahi, accompanied by some of his relatives and mulazemin, entered the prison and walked about among the prisoners, ordering a few to be released. When he came to Slatin he nodded and asked, 'Abdel Kader, are you well?'

'I am well, Sidi,' Slatin answered.

The Khalifa passed on, but Yunes Wad Dekeim, one of the Khalifa's relatives, pressed Slatin's hand quickly and whispered, 'Keep up your spirits. Don't be downhearted, everything will be all right.'

From that day Slatin's condition was distinctly improved. Zenoba was permitted to send him a little food and he was allowed to spend the day with Sheikh Mohammed Wad el Taka, once head of the Hawara tribe and now in prison on suspicion of having been friendly with the Turks. The suspicion was well founded, for the old sheikh spent much of his time with Slatin criticizing the Dervishes and their ways. Almost daily they were visited by the good sheikh's wife, a Xantippe who never failed to bring them food but made each mouthful bitter for her husband by her sharp tongue. She would set down a large dish of baked durra bread and a pan of sauce and then begin the quarrel: 'Yes, old women are quite good enough to cook and do all the hard work, but when men have their freedom and can do as they like, they always turn their eyes on the young and pretty girls.' The sheikh had two younger wives who were staying in the country with the herds, and Slatin was soon well versed in the domestic habits and sexual lapses of his friend. The longer the old woman talked, the more bitter she grew and the more piquant and intimate her details.

The old sheikh, who was always famished when his wife arrived, ate his meal in silence, suffering her criticism, but as he ate and his hunger left him he became more and more angered by her sarcasm and ridicule. As soon as he was full, he would turn on her. 'You who neither fear Allah nor man, leave me and let me starve,' he yelled. 'Some women as they grow old get silly instead of wise. This is the case with you. I think you are possessed of the devil. Get away, and never come near me again!'

Slatin always tried to act as mediator, for he too ate her food and he was always afraid that some day the woman would take her husband at his word and not return. When she was away, Slatin assured her, the sheikh had nothing but good words for her. However hot the argument and bitter the parting, the good woman always returned with her dish full of food.

Slatin was sometimes allowed to speak to Lupton. Although he was a young man, Lupton's hair and beard had grown white during his captivity. He was bitter and impatient, often alarming Slatin when he expressed his feelings without bothering to lower his voice. Slatin tried to calm him and induce him to accept the kind of advice he himself had received from Madibbo: to accept his miserable treatment and try to profit from the experience. But Lupton grew daily more depressed.

Then one day the Khalifa Abdullahi returned to the prison. This time, instead of walking about, he had his angareb put under a shady tree and ordered all the prisoners to be brought to sit in a semi-circle around him. He spoke to several and freed some who had been imprisoned by his personal orders; among those freed was Slatin's friend, the sheikh of the Hawara. The Khalifa promised others, who complained of the sentences they had been given, that he would talk to the kadi about their cases. But he appeared to take no notice of Lupton and Slatin. Lupton glanced at his friend once and shook his head, but Slatin put his finger to his lip to warn him against saying anything foolish. At last the Khalifa seemed to be finished. 'Have I anything else to do?' he asked Idris es Saier.

'Sidi, I am at your service,' replied the Idris.

Then the Khalifa turned and looked at Slatin and asked the same question he had asked during his last visit: 'Abdel Kader, are you well?'

'Sidi,' said Slatin, 'if you will allow me to speak, I will tell you of my condition.'

Sitting at his ease on the angareb, the Khalifa gave his permission.

'Master,' Slatin began, 'I belong to a foreign tribe. I came to you seeking protection, and you gave it to me. It is natural for man to err, and to sin against Allah and each other. I have sinned. But I now repent, and regret all my misdeeds. I repent before Allah and His Prophet. Behold me in irons before you! See, I am naked and hungry. I lie here patiently on the bare ground waiting for the time to come when I may receive pardon. Master, should you think it well to let me continue in this sad plight, then I pray Allah for strength to enable me to bear His will, but now I beg of you to give me my freedom.'

Slatin could see that this speech, which he had carefully composed and practised in his mind, made a favourable impression on the Khalifa. Turning to Lupton he asked, 'And you, Abdullahi?'

'I can add nothing to what Abdel Kader has said,' muttered Lupton. 'Pardon me and grant me liberty.'

The Khalifa turned to Slatin and said, 'From the day you came from Darfur I have done everything I possibly could for you, but your heart has been far from us. You wanted to join Gordon, the infidel, and fight against us. As you are a foreigner, I spared your life; otherwise you would not be alive now. However, if your repentance is real and true, I will pardon both you and Abdullahi. Saier, take off their irons.'

The gaolers took them both away and, after much effort, removed the heavy irons from their legs. Then they were led back to the Khalifa, who had been patiently sitting on his angareb waiting for them. He ordered Idris es Saier to bring him a Koran. When this was put on his sheepskin he called on Slatin and Lupton to swear eternal allegiance to him and to serve him honestly in the future. This done, they followed in his footsteps as he walked out of the prison. Slatin had been in chains for eight months.

Outside the prison, the Khalifa was helped on to his donkey by his servants and Slatin and Lupton were ordered to walk by his side. After shuffling in their chains and irons for so long, they found it difficult to step out and they had a hard time keeping up. When they arrived, panting, at the Khalifa's quarters, he took them inside; he had something important to tell them. He had received from the commander of the army in Egypt a letter stating that he had seized all of the Mahdi's relatives in Dongola and demanding that they be exchanged for all the Christian captives of the Khalifa. 'We have decided to reply,' said the Khalifa, 'that you are now all Mohammedans, that you are one with us, and that you are not willing to be exchanged for people who, though the relatives of the Mahdi, are far from us in thought and deed; that they can do what they like with their captives. Or perhaps you would like to go back to the Christians?'

Slatin assured him that they would never leave him of their own volition; that all the pleasures of the world would never tear them from his side; and that it was only by being constantly in his presence that they had learned to act in such a way as would lead to their salvation. The Khalifa accepted this and promised to present them that very day to the Mahdi.

They waited in an outer room until evening, when the Khalifa finally came to them and led them into an inner room where the Mahdi was seated on an angareb waiting to receive them. He had grown so fat that Slatin hardly recognized him. He held out his hand to be kissed, and while Slatin and Lupton knelt before him, he told them that his only wish was for their good. When men were placed in irons, he said, it exercised a lasting and beneficial effect on them. Speaking of his captured relatives, he said with a smile: 'I love you better than my own brethren, and therefore I refuse to exchange.'

Slatin replied by a paraphrase of the Mahdi's own words, which had been suggested to him by a clever friend while he had been waiting outside: 'Sidi, the man who does not love you more than himself, how can his love proceed truly from his heart.'

'Say that again,' said the Mahdi, and turning to the Khalifa he said, 'Listen.'

When Slatin obediently repeated the words, the Mahdi took his hand and said, 'You have spoken the truth. Love me more than yourself.'

He then called up Lupton and took his hand. He made them both take the oath of allegiance again, saying that as they had not been faithful to their first oath, it must be renewed. When this was over, the Khalifa signalled for them to retire. It was some time before the Khalifa came out to where they waited for further orders. He at once dismissed Lupton and sent him to join his family. 'And you,' he asked Slatin, 'where do you wish to go? Have you anyone to take care of you?'

Lowering his eyes to the ground, Slatin said, 'Besides Allah and yourself, I have no one. Deal with me as you think best for my future.'

'I had hoped and expected this answer from you,' said the Khalifa. 'From this day you may consider yourself a member of my household. I shall care for you and shall never allow you to want for anything. And you will have the benefit of being brought up under my eye, on condition that, from this day forth, you absolutely sever your connection with all your former friends and acquaintances, and associate only with my relatives and servants. You must, moreover, obey implicitly every order you receive from me. During the day, your duty will be to stay with the mulazemin employed in my personal service at the door of my house. At night, when I retire, you will be permitted to go to the house which I shall assign to you. When I go out, you must always accompany me; if I ride, you must walk beside me, until the time comes when, should I see fit, I will provide you with an animal to ride. Do you agree to these conditions, and do you promise to put them into full effect?'

'Master, I agree with pleasure to your conditions. In me you will find a willing and obedient servant, and I hope to have strength to enter upon my new duties.'

All this talk of loyalty, love and devotion between Slatin and the Khalifa was sheer hypocrisy. Both men knew it and each suspected that the other knew it. Certainly Slatin did not trust the Khalifa, and, in view of the orders he had just received regarding his future activities, it was obvious that the Khalifa did not trust Slatin. Why, then, did the Khalifa keep Slatin by him? Why did he not leave him in prison or, in view of his broken vows and correspondence with the enemy, why was he not killed?

Slatin's position was to Western eyes a peculiar one, though in Oriental history not unique: he was a slave who walked in the dust beside his mounted master, and he was an adviser who sometimes counselled on the highest matters of state. It flattered the vanity of the once lowly Abdullahi to have a former high government official as his slave. He often pointed out Slatin when speaking to Western Arabs: 'See, this is the man who was formerly our master, and under whose arbitrary rule we suffered. Now he is my servant, and must obey my commands at all times. See, this is the man who formerly indulged in the pleasures and vices of the world, and now he has to wear an unwashed jibba and walk barefoot. Allah is indeed merciful and gracious!'

Slatin and Lupton were the highest ranking prisoners of the Mahdists. But Lupton, although of equal rank, was not kept as a personal slave. Slatin may have seemed the higher official because he had once ruled over the Khalifa's own tribe, but this cannot account for the seemingly inordinate amount of time which the Khalifa devoted to his European slave. The Khalifa was, after all, the executive head of the secular affairs of the Mahdist state, its prime minister. He had many other things to do besides concerning himself with the activities, loyalty and religious convictions of one member of his numerous household.

While the exact thoughts of the Khalifa on this subject will never be known, much can be inferred from his actions and his reported conversations. A study of their relationship makes it difficult to escape the conclusion that in spite of Slatin's proved infidelity and the Khalifa's distrust, the Khalifa actually liked Slatin. He enjoyed talking with him and matching wits with him. Slatin's knowledge of and interest in Sudanese affairs combined with his Western logic must have given the Khalifa a unique viewpoint. Then, too, the Khalifa was probably flattered by having such a keen intelligence focused on the study of his every whim; he, in turn, took a great interest in many small details of Slatin's existence.

The morning after his release from prison, the Khalifa turned Slatin over to his brother Yakub, whom he instructed to find a place for him to build his hut, adding that it should be as near his own house as possible. This proved difficult, as most of the available land in the vicinity was already taken up by the houses of the Khalifa's relatives, so a place was found near Yakub's house and about 600 yards from the Khalifa's. Slatin now set about to make himself as comfortable as possible in his new position. His servants were gone: some had remained in Darfur; others, who tried to join him, had been held in El Obeid; those whom he had brought with him to Omdurman had been carried off by Abu Anga. He could locate only one of his former servants, an old Nubawa named Saadalla. With the Khalifa's permission, Slatin took him back and put him to work building a hut. The Khalifa directed Fadl el Maula to give him back his own possessions as well as those of Oliver Pain, all of which had been deposited in the Beit el Mal. It was little enough. From Pain's effects, Slatin received only an old jibba, a well-worn Arab cloak and a Koran in French. Fadl el Maula told him the rest had been lost. His own wealth consisted of £40, a few sequins and some gold nose-rings he had collected as curios.

One day the Khalifa asked, 'Are you not a Muslim? Where, then, did you leave your wives?'

'Master,' said Slatin, 'I have only one and I left her in Darfur. I am told she was arrested with all my other servants by Said Mahmud and is now in the Beit el Mal in El Obeid.'

'Is your wife of your own race?'

'No, she is a Darfuri. Her parents and relatives were killed in the battle with Sultan Harun. She and several others had been captured by my men. I gave most of them to my servants and soldiers to marry. This orphan alone was left, and she is now my wife.'

'Have you any children?' asked the Khalifa. When told he had none, he said, 'A man without offspring is like a thorn-tree without fruit. As you now belong to my household, I shall give you wives so that you may live happily.'

Slatin thanked him, but asked that this mark of his favour be postponed until he had erected his huts and could accommodate them. The request was granted.

At this period in the Sudan, it was difficult to sort out the exact position of the women. The line was often blurred between wives, concubines, servants and slaves. In the conversation reported above, Slatin speaks of his wife and 'other servants'. This is the only mention he ever made of a wife whom he had voluntarily married, and he never mentioned her name. She was, by other accounts, a woman named Hassanieh, and she was said to be of the ancient royal family of the Sultans of Darfur. There is also mention – though not by Slatin – of a second wife, an Abyssinian girl named Desta, whom he acquired at a later period. Whether Desta was one of the wives given him by the Khalifa is not known.

Returning home late one night from his post at the Khalifa's gate, Slatin was met by old Saadalla, who informed him that a female slave had been brought to his house. He ordered Saadalla to light a lantern and went to look at his gift, a closely muffled-up figure huddled on a palm mat. Slatin seated himself on his angareb and gently asked her where she came from. She said that she was from southern Kordofan, had been captured and held in the Beit el Mal, and that just now she had been selected and dispatched to him. As she spoke she removed her scented white drapery, as slaves always did when speaking with their masters, revealing her face, bare shoulders and part of her breasts. Slatin made a sign to Saadalla to bring the lantern closer. When he saw the face before him he nearly fell off his angareb: 'Out of her ugly black face, peered two little eyes; a great flat nose, below which were two enormous blubber-shaped lips which, when she laughed, were in danger of coming in contact with her ears, completed one of the most unpleasant physiognomies I had ever beheld. Her head was joined to her enormously fat body by a bulldog-like neck; and this creature had the audacity to call herself Maryam (Mary).'

This was the Khalifa's first gift, and Slatin was not pleased. He complained: 'He had not given me a horse, a donkey, or even a little money, which would have been of some use to me, but had presented me with a female slave, for whom, even had she been fair, he knew well I should not have cared, as, let alone her disagreeable presence, her food and dress were items of expense which I by no means relished.' The Khalifa must have been looking forward with amusement to hearing his gift praised. He asked Slatin if Ahmed Wad Suleiman had carried out his orders and delivered the slave girl to him. Slatin replied that he had, and then candidly gave the Khalifa an exact description of the girl. The Khalifa pretended to be indignant, and that evening Slatin found a second, less ugly, young girl in his house. Both were turned over to Saadalla.

In June 1885, six months after the fall of Khartoum, the Mahdi fell sick of typhus and did not appear at the mosque for prayers. For a week the Khalifa Abdullahi watched at his bedside as he grew steadily worse. When the end came, the three khalifas, the Mahdi's relatives, and his closest friends and advisers were with him. Just before he died, he said, 'Khalifa Abdullahi has been appointed by the Prophet as my successor. He is of me, and I am of him. As you have obeyed me and have carried out my orders, so should you deal with him. May Allah have mercy on me!' He then recited the creed a few times and died. Aisha, the Mahdi's principal wife, who had sat closely veiled in a corner, arose and went to tell the other wives.

In spite of the Mahdi's explicit command that the Khalifa Abdullahi should succeed him, there was not, at first, agreement among the notables present. In fact, there was a discussion, if not an actual argument, held over the still warm body of the Mahdi. The reluctance, for the most part, came from the Ashraf (relatives of the Mahdi) who would have preferred to see one of their own people, such as Khalifa Sherif, take the reins of power. Their position was weakened, however, not only by the last wishes of the Mahdi, but by the fact that in his final appearance in the mosque the Mahdi had publicly rebuked the Ashraf for their luxurious living and for disregarding some of his more puritanical edicts; he had then warned them that the Mahdiya had not been created for their benefit. There was nothing they could do: first one and then another of those present swore allegiance to the Khalifa Abdullahi, until all, even the Ashraf, had given him their oath. They then went outside and announced to the waiting crowd that the Mahdi was dead and that the Khalifa Abdullahi, henceforth to be known as Khalifat el Mahdi, 'Successor of the Mahdi', had demanded the oath of allegiance from the entire population.

Among the first to take the oath were his principal mulazemin, which included Slatin. The Khalifa, with tears rolling down his face, then proceeded to the mosque and there began accepting the oath of allegiance from the masses. Only a few could be given the oath at one time, so the crowds milled about him all day until nightfall. The Khalifa, exhausted, but visibly excited by the crowds surging about him and pledging their eternal allegiance, kept on until far into the night. Slatin, too, was exhausted; as he lay down on the ground to sleep he heard the voices of the passers-by praising the dead Mahdi and assuring each other of their intention to support his successor.

During the reign of the Mahdi, the Sudanese had been united in their efforts to drive out the Turk and they had obeyed the commands of the Mahdi and his lieutenants. The Khalifa inherited a united country and strong forces to maintain his rule, but he could never acquire the same spiritual force that gave the Mahdi the power to unite feuding tribes and overcome the distrust of one region for another, the Nile dweller from the desert Arab. Almost immediately, things began to come unstuck around the edges of the empire and suspicion and intrigue made itself known in the centre of authority. As soon as the news of the Mahdi's death was made public, proclamations by the Khalifa Abdullahi, the other khalifas, and the Ashraf were sent out in all directions to prevent panic and consolidate authority under the new ruler. But it was never quite the same, for in spite of the physical power of the Dervishes it was the spiritual power of the Mahdi himself that had held the state together. The Mahdi had thought of government in moral and religious terms and had established a theocracy in which government was subordinate to religion; the Khalifa converted religion into a tool of government which he used to maintain his dictatorship. This is not to say that the Khalifa was not a religious man, for he was, but his primary interest was in ruling the Sudan rather than reforming Islam. When the Mahdi died, the British and Egyptians hoped the Madhist régime would collapse. It might have happened. But the Khalifa Abdullahi was a clever and ruthless man; he knew both how to acquire and how to maintain political power.

One of his first moves was to place his brother Yakub in command of his own troops of the Black Flag. Another step in his gathering of power into his personal charge was to remove Ahmed Wad Suleiman from his post of treasurer. He did this easily enough by demanding a full accounting of the wealth in the Beit el Mal and of the disbursements that had been made. As the Khalifa well knew, few accounts had been kept and many disbursements had been made on the verbal orders of the Mahdi. The unfortunate Ahmed Wad Suleiman, unable to comply, was dismissed from office and all his property was confiscated. In his place, the Khalifa put the clever Ibrahim Wad Adlan, one of his own trusted men who had once been a merchant in Kordofan.

The Khalifa recognized that the Ashraf constituted the main threat to his rule. He made little attempt to placate them, but set about systematically undermining their power to harm him. He had a particular aversion to the Mahdi's cousin, Abdel Kerim, whom he believed to be plotting to overthrow him and put Khalifa Sherif in his place. Abdel Kerim, as one of Khalifa Sherif's emirs, had command of 600 Black soldiers whom he had taken with him to capture Sennar, one of the few garrisons of the Egyptian government remaining after the fall of Khartoum. The Khalifa ordered Abdel Kerim to come to Omdurman.

When Abdel Kerim arrived with his troops, the Khalifa had them parade before him and complimented them on their valour and loyalty. That evening Abdel Kerim and the other Ashraf were invited to the house of the Khalifa Abdullahi. When they arrived they were shown into an inner room where the Khalifa Abdullahi was seated upon an angareb; the other two khalifas, already there, had been given sheepskins, but Abdel Kerim and his friends were forced to sit on the floor. The Khalifa first ordered his secretary to read a proclamation which the Mahdi had made several months before his death. Throughout the reign of the Khalifa Andullahi this proclamation was much used, but particularly in the early days when he was consolidating his power. It stated in the most unequivocal terms the complete trust which the Mahdi placed in his principal khalifa:

> He is of me, and I am of him. Behave with all reverence to him, as you do to me. Submit to him as you submit to me, and believe in him as you believe in me. Rely on all he says, and never question any of his proceedings. All that he does is by order of the Prophet, or by his permission. . . . The Khalifa Abdullahi is the representative of the righteous. . . . If any one of you speaks or thinks ill of him, you will suffer destruction, and will lose this world and the world to come. . . . He has been given wisdom and right judgment in all things. If he sentences any of you to death . . . it is for your own good.

When the clerk had finished, the Khalifa announced that Abdel Kerim had been unfaithful to him. Abdel Kerim vigorously denied this, but, naturally, he was declared to be guilty. The Khalifa dared not go too far, however, and he hastily granted Abdel Kerim a full pardon. But he did demand that Abdel Kerim turn over to him all of his Black soldiers. Khalifa Ali Wad Helu on this occasion declared in the strongest terms his affection for and devotion to the Khalifa Abdullahi, saying that as he had been a most faithful adherent of the Mahdi, he was now the Khalifa Abdullahi's slave. Then, on a wink from the Khalifa Abdullahi, he suggested that it was a fitting moment for all present to renew their oath of allegiance; he also averred that it was the duty of all of them to turn over to the Khalifa their armed Blacks. Khalifa Sherif and his relatives were thus forced, however unwillingly, to give up their most valuable weapons: the splendid Blacks, the jihadia.

The following morning, in a ceremony in front of the Khalifa's house, all the Black soldiers were turned over to Yakub, so that all the jihadia in Omdurman were placed directly under the black flag of the Khalifa Abdullahi. Not content with this, the Khalifa now demanded that the subordinate khalifas give up their war-drums and plant their flags in front of Yakub's quarters. It was clear to all that there was to be one ruler of the Sudan and that he was determined to be obeyed.

The Khalifa now dispatched his relative, and Slatin's friend,

Yunes Wad Dekeim, to Kordofan, to take over the Blacks stationed there and to move a reluctant tribe to Omdurman. Yunes asked the Khalifa's permission to take Slatin with him to assist with the transport arrangements. After some hesitation, the Khalifa told Slatin, to his great delight, that he could go.

By this time, Slatin was beginning to live on a comfortable scale: his house was completed and filled by a large household. His remaining servants from Darfur had arrived and he had taken back all who wanted to stay with him. He now had four male servants and their many wives and probably – although Slatin never mentioned it – his own wife, Hassanieh. He asked if he could take three of his male servants with him on his journey, but the Khalifa told him he did not need them as Yunes would look after him.

Before leaving, the Khalifa had a long talk with him, reminding him of his promise to be faithful and adjuring him to give Yunes good advice. As he was about to ask permission to leave, the Khalifa beckoned to one of his eunuchs and whispered something in his ear. Slatin knew his master well, and he had a foreboding of ill.

'I have already ordered you,' said the Khalifa, 'to leave behind all the members of your household. Yunes will give you a servant, but I am giving you a wife, so that in case of illness you may have someone on hand to attend you. She is pretty, and not plain like the one Ahmed Wad Suleiman sent you,' he said with a smile. The girl entered and removed her veil. Slatin saw at once that she was indeed a pretty girl, but pretty or not, he did not want her; she was only another mouth to feed.

Just how Slatin managed to feed and clothe himself and the people in his household is something of a mystery. In principle, the Khalifa was to provide for him, but Slatin frequently complained that this was not done. 'The Khalifa contributed very little towards the support of my household,' he said, 'and only occasionally gave orders for me to be supplied with a few ardebs of durra, or a sheep, or a cow.' Yet, as one of the Khalifa's principal mulazemin, he managed to live quite well, even when the other European prisoners and the Sudanese population itself were in great want. It is known that Ibrahim Adlan, head of the Beit el Mal, gave him ten to twenty dollars a month, and some of the officials and merchants secretly sent him sums from time to time, and perhaps as a mulazem standing always in front of the Khalifa's door or by his side, he was in a position to accept bribes. But his living was too precarious to regard wives as an asset, and he did not want this one, pretty or not.

'She was my wife,' said the Khalifa. 'She is very good and patient, but I have so many that I gave her her freedom. But you may now call her your own.'

'Sidi, allow me to speak candidly,' said Slatin.

'Certainly. Here you are at home. Speak!'

'I am at home where I need fear nothing,' Slatin began hastily. 'This woman was your wife, and thus has a right to be treated with consideration for your sake. This, of course, is an easy matter. But, Sidi, how can I, your servant, take your own wife for myself? Moreover, you said yourself that you look upon me as your son.' Slatin now dropped his head and continued: 'I cannot accept this gift.'

He was not too sure what the reaction would be to this speech, but the Khalifa was in an agreeable mood and simply said, 'Your words are good, and I pardon you.' Signing to the woman to withdraw, he called to eunuch: 'Almas! bring my white jibba!' When it was brought, the Khalifa said, 'Take this jibba, which I have often worn myself, and which was specially blessed by the Mahdi for me. Hundreds and thousands of people will envy you this. Guard it carefully, for it will bring you blessings.'

Slatin was delighted to exchange a wife for a jibba, and he fervently kissed the Khalifa's hand.

The next day, Slatin, with Yunes and a force of more than 10,000 set off in the direction of Sennar. Yunes was extremely kind and considerate. He gave Slatin three female slaves and two old soldiers to act as servants, and a horse to ride. Slatin had hoped to find an opportunity to escape, but it soon became apparent that with the populace thoroughly in sympathy with the Mahdist cause, there was little chance. They had been gone only a few days when Slatin received a disturbing letter from the Khalifa:

In the name of Allah, the All-bountiful and Merciful, from the noble Sayed Abdullahi Ibn Sayed Mahmud, by the grace of Allah, Khalifat el Mahdi, on whom be peace, to our brother in Allah, Abdel Kader Saladin.

After this greeting of peace, this is to inform you that I have not received any letter from you since your departure. But I hope that, by the grace of Allah, you are in good health. You know my instructions, and you have drunk from the river of my eloquence. I have urged you to remain faithful, and I know you will uphold your promise. This day I received a letter from one of the Mahdi's friends, who tells me that your wife, coming from the land of the unbelievers, has reached Korosko, and is at this moment trying to bribe people to induce them to fly with you, in order to bring you to her. I have been told that you know all about this. I therefore again urge you to adhere steadfastly to the faith of the Prophet, and to perform with honesty the duties upon which you have entered. But I wish to add that no doubt has entered into my heart of your fidelity. I only wish you peace, and I greet you.

Slatin knew that doubt had indeed entered the Khalifa's heart when Yunes's secretary told him in confidence that a letter had also been sent to his master telling him of the news from Berber and ordering Yunes to keep a strict watch over him. Yunes continued to be friendly, but Slatin was aware of the fact that he was being carefully guarded and was not surprised when, a few days later, Yunes ordered him to return to Omdurman, ostensibly to give the Khalifa a verbal report of their progress. He asked if he should return after giving the Khalifa his report, but Yunes thought not: 'Perhaps you wish to remain with our master the Khalifa, or perhaps he may require your presence in Omdurman.'

Slatin now understood perfectly that Yunes wanted to avoid the responsibility of having him with him. Yunes, kind to the last, gave him 100 hides as a parting gift and a token of his friendship.

When Slatin returned to Omdurman, the Khalifa affected surprise at seeing him, but in the evening, when the two were alone, he spoke of the letter he had received from Berber. Slatin told him, truthfully enough, that he had no wife in Europe and therefore no wife could be attempting to rescue him. He promised that should anyone attempt to induce him to leave, he would at once report it. The Khalifa assured him that he had not believed the story, but speaking in a serious tone, he reminded him to be faithful and warned him to have nothing to do with people other than his own household. He then ordered him to leave and take his usual place before the gate. Slatin had no doubt that his suspicions had been very much aroused.

The Khalifa Abdullahi, from the moment of his accession to power, was never free from revolts, wars and intrigues. From the north he always feared an invasion from Egypt, but, fortunately for him, the Egyptians equally feared an invasion by the Dervishes. In the east, Osman Digna continued his series of running fights with the Egyptian and British forces around Suakin. In the southeast, there was a senseless and bloody war with Abyssinia. In the south and south-west, his able emir, Karamallah, who ruled Bahr el Ghazal, began an invasion of northern Equatoria before he was recalled to Omdurman. In the west there was continuing trouble in Darfur where Slatin's old enemy Madibbo revolted. Eventually he was defeated, captured and sent to Kordofan, where he was placed at the untender mercy of Abu Anga.

Before the Mahdiya, Abu Anga had fought for Sultan Zubair and had once been captured by Madibbo, then an official of the Egyptian government. Madibbo had made him carry a heavy box of ammunition on his head for several days; when he complained about it, Madibbo had him flogged. Although the old warrior knew he could expect neither mercy nor justice from Abu Anga, he made an attempt to plead his case. He had been forced to take up arms, he said, but he had never revolted against the Mahdi; he was innocent and faithful. To all this Abu Anga said simply, 'And yet I will kill you.'

Madibbo, knowing now that he must die, lost his temper: 'It is not you who will kill me, but Allah. I have not asked for mercy, but for justice. However, a slave like you can never become noble. The traces of the lashes of my whip, which can still be seen on your back, were well deserved. In whatever form death may come to me, it will always find me calm and a man. I am Madibbo, and the tribes know me!'

The next morning Abu Anga had him executed in front of his entire army. When Madibbo was marched out in chains, he sneered at the soldiers and before kneeling to receive the sword on his neck he called on those present to report faithfully how he had borne himself at this moment. A few moments later he was headless. Thus ended the life of a man whom Slatin described as 'one of the ablest Arab sheikhs in the Sudan.'

The Khalifa now decided that the Kababish tribe, one of the largest in the Sudan, was not sufficiently submissive. They had been ordered to make a pilgrimage to Omdurman and most had refused to comply. He therefore ordered Ibrahim Adlan, head of the Beit el Mal, to confiscate all of their property. The Kababish lived, then as now, in the vast desert of northern Kordofan where they raise camels and sheep; they were at this time the main carriers of the gum trade in Kordofan, and therefore possessed considerable sums of money, which they buried in secret places in the desert. Ibrahim Adlan sent out a force to make them comply with the Khalifa's orders. For the most part the tribe submitted without too much fighting, but they were maltreated and tortured to make them give up their hidden treasures. The head sheikh of one of the largest sections of the tribe fled into the desert with his relatives to the wells of Om Badr, where it was exceedingly difficult for the Dervishes to pursue them. His name was Saleh Fadlallah Salem, and his brother had been beheaded by the Mahdi four years earlier.

In January 1887 the Khalifa sent two prominent sheikhs as his emissaries to Om Badr to entice Sheikh Saleh to come to Omdurman. They assured him that if he did, he would be granted a full pardon and would be named emir of the Kababish. Sheikh Saleh listened quietly to all they had to say. Then, to their horror, he carefully took out some tobacco and put it in his mouth. Before they could recover from their shock, he said, 'I have well understood what you have said. The Khalifa forgives me entirely, and desires me to come to Omdurman. Suppose that on my arrival the Prophet should appear to the Khalifa – for we all know that the Khalifa acts altogether on the inspiration of the Prophet – and instructs him not to forgive me. What then?'

Not being able to give Sheikh Saleh a satisfactory answer to this question, the emissaries were politely dismissed and each was given a present of a camel. Sheikh Saleh remained at Om Badr, where he was soon joined by embittered Kababish whose property had been confiscated. Before long he had a force large enough to be of considerable annoyance to the Mahdists.

For the Khalifa, tribal revolts were minor matters compared to the potential threat to his power by the very existence of the Ashraf, and he took pains to make certain that no relative of the Mahdi's remained in any position of power anywhere in the Sudan. He did not forget that Khaled, Slatin's former lieutenant and successor in Darfur, was related to the Mahdi. Letters were sent to him instructing him to come to Omdurman. When Khaled stalled, more letters arrived from the Khalifa, urging him to come and act as mediator between himself and the Ashraf; with his practical common sense, he said, he was sure a reconciliation could be arranged.

Khaled, believing the Khalifa's words and being anxious to help his relatives, set out for Omdurman. He took with him a large force: 1,000 cavalry, 3,000 rifles and more than 20,000 Baggara tribal levies and followers. He was near Bara when he awoke at sunrise one morning to find himself surrounded by 5,000 riflemen under Abu Anga. Summoned to appear before Abu Anga, Khaled was shown the Khalifa's secret instructions: As a sign of his submission and fidelity, he was to turn over all his troops to Abu Anga. When he had digested this, he was instructed to give the necessary orders at once, and within a few hours the whole of the Darfur troops were under the command of the subordinates of Abu Anga.

This over, Abu Anga called before him all of Khaled's emirs and read them a flattering statement from the Khalifa; they were then given the option of returning to Darfur or going on with Abu Anga. Khaled and his relatives were given no option: they were arrested and all their property confiscated.

Perhaps the man most pleased by this operation was Said Bey Guma, now Abu Anga's chief of artillery. He received permission to re-annex all his slaves, wives and property which Khaled had taken from him at El Fasher. Doubtless, too, he enjoyed seeing Khaled himself put in chains and sent to El Obeid to consider the value of a promise made by the Khalifa Abdullahi.

9

Slatin: Under Suspicion

Although Slatin found life often difficult and sometimes dangerous, he also found it intensely interesting. He had an inside view of all the principal events that took place during the Mahdiya. For the other European prisoners, who lived outside the vortex of Sudanese power politics, life was harder and more dreary. Gustav Klootz, the ex-orderly, being unable to make a living in Omdurman, tried to escape to Abyssinia, but died on the way. Frank Lupton had considerably more freedom than Slatin – he was allowed to wander about Omdurman, talk with whomever he pleased and he was not required to attend the five daily prayers at the mosque – but he found it difficult to earn enough for food. He had no trade, but he tried to earn a livelihood by mending old weapons. Slatin was able to persuade Ibrahim Adlan to give him small sums of money from time to time, but Lupton found life hard.

One day Slatin encountered Lupton at the mosque. When Lupton complained bitterly of his wretched condition, Slatin, remembering that he had once been a sailor, suggested that it might be possible for him to work in the Khartoum dockyard. Lupton was enthusiastic, and Slatin promised to try to find a job for him.

A few days later, Slatin found the Khalifa in a good mood – Abu Anga had sent him a young horse, money and some of Mohammed Khaled's slaves. That evening the Khalifa commanded Slatin to dine with him and Slatin found an opportunity to bring up the subject of the steamers.

'The steamers require competent men to look after them and repair damages,' Slatin began. 'As most of the workmen in the dockyard were killed during the siege of Khartoum, I suppose you have had some difficulty in replacing them?'

'But what is to be done?' said the Khalifa. 'These steamers are of the greatest value to me, and I must do all I can to preserve them.'

'Abdullahi Lupton was formerly engineer on a steamer. If he received a good monthly salary from the Beit el Mal, I believe he would be really useful for this work.'

The Khalifa seemed pleased with the idea, and asked, 'Then will you speak to him? If he undertook this work of his own free will and accord, without being forced into it, I believe he would be of some use in these matters, of which, I admit, I know absolutely nothing. I will order Ibrahim Adlan to pay him well.'

'I do not know where he is,' lied Slatin. 'I have not seen him for a long time, but I will make inquiries. I feel confident that he will be only too glad to serve you.'

The next day, Slatin sent for Lupton and told him of his conversation with the Khalifa. He also asked him to do as little as possible to repair the steamers, and Lupton assured him this would not be difficult as he had only a very superficial knowledge of machinery. Lupton was given a post at the dockyard, but he was paid only forty dollars a month: just enough to live without starving.

Towards the end of April 1887 another European prisoner was brought to Omdurman. He was Karl (or Charles) Neufeld, a German merchant who had been captured by Wad Nejumi's men not far from the Egyptian frontier. Although Slatin and Neufeld were in the same city for more than seven years, they never saw each other after the first few days of Neufeld's arrival. Slatin often tried through friends to help Neufeld, but he was able to do very little and was forbidden by the Khalifa to visit him.

Omdurman, on the west bank of the Nile, was now the capital of the Mahdist empire; Khartoum, except for the dockyard and a few former government buildings, was allowed to lapse into ruins. The Khalifa decided to show his veneration for the Mahdi by building a tomb for him in Omdurman. All the other buildings in the Mahdist capital were of mud brick, but the walls of the Mahdi's tomb were made of stone, brought across the river from Khartoum. The tomb was a square building, thirty-six feet on the sides and thirty feet high, topped by a forty-foot dome. The walls of the building were more than six feet thick and were pierced by ten arched windows and two doors. When completed, it was whitewashed and surrounded with a trellis-work fence. Although supposedly designed by the Khalifa himself, an Egyptian architect made the plan, following a design of Neufeld's, and supervised the construction. It was the only monument built during the Mahdiya.

Late one evening in April 1888 the Khalifa summoned Slatin and handed him a letter that had just reached him. It was addressed to Slatin and had been sent by the Governor of Suakin through Osman Digna. The Khalifa demanded that he open it at once and tell him what it said. Quickly glancing through it,

Slatin saw with sorrow that it was from his brothers and sisters telling him that his mother had died. Having no reason to conceal its contents, he translated the letter for the Khalifa. When he came to the part where they told him how his mother had said, 'I am ready to die, but I should have loved to see and embrace my Rudolf once more,' he almost broke down. The Khalifa interrupted him: 'Your mother was not aware that I honour you more than anyone else, otherwise she certainly would not have been in such trouble about you; but I forbid you to mourn for her. She died as a Christian and an unbeliever in the Prophet and the Mahdi, and cannot therefore expect God's mercy.'

Slatin felt the blood rush to his face, but even this affront could not draw from him any expression of indignation. He read on: his brother Henry was married; his brother Adolf and his sisters were well. At the end they begged him to try to write. When Slatin had finished translating the letter, the Khalifa told him: 'Write and tell at least one of your brothers to come here. I would honour him and he would want for nothing. But I will talk with you about this another time.' He then signed to him with his hand that he should leave.

He had to wait outside until the Khalifa retired and he was free to go home and be alone. Then he threw himself on his angareb and cried.

The next morning the Khalifa made Slatin read the letter to him again. He then told Slatin to answer the letter and to tell his family how perfectly happy he was in his present position. Slatin wrote and asked his brothers and sisters to have a letter written in Arabic sent to the Khalifa thanking him for his kindness and to send him a travelling bag, twelve watches – these to be used as gifts – and £200 for his own needs. He also asked for a copy of the Koran in German. Why the only book Slatin took with him from Dara was a Koran in French and why he now asked as the only present for himself, besides the money, a copy of the Koran in his mother tongue, has never been explained. It was certainly not to impress the Khalifa, since any foreign book was suspect. Although never a true Mahdist, there appears to be a possibility that Slatin was indeed a true and not a pretended convert to Islam.

It was many weeks before his letter found its way to Austria and many more weeks before he received a reply. He was at his post before the Khalifa's door one morning when a man came up on a laden camel and asked to see the Khalifa; he had letters and goods from Osman Digna. Suspecting that they might be for him, Slatin was wild with impatience, but the Khalifa simply consigned the boxes to the Beit el Mal and the letters to his clerks. It was not until after sunset that he summoned Slatin and gave him the letters. They were, as he thought, from his brothers and sisters. They had enclosed a letter in Arabic to the Khalifa written by a German professor at the request of Slatin's family. It was so flowery and flattering that the Khalifa had it read aloud in the mosque and in a burst of generosity gave Slatin his boxes from the Beit el Mal.

The boxes contained all he had asked for and more – there were even newspapers. The fitted travelling bag was Slatin's present to the Khalifa, who was properly astonished when he opened it and saw the little crystal boxes, silver-topped bottles, brushes, razors, scissors and other marvels it contained. He at once sent for the kadis and showed it to them; they, of course, were duty bound to express even greater astonishment, although Slatin was sure that one or two had seen such things before in other days. The Khalifa then called in his clerks and dictated a letter to Slatin's brothers, describing the high position their brother held in his service and inviting them to come and visit him; he told Slatin to write, too, in his native language. Slatin did, carefully warning them not to think of accepting the Khalifa's invitation.

Occasionally, Father Ohrwalder, who with other Catholic missionaries had been captured in Kordofan, would come and secretly visit Slatin. Now the two of them sat up late for many nights reading and re-reading the newspapers. It was the first world news they had had in six years. Much had happened outside the Sudan in that time: Tsar Alexander II of Russia and President Garfield of the United States had been assassinated; Louis Pasteur had demonstrated the principle of immunization through inoculation and had developed a treatment for rabies; the electric fan, the fountain pen and Maxim's machine gun had been invented; Gottlieb Daimler developed a high-speed internal combustion gasoline engine suitable for automobiles and the first motor-cycles were introduced in France and Germany; the first skyscraper was built; Queen Victoria celebrated fifty years on Britain's throne; gold was discovered in South Africa; and the tuxedo was introduced. Slatin and Father Ohrwalder devoured every scrap of news and read every advertisement. Even years later, a short notice Slatin read then of a woman seeking a kindred spirit with a view to matrimony stuck in his mind.

One day an acquaintance of Slatin's who had travelled to Egypt gave him an Egyptian newspaper he had picked up. It contained an account of the strange death of Archduke Rudolf, crown prince of Austria, who, although married, had a mad attachment for Baroness Marie Vetsera. In January 1889 their bodies were found together at his hunting lodge of Mayerling, near Vienna. Slatin was greatly affected:

> I cannot describe the distress which this news caused me. I had served in his regiment; and I had never given up hope that some day I should return home, and have the pleasure of assuring him that, under all the strange and sad circumstances of my eventful life, I had always endeavoured to uphold the honour of an officer belonging to the Imperial regiment. But what were the trials and troubles of one obscure individual in comparison with this great national calamity – nothing! Again and again my mind turned to the grief of our beloved Emperor, to whom we Austrians look up as to a father. What must he have felt and suffered!

Slatin felt that his acquaintance would have done him a greater favour had he not shown him the newspaper.

On 8 May 1888 Frank Lupton died of typhus. Slatin, with the Khalifa's permission, was able to be with him during his last hours. Barely conscious, he begged Slatin to take care of his wife and daughter. Slatin arranged for his body to be washed, wrapped in a shroud and carried to the mosque for the usual prayers for the dead. He was buried in a cemetery near the Beit el Mal. Father Ohrwalder and most of the Greek colony attended the funeral.

The Khalifa continued to be plagued by minor rebellions in various parts of his empire. Some of these were religious in nature – one rebel leader claimed to be Jesus Christ – while others were inspired simply by resentment against the Khalifa's orders. The Batahin tribe, who lived in the country north of the Blue Nile, resisted the Khalifa's tax collectors, refused to obey an order to move elsewhere and resisted when force was applied to make them comply. Sixty-seven men of this tribe, together with their wives and children, were rounded up and brought to Omdurman to be tried.

The Khalifa, after giving his own views to the judges, had the tribesmen brought before a public court where they were promptly found guilty of the charge of disobedience. 'And what is the punishment for disobedience?' asked the Khalifa.

'Death,' said the kadis.

Three scaffolds were erected in the market-place, and, after midday prayers, the ombeÿa was sounded and the great war-drum beaten to summon the inhabitants of Omdurman. The Khalifa rode to the parade ground and seated himself on an angareb. The sixty-seven Batahin, heavily guarded and with their hands tied behind their backs, were brought before him. Their women and children ran screaming behind. The Khalifa called three of his emirs to him and talked with them in an undertone. One of the emirs then ordered the escort to follow him with their prisoners, and led them off to the market-place.

The Khalifa continued to sit on his angareb for another fifteen minutes, and then stood up and walked with his escort, which included Slatin, to the market-place. A ghastly scene awaited them. The Batahin had been divided into three groups. The first group had been hanged, and the Khalifa stopped in front of the scaffolds, almost broken by the weight of the bodies suspended from them. Near by was the second group, which had been decapitated. The Khalifa then walked over to the third group, whose right hands and left feet had been chopped off. Heads, hands and feet were scattered over the blood-soaked dust of the market-place. The Batahin tribe had always been noted for its bravery, and the mutilated men who were still alive did not make a sound, but stared ahead of them, trying to conceal from the crowd any signs of their suffering. The Khalifa called to him one Osman Wad Ahmed, a Mahdist official who was of the Batahin tribe and an intimate friend of Khalifa Ali Helu. 'You may now take what remains of your tribe home with you,' he said.

It is easy for dictators, omnipotent, flattered and unquestioned in their own countries, to overestimate their power and influence outside the range of their effective physical force. Such was the case with the Khalifa Abdullahi. He believed that Egypt was eager to accept Mahdism and that his army could easily conquer the forces he would encounter there. In July 1889 he therefore dispatched an army under Wad Nejumi to invade Egypt. The army consisted of about 16,000 people, most of whom were camp followers, and it did not include the best fighting men. Still, the Khalifa hoped for success.

He had not long to hope. He was praying by the Nile one day when mounted messengers arrived in haste from Dongola. Their letters were handed to one of the Khalifa's secretaries, who decided to wait until he returned to his house before telling him the news: Wad Nejumi was dead and his army annihilated near the village of Toski (or Tushki) in southern Egypt. The blow had been dealt by Francis Grenfell Pasha, Sirdar of the new, British-trained, Egyptian army. It was a terrible blow to the Khalifa, who now feared that British and Egyptian forces would invade the Sudan. For three days he did not go near his harem and Slatin and the other mulaze-min did not dare leave his door.

The Anglo-Egyptian army did not advance into the Sudan, but a disaster of a different order struck the country: famine. There had been practically no rain for a year. Crops failed and grain became increasingly scarce. Refugees from famine-stricken areas wandered into Omdurman, which was already overpopulated, and here in the last months of 1889 the situation grew critical. The Khalifa sent armies to sweep the countryside for food, but little could be obtained even by force. In Omdurman, the price of grain rose to forty dollars an ardeb, then to sixty. The rich could buy it; the poor died.

Ibrahim Adlan, head of the Beit el Mal, was ordered personally to go to the Gezira district and convince the inhabitants that they should voluntarily give up their grain. The needed grain was to be given to the Khalifa's own tribe, the Taaisha, whom he always favoured and whom he considered the main source of his strength. Adlan was an able official who had, through his efficiency and wisdom, risen high in the Khalifa's favour. He was described as being about thirty-five years old at this time, with a black skin and an aquiline nose. He was liberal and kind to those who were submissive to his will, but he was a bitter enemy to those whom he suspected of finding fault with his work or attempting to obtain favours without consulting him. He was greedy for money and, as head of the Beit el Mal, the means for acquiring wealth were not difficult to find. He was, therefore, a very rich and influential person, but he did have enemies and his absence gave them an opportunity to plot his downfall. Unfortunately for him, among his enemies was Yakub.

When he had left Omdurman, Yakub and several of his friends informed the Khalifa that Adlan's influence in the country was nearly as great as his own; that he often spoke disparagingly of the Khalifa; and that he even went so far as to attribute the famine to the Khalifa's generosity to his own tribe. When Ibrahim Adlan returned, the Khalifa summoned him and accused him of infidelity and abuse of his confidence. Made incautious by anger, Adlan forgot that he was, after all, only the slave of the Khalifa, and replied sharply: 'You reproach me now – I who have served you all these years. And now I do not fear to speak my mind to you. Through preference for your own tribe and your love of evildoing, you have estranged the hearts of all those who have hitherto been faithful to you. I have ever been mindful of your interests, but as you now listen to my enemies and to your brother Yakub, who is ill-disposed towards me, I cannot serve you any longer.'

The Khalifa was shocked. No one had ever before dared to use such language to him. He controlled himself with an effort, and then said simply, 'I have taken note of what you have said, and will think it over. Leave me now, and I will give you an answer to-morrow.'

After sunset the next day, the Khalifa summoned the other khalifas, all the kadis and Yakub to hear his reply. When Adlan stood before him, he began severely, 'You spoke against Yakub and said I had estranged myself from the hearts of my followers. Do you not know that my brother Yakub is my eye and my right hand? It is you who have estranged the hearts of my friends from me. And now you dare to do the same with my brother. But Almighty Allah is righteous and you shall not escape your punishment.'

The Khalifa made a sign to his waiting mulazemin; Adlan was quickly seized and carried off to prison. Adlan said not a word, but carried his head high, determined that he would not give his enemies the satisfaction of seeing him downcast or afraid. The Khalifa at once gave instructions for his house and property to be seized. In Adlan's pocket was found a piece of paper on which was mysterious writing in which the name of the Khalifa was seen. This was declared to be sorcery. Adlan was condemned to mutila-tion or death – he could make his own choice. He chose death. To the baying of the ombeÿa he was taken to the scaffold in the market-place. He put the noose around his neck by himself, and when the angareb was pulled out from beneath his feet he swung stiff as a statue with his index finger outstretched in the sign that he died in the true faith of Islam. Ibrahim Adlan had been good to Slatin. Of his execution Slatin said, 'I lost a true and kind friend and protector.'

Slatin knew that Adlan's fate could be his own. The Khalifa summoned him one day and complained that neither of Slatin's brothers had come to him as a result of his letters. The Khalifa therefore forbade him to ever have any further communication with his relatives. Slatin agreed. Then the Khalifa looked at him fixedly and asked, 'Where is the Gospel that has been sent to you?'

'I am a Muslim,' Slatin replied. 'I have no Gospel in my house. My brothers sent me a translation of the Koran, the Holy Book which your secretary saw when the box was opened, and which is still in my possession.'

'Then bring it to me tomorrow,' ordered the Khalifa.

The next day Slatin brought the book and gave it to the Khalifa, who examined it carefully. 'You say that this is the Koran,' said the Khalifa. 'It is in the language of unbelievers, and perhaps they have made alterations.'

'It is a literal translation into my own language,' Slatin said calmly. 'Its object is to make me understand the Holy Book which has come from Allah and was made known to mankind by the Prophet in the Arabic language. If you wish, you can send it to Neufeld, who is in prison and with whom I have had no intercourse. You can find out from him if what I say is correct.'

'I do not mistrust you, and I believe what you say,' replied the Khalifa in somewhat kinder tone. 'But people have spoken to me about it, and you had better destroy the book.'

Slatin said he would, and the Khalifa added, 'Also, I wish you to return the present your brothers and sisters sent me. I can make no use of it, and it will be a proof to them that I place no value on worldly possessions.'

Slatin did not know who was intriguing against him, but he knew well enough that it was not difficult to arouse the Khalifa's suspicions. He was extremely circumspect, but he never discovered exactly who his enemies were. One day, not long after Adlan's execution, the Khalifa called all his mulazemin before him and openly announced the charges that had been made against Slatin: He was told that he was suspected of being a spy; that he questioned the camel postmen when they arrived; that he received visitors in his house at night who were out of favour with his master; and that he had even inquired as to what part of the house the Khalifa's bedroom was located. The Khalifa ended with the warning words: 'I am afraid that if you do not change your line of conduct, you will follow in the footsteps of my old enemy Adlan.'

Slatin knew that now if ever in his life he needed to be calm, collected and clever, it was at this moment. He answered firmly, 'Sidi! I cannot defend myself against unknown enemies, but I am perfectly innocent of all they have told you. I leave my detractors in the hands of Allah. For more than six years, in sunshine and in rain, I have stood at your door, ever ready to receive and carry out your orders. At your command, I have given up all my old friends, and have no communication with anyone. I have even given up all connection with my relatives, and that without the slightest remonstrance. Such a thing as conspiracy has never entered my heart. During all these long years, I have never made a complaint. Sidi, what have I done? All that I do is not done out of fear of you, but out of love for you, and I cannot do more. Should Allah have further trials in store for me, I shall calmly and willingly submit to my fate, but I have full reliance on your sense of justice.'

There was a moment's silence after Slatin had finished his speech. Then the Khalifa asked of all those present, 'What have you to say to his words?'

All protested that they had never noticed anything suspicious in his behaviour. Mollified, the Khalifa turned to Slatin and said, 'I forgive you, but avoid in the future giving further cause for complaint,' and held out his hand for him to kiss.

The next day he talked with Slatin kindly, but warned him to be careful as it required only two witnesses appearing against him before the kadis and he was lost. Slatin well knew this. That night the Khalifa sent him, as a sign of his forgiveness, another wife.

Although Slatin was not involved in any conspiracy against the Khalifa, others were. The Ashraf had been shorn of most of their power, but not of their hatred for the Khalifa, nor of their desire to hold power themselves. The Khalifa Mohammed Sherif and two of the Mahdi's sons, all young men in their twenties, plotted to overthrow the Khalifa. The plot was hatched in Omdurman, and their friends and fellow tribesmen were taken into their confidence. They also sent letters to the Danagla living in the Gezira, asking them to come to Omdurman and join them. They were betrayed by a Jaalin emir. He had been bound by an oath to tell only his brother and his best friend, but he at once informed the Khalifa, justifying his perfidy by saying that he considered him his best friend.

The Khalifa Abdullahi at once moved to thwart the coup, but the spies of the conspirators warned them that the Khalifa knew of their plans. All the Ashraf and Danagla in Omdurman, together with a number of sympathizers, assembled in the houses around the Mahdi's tomb. Hidden arms and ammunition were brought out and distributed.

It was on a Monday evening after prayers that the Khalifa summoned his special mulazemin and warned them of the trouble. They were instructed to arm themselves and on no account to leave their posts in front of his gate. Ammunition was issued to the jihadia; more than 1,000 rifles were passed out to tribesmen of the Khalifa's own Taaisha; spearmen and cavalry were assembled by Yakub in the mosque. At sunset the next morning the Ashraf and their followers found themselves surrounded.

The Khalifa Abdullahi was anxious to avoid an open fight. He had no doubt that his men could easily overwhelm the Ashraf, but he feared the victory, knowing as he did the wild nature of his western Arabs – they would surely use the fight as an excuse to sack Omdurman, plundering friend and foe in the excitement and lust for loot. He therefore sent a kadi to Khalifa Sherif and the Mahdi's sons, reminding them of the Mahdi's proclamation and of their own oath of allegiance; the kadi was also instructed to inquire into their grievances and to promise that they would be rectified. Khalifa Sherif's curt reply to the kadi was that they preferred to fight. Some desultory fighting did break out and a few men were killed, but no outright attack was made by either side. The Khalifa Abdullahi sent Khalifa Ali Wad Helu to talk with Khalifa Sherif. He returned with a more favourable reply: Khalifa Sherif had asked what terms they would be given if they surrendered. Negotiations were carried on all that day and far into the night. At last an agreement was reached: the Khalifa promised under a solemn oath to completely forgive all those who had taken part in the insurrection; to give Khalifa Sherif a position worthy of his dignity; to allow Khalifa Sherif to take back his flag and to recruit his own followers and to give pecuniary support to the Mahdi's family. In return, the Ashraf agreed to give up all their arms and submit to the Khalifa's orders. Even after all had agreed to these terms, no one seemed in a hurry to carry out the agreement, and an uneasy truce settled over Omdurman. It was nearly three weeks before the Khalifa managed to collect all the arms of the Ashraf, but once this had been accomplished he set about his revenge.

He summoned the kadis, the other khalifas and the leaders of the Ashraf and Danagla. He accused the latter of being reluctant to obey his orders, seldom attending prayers and failing to attend the Friday morning parades. He then announced that the Prophet had come to him in a vision and commanded him to punish thirteen of them, whom he named. As each name was pronounced, the man was seized and his arms were bound behind him. They were led off, put in chains and in a few days shipped off to Zeki Tummal at Fashoda. There they were kept in a zariba for eight days with just enough food and water to keep them alive; then, following the Khalifa's secret orders, they were beaten to death with freshly cut branches of thorn trees.

Almost 1,000 Danagla were seized in their own country, the Khalifa claiming that they had been in sympathy with the insurgents and that they were excluded from his pardon of the rebels in Omdurman. They were brought to Omdurman and thrown in prison, and only released after they agreed to give up the bulk of their property to the Khalifa. This was done and after the Khalifa and Yakub took what they wanted, the rest was given to the Baggara Arabs. This move aggravated the general discontent of many of the eastern tribes who resented the fact that the Khalifa always gave preference to the western Baggara and particularly to his own tribe, the Taaisha.

The Khalifa's next move was to arrest two of the Mahdi's uncles and ship them off to Zeki Tummal to be murdered. When Khalifa Sherif learned of this, he openly protested. His complaint gave Khalifa Abdullahi the excuse he was seeking. He assembled the kadis and principal emirs and they decided that Khalifa Sherif himself should be arrested. The following day the mulazemin were formed into a square in the open space between the Khalifa Abdullahi's house and the Mahdi's tomb. The kadis were sent to Khalifa Sherif; they told him he was under arrest and counselled submission. Walking out of his house, Khalifa Sherif was met by mulazemin who would not even permit him to put on his shoes but hustled him off to prison so fast that he twice fell to the ground. At the prison, six irons were hammered on to his legs.

In the midst of all this uproar, Father Ohrwalder made a daring attempt to flee Omdurman, taking two nuns with him. On the Sunday afternoon preceding the affair with the Ashraf, Slatin had sent one of his servants to Father Ohrwalder. When the servant reported back that he could not find him, Slatin foolishly sent him back to inquire among Father Ohrwalder's neighbours. Too late, it occurred to him that perhaps his friend had found a means to escape. That evening, George Stambuli and the Greek called Abdullahi, who was the emir of the muslimania, anxiously waited upon the Khalifa. As the Khalifa was then much preoccupied with the plot of the Ashraf, he did not see them until after evening prayers. When told of Father Ohrwalder's flight, he immediately called for the chief of his police force and commanded him to find the fugitives and bring them or their bodies back.

Father Ohrwalder: a Priest in Purgatory

When he left Cairo on 28 December 1880 Father Joseph (or
Giuseppe) Ohrwalder was a tall, strikingly handsome young man,
excited by his assignment to a mission station in the remote Sudan.
He had no inkling that he would be caught up in a Muslim religious
reformation and a jihad. Travelling with Bishop Daniele Comboni
and two other priests by way of Suakin, he crossed the desert to
Berber, then went up the Nile to Khartoum, arriving there in early
February 1881. On 29 March he and Bishop Comboni left with
Slatin and Dr Zurbuchen for El Obeid.

Ohrwalder remained in El Obeid while Bishop Comboni made a
tour through the Nuba Hills and then returned to Khartoum,
where he died shortly after. On 28 November Father Ohrwalder
left El Obeid for the small mission station of Dilling in the Nuba
Hills, five days' march to the south. A short time before, the government had established a post at Dilling and a company of Sudanese
soldiers was garrisoned there. Father Luigi Bonomi, a forty-year-
old priest from Verona, was the superior and Sister Teresa Grigolini
was the mother superior of a small group of nuns.

Father Ohrwalder was happy at Dilling. Working with Father
Paolo Rossignoli and Brothers Domenico Polinari and Giuseppe
Rognotto (called Beppo), he helped to make bricks for the ex-
pansion of the mission and taught the Catholic faith to the Nubas.
In his spare time he collected insects and skinned birds and snakes.
He took a great interest in the civilization of the Nubas and made a
collection of their artifacts.

His time of peace and tranquillity at Dilling was short. On 8 April
1882 cries of alarm rang through the hills and a band of mounted
Baggara Dervishes with broad lances swept through Jebel Nuba.
For the first time, the young priest saw the swift and horrible
violence of the Sudan. It was only the first of a series of Dervish
attacks. As time passed, the priests, brothers and nuns at Dilling
heard less and less news from El Obeid, but many confused and
disturbing reports concerning the Mahdi. For more than five

months they lived in a state of uncertainty and fear, cut off from the rest of the world, not daring to leave their hills and venture into the plains.

In September the Mahdi advanced into Kordofan, and an Arab emir named Mek Omar was sent with fifty men to take possession of Dilling. He camped on a neighbouring hill, beat his war-drum and sent messages to the mission and garrison demanding their surrender. The missionaries wanted to try making their way south to Equatoria, but as the soldiers would not join them they abandoned the project, fearing they would have little chance of getting through without the protection of the Remingtons. On 15 September 1882 they rang the ave-bell for the last time and surrendered to Mek Omar.

The missionaries were herded north by Mek Omar's son, Naser, and after several days' marching they reached the Mahdi's camp near El Obeid. Contrary to what they had been told by Mek Omar, the inner fort of El Obeid had not yet fallen, although the city was surrounded and completely cut off. As they approached the Mahdi's camp, they could hear the rattle of musketry and the occasional boom of a cannon. Almost within sight of the camp, they halted to rest under a large Adamsonia tree. Here they were set upon by a band of Dervishes who stripped them of their watches and money, and the men of their outer garments. They even tried to tear off the veils and clothes of the nuns, but the priests and monks seized sticks and, with the help of Naser and their escort, drove them off. Father Ohrwalder had sewn thirty Maria Theresa dollars into his clothes. These were now gone and he was left penniless and with only his shirt and drawers.

As soon as they entered the Mahdi's camp, a crowd collected around them. As they were prodded into the centre of the camp, the crowd grew denser. Exhausted from their long march, the missionaries were driven in the intense heat through the clouds of dust and the swarms of hostile people towards the tent of the Mahdi. Brother Mariani, who had been sick when they left Dilling, could now hardly stand and had to be carried along by the others. The crowds pressed in upon them, threatening them with clubs and spears, until Naser and his escort drew their swords and formed a square to protect them.

At the tent of the Khalifa Sherif, their tormentors were driven off and they were given some water to wash the dust from their swollen tongues. After a short rest they were taken to a small hut, open on two sides, and filled with flies. Close by was a captured government army tent from which the Mahdi soon emerged and, crossing over to their hut, seated himself with dignity on a straw mat in front of them. He was wearing a dirty jibba with parti-coloured patches; on his head was a white skull cap around which was wound a broad white turban. He greeted the missionaries in a friendly manner, asking them in a gentle voice why they had come to the Sudan, what was their nationality and whether they had heard of the Mahdi. He then briefly explained to them the nature of his divine mission and recounted the success of his campaign against the hated Turk. Seeing that they were exhausted, he gave them some dried apricots mixed in water. Before they could raise the cup to their lips it was full of flies.

George Stambuli was summoned and told to explain to them the merits of Islam and of Mahdism. The Mahdi did not, however, ask them outright to renounce their Christian faith and adopt Islam. After talking with them for some time, he stood up abruptly and left them, returning shortly wearing a clean jibba patched with pieces of vestments taken from the Catholic mission in El Obeid. He again tried to talk to them of Islam, but seeing what little interest they took, he broke off his sermon and ordered them to be taken to the Khalifa Abdullahi.

At the Khalifa's hut they found themselves in the company of about twenty criminals, bound hand and foot with chains. The large crowd by the hut looked threatening, but the guards, armed with Remingtons, kept them back. The Khalifa appeared in a few minutes. Father Ohrwalder thought he looked to be about thirty-five years old and later described him as being 'of middle height, very thin – in fact, little else but skin and bone'. He greeted them kindly, but soon began to harangue them on the glories of Islam, urging them to renounce their faith and become Muslims. Their lack of interest was so apparent that he grew angry as he talked and ended his speech with the terse statement that if they refused to be converted they would be killed. They were taken away.

Shortly after this interview, George Stambuli came to them and advised them to adopt Islam as he had done, warning them that they would surely die if they refused. They listened to him quietly and when he had finished told him that if they must die, they must – they would never become Muslims.

During the next few days the Mahdi tried repeatedly to make them change their minds, sending a variety of people to instruct and to woo them. They were immovable. The Khalifa Abdullahi was sent to make the final attempt, and when they refused him too, he announced that this was the end of his forbearance: they would be beheaded in the morning.

At midnight that night, George Stambuli came to them greatly agitated; he had heard that a large ransom had been offered for their release and refused. They would surely die. The missionaries spent the remaining hours of the night in prayer. Just before dawn they saw a large comet with a long golden tail in the clear desert sky. This was the Great Comet of 1882, one of the brightest comets ever seen on earth. It reminded them of the star of the east that had shone over Bethlehem and it moved them greatly that such a heavenly reminder should appear on the morning of their martyr- dom. The Dervishes saw it too, and called it Star of the Mahdi.

Early in the morning, the great war-drum of the Mahdi began its booming and the braying ombeÿa sounded through the camp. The drums of the khalifas and the emirs took up the call and soon men were rushing in all directions to take their stations by the flags of their chiefs. George Stambuli arrived and, weeping bitterly, told the band of priests, nuns and monks that their sufferings would soon be over. They gave him letters of farewell to their relatives and he promised that if it were ever possible he would send them out.

About nine o'clock a party of thirty Dervishes armed with lances arrived and the missionaries were ordered to follow them. They were taken to an area east of El Obeid where the Mahdi had assembled an army which Father Ohrwalder estimated to be about 40,000 men. Thousands of other people were also swarming about. Led before the massed warriors, the missionaries were told to bend their heads for the death-blow. Without the slightest sign of hesita- tion they did so, and waited calmly for the sword to descend on their necks.

There was a disturbance around them of which they were hardly conscious. They were jerked to their feet and stood looking about them dazedly until they became aware that the Mahdi had come up, mounted on a magnificent white camel, and they were being ordered to go to him. When they had stumbled over to him, he looked down upon them and said, 'May Allah lead you into the way of truth.' They were spared.

The troops were dismissed and the missionaries found them- selves surrounded by such a dense crowd of curious people that they seemed in danger of being crushed to death until the Mahdi turned back and told them to walk in front of his camel for protection. They tried, but weak, exhausted and swept about by the crowd, they were unable to keep up the pace. Seeing their plight, the Mahdi ordered several of his emirs to hold them back until he and the crowd had passed on. Their escort formed a square about them and amused themselves by asking each of them in turn whether they preferred Islam or death. Each of them answered resolutely, 'Death!' They were then pushed on, exhausted and covered with dust, to the Mahdi's hut. There he spoke to them: 'Have you not seen my army?' he began. He then talked to them of the vast number of his followers and of their great bravery. When the missionaries did not reply, he ordered them taken to the Khalifa Abdullahi's hut.

While they waited, a council was held to determine their fate. As they learned later, the majority of those present were in favour of killing them, but a man whom Father Ohrwalder described as 'a certain Hajji Khaled' – probably Khaled Ahmed al Omarabi, a devout notable of the Jaalin tribe – pointed out that according to Islamic law it was not proper to kill captive priests who had not offered armed resistance. The Mahdi apparently agreed with this view and it was finally accepted.

They were now turned over to George Stambuli, who was made responsible for them, and were moved to his hut. As Stambuli's hut was barely large enough for himself and his family, the missionaries were forced to live in the open. There they remained for fifteen days, exposed to the continual insults of the Dervishes while they worked to build some shelter for themselves.

Father Ohrwalder and his friends were in the middle of an enormous camp spread out over a vast plain. It must have been an impressive but frightening sight. There was a constant welter of confused and discordant noises created by tens of thousands of people living in close proximity in temporary shelters, many with their animals about them. The huts were built so close together that fires were frequent, spreading rapidly and causing great destruction. The congestion created appalling sanitary conditions: no attempt was made to keep the area clean; filth was simply piled behind the huts; dead animals remained unburied beneath the scorching sun; and the entire population of the camp lived amid an ever-increasing heap of filth swarming with masses of flies.

These living conditions, combined with the missionaries' physical and mental exhaustion and the bad food, soon affected their health. All had diarrhoea and some were consumed with burning fevers. Filthy and covered with lice, they lay helpless and despairing on their palm mats. Within a month three died: two nuns and a lay brother. The survivors found it almost more than they could do to sew the quickly decaying corpses into mats and drag them to the door of the hut. It was some time before some slaves could be persuaded by promises of pay to remove the bodies and bury them. No one wanted to help the 'Christian dogs'. The bodies were carried away without prayer or chant and the priests were too miserable and sick to know if they were ever really buried or simply carried beyond the huts and left rotting on the ground.

In early November, Mek Omar arrived in camp with the Sudanese converts of the Dilling mission. The young men were drafted into the army, two of the girls were made concubines of the Mahdi and the rest were sold as slaves. Shortly after, Mek Omar himself was thrown in chains on the charge that he had concealed some of the booty from the mission. Father Ohrwalder and Father Bonomi went to visit him, and Father Bonomi was so touched by his wretched condition that he went to the Mahdi and pleaded for his release, telling him, as Mek Omar had told them, that it was really the Nubas who had stolen the booty.

When the missionaries began to recover from their illnesses, their thoughts turned to how they might escape. As flight seemed impossible, they decided to appeal to the Mahdi for permission to leave. Petitioners and devotees crowded about the Mahdi's hut night and day, and it was not easy for them to gain an audience. Several times they succeeded in reaching the doorway, only to be pushed back by the guards. When at last they managed to obtain an interview, the Mahdi listened sympathetically, but told them that the roads were too dangerous now, and that he did not wish them to be harmed. He told them to wait, and promised that after El Obeid had fallen he would permit them to return to their own country. He also gave them some good advice: wear Arab dress to avoid being conspicuous and attracting the curses and clods of his followers.

Martin Hansal, the Austrian Consul in Khartoum, wrote to the Mahdi offering to ransom the missionaries, but the Mahdi refused. The missionaries put little faith in the Mahdi's promises and all their hopes were now pinned on Khartoum; when word circulated that an army was on its way into Kordofan, their hopes rose. Then, one day they heard that an English officer had been captured. Stambuli, Bonomi and Ohrwalder were summoned by the Mahdi to translate for him. In the Mahdi's tent they found a young man with blond hair, blue eyes and a sunburnt face with a nose red and peeled. He was dressed in a dirty tarbush, rough canvas clothes and so dirty that he reminded Father Ohrwalder of a fireman on a locomotive.

Father Ohrwalder opened the conversation by telling the young man how sorry he was that he had fallen into the hands of the

Dervishes. But the young man was Gustav Klootz and he had deserted the army of Hicks Pasha. The story he told of the condition of the army dismayed the priests, and they tried to translate as little as possible of the information they thought to be of military value. The Mahdi and his advisers questioned Klootz closely. The Mahdi asked whether he thought Hicks Pasha would surrender if he wrote to him. Klootz said he would not. The Mahdi asked which he thought the more powerful and Klootz said he thought the Mahdi more powerful. The Mahdi told Ohrwalder to explain to Klootz that he would receive the best of treatment if he would turn Muslim, but that if he did not he would be killed. Klootz said he was prepared to do anything the Mahdi required. The Mahdi then gave him the Muslim name of Mustafa, as he thought it sounded something like Gustav.

When they were dismissed, Klootz was turned over to Stambuli, and they all went together to his hut. Father Ohrwalder, thinking that perhaps Klootz had invented his report to save his skin, now asked for the true story. To his dismay, Klootz swore that it was all true; that the army marching into Kordofan was really in a miserable condition; and that he had indeed deserted to the Mahdi of his own free will.

When the Dervishes went out to annihilate Hicks and his wretched army, Klootz was taken along. He appears to have felt no emotion other than relief that he had had the good sense to desert. After the battle, when he wandered among the corpses and witnessed the work of the vultures and hyenas, even he was affected by the sight of the mangled bodies of the Europeans who shortly before had been his comrades.

From the clothing taken off the dead bodies of the officers and men of Hicks Pasha, the priests and nuns managed to earn a little money. They washed off the blood from the uniforms and the sisters cut them up and made jibbas from them. George Stambuli sold them and gave the money to the missionaries. The missionaries had only praise for Stambuli, who, through his kindness and generosity, probably saved their lives many times.

An interesting character was George (or Georges) Stambuli (or Istambulia or Istanbuliya). He was at this time a man in his early forties, a Syrian (or perhaps a Greek) who had lived in El Obeid as a merchant, and had once been Emin Pasha's agent in Khartoum. Although a Christian, he went over to the Mahdist side with his family before the siege of El Obeid began. He became, or pretended to become, a Mahdist, and the Mahdi trusted him. Only once did he fall under a cloud. Towards the end of January 1884 one of his female slaves denounced him to the Khalifa Abdullahi, swearing that he was a Christian. The ever-suspicious Abdullahi had his house searched. Stambuli was apparently warned, or was sufficiently cautious to hide everything that might be incriminating; he only overlooked a small silver cross that hung around the neck of his little daughter. The cross was found and Stambuli was thrown in irons. He had managed to store up a quantity of gum and ostrich feathers, and these, with the rest of his property, were confiscated and taken to the Beit el Mal. It was rumoured that he was to be beheaded, but a group of his friends petitioned the Mahdi, and Stambuli, after appearing before him in a shebba and begging his forgiveness, was finally released. His property was never returned and after that he was no longer in a position to assist the missionaries.

After the fall of El Obeid, Father Bonomi wrote to the Mahdi and reminded him of his promise to release them. The Mahdi replied that because of the affection he had for them, he could not bear to let them go. However, he did instruct Wad Suleiman to give them some food from the Beit el Mal from time to time. This was on 5 February 1884. Shortly after this, news reached El Obeid that Gordon had arrived in Khartoum, and the captives felt that at last they had some hope of deliverance, for it was assumed that he had arrived with troops.

Their hopes were dashed when the Mahdi received Gordon's first letter, offering to make him the Sultan of Kordofan. The Mahdi rightly interpreted this as a sign of weakness and had the letter read aloud to the people. When it was later learned that no troops had accompanied Gordon, all knew that Khartoum was practically in the hands of the Dervishes.

On 23 March the missionaries received a note in French smuggled to them by Frank Power from Khartoum: 'Courage pour un peu. Gordon est ici. Courage tout ira bien.' Power also asked for the names of the survivors of Hicks Pasha's expedition and the names of the other prisoners in Kordofan. The priests answered his questions as best they could, although they did not share his optimism: courage they had in plenty, but they doubted that all would go well.

The Mahdi now decided to move to Er Rahad, probably because of the more ample supply of water there. The camp was thrown into a fever of preparations and in the days of confusion that followed, the priests managed to find camels and guides for an attempted flight. Their plans were inadvertently thwarted by the Khalifa Abdullahi, who chose this time to reopen the dispute over their religion. On 28 March he sent for Fathers Ohrwalder and Bonomi and Brother Rognotto and, seated on a palm mat in the midst of a group of emirs, once again enjoined them to adopt Islam. When they again refused, he dismissed them. This time he made no threats.

About sunset that evening, some thirty horsemen rode up to their huts and broke in on them. They had orders to take the nuns. The priests and monks made a valiant effort to prevent them, but thirty armed men were bound to prevail. The Dervishes mockingly assured the priests that no harm would come to them. The nuns were taken to the Khalifa, who, expecting to find them more amenable than the priests, commanded them to declare themselves Muslims. They refused. The young Khalifa Sherif was also present and at one point in the scene that followed he seized the scissors one of the nuns had dangling from her waist and with them cut the partition between her nostrils. They still refused to renounce their faith. When all else failed, the Khalifa Abdullahi's wives were called in to see what female abuse could do. It could do nothing. The nuns were finally sent off under guard to Er Rahad, there to be distributed among several emirs.

The morning after the kidnapping of the nuns, the priests and monks were presented as slaves to various emirs. Father Ohrwalder passed through the hands of several masters in the next few days until he was finally turned over to Idris Wad el Hashmi, whose household was already packed and ready for the journey to Khartoum; the Mahdi himself had already started. In one of the rooms he found a number of well-bound books strewn on the floor. They had been dumped out of a captured leather trunk. He picked one up. It was *The Soldier's Pocket Book* by Lord Wolseley. He wanted to see if there were any diaries among them, but he was hustled out.

On the march, Father Ohrwalder served as a camel driver. The route to Er Rahad was crowded with thousands of men, women, children, heavily laden camels and donkeys, and flocks of sheep. The sun beat down mercilessly and the greatest confusion prevailed: in the heat and dust animals fell, children cried for lost parents and slaves looked for lost masters. During the three-day march to Er Rahad, Father Ohrwalder was forced to share the meal of his master's horse and to beg an occasional drink from a slave. The burning sand made his feet blister and his legs swelled.

At Er Rahad a huge camp had already sprung up. The Mahdi had ordered his quarters to be set up between two large trees. Around him were his khalifas, and in ever-widening circles beyond were his emirs and their wives, concubines, children, slaves, servants and followers, representing countless tribes and districts from all over the Sudan. At prayer time the men sat in well-ordered rows, and Father Ohrwalder was impressed by the sight of these thousands of people performing their prayers in concert.

Just before noon one day Father Ohrwalder was summoned by the Mahdi. It was nearly prayer time and the men were ranging themselves in rows. When the Mahdi came out to where his sheepskin had been laid out on the ground, Ohrwalder, who had not seen him since the interview with Klootz, was struck by how stout he had become. After leading the prayers and handling some petitions, he turned to Father Ohrwalder and questioned him about the Christian religion. He asked if Christians used the 'Hamdu' (a Muslim prayer). Father Ohrwalder told him that Christians had several such, and repeated the Lord's Prayer in Arabic. This excited astonishment among several of those around who had thought Christians did not know how to pray. They then had a long conversation on the Psalms of David. The talk went on until Aser, or afternoon prayers.

After Aser, a dwarf was brought before the Mahdi. The Mahdi questioned him and asked if he were married. The dwarf replied that this was the reason he had wanted to talk with the Mahdi: he badly wanted a wife. The Mahdi at once ordered that one be given him. After this interview, the Mahdi rose and Father Ohrwalder was permitted to go back to his hut.

The next day Father Ohrwalder was again summoned for another long talk. Asked if he ever had dreams, Father Ohrwalder replied that he did, but he certainly did not believe in them. The Mahdi turned to those around him and said, 'Assuredly the Turks do not believe in dreams, or they would admit that I am the Mahdi.'

On the following day, when Father Ohrwalder was summoned once again, he pleaded illness and escaped the interview. He found these talks with the Mahdi uncomfortable and exhausting – disputing religion with a messiah was a tricky business – but they gained for him considerable status in the eyes of Sheikh Idris, his master, who, after this, made some attempt to shield Father Ohrwalder from some of the insults which daily assailed him, and once even invited the priest to have breakfast with him. The breakfast was particularly satisfying, as Father Ohrwalder was used to getting his food from the horses' nose-bag and quenching his thirst from the water allotted to the animals. He slept on the bare ground, and each morning shook the scorpions from his clothes.

At Er Rahad Father Ohrwalder was again able to see his friend, Father Bonomi, for since the missionaries had been separated, they had lost all contact with each other. The nuns were also in Er Rahad, but the priests could not visit them. They had suffered greatly on the march from El Obeid, walking the entire way barefooted over hot sand and thorns; they endured hunger and thirst, and some were forced to carry loads. One of them was suspended from a tree and the soles of her feet were beaten so badly that later the toe-nails dropped out. But in spite of their tortures – which for the most part were torture only because they did not possess the constitutions of Sudanese women – they were not sexually violated. One day they managed to make their way into the Mahdi's presence and complain of their ill-treatment. He protested that he knew nothing about it and brought them all into his own enclosure. Eventually they were turned over to some Greeks who were in the Mahdi's favour.

After the defeat of Hicks Pasha, the missionaries had been able to send off to Khartoum one of their Black converts, a girl they had given the name of Marietta Combotti, with news of their condition and of the assembled power of the Mahdi, and with the advice that everyone should flee Khartoum. The messages were sewn into the end of a mat, which she carried. Seven months later she returned. After considerable difficulty she had been able to reach Khartoum, where Consul Martin Hansal had welcomed her with great kindness and helped her in every way he could. She had then started back, carrying with her letters describing the conditions in Khartoum and news of the defeat of Valentine Baker Pasha. She also brought a copy of a newspaper, the *Tyroler Volksblatt*, in which Father Ohrwalder read an account of his own death – from fatigue and ill-treatment at the hands of the Dervishes.

The state of mind of the priests at this time is reflected in a statement later made by Father Ohrwalder:

> The state of moral darkness in which we lived, the constant insults, being gazed upon by such multitudes, being at the mercy and sport of these savages, just as if one were a monkey or other curious animal, all had a dulling effect on one's spiritual nature, and I felt that I must be losing my mind; but yet in all these trials and afflictions God did not leave us.

After passing the month of Ramadan in Er Rahad, the Mahdi decided to go himself with all his people to Khartoum, where Wad Nejumi was already attacking the city. Treating his nation as though it was a vast tribe, he sent out proclamations for one and all to join him, and a huge migration of people and animals now began. Father Ohrwalder estimated that there were more than 200,000 people on the march towards Khartoum.

Father Ohrwalder himself did not go at this time. Just before the Mahdi left, he was turned over to a new master, Sherif Mahmud, the Mahdi's uncle and the newly appointed Governor of Kordofan, who took Father Ohrwalder with him when he went back to El Obeid to take up his new duties. Fortunately, his new master allowed him to ride a mule that had survived the Hicks Pasha expedition, for insufficient and inadequate food, combined with the other hardships of his captivity, had broken his health. He had a constant fever, his teeth were chattering and loose, and when one day he discovered black spots on his body he was certain that he had scurvy. He felt that he could never have survived the journey on foot. A few days after their arrival in El Obeid, Father Bonomi was brought in from Er Rahad and the two priests were assigned a small hut in the middle of Sherif Mahmud's slave quarters.

About two o'clock in the afternoon of 15 August 1884 a European and three Arabs rode into the yard in front of the mudiria where the European dismounted and boldly advanced towards the crowd. His arrival in El Obeid created a sensation and wild rumours began to fly. Father Bonomi was summoned to translate the stranger's words, as the latter spoke little Arabic. The man who had rashly ridden into the capital of Kordofan was Oliver Pain. He said that he came in the name of France to help the Mahdi, but the Dervishes did not believe him, and the European captives also found it hard to imagine that anyone would willingly put himself in the Mahdi's hands. He was questioned for several days, but as none of his answers made sense to the Dervishes, he was passed on to Er Rahad under heavy guard.

Early in September, Lupton Bey arrived in El Obeid. Like Slatin, he had been well treated immediately after his capture and he still had with him a kavass and a clerk and much of his property. He was generous and helpful to the two priests – among the things he gave Father Ohrwalder were two volumes of *The Popular Educator* – but of all the Europeans in the hands of the Mahdi, Frank Lupton found the indignity of captivity hardest to bear and frequently gave way to bursts of rage and fits of depression. He remained in El Obeid for a month before being passed on to the Mahdi.

For some time the priests had been following the progress of the relief expedition. Fresh news and fresh rumours came daily, but not always in the proper sequence. News of the British victory at Abu Klea arrived in El Obeid on the same day as the news of the fall of Khartoum. On 4 June 1885 news of a very different sort reached the priests. A Copt came to El Obeid and handed Father Bonomi a small note, telling him at the same time that a man was ready to carry him to Dongola.

Fathers Bonomi and Ohrwalder read the note together. It said: 'Dear friend, I am sending this man so that you may escape with him. Trust him. He is honest. Monsignor Sogaro awaits you in Cairo with outstretched arms.' It was signed, 'Your fellow country-man, Alois Santoni.' Santoni was an Italian who had joined the Egyptian postal service in 1865; he had accompanied Gordon to the Sudan in 1878 and he had organized the postal service of the relief expedition. He was now Director of Posts for Upper Egypt and Nubia.

Father Bonomi was delighted, but Father Ohrwalder, while happy for his friend, could not understand why he, too, had not been included. Why had Father Bonomi only been sent for? The next morning, when Bonomi went alone to meet his guide, Father Ohrwalder begged him to ask the guide to take him as well. When he returned, Father Ohrwalder was crushed to learn that the guide had positively refused. However, he promised to return in two weeks if he succeeded in getting Father Bonomi out safely. Late that after-noon, the priests went together to the edge of town. Father Bonomi took with him only a large knife. It was just sunset when they said good-bye, and the dull plain looked beautiful. In his parting words, Father Ohrwalder asked his friend not to forget him.

As he walked slowly back into town, Father Ohrwalder began to wonder what would be his own fate when it was discovered that his companion had escaped. He was questioned when he returned to his hut, but he said he had been looking for grain – a plausible excuse, since there was now a famine in Kordofan and little was to be had in the markets.

Father Ohrwalder threw himself on his angareb and tried to sleep. It was a hot, sultry night, but soon it began to rain, giving some relief. While the rain was falling, Father Ohrwalder, half asleep, thought he heard the sound of Father Bonomi's voice in the hut, but this, he thought, was impossible. He lay still on his mat, wondering what, if anything, was happening, but he was too blurred with sleep to get up. The next morning he searched about the hut, but could find no trace of his companion. Father Bonomi was definitely gone. It was not until six years later that Father Ohrwalder solved the mystery of Father Bonomi's voice in the night.

After leaving Father Ohrwalder, Father Bonomi had tried to make his rendezvous with his guide, but neither guide or camels appeared. Discouraged, he had returned to the hut. There he encountered the Copt who had given him the note. The Copt then led him to the proper place.

It was also not for many years that Father Ohrwalder learned why no arrangements had been made for his escape along with Father Bonomi: it was believed by those in Cairo that Father Ohrwalder was in Omdurman and that Father Bonomi was alone in El Obeid.

Father Bonomi's escape was not detected. After he had been gone for four days, Father Ohrwalder reported to the man in charge of the Beit el Mal that Father Bonomi had gone to Khartoum to get some medicine. Father Ohrwalder was immediately put under surveillance while letters were written and sent to Khartoum. A few days later he was imprisoned in the zariba of the Beit el Mal.

As there was no hut for him, he was housed with a group of slaves suffering from smallpox, then prevalent in El Obeid. It was a disease much feared in the Sudan. He had seen its victims lying under the trees in the market-place, shunned by everyone. When dead, their bodies were dragged off at the end of ropes out of town, then left to be devoured by hyenas – sometimes they were dragged off before they were dead. But life in the zariba was not as bad as it might have been. He did not catch the disease and he made friends among some of his warders, Blacks who had been government soldiers; they often did small favours for him, and he was not ill-treated. Eventually, he was separated from the diseased slaves and given a hut of his own.

Father Ohrwalder was anxious to be available when the guide who had helped Father Bonomi to escape returned for him. Working by night, he worked loose a section of the zariba thorn hedge so as to be able to get out easily when the time came. But a month passed, and the guide did not return. Once he heard that a man had come asking for him, but on learning that he was in the zariba had disappeared. Hope faded away.

It was while confined in the zariba of the Beit el Mal in El Obeid that Father Ohrwalder witnessed the revolt of the Blacks. Dissatisfaction with the Mahdist way of life was perhaps strongest among the Sudanese soldiers who had served in the Egyptian army – 'had eaten the Khedive's bread', as it was said in the Sudan. Many of those in El Obeid had once proved their bravery fighting under Slatin against the Dervishes. There were about 200 Black soldiers in El Obeid and about the same number of bazingers who were equally disenchanted with the Mahdist régime.

The revolt started at noon one day in the middle of October 1885. Father Ohrwalder was in his hut when he heard the sound of musketry. He rushed out to find that there was not a single soldier in the zariba. He shouted, but there was no reply. Even the women of the soldiers were gone, as were the slaves who had been in chains. The gate was open and unguarded. He walked out of the zariba without being challenged and went to the house of the Emir Abdullah, who was in charge of the soldiers. He found him standing by the door with two soldiers. When Father Ohrwalder asked him what was happening, he replied in a surly tone, 'These Beit el Mal slaves have destroyed everything.'

At that moment about fifty Dervishes rushed up, overpowered the emir and the soldiers, and dragged them off to the courtyard of the mudiria. Father Ohrwalder followed. An enormous crowd had collected and they almost pulled the hapless emir to pieces. He was immediately charged with having incited the Blacks to revolt. Although he protested that he knew nothing of the affair, the crowd wanted blood and there were cries of, 'Cut off his head!' He was forced to kneel down, and in a moment his head was rolling in the sand. The two soldiers were similarly treated and their headless bodies were thrown on the ground near the mosque where everyone could see them.

The powder magazine, which the mutineers had seized, consisted of a square yard with four small towers at the corners. All arms and ammunition were stored there, and there too a few Egyptians worked at moulding bullets and filling cartridges. An attempt was quickly made by the Dervishes to storm the magazine, but the attackers were easily driven back by the Remingtons of the Blacks. The Dervishes rallied and attacked once more, but again they were beaten back and several emirs fell. Father Ohrwalder was not a man of war; he fled to the home of a clerk he knew who lived in a house with walls strong enough to withstand rifle bullets.

That night, feeling feverish and restless, he wandered out to see what was happening. He went back to the zariba and found it deserted; even the cattle kept there had escaped. He went on to the mudiria where an angry, exasperated crowd had collected. Defeat by a band of 'slave soldiers' was humiliating. One of the emirs caught sight of Father Ohrwalder and ordered him back to the zariba, threatening to kill him if he left it again. He was escorted back by four Dervishes. Throwing himself on his angareb in the deserted zariba, he wondered what, if anything, it would mean to him even if the rebels succeeded. He wished that they had some experienced leaders. Still, while there was rebellion, there was hope, and he drifted off to sleep.

He was awakened by a prod from the rifle-butt of one of his guards: 'How can you sleep when everyone else is in terror of his life?' Ohrwalder roused himself and sat up. The powder magazine was not too far from the Beit el Mal and they could hear the sounds of revelry going on inside as the Blacks celebrated their freedom. Together with the women and the slaves who had joined them, there were perhaps a thousand people laughing, singing and drinking the marissa forbidden by the Mahdi. Early the next morning the sounds of the Khedival salute rang out over El Obeid for the first time since the city had fallen to the Mahdi. Firing broke out at sunrise and continued until nine o'clock. The Blacks made a few sorties to capture camels and donkeys, but they made no attempt to attack the main body of the Dervishes. The chief Dervish emir sent an imam to tell them that if they surrendered they would be pardoned. The Blacks jeered at this offer. Knowing the value of a Dervish promise, they took the imam about fifty paces from the magazine and killed him with his own spears.

That afternoon the Blacks marched out of the magazine in good marching order with the band playing a lively air. The Dervishes rushed for the magazine, but found it empty. The Blacks had dumped all the powder they could not carry down the well before they left the magazine and set off in the direction of the Nuba Hills. The Dervishes ran to attack them on the march, but were driven off with a few well-directed volleys.

The rebels reached the hills in safety. There they established their own government and withstood several Dervish expeditions sent against them until at last, after many months, they were overwhelmed and died fighting.

Sherif Mahmud was killed fighting the rebel Blacks in the Nuba Hills. All his people, including Father Ohrwalder, were then ordered to be transported to Omdurman. They left El Obeid on 25 March 1886, and Father Ohrwalder was not sorry to leave, for El Obeid, which had once had civilized pretentions, had now become simply a 'dirty Arab village'. There was still a great shortage of food and Father Ohrwalder had long been suffering from dysentery. Their route took them past the site of the El Obeid mission-house, of which not a trace now remained.

It took them exactly one month to make the move from El Obeid to Omdurman, and it was not until 25 April that they camped just outside the town while a wild sandstorm enveloped them. The next day, still covered from head to foot with sand and dust, they entered the Dervish capital of the Sudan. The Mahdi was dead now and the Khalifa Abdullahi was consolidating his power. Omdurman looked prosperous and happy after El Obeid, and Father Ohrwalder estimated the population to be about 150,000. There was a vast maze of a market and plenty of goods to be bought at reasonable prices; a number of Greeks and Syrians, all converts or pretended converts to Mahdism, had started small businesses and they were thriving. The market was always crowded, not only with buyers and sellers but with idlers and those searching for the latest news or the latest rumour, for here was the starting-place and the distribution centre for all information and misinformation. Every race, nationality and tribe represented in the Sudan could be found in the market: Niam Niam, Dinka, Baggara, Rizegat, Kababish, Jaalin, Hadendowa, Abyssinian, Indian and European.

Not long after he arrived in Omdurman, Father Ohrwalder had a chance to visit Khartoum across the Nile. At that time very few houses had been destroyed and people were still living there. He walked along the ramparts and on one parapet he counted nearly 150 bodies, shrivelled up like mummies, in some of which rats and mice had made homes. In the European cemetery, crosses had been smashed and many graves had been opened. The grave of Bishop Comboni in the garden of the mission had been dug up, but the stone put up for him was intact. The mission's church bells had been pulled down, but they lay undamaged in the garden. Four months after Father Ohrwalder's visit, the Khalifa Abdullahi ordered that the town be vacated. Houses were pulled down and the wood and stones transported to Omdurman. Only the arsenal, shipyard and a few other buildings were still used; the rest of the town was soon in ruins and large prickly thorn bushes began to appear everywhere among the rubble.

There were some forty or fifty Europeans in the Sudan at this time, most of whom were Greeks. When Father Ohrwalder first arrived in Omdurman, he was taken in by a kindly Greek with whom he stayed for about eight months. Then he built himself a small straw hut and lived there with one of the mission brothers. His greatest problem was food, and this meant finding some way to make a living. For a while he was in the soap-boiling business with Frank Lupton, and at this time he moved to a house on the edge of the Greek and Syrian quarter. Two of the mission sisters were living near by, earning a precarious living by needlework. The nuns were able to earn very little by this work, as a number of the formerly well-to-do women who had survived the Khartoum massacre had also taken up sewing and the competition was considerable. When Lupton died, Father Ohrwalder abandoned soap-boiling and conceived the idea of making hooks out of telegraph wire; the nuns sewed these on to purses and other articles, and for a time they did a thriving business. But gradually the novelty wore off, and business declined.

It was the fashion in Omdurman for women to wear long garments trimmed with various sorts of ribbons. Father Ohrwalder decided to become a ribbon-maker, and he acquired a small, simple loom. There was a group of men in the market who had a monopoly in this industry and they refused to teach their trade to anyone for less than forty dollars. As this was a sum too large for him to raise, he set out to teach himself. He carefully unravelled a piece of ribbon and studied the way in which it was made. He then tried to repeat the method on his loom and with much patience he succeeded, but he found it slow, back-breaking work. At first he was only able to make four yards a day. This he sold in the market for four piastres, out of which he had to buy thread for more ribbons. After practising continually for a month, he was able to make sixteen yards a day, which he sold, earning enough to support himself and help the nuns. But it was a very low standard of living. For seven months, during the terrible famine of 1889, they lived on durra bread and a few boiled potatoes. Even so, they were better off than thousands of others.

During these hard times in the Sudan, hundreds willing to do any kind of work were unable to find employment, and starved to death. Father Ohrwalder was witness to the most appalling scenes of poverty and degradation. In the yard where animals were slaughtered, hundreds of men and women stood around with bowls to catch the blood of slaughtered animals. With the animal on the ground writhing in its death agony, the starving people fought over the body, spilling the blood on themselves and each other and quarrelling over bits of bloodstained dust. Leather and skins were boiled and eaten, while old bones were ground into powder and made into a sort of bread.

It was even unsafe for small children to be alone on the streets at night. One evening Father Ohrwalder heard a cry and ran out to see a starving man trying to drag away a small boy. Father Ohrwalder and his neighbours chased after him, and the man dropped the boy and fled. He had apparently intended to feed on him that night.

Entire districts were depopulated. Father Ohrwalder thought it was 'Heaven's terrible retribution on a people who had practised untold cruelties and shed rivers of innocent blood.' Thin, starving wretches roamed the streets, eating anything they could find, however disgusting: skins of long-dead animals, leather strips from angarebs, decaying carrion. The dead lay by the hundreds in the streets, and no one could be found to bury them. The poor who had any strength left stole.

In the market-place, those with anything for sale had to fight to defend their goods. Market women would sit or lie on their produce to protect it. There were incessant cries of 'Gayekum! Gayekum!' (He is coming!) – meaning that some famished creature was stealing up on a merchant. Slatin once saw a man seize a piece of tallow and cram it in his mouth. Its owner jumped at his throat before he could swallow it, choking him to make him spit it out. The man's eyes nearly started from his head, but he held the tallow in his mouth until he fell unconscious to the ground.

At night the space between the houses of the Khalifa and his brother Yakub was filled with starving people crying piteously for food. Slatin dreaded going home, for he was always followed by famished beggars who often tried to force their way into his house, and he had all he could do to provide for his own household and his friends. Late one bright moonlit night he was on his way home when he noticed something moving on the ground. As he came nearer he saw three nearly naked women, their long, tangled hair hanging about their shoulders, squatting around a baby donkey lying on its side. The little donkey had strayed from its mother or been stolen by the women, and they had torn open its bowels with their nails and teeth and were eating its intestines while it was still breathing. The women looked up at Slatin with wild eyes, while the beggars who were following him fell upon them, pushing them aside to get their prize.

One woman was brought to trial for eating her own baby; she went mad and died two days later. Many women sold their children, claiming they were slaves. Often they did this less to get money than to save their children from starvation. One day such a woman came to Slatin with her only daughter, a lovely young girl. She was of the Jaalin tribe, perhaps the most moral Arab tribe in the Sudan. With tears streaming down her cheeks and in a barely audible voice, she begged Slatin to take her daughter as his slave. 'Do not fear that I shall molest you any further,' she said. 'Only save her! Do not let her perish!' Slatin gave them what he could and told them to go away, but to come back when they were again in want. He never saw them again.

At long last the rain fell on the thirsty land. Crops sprang up and finally harvest time was near. The entire Sudan, from Darfur to the borders of Abyssinia, everyone from the Khalifa to the lowest starving tribesmen, looked forward to deliverance. But now the sky over the Gezira and the fertile banks of the Nile was clouded by swarms of locusts of exceptional size. The prospects of a rich harvest vanished. The only consolation for this plague was that the locusts could be eaten; they were considered a great delicacy by the Sudanese. What grain the locusts did not eat, the mice consumed. To Catholic priest and Dervish peasant alike, it seemed that the entire Sudan lay under a curse.

Through all the months and years, Father Ohrwalder, like Slatin and the other prisoners, dreamed and schemed; uppermost in their minds always was the thought of escape. One day in 1890 an Ababdeh Arab named Ahmed Hassan came to Father Ohrwalder and volunteered to carry a letter to his friends in Cairo. Father Ohrwalder sent him away, telling him that he would think about it. Spies were everywhere and he did not trust the Arab. He had sent a number of letters before and nothing had happened; besides, it was dangerous to write; if the letter fell into the hands of the Khalifa, he would surely be thrown in prison. However, he made discreet inquiries about the man and in the end decided to trust him with a letter to the Reverend Vicar Apostolic, Franz Sogaro.

Ahmed Hassan represented only one of many plans to escape which Father Ohrwalder had made over the years, and no sooner was he gone from Omdurman than he was nearly forgotten. There was little hope to be derived from such attempts and fear of discovery almost drove out the little hope offered. Meanwhile, there was work to be done, making a living for himself and the nuns and helping other captives. One of the mission brothers, Domenico Polinari, was sent to prison on a false charge of possessing tobacco and Father Ohrwalder often visited him and took him food. He also visited Charles Neufeld, the German merchant, during his long imprisonment, bringing him such food and money as he could spare – and even more than he could spare. Often he was turned away from the prison gates, even after he had bribed the guards, but he managed to get in every month or two. Neufeld later paid tribute to Father Ohrwalder's kindness: 'That my reason did not give way during my first period of imprisonment I have but to thank Father Ohrwalder. . . .' Father Ohrwalder also did all he could to obtain his release. Enlisting the support of all who would listen, the priest and his friends even won the support of the Mahdi's chief widow, but the Khalifa would not listen.

If life in Omdurman was hard and dangerous, it was seldom dull. Father Ohrwalder followed the news and rumours that ran through the market-place and the town. He knew of the Mahdi's campaigns on the Abyssinian frontier and even planned an escape into Abyssinia, but changed his mind at the last minute. He was witness to the horrible slaughter of the Batahin and the execution of Adlan. He was also in Omdurman when the powder magazine exploded.

The Khalifa was running out of gunpowder. The barrels captured at Khartoum, having been left in the damp, had now crusted over. Many tried to make new powder, but failed. At last a Greek, Joseph Pertekachi, succeeded. But on 26 January 1891, the anniversary of the fall of Khartoum, Father Ohrwalder was working at his loom when he heard a tremendous explosion. He ran up to the roof of his house and saw a great column of smoke rising near the Beit el Mal. Running to the scene, he learned that Pertekachi had blown up himself and several of his helpers. A pair of legs was found fifty yards away, a head was found half buried in a mud wall, but no other remains were found anywhere. The prisoners now hoped that the secret of making gunpowder would be lost, but one of the men Pertekachi had trained escaped the blast and the work went on.

Although Islam allows four wives and any number of concubines, and in spite of the large harems of the Khalifas and their emirs, constant warfare had so diminished the number of males in Omdurman that there were a large number of women in the town who had neither husband nor male relations. To correct this situation, the Khalifa once ordered every unmarried woman to be provided with a husband within three days. Consequently, the entire town was taken up with wedding ceremonies; many women were forcibly seized and made to marry. Most of the nuns lived with Father Rosignoli and Brother Beppo Rognotto, who ran a cookshop in the market-place, and were able to escape this marrying spree. But one, Sister Teresina Grigolini, who had formerly been the mother superior at Dilling, voluntarily married a Greek named Kakorembas (or Kocorombo) and had two sons by him.

At another time the Khalifa arbitrarily ordered all males to be circumcised and there was an orgy of foreskin cuttings in Omdurman, but this was later and by then Father Ohrwalder was gone.

By 1891 nearly half of the Europeans and Syrians who had survived the fall of Khartoum were dead. In October of that year, one of the nuns who lived with Father Ohrwalder, Sister Concetta Corsi, was carried off by typhus. On 28 October 1891, about three weeks after her death, Ahmed Hassan suddenly reappeared at Father Ohrwalder's door and said simply, 'Here I am. Are you coming?'

Father Ohrwalder: Flight into Egypt

Archbishop Sogaro had worked unceasingly to free the missionaries trapped in the Sudan, enlisting the support of both Muslims and Christians, of government, army and Church. Pope Leo XIII himself was interested in their fate. A missionary father was stationed on the Egyptian frontier with the special task of trying to effect their escape. Money and letters were sent into the Sudan, but they seldom reached the person for whom they were intended; the Arabs by whom they were sent seldom returned.

The good archbishop and his people never became discouraged, and when Ahmed Hassan arrived in Cairo with the letter from Father Ohrwalder, they at once began to discuss with him ways and means of bringing out Father Ohrwalder and the two nuns who were with him. A contract was drawn up in Arabic:

I, the undersigned, Ahmed Hassan el Abbadi, of Bashri Mohammed Ali's Arabs, agree to proceed at once to Omdurman to bring Father Ohrwalder and the two nuns from Omdurman to Cairo. I agree to take care of them on the journey, and to do all in my power to bring them here and to give them every satisfaction. As a reward and to compensate me for the expenses which I shall incur between Omdurman and Cairo, Monsignor Sogaro has agreed to give me:

1. All the goods to the value of £100 now in possession of Sheikh Abdel Hadi at Korosko.

2. £20 in advance before leaving Cairo.

3. On my return from Omdurman with Father Ohrwalder and the two nuns, a sum of £300, i.e. £100 for each person.

This is the agreement between me and Monsignor Sogaro, and I have made it of my own free will and accord, and I have been in no way forced to do so by any one. Monsignor Sogaro and myself signed this agreement, and Wingate Bey, Assistant Adjutant-General, Intelligence, stands as witness. This agreement will be kept in the War Office until I return from Omdurman with the three persons above named, and I shall be dealt with in accordance with its contents.

Ahmed Hassan el Abbadi
of Sayala, Frontier Mudiria
Leon Henriot (for Monsignor Sogaro)

Cairo, 9 July 1891.

Below this, in English, is written:

> This is a private agreement between Monsignor Sogaro and Ahmed Hassan el Abbadi, who leaves Cairo for Omdurman on Friday, the 20th July, 1891, and will attempt to bring Father Ohrwalder to Egypt.
>
> Witnessed by me,
> *F. R. Wingate*
> Kaimakam
>
> A.A.-G., Intelligence, Egyptian Army
> War Office
> 9th July, 1891.

This document and all correspondence connected with it were kept sealed in the Intelligence Office of the Egyptian army.

Ahmed Hassan was given free transportation by government steamer as far as Korosko. From that point to Omdurman he was on his own, left to work his way south and make his own arrangements for the dangerous return trip. When he reached Omdurman and contacted Father Ohrwalder, the priest was so stunned that at first he did not reply when Ahmed Hassan asked him if he were coming. His mind was suddenly crowded with thoughts of the difficulties, dangers and hopes that lay in the simple statement of the Arab standing before him. Then, collecting himself, he stammered that of course he would go.

Father Ohrwalder took Ahmed Hassan into his hut and questioned him. He told of his visit to Monsignor Sogaro, who, he said, had written a letter to Father Ohrwalder, but he had not brought it with him; he had left it in Berber. He asked about the nuns and when Father Ohrwalder told him that one had just died three weeks earlier, he struck his forehead with his hand and almost wept – one-third of his reward gone; but Father Ohrwalder assured him that he would get another nun. They discussed the details of the flight and all that would have to be done before they could start, then Ahmed Hassan left him.

When he had gone, Father Ohrwalder began to have doubts of the Arab's trustworthiness. It seemed suspicious that he should arrive without a letter. Nevertheless, he at once began to scheme and plan. His first object was to get one of the sisters who was staying with a Greek to come and live with him. He feigned illness – not difficult since he was indeed overworked and so nervous that the slightest knock at the door made him jump and the sound of the ombeÿa actually made him tremble. He begged the Greek to let the nun come to help him in his work and take care of him. This was permitted.

Father Ohrwalder now had with him three women whom he proposed to take out of the Sudan: the two nuns, Sister Catarine Chincharini and Sister Elizabetta Venturini, and a little Black girl named Adila, who had been born in the mission house in Khartoum. After the fall of Khartoum, Adila and her mother had been sold as slaves and sent to Gedaref, where Adila was resold to one of Abu Anga's men for five Dervish dollars. The Dervish knew Father Ohrwalder and had once been helped by him. When he returned to Omdurman, he made him a present of the girl together with a packet of coffee. Father Ohrwalder felt it would be impossible to leave her behind.

Ahmed Hassan managed to procure camels and also to have the letter from Monsignor Sogaro brought from Berber. The letter contained only a few lines wishing him well, but Father Ohrwalder was encouraged and now had complete faith in his guide. He was also impressed by the shrewdness of Ahmed Hassan, who had not risked arousing suspicion by buying camels in the market but had kept his eyes open for a man with a good camel; when he saw one, he followed the man home, noted the place, then came back later to buy the camel. Ahmed had also engaged two trustworthy friends as camel drivers.

On 24 November the town was in an uproar over the quarrel between the Khalifa Abdullahi and the Ashraf. With the attention of the Khalifa and his people focused on the rebellion of the Ashraf, the time seemed ripe for flight. Father Ohrwalder and the nuns waited impatiently for Ahmed Hassan for three long days. On Friday the 27th, he finally appeared and said that all was ready for departure on Monday. When Father Ohrwalder reproached him for not coming earlier, he explained that one of his friends had been locked up because of a quarrel and he had had to wait until he was released. He brought good news, however: all the riding camels had been dispatched from the Beit el Mal on business connected with the Khalifa's problems with the Ashraf. Thus, immediate pursuit would be impossible.

On Sunday evening, 29 November 1891, Father Ohrwalder returned home about nine o'clock in the evening and found Ahmed Hassan waiting for him. He said his friends had made a mistake and had brought in the camels a day early. They should start at once. Father Ohrwalder locked his house and took the key with him.

The two nuns each mounted behind an Arab and Father

Ohrwalder took Adila behind him on his camel. The camels were restive and the Arabs had difficulty keeping them quiet. Fortunately, it was a cold night and most of the people were in their huts. A few women were cooking at open fires, but there was no alarm. The camels ran swiftly. Father Ohrwalder listened intently for possible pursuers, but there were none. They were soon hurrying along in the darkness out of Omdurman and along the bank of the Nile: northwards towards Egypt.

A cold north wind was blowing in their faces, and Father Ohrwalder wrapped a large turban around his head so that only his eyes were exposed. They came upon several villages, but the barking dogs always gave them warning and they skirted the houses. The track narrowed and led them through thick bushes; hands, feet and clothes were torn by thorns; they dared not check their pace. They crossed dry stream-beds and the camels stumbled on the stones in the dark; sometimes camels and riders fell, but there was no time to think of cuts and bruises; they picked themselves up and re-mounted as quickly as possible. Their life depended on the speed of the camels and the endurance of men, women and beasts.

Just at dawn they neared the village of Wad Bishara, which was considered a normal two days' march from Omdurman. They beat their camels to get past the village before daybreak. Then they left the banks of the Nile and detoured into the desert, for they dared not be seen along the banks of the river during the day. Up and down hills and across long stretches of sandy plain they rode, tense and fearful. With daylight, they could see in the distance off to their right the thin strip of green that marked the course of the Nile. The sun beat down on them and the heat rose from the sand; their eyes grew red, swollen and painful.

It was nearly mid-morning before they made their first halt, and that was brief: a little biscuit, a drink of water, the saddles re-adjusted, and they were again up and on their way. Father Ohrwalder's thoughts returned to Omdurman. Had their flight been discovered yet? What would happen to the other Europeans when their escape was known? How long would it take them to find riding camels and start the pursuit? His thoughts were broken by the fall of one of the exhausted nuns from her camel. She lay unconscious on the ground. They stopped, picked her up, splashed a little water on her face until she revived and then lifted her back on the camel and tied her firmly to the saddle. They had to go on.

Occasionally they came across Arab shepherds tending their herds of goats in the desert. Ahmed always rode somewhat behind the others and it was he who stopped to answer the questions of curious shepherds. He painted a picture of great confusion in Omdurman, with the two khalifas fighting openly for power; he told how all day and night the sound of rifle and cannon echoed through the streets. He said that the fleeing group was composed of fugitives from this disorder who, fearing the disturbed state of the country, had decided to avoid the brigands that would doubtless be on the main routes. Ahmed was believed; they were wise to fly, they said; and they gave him milk for his party.

Although the guides knew the main road well, they had never been over this exact route. In their haste they suddenly found themselves close to the Nile again and among the houses of a village before they knew it. On Ahmed's advice, they slowed their camels to a walk to avoid the appearance of undue haste, but even so a party of Gellabas eyed them suspiciously when they passed. When they had cleared the village, Father Ohrwalder reproached Ahmed for misguiding them, but he replied cheerfully, 'Allah marakna!' (Allah has delivered us!).

When they had again made their way a safe distance from the river, they stopped to eat a light meal of dates and water and to stretch their cramped legs, which were so stiff they could not stand up straight. Although they longed for sleep, they were off as soon as the camels had finished eating their durra. They watered at Gubat and then cautiously skirted the town of El Metemma.

Father Ohrwalder and Ahmed discussed how and where they would cross the Nile. Ahmed had a friend in a village just south of Berber, and he thought they would be able to cross there. They were trotting towards this village when suddenly a man sprang up in front of them and cried, 'Who are you?' Ahmed halted to answer, while the rest of the party rode on. As it turned out, the man was simply afraid they were robbers and their sudden appearance had startled him. When they drew close to the village, they dismounted and hid in some thick bushes while Ahmed went in search of his friend. He came back in half an hour with discouraging news: it was impossible to cross the river here at this time because the one boat that could take them was on the other side; he also learned that two steamers had recently passed down river carrying the news that the disturbances in Omdurman had ended; however, the villagers apparently had heard nothing of their flight.

That evening, after their third day, they came down to the river to water the camels and fill their waterskins almost directly opposite Berber. Then they retreated again into the desert. About midnight they stopped, as Ahmed was unsure of the route in the dark. The camels were fed and the weary fugitives ate a few biscuits. From his friend in the village, Ahmed had obtained tobacco and some earthenware pipes. The men smoked and for a few minutes relaxed. They began to feel that their escape was now almost assured. But they still had to cross the Nile.

They were in the saddle again at dawn and on their way, travelling now over a stony plateau which was unfamiliar to their guides. All day they plodded through narrow valleys filled with large stones washed down by torrents. Towards evening they sighted the river again and descended towards it through a narrow gorge. Once on the plain, the guides recognized the road. They were near the village of Benga just south of Abu Hamed, where they hoped to find boats to carry them across.

As they approached Benga, looking carefully in all directions, they spied three camelmen making off in the direction of Abu Hamed. Fear gripped the Arab guides: they felt sure that word of the escape had been carried to Berber and that now camelmen were dashing ahead to warn the emir of Abu Hamed to intercept them. Father Ohrwalder tried to convince them that this was impossible, but the Arabs gloomily remained unconvinced.

Hiding in a khor among some bushes while Ahmed's companions went to the river, some four miles away, to reconnoitre, Father Ohrwalder, Adila and the nuns, numbed with fatigue, stretched themselves out to sleep. During the three and a half days they had been travelling, they had slept only four hours. They were thoroughly exhausted; the biscuits, dates and water were not enough to keep up their strength, the unaccustomed camel riding had made them so stiff they could scarcely move, and the cuts they had received the first night plunging through the thorn bushes had produced painful wounds. But for Father Ohrwalder, the alarm of the guides at the appearance of the camelmen and his own anxiety about the river crossing drove away all sleep.

Just as the sun was setting, their two Arab friends returned. They had learned that nothing was known of their flight and that the three fast-riding camelmen had had nothing to do with them; also, they had made arrangements with a boatman to ferry them across the Nile, telling him that they were conducting a small party of slaves to the emir of Abu Hamed.

As soon as it was dark, they moved to the river and dismounted close to the bank. They saw boys rowing a rather large boat, but there was no sign of the boatman. When eventually he arrived, he declared it was too late to take them across the river that night; they would have to wait until morning. Ahmed argued with him, but he would not be moved.

Meanwhile, the two boys in the large boat had landed and offered to take them across. The offer was eagerly accepted, and all were soon crowded on board. When they reached the opposite bank, Ahmed gave the boys two Dervish dollars and they kissed his hand in gratitude. After watering the camels and hurriedly filling the waterskins, the fugitives pressed on their way north.

They rode all that night and all the next day over lonely desert without seeing a soul; only the antelopes and hyenas looked at them inquisitively as they passed. The weather turned oppressively hot and they were frequently deceived by mirages. The camels, so high-spirited when they left Omdurman, now had to be flogged forward. Their high, fat humps had shrunk to half their original size, and their feet were so worn that treading on a stone made them jump sideways. During the night the lead camel suddenly swerved and they heard the hiss of a snake in the dark. No one was hurt, but to the Arab guides the encounter was a bad omen.

About nine o'clock the next morning they sighted the hills which were their landmark, indicating the place where they hoped to water. They expected to reach them in about three hours, but somehow they went too far east, and failed to discover the mistake for several hours, so that it was nearly midnight instead of midday when they reached the hills. The road here passed through a narrow funnel-like valley through which the wind blew fiercely, cutting their faces. They moved down the rocky path through the valley to the river. At this point the Nile flowed rapidly and silently at the foot of a great cliff. They were about six miles south of Abu Hamed. This was to be their last watering before plunging into the great Nubian desert. A few dom palms and shrubs had gained a slender footing on the steep bank, and the reflection of the bright stars on the silent river gave an impression of solitude and peace.

Father Ohrwalder scooped up the water in his hands and cleaned the dust from his parched throat. Then he helped unsaddle and water the camels; he filled the water-bags and, last of all, ate a few biscuits. His face and eyes burned and ached and he longed to bathe them in the river, but there was no time. Ahmed gave the word to saddle the camels and mount, and he did not protest. The nuns were too stiff and exhausted to move unaided and had to be lifted on to the camels. But everyone felt that the worst was over now. It was past midnight; they would soon be deep in the desert and before them lay Egypt and safety.

The sound of a camel jerked them into alertness. Egypt and safety were still far away. They were only twenty paces from the river. In the starlight they could see the camel's rider, half hidden by the dom palm he was using as cover. He was armed with a Remington. They halted and Ahmed and his two friends dismounted and walked towards the stranger, Ahmed switching his rifle to his left hand and holding his right out in a friendly greeting. Father Ohrwalder and the nuns sat numbly on their camels and watched as the stranger dismounted and joined the guides. It was fortunately too dark for him to notice the white skins of the priest and the women, so that when he asked if they were slaves, Ahmed answered readily that they were. It was the wrong answer. The stranger was a guard set there to prevent the very thing Ahmed claimed to be doing. No merchant was to export slaves into Egypt by order of the emir of Abu Hamed. With a slight motion of his Remington, the guard said that they would have to go to the emir.

While Ahmed argued and cajoled, one of the guides returned to where Father Ohrwalder and the nuns sat on their camels doing their best to look calm. When he told them what had happened, Father Ohrwalder groped in his robes for the long knife he had carried with him and handed it to the guide. He must do his best to bribe the guard, he told him, but if that failed – 'Well, we are four men to one.'

They watched in apprehension as the guide rejoined the gesticulating group. It seemed to Father Ohrwalder that they would never stop talking, but at last Ahmed and the other guides crossed briskly to where they waited, and, hurriedly mounting their camels, gave the signal to go on. He had given the guard twenty Dervish dollars, Ahmed said, for a promise not to betray them, but he did not trust him – perhaps rightly, for he was of the same tribe that had lured Colonel Stewart and Frank Power to their deaths.

This incident was a forcible reminder that they were still in the Sudan, and the Sudan was ruled by the Khalifa Abdullahi. Fear drove away fatigue and they raced off into the desert night, beating their tired camels. They rode all that night and all the next day. Evening found them in some hills where they dismounted and ate their last mouthful of biscuit. A short rest and they were off again.

Sleep was their worst enemy. They shouted at each other to keep awake. They told stories; they pinched themselves; they made sudden jerks. 'Don't sleep,' Ahmed kept saying. 'Don't sleep.' They rode through the night and on through the next day. Father Ohrwalder's arm ached from beating his camel, but the poor beast could hardly keep moving. Hunger, fatigue and sleeplessness were having their effect. They could not go on like this much longer.

Shortly before sunset they turned down a khor leading to the wells at Murat. A fort protecting the wells was just visible on a hill. Over the fort they could make out the flag: red with the white crescent and star. 'Ahmed!' Father Ohrwalder shouted, 'Greet the flag of freedom!' Ahmed seized his rifle and fired a series of shots in the air. The camels seemed to sense the end of the journey and pulled themselves together for the last effort.

Ahmed's shots created a stir in the fort, where at first the soldiers thought they were being attacked. Then they saw the little band of refugees and rode out to meet them. It was 8 December – the Feast of the Immaculate Conception, as Father Ohrwalder always remembered. Their ten-day flight was over. It was, as Father Ohrwalder later described it, a 'delicious moment'. They were free.

They were taken to the commandant's house where they were showered with questions and kindness. A week later they were aboard a steamer for Assiut, where they were met by two representatives of the Cairo mission. On 21 December 1891 they reached Cairo by train. Ahmed Hassan and his companions went with them and were given their reward.

Father Ohrwalder wrote:

The rapid transition from barbarism to civilization, our pleasant journey from Korosko to Cairo, intercourse with educated people, the incessant change of scene, all affected us greatly; but our joy and delight at being free was somewhat saddened by the thought of the sufferings of our poor companions in our adversity, whom we had left behind in slavery and captivity.

Slatin: The Man with the Needles

'He who lives long sees much,' Madibbo had said, and Slatin, though still a young man, was learning how very true this was, for in his twelve years of captivity he had indeed seen much. He had witnessed the rise of the first African state in modern times to be created by the will and power of its own people. He had seen, too, at first hand this vast nation effectively ruled by a man who could neither read nor write, and who until the age of thirty-five had been a simple tribesman; Abdullahi had not even been a sheikh in his own tribe before the trust placed in him by the Mahdi catapulted him to a position of power and influence, a position he was able to maintain and strengthen when the Mahdi died, and he was forced to rely solely upon his will and abilities.

Slatin saw the Khalifa as an immoral, unjust, barbaric tyrant, cunning, cruel and vain – which he was. But his political accomplishments were astonishing. Without ever leaving his self-made capital of Omdurman, he ruled a wild array of diverse people scattered over hundreds of thousands of square miles. If he was cruel, it must be remembered that he ruled barbarous peoples; if he was cunning, this was a necessary attribute for such a ruler; if he was vain, this is, after all, a very human quality – and Abdullahi had reason enough to be vain and flatterers enough to cultivate his vanity. Despite his faults and his handicaps, he controlled the Sudan more effectively than had Gordon or any of the Egyptian governors who preceded him.

The difficulties in administering such an empire were, of course, immense; and in addition to keeping the Sudan, the Khalifa wanted to keep the promises of the Mahdi to extend Mahdism beyond the Sudan. Attempts were made to do this in the direction of Abyssinia and Egypt.

On 12 April 1887 four Dervishes appeared at the outpost of the Anglo-Egyptian Frontier Field Force at Wadi Halfa. They were bearers of letters from the Khalifa addressed to the Khedive of Egypt, the Sultan of Turkey and the Queen of England. The messengers were sent on to Cairo. All their letters were to the same end, calling upon these rulers to believe in the Mahdi and submit to the will of his successor, the Khalifa Abdullahi. The language was beautiful, terrible and naïve. The letter to Queen Victoria read in part:

> If you will believe and testify that there is no god but Allah, and that Mohammed is the apostle of Allah, and if you follow the Mahdi – grace be on him – and become subject to my rule, I will receive you and give you tidings of prosperity and safety from the torments of the fire. You will be secure and content. What is for me will be for you; what is against me will be against you. A love in Allah will arise between us, and He will pardon you all the sins you have committed in the time of your unbelief. . . . But if you refuse . . . trusting to your supplies of war and your armies, then know that you are in great error, and against all your preparations and plans we have where-withal to meet them – the true faith, to which Allah the almighty king assures victory and support. . . . None have strength to resist Him, and none have means to overthrow Him, for the might of Allah is victor-ious, not to be withstood, and His force is terrible, and not to be clashed against. . . .
>
> For the men of the Mahdi are men of iron. Allah gave them a nature to love death. He made it sweeter for them than cool water to the thirsty. Hence are they terrible to the unbelievers. . . . They regard in everything nought save Allah by reason of their trust in their mighty Lord. They care not for the life of this world, the transient, the enchanted with magic, but they look instead for eternal bliss and dainty living to be allotted to them in the world to come. . . .

Queen, Sultan and Khedive ignored the letters and the call to become Mahdists. Two years later the Khalifa sent another letter to Queen Victoria, as well as more letters to the Khedive and to Baring. It was shortly after this that the Khalifa ordered the abortive invasion of Egypt that ended with the defeat of Wad Ne-jumi at the battle of Toski on 3 August 1889.

In November 1893 the Khalifa dispatched an army under Wad Ali to the south-eastern Sudan. But Wad Ali had no greater success than Wad Nejumi. He encountered Italian troops at Agordot who defeated his army and killed him. The Italians then advanced and occupied Kassala.

The management of his vast country was particularly difficult for the Khalifa since he had seen nothing of civilization and, with the exception of a few ex-government clerks, he had no administrators to assist him. But he did remarkably well. He appointed emirs to be in charge of various regions and different elements of his army; he established a system of courts, with lesser courts in the provinces and a kind of supreme court in Omdurman, and appointed their kadis; he also appointed officials to be in charge of the principal government functions, of which the chief was probably the treasurer in charge of the Beit el Mal. The only model for government administration that he or any of his people had seen was the corrupt, inefficient and discredited Egyptian government in the Sudan. If Abdullahi did not improve on this system, his government was not much worse; it was certainly designed for maximum personal control, and this was his aim.

Slatin described the postal system as 'very primitive', but it worked. The Khalifa kept from sixty to eighty riding camels and built up a specially selected staff of postmen whom he dispatched to all the parts of his empire. Ibrahim Adlan once suggested to him that he should establish a system of post stations with relays of camels and riders, but the Khalifa rejected this idea. In this he was undoubtedly wise, for he placed a special value on the verbal reports of the postmen. He questioned them personally and often learned more than was contained in the dispatches concerning the attitudes, actions and personal behaviour of his emirs. Illiteracy has its advantages and the Khalifa avoided the common error of most administrators: over-reliance on the written word.

The Khalifa's justice, administered by his kadis, was founded upon Muslim religious law as modified by the 'instructions' of the Mahdi and, from time to time, by the visions of the Khalifa. Under this system, the evidence of witnesses was inviolable, but it was the prerogative of the judges to accept or refuse witnesses, and the accused was not permitted to protest. As the salary was low and the judges venal, the rich and influential had much less to fear than the poor and unknown.

The Khalifa imposed a wide variety of taxes on various types of products and activities. Stable businesses and industries, being the easiest to reach, were the most heavily taxed – to their detriment – a mistake frequently made by more sophisticated governments both before and since. The taxes, though often oppressive and collected with a ruthless efficiency, do not appear to have been much worse, nor collected with greater brutality, than under the Egyptian administration.

There was, however, comparatively little industry or trade, certainly less than there had been under the old régime. A surreptitious trade with Egypt was gradually resumed and a few European goods trickled into the country, but for the most part, the

Sudan was cut off from commercial dealings with the outside world. There was one business, though, that prospered mightily: slavery. The main trade was in women and children; male slaves were generally the property of the Khalifa. In Omdurman anyone with a male slave to sell took him to the Beit el Mal, where he was paid only a nominal price; the slave was then incorporated into the army or, if unsuitable for this purpose, was sent off to work on one of the Khalifa's private estates. Women were bought and sold everywhere and were regarded as the principal measure of wealth.

The slave market in Omdurman was located a short distance to the south-east of the Beit el Mal in an open space in the centre of which was a mud-brick building. Here professional slave dealers displayed their wares and buyers inspected the merchandise offered. Slatin visited the market several times, with the Khalifa's permission, under the pretext that he wanted to buy or sell slaves. He has left a graphic picture of the way in which the market operated:

> Round the walls of the house numbers of women and girls stand or sit. They vary from the decrepit and aged half-clad slaves of the working class to the gaily-decked Surya (concubine); and as the trade is looked upon as a perfectly natural and lawful business, those put up for sale are carefully examined from head to foot, without the least restriction, just as if they were animals. The mouth is opened to see if the teeth are in good condition. The upper part of the body and the back are laid bare; and the arms carefully looked at. They are then told to take a few steps backward or forward in order that their movements and gait may be examined. A series of questions are put to them to test their knowledge of Arabic. In fact, they have to submit to any examination the intending purchaser may wish to make.
>
> Suryas, of course, vary considerably in price; but the whole matter is treated by the slaves without the smallest concern. They consider it perfectly natural, and have no notion of being treated otherwise. Only occasionally one can see by the expression of a woman or girl that she feels this close scrutiny; possibly her position with her former master was rather that of a servant than a slave, or she may have been looked upon almost as a member of the family, and may have been brought to this unhappy position by force of circumstances, or through some hateful inhumanity on the part of her former master. When the intending purchaser has completed his scrutiny, he then refers to the dealer, asks him what he paid for her, or if he has any other better ware for sale. He will probably complain that her face is not pretty enough, that her body is not sufficiently developed, that she does not speak Arabic, and so on, with the object of reducing the price as much as possible; whilst, on the other hand, the owner will do his utmost to

show up her good qualities, charms, etc., into the detail of which it is not necessary to enter here. Amongst the various 'secret defects' which oblige the owner to reduce his price are snoring, bad qualities of character, such as thieving, and many others; but when at last the sale has been finally arranged, the paper is drawn out and signed, the money paid, and the slave becomes the property of her new master.

Slaves were always paid for in local currency, called Omla Gedida dollars. Although the rates varied according to the market or special demands for a particular race, in general prices ran something like this:

Old working slave	50–80	dollars
Middle-aged woman	80–100	
Little girls (8–11)	110–160	
Concubines	180–700	

As a comparison, here are some prices of other chattels:

Baggage camel	60–80	dollars
Riding camel	200–400	
Abyssinian horse	60–120	
Cow	100–160	
Calf	30–50	
Sheep	5–20	

Under the Egyptian government, both Maria Theresa dollars and Medjidie (Turkish or Egyptian dollars) had circulated in the Sudan. There were at least nine different 'Dervish dollars' minted at various times, the latest being the Omla Gedida, or 'new money'. In the Sudan at this time it took eight Omla Gedida dollars to equal one Medjidie and five to equal a Maria Theresa dollar, that hardy coin with the buxom Queen of Hungary and Bohemia stamped on it which is still minted and which still circulates in many Middle East countries.

Sexual morality, by European standards, was extremely low. Slatin knew of many men who had married forty or fifty times in the space of ten years, never having more than the authorized four wives at any one time. There were also many women who had had almost an equal number of husbands. Merchants sometimes pimped for their female slaves, taking a percentage of their income. According to Slatin, the greatest immorality existed among the mulazemin. They frequently exchanged wives and there was a considerable amount of homosexuality among them.

Originally the mulazemin constituted a relatively small group of men who were part of the Khalifa's household. Later, he expanded this body into a small army of about 12,000 men which was considered his personal bodyguard. It was divided into three corps under the command of the Khalifa's younger brother, a nephew and his own son, Osman. The mulazemin, with their women and children, camped around the house of the Khalifa, guarding him and his personal household of 400 wives and concubines, eunuchs, servants, personal mulazemin and close relatives. And beyond the bodyguard was his own tribe and then other Baggara tribes, shielding him from the Danagla and the other Nile tribes whom he distrusted.

Living in the centre of this spider's web of power, Slatin had a unique opportunity to see what no other European and few Sudanese were able to see. And what he saw was not conducive to a sense of personal security, for he saw the Khalifa ruin not only his enemies but his friends as well when they grew powerful and in a position to do him harm. Only his relatives remained in his confidence. Even Zeki Tummal, who had done so much of the Khalifa's dirty work, at last ran foul of Yakub; he was thrown into prison and slowly starved to death. Things were never done by halves in the Sudan; seven of Zeki's brothers and close relatives were also killed, and his sister was flogged to death.

Over the years Slatin had constantly dreamed of ways and means of escaping, but he was closely watched and the Khalifa had forbidden him to move about the city or to talk with those with whom he might have plotted. When Slatin learned of Father Ohrwalder's escape, he fervently hoped that it would be successful, but with Lupton dead and Father Ohrwalder gone he felt completely deserted. 'He was the only man with whom I was intellectually on a par,' Slatin said of Father Ohrwalder, 'and with whom I could – though very rarely – talk a few words in my mother tongue.' The day following Ohrwalder's escape the Khalifa accused Slatin of helping the priest to escape. 'He is of your own race and is in communication with you,' said the Khalifa. 'Why did you not draw my attention to the possibility so that I could have taken precautions? I am positive you knew of his intention to escape!'

'Sidi, pardon me!' Slatin exclaimed. 'How could I know of his intention to escape? And how could I tell you that he had done so? Since the outbreak of the revolt attempted by your God-forsaken enemies, and which, thanks to the Almighty, you have now defeated by your wisdom, I have not moved day or night from my post. Had I known that he was a traitor, I should have at once told you.'

Slatin was forgiven this time, but not long after the arrest of Khalifa Sherif a more serious charge was made against him. A man arrived in Omdurman from Cairo, having been passed on by Yunes, who was now in charge of the area around Dongola. He was received personally by the Khalifa in the presence of all the kadis. Slatin, who had a foreboding that this man had something to do with him, tried to find out from one of the kadis what the messenger had said. The kadi told him not to be afraid, but to pretend to have no interest in the matter. After prayers, the kadis and messenger were again with the Khalifa. When they had finished, Slatin saw that the messenger had been bound and sent off to the prison.

The next day the Khalifa summoned Slatin and in the presence of all the kadis he said, 'Where there is no fire there is no smoke, but with you there is a great deal of smoke. The messenger said yesterday that you are a government spy, and that your monthly salary is paid to your representative in Cairo who forwards it to you here. He says he has seen your signature in the government office in Egypt, and that you assisted Yusef el Gasis (Joseph the Priest), to escape. He also says you are pledged to the English, in case of an attack on Omdurman, to seize the powder and ammunition stores, which they know are situated opposite your house. What have you to say in your defence?'

Once again Slatin's quick mind and glib tongue saved him; but he was almost too glib. He ended his speech to the Khalifa by asking rhetorically: 'Sidi, I rely upon your justice, which is well known to all; will you sacrifice one who has been for so many years your devoted servant to the whim of a Dongolawi who is one of your enemies?'

'How do you know the man is a Dongolawi?' asked the Khalifa quickly.

By the merest chance, Slatin had heard the man's name and knew that he was a Dongolawi who had once before been in Omdurman with Nejumi, so he replied, 'Some time ago, I saw the man at your gate with Abderrahman Wad Nejumi. Because of his forwardness and impudence, I had to call on your mulazemin to remove him by main force. No doubt he now wishes to revenge himself, and at the same time curry favour with you, by casting suspicion on me. You to whom Allah has given wisdom to govern your subjects, will also judge me righteously and fairly.'

With a warning to be more careful in the future, the Khalifa repeated the Arab proverb: 'Where there is no fire, there is no smoke.' He then signed to Slatin that he was dismissed.

That night Slatin talked with a friend whom he could trust and asked what had happened after he had left. The Khalifa had admitted the man was a liar, his friend told him, but he had added that there might still be some truth in what the man had said.

The following morning after prayers, Slatin was on his way home when he was overtaken by Gereifawi, the man who had succeeded Adlan as head of the Beit el Mal. Slatin knew him well and was on friendly terms with him.

'You are a rare visitor,' Slatin greeted him. 'Please Allah you have good reason for it.'

'Yes, but I come to disturb you,' Gereifawi said. 'I require your house, and I must ask you to leave it today. I will give you one in place of it which lies to the south-east of the mosque and in which the Khalifa's guests are usually housed. It is somewhat smaller than your own, but you have only the road between it and the mosque, and this will thoroughly suit a religious man like you!'

'All right, but tell me privately who sent you here, the Khalifa or Yakub?'

'Ah! That is a secret!' he said, laughing. 'But after your conversation with the Khalifa yesterday, I'm sure you can understand the reason. Probably,' he said ironically, 'our master, out of his great love for you, wishes to have you close to him. Your house is about two hundred paces from his. When may I take over your old house?'

'I shall be finished moving by evening, but it will take me some time to move the fodder for my horse and mule. Is the new house vacant?'

'Of course. I have given orders for it to be cleaned, and I will now go back and make the necessary arrangements. You had better begin moving at once. I hope your new house brings you better luck than your old one.'

So the Khalifa, although he did not believe the Dongolawi, thought it best to move Slatin away from the ammunition stores. Slatin's household cursed when told of the move. Little by little, year by year, they had made themselves more comfortable. A well had been dug, lemon and pomegranate trees had been planted, and the house itself made quite liveable. Slatin, although he lived perilously, now lived comfortably. Even in his work he was no longer required to walk barefooted in the dust beside the Khalifa's horse but rode a horse of his own. Still, the suspicions of the Khalifa made his existence precarious.

One of Slatin's duties was to wind and generally take care of the

Khalifa's numerous watches and clocks, of which he was very fond. Under the pretext of having a watch or clock repaired, he would sometimes visit an Armenian watchmaker named Artin and arrange to meet friends there from time to time and exchange news. Sometimes, too, he was able to meet friends at the mosque. At first the only person to whom he confided his longing to escape was Ibrahim Adlan, who promised to help him. But Adlan was executed shortly after Slatin's confidence. Later he told his desire to two other influential friends, but they were too frightened of the Khalifa to risk helping him. Help would have to come from the outside.

In September 1886 the British government allotted £500 for the rescue of Slatin and Lupton, although there was some dispute over the sum: Captain H. Fitzgerald, Intelligence Officer with the Frontier Field Force understood that he could spend £500 for Lupton and £450 for Slatin; General Frederick Stephenson thought it was only £500 for the two of them. Sheikh Saleh of the Kababish was offered £450 if he could bring Lupton out, but nothing came of this. Slatin's family had placed a considerable amount of money with the Austrian Consul-General in Cairo, begging him to do all he could to aid him and, if possible, effect his escape. Many diplomatic and military people in the officialdom of Cairo interested themselves in aiding Slatin and the other European prisoners, but those who took the most pains and were the most helpful were Major Francis Reginald Wingate, chief of the Intelligence Department of the Egyptian army, and Baron Heidler von Egeregg, Austrian Consul-General and later an ambassador. It was they who were successful in smuggling sums of money to Slatin from time to time. He never received the whole sum, but he usually got a part of it and he was always grateful for that.

One day early in February 1892 only two months after Father Ohrwalder's escape, a man named Babakr Wad Abu Sebiba, former chief of the Dongola camel postmen, arrived in Omdurman from Egypt. He claimed to have escaped from Aswan and begged the Khalifa to allow him to live in Berber. His request was granted. As he was coming out of the mosque, he nudged Slatin and whispered, 'I have come for you. Arrange for an interview.'

'Tomorrow after evening prayers, here in the mosque,' Slatin said quickly.

The next evening, when everyone else had left the mosque, Babakr appeared and Slatin followed him to the thatched portion of the building, in the shade and out of sight and hearing. Babakr handed him a small tin box which smelled of coffee. 'This box has a double bottom,' he said. 'Open and read the papers inside. I shall be here tomorrow at the same time.'

Concealing the box under his jibba, Slatin returned to his post in front of the Khalifa's door. That evening he was summoned to have dinner with the Khalifa. The box was large enough to make a sizeable bulge under his jibba and he had to sit opposite the lynx-eyed Khalifa, but fortunately the Khalifa was tired and noticed nothing. He rambled on, talking of general subjects, but not omitting to adjure him to be loyal. After eating a little meat and durra, Slatin pretended to be taken suddenly ill. The Khalifa excused him and he hurried home.

Once inside his house, he lit a small oil lamp and with his knife tore open the false bottom of the box. Inside was a tiny slip of paper that simply said that Babakr Wad Abu Sebiba was a trustworthy man. The writer had wisely omitted his own name in case the paper should fall into Mahdist hands.

The next evening Slatin again met Babakr in the mosque. Babakr whispered that he had come to arrange his escape. Having now contacted him, he would return to Berber and make the arrangements. Slatin assured him that he was ready to make the attempt at any time; Babakr promised to return in July.

Slatin impatiently waited the five months for Babakr's return. When at last he came, there was another secret meeting in the mosque. As his first piece of news Babakr told him that in order to avoid suspicion he had taken a wife in Berber. He had not yet completed all the arrangements, he confessed, but he had planned the route: they would go through the Bayuda desert and west of Dongola to Wadi Halfa. Slatin listened with a sinking heart. He knew that camels could not possibly make a forced march over this route in the height of summer; he saw all too plainly that the man was not eager to make the journey and preferred to spend more time in the Sudan with his new wife. Slatin sadly agreed that the trip would have to be postponed until December.

Months passed; December came and went; Babakr did not return until the following July. This time he brought two camels with him, but he well knew that flight was impossible at this time of year. Shortly after, Babakr came under suspicion and fled alone to Egypt, where he reported that although he was frequently in Omdurman, Slatin had persistently refused to attempt the flight.

Fortunately Major Wingate and Baron Heidler did not believe Babakr's story. A more elaborate scheme was set up by the summer of 1894. In June of that year, a man called Ahmed came to Slatin and told him that all was arranged for his flight and that a change of camels was set up in the desert. On 1 July Ahmed informed him that the camels for the first stage of the journey had arrived with the guides and that they should be ready to leave the following evening. It was the wrong time of year, but by now Slatin was willing to take a chance.

That evening Slatin told his servants that he had the Khalifa's permission to visit a sick friend and that they should not be concerned if he stayed with him all night. As soon as the Khalifa retired for the night, Slatin met Ahmed and set off for the edge of town where the camels and the Arab guides were to meet them. Barefoot and armed with only a sword, Slatin hurried through the darkness past the parade ground and through the cemetery. Rain had fallen during the day and had washed out some of the shallow graves. Slatin stepped into one and caught his foot in the bones of a skeleton, twisting his ankle. It seemed to him that the dead as well as the living were conspiring to prevent his escape.

In spite of the pain, Slatin hurried on after Ahmed until they reached the spot where the camels and guides were to be. No one was there. They searched the whole area, their bodies bathed in sweat from their efforts and from fear that their plans had been discovered. Just before dawn they gave up. Slatin hurried back to his house, where he found one of his fellow mulazemin with a message from the Khalifa asking why he had been absent from morning prayers. Slatin told him he was ill, and his wretched appearance from lack of sleep, the pain in his foot and his bitter disappointment made the excuse plausible enough. It was not until two days later he learned that the Arab guides had decided at the last moment that the venture was too dangerous.

Slatin's family were never daunted by the many unsuccessful escape attempts for which they supplied the money. They went on paying anyone who seemed able to make a try, sure that some day a plan would succeed. Father Ohrwalder, after his own escape, visited the Slatin family in Austria and brought back to Egypt with him a supply of mysterious 'ether pills' compounded by a Professor Ottokar Chiari. They were supposed to be strengthening for a hard journey and to ward off sleep. With great difficulty and at considerable risk to the bearer, these were sent to Slatin in Omdurman. When they finally arrived, Slatin carefully buried the small bottle in the ground near his house until the time when they would be needed.

One day Slatin was given a slip of paper by a Suakin merchant who came to Omdurman. On it was written:

> We are sending you Osheikh Karrar, who will hand you some needles, by which you will recognize him. He is a faithful and brave man. You can trust him. Kind regards from Wingate.
>
> Ohrwalder

It was about the middle of January 1895 when a man passed Slatin in the street and made a sign to follow him. As Slatin brushed against him he said, 'I am the man with the needles.'

Slatin had a feeling that this time he would really be able to make his escape. He led the man into a small niche in the outside wall of his hut. There the man gave him three needles and a slip of paper which vouched for his trustworthiness. He said that although he had come with the intention of taking Slatin out by way of Kassala, he was now unable to do so. Slatin's hopes dissolved as he explained that there was now a string of forts along the way he had intended to go; that one of his camels had died; that he had lost money in a business transaction and now did not have enough to make the escape arrangements. He begged Slatin to give him a paper for Major Wingate asking for more money.

Sick with disappointment, Slatin was returning to his house when he found a man named Mohammed walking beside him. Mohammed whispered, 'We are ready. The camels are bought; the guides are engaged. The time arranged for your escape is during the moon's last quarter next month. Be ready!' Then, without waiting for a reply, he vanished.

It suddenly seemed that people were trying to help him from all directions. Major Wingate and Father Ohrwalder had engaged the first man and Major Wingate with Baron Heidler had engaged the second. Slatin now began to be alarmed that with so many people plotting his escape he would be betrayed. If the Khalifa discovered the plan, he was a dead man.

On 17 February 1895, a Sunday, Mohammed again appeared. The camels would arrive the next day, he announced; they would have to rest for two days, so the attempt would be made on the night of the 20th. He would contact Slatin again on Tuesday and tell him if all was ready. He emphasized that Slatin must do all in his power to give them as long a head start as possible.

Tuesday night Mohammed was waiting for Slatin at the door of the mosque. In a hurried whisper he said that all was ready. That night, Slatin was too excited to sleep and only managed to doze for a couple of hours towards dawn. In the morning he asked permission of the head mulazemin to stay at home. He was sick, he said; too sick to get up. Permission was granted and Slatin took a dose of senna tea and tamarind to calm his nerves and rested as quietly as he could in his house.

Just before sunset he assembled his servants and made them promise to keep secret what he was about to say. He then told them that the man who seven years earlier had brought him letters, money and watches from his relatives had again arrived in Omdurman with another consignment for him. He said the Khalifa did not know about the visit and that he intended to secretly meet with the man that night. He anticipated receiving a considerable amount of money, he said, and gave them each several dollars, with a promise of more to come. To make the story seem even more authentic, he asked one of his servants, Ahmed, to meet him at sunrise at the northern end of the city with his mule. He told them not to worry if he was late, but to tell any of the mulazemin that might ask for him that he had been sick during the night and had ridden off with Ahmed to seek the advice of a man, whose whereabouts they did not know, but whom they supposed would cure him. Slatin knew, of course, that the deception would be discovered soon enough, but he also knew that every hour was precious to him and he wanted every minute he could get, even at the possible expense of his servants' lives.

That night, three hours after sunset, Slatin took a rifle, his prayer rug and his farda, and went across the mosque to the road that led north. The night was dark and there was a cold northerly wind. He heard a low cough, Mohammed's signal, and he stood still. Mohammed had brought a donkey. Slatin quickly mounted behind him and they rode off. They reached the edge of town without meeting a soul. From behind a small ruined house standing obliquely to the road came a man with a saddled camel. Mohammed quickly introduced him: 'This is your guide. His name is Zeki Belal. He will guide you to the riding camels that are waiting concealed in the desert. Make haste. A happy journey, and may Allah protect you!'

Zeki mounted and Slatin climbed on behind him. After an hour's ride they came to the place where another man was waiting with more camels hidden among some low trees. As Slatin mounted the camel assigned to him, he suddenly remembered something. 'Zeki,' he said, 'did Mohammed give you the medicine?'

'No. What medicine?'

'They call them ether pills. They keep off sleep and strengthen you on a journey.'

'Sleep!' said Zeki. He laughed. 'Do not worry about that. Fear is the child of good folk, and will keep sleep from our eyes. And Allah in his mercy will fortify us.'

He was right. There was no thought of sleep as they hurried their camels north through the halfa grass and desert. With daylight Slatin was able to see the faces of his two guides: Zeki was a young man with a downy beard; the other man, Hamed Ibn Hussein, was in the prime of life.

'How long a start have we got from your enemies?' Hamed asked. 'When will they miss you?'

'They will look for me after the morning prayer. But before all doubt is over as to my escape, and before the men and beasts are found to pursue me, some time must elapse. We can count on at least twelve or fourteen hours' start.'

'That is not much,' said Hamed, 'but if the animals are up to their work, we shall have left a good bit of ground behind us.'

'Don't you know your animals? Haven't they been tried?'

'No. Two of them are stallions of the Anafi breed, and the third a Bisharin mare, bought from friends for your flight. We must hope for the best of them.'

All morning long they rode without stopping over flat country broken only by solitary shrubs and an occasional small stony hillock. It was near midday when suddenly Zeki called, 'Halt! Let the camels kneel down. Quick!'

The camels knelt. 'Why?' asked Slatin.

'I see camels and two led horses. I fear we have been seen.'

Slatin began to load his Remington. 'But if we have been seen, it is better to ride quietly on. Our making the animals lie down will excite their suspicion,' he objected.

Hamed agreed. They raised their camels and rode on. The other party was about 2,000 yards away marching north-west, so Slatin and his guides altered their line of march to go north-east. For a few minutes they thought they had escaped detection. Then they saw one of the men in the other party mount a horse and ride swiftly towards them. Slatin gave the orders: 'Hamed, I will go slowly on with Zeki. You stop the man and answer his questions. In any case, prevent him from seeing my face. You have the money on you?'

'Yes. Good. But march slowly.'

Slatin and Zeki rode slowly on; Hamed turned back and met the horseman. About twenty minutes later, Hamed caught up with them again. 'You must thank Allah for our safety,' he cried as he rode up. 'The man is a friend of mine, a sheikh on his way to Dongola to buy dates to take to Omdurman. He asked me where I was going with the "white Egyptian". The man has the eyes of a hawk.'

'And what did you answer?' Slatin asked.

'I begged him as my friend to keep our secret, and gave him twenty Maria Theresa dollars. We Arabs are all a little avaricious. The man swore a sacred oath to me to hold his tongue if he happened to fall in with our pursuers. Urge the camels on. We have lost time.'

On they rode, all day long, not stopping until an hour after sunset, when they were about a normal day's march west of the Nile. They had ridden twenty-one hours without stopping to eat, and had only once drunk water. Now they stopped to rest the camels and to eat some bread and dates. They also tried to feed the camels, but to their dismay, the camels refused to eat. Hamed made a little fire, took a burning stick with resin on it and walked around the camels muttering some incantation.

'What are you doing?' Slatin asked.

'I fear the Khalifa's holy men have bewitched our camels. I am trying an Arab antidote.'

'For my part, I fear they are second-rate market camels, or are sick,' Slatin said. 'Let's give them a little more rest. Perhaps they will pick up.'

Another half-hour's rest and the camels still refused to eat. They tightened the saddle-girths and mounted. The camels rose obediently, but they refused to trot. All that night they rode at the camels' slow pace, and dawn found them on the high ground northwest of El Metemmeh. Fresh camels were waiting for them about a day's march north of Berber, but it was obvious that their present camels would never last that far. They forced the exhausted beasts on until they came to a place where they could stop in the shade of some trees. They discussed their situation and what they should do. It was finally decided that they should make for the Gilif Hills. Zeki and Hamed were both from the Kababish tribe, which explained their lack of love for the Khalifa, and the Gilif Hills were in their own tribal territory; they were familiar with every path.

After an afternoon's rest the camels revived sufficiently to walk at a good pace and they set off for the Gilif range, a normal day's march away. When they reached the hills, they dismounted and drove their camels before them for three hours over extremely difficult country, a valley hemmed in by sheer rock. At last they stopped and Slatin and the camel saddles were hidden among some rocks while his guides went off to water the camels. Slatin, tired and alone, was depressed. He had hoped to make a straight dash to the Egyptian frontier and outdistance his pursuers by speed. Now, because of the wretched camels, the news of his escape would fly ahead of them and the remaining portion of the journey would be slower and more dangerous.

It was decided that Slatin and Hamed should remain concealed here while Zeki rode to where the fresh camels were waiting, a two days' march away, and returned with fresh mounts. When Zeki had gone, Hamed proposed that he go to the local sheikh, who was a relative of his, and, without telling him Slatin's name, inform him of the situation. As a kinsman, he was bound to offer asylum and, in case of pursuit, he could warn them of danger. Slatin agreed, but told Hamed to take along a gift of twenty dollars. Hamed left at sunset and Slatin fell asleep among the rocks on the hard ground. In the morning Hamed returned to report that all was well.

That afternoon, while Slatin and Hamed were talking together in low tones, Slatin heard a noise behind him. He turned to see a man about 150 yards away climbing the slope opposite him and covering his face with his farda. They had obviously been seen. Hamed ran after him and a few minutes later he returned, smiling, with the stranger beside him. 'We are in luck,' Hamed called as he came up. 'He is one of my numerous relations. Our mothers are children of two sisters.'

The stranger shook hands and sat down. Slatin offered him some dates and asked, 'Who are you?'

'They call me Ali Wad Feid,' he replied. 'To be honest with you, my intentions were not well disposed to you. I was changing my pasture ground, and arrived a few days ago with my flocks at the foot of those hills which you can see from here to the south. I went to the cleft in the rocks to see if there was much water there. I found traces of a camel and followed them. When I saw the white skin of your feet sticking out of your hiding-place, I knew that a stranger was there and I tried to get away without being seen. I intended to return with a few friends at night to make your journey easier by removing your superfluous baggage. I thank Allah that my cousin here caught me up. By night I should probably not have recognized him.'

'Ali Wad Feid,' said Hamed, who had listened in silence, 'I will tell you a little story. Listen! Many years ago, when I was a little boy, in the days when the Turks ruled the land, my father was sheikh of these hills, which were then thickly peopled. One night there came a man, a fugitive, who sought asylum with my father. He was closely pursued by government troops. His women fell into the hands of his pursuers, but he himself found protection with my father, who hid him. A long while after, my father went to the seat of the government at Berber, and by money and fair words succeeded in obtaining a pardon for him and in setting his women free. That man's name was Feid . . .'

'And he was my father,' interrupted Ali, his face solemn. 'I was born later, and heard the story from my mother. What your father did for mine, his father's son will do for your father's son. In peace or in peril, I am with you. But follow me and I will show you a better hiding place.'

He led them some 2,000 yards back around the hill to a grotto formed of rock slabs and just big enough to hold two men. He left them here and it was decided that Slatin should stay in the grotto while Hamed climbed the hill and acted as a lookout. When their bread gave out and they had only dates to eat, Ali Wad Feid returned and brought them bread and milk. Ali also reported that he had been to the wells and talked with people there, but had heard nothing to make them uneasy.

They had been in hiding five days when Zeki Belal returned with fresh camels. They started out again just before sunset and rode all that night without stopping. After a brief halt, about dawn, to eat some dates and rest the camels, they rode on all that day. Slatin's guides considered this the most critical day of their flight, for they were near the Nile and had to pass through pasture grounds of river tribes. Towards evening, Slatin could see the Nile, about two miles away in the distance. They halted and took off the saddles. 'Our mission is almost over,' said Hamed. 'Stay here with the animals. We will go to a spot we know near the river. There we will find your friends, who will guide you on.'

Slatin was left alone. Tired, but feeling confident of success, he went to sleep. It was past midnight when he awoke. He was immediately concerned to find that his friends had not returned. If they did not come soon, he would not be able to cross the river that night. It was not until two hours before dawn that he heard footsteps and at last Hamed appeared.

'What news?' Slatin asked.

'None!' was the reply. 'We could not find your friends. I returned because you cannot stay here after daybreak. You are too near human habitations and run the risk of being seen. I left Zeki behind to look for your people. Take the waterskin on your shoulders and some dates. I am too exhausted to carry anything. We must go back to the plateau. You must stay hidden there among the stones until tomorrow night.'

Slatin did as he was told and followed the weary Hamed. Hamed found a spot, told Slatin to hide himself and left. Slatin made a ring of stones about a foot and a half high, as camel-herds do to keep out the cold. He left just room enough for himself, his gun and the waterskin. The sun rose and Slatin stayed hidden behind his small rock enclosure. His mind kept going backward and forward in time. He thought of his years with the Khalifa and pictured his former master's anger when he discovered that he had fled. He thought of his friends and relatives in Egypt and Austria and longed desperately to be with them. As the day of inactivity wore on, he began to despair that he would ever escape the Sudan. A sense of fear came over him, and he wondered if the sand and rocks on which he was lying were to be his grave. He prayed. Over and over he repeated, 'God have mercy on me!'

Early in the afternoon, he heard a low whistle and looked up to see Hamed. He was smiling. 'Good news!' he cried. 'We have found your people.'

Slatin's hopes soared. That evening he rejoined Zeki and Hamed and was introduced to two strangers who were to take him to the river. Slatin bade a warm good-bye to Zeki and Hamed, both of whom were soon to be caught, tortured and imprisoned in Omdurman for their bravery. Slatin mounted a camel behind one of his new guides, who told him to keep his face covered, even in the darkness, for all the roads and ferries were being watched. They rode for about two hours until they came to a clump of bushes where four other men were waiting. The arrangements had been carefully made. The camels were unsaddled and waterskins were filled with air and tied around their necks. The saddles and men were taken across the Nile in a small boat. When they reached the far shore, one of the men took the boat into the river again and sank it. Slatin was given bread and milk and introduced to Ibrahim Ali, who was to be his guide through the desert. Then he was taken inland for some distance and again hidden. Another long day alone under the sun, but now he felt close to his goal and that it would not be long until he was safe.

An hour after sunset his friends reappeared. 'Thank Allah you are safe!' cried one. They told him that sixty Dervishes on horses had passed through their village that morning. They had taken the sheep the villagers were preparing for him and then had scattered to look for loot. His friends feared that the mounted Dervishes had found him. Now there was a delay because the camels had been sent out in the desert to keep them from being taken as well. They asked Slatin if he wanted to wait another day until they could prepare provisions, but he said that dates and meal were enough. He wanted to press on. It was near midnight before the camels were brought and he could start off with Ibrahim Ali and another man. Slatin found that his new guides were entirely different from Zeki and Hamed. They grumbled constantly and were afraid their absence would be noticed. They also managed to lose Slatin's sandals, leaving him barefoot. They were supposed to take him to Aswan, but instead they turned him over to an old man who they said could guide him. His name was Hamed Garhosh and he began by saying, 'Every man looks to his own advantage and profit. Your guides, whom I know well, wish me to take you to Aswan, but what shall I earn by doing it?'

'On the day of my arrival, I will pay you there 120 Maria Theresa dollars, and in addition, a present, which I shall calculate according to the manner in which you accomplish your duties.'

'I accept,' he said. 'Allah and the Prophet are my witnesses that I trust you. I know your race. A white man does not lie. I will bring you to your own people, across untrodden mountain ways, known only to the fowls of the air. Be ready. After the sun is down we start.'

They had only one camel between them, but the old man had spoken the truth: the route they took was indeed mountainous and the camel could not go faster than a foot's pace anyway. They set off at night and marched for the first two days through extremely difficult country. Slatin said: 'We traversed a well-nigh impassable road, moving on without resting, impelled by my desire to see my own folk and to finish the weary journey as quickly as possible.'

Old Hamed Garhosh was willing enough, but his flesh was weak. He fell ill, and because he felt the cold mountain air so much Slatin gave him his jibba. Since his former guides had lost his sandals, his bare feet were badly bruised and cut. The camel, too, had a raw spot on his off fore-foot and he could hardly walk on it. At last, after a six-day march, with Slatin and the camel limping after the sick old guide, they descended from the heights at sunrise on 16 March 1895, and saw before them the Nile and the town of Aswan. They were in Egyptian territory at last.

Five officers were sitting in the British officers' mess that day in Aswan waiting for lunch when the Nubian waiter came up to one of the officers, H. W. Jackson, and said, 'There is a man outside who asks to see Your Excellency.'

'Tell him he can wait till I have had lunch,' Jackson said.

The waiter went out, but returned in a few minutes, saying, 'The man insists. He begs in Allah's name to be allowed to see Your Excellency.'

'I'm damned if he can't wait. Who is he? What does he want?'

Again the waiter went outside and returned. 'The man won't say anything. He is a wretched, poor man, and he is dirty. He is squatting outside.'

Jackson was intrigued. It was certainly unusual for a native to insist on disturbing a British officer at his lunch. With the consent of the others present, he ordered the man brought in. They saw before them a dirty, bare-footed Arab who stood with his hands on his chest and his eyes on the ground. Jackson spoke to him in Arabic.

'Who are you?' he asked.

Without lifting his eyes from the ground, the man whispered, 'I am Abdel Kader.' Jackson asked other questions, but that was all he could get from the man. Arcihbald Hunter, another officer present, then asked, 'Have you any other name?'

There was no reply.

Then Hunter, remembering the rumours that had recently been going about, exclaimed in English, 'Good God Above!' Then, remembering Slatin's Arabic name, he asked in Arabic, 'Are you Salatin?'

Still in a whisper the man replied, 'Yes. I am Salatin.'

Hunter shouted for a bottle of beer and poured it down Slatin's throat. The bandmaster was sent for and ordered to play the Austrian national anthem. The officers set about making Slatin a European again. While he was bathing and sleeping, they collected together a fair substitute for an officer's kit. By dinner-time, when Slatin entered the mess as the band played *Gott erhalte Unsern Kaiser*, he again resembled a European officer. Everyone stood to do him honour, and Slatin wept.

The telegraph wires hummed with the news, and messages of congratulations poured in. The next afternoon Slatin boarded the postal steamer and started down the Nile to Cairo. At Luxor there was a hero's welcome from the Europeans there and messages from his sisters. At Girga, then the southernmost station of the railway, he transferred to the train, arriving in Cairo at 6 a.m. on 19 March. On hand to meet him were Baron Heidler von Egeregg with his staff, Major Wingate, Father Rosignoli and a reporter from *The Times*.

Baron Heidler carried him off to his home and gave him a room decorated with flowers and Austrian flags. Over the door was a sign that said, 'A hearty welcome home'. He was received with open arms everywhere. Everyone wanted to meet him. Father Ohrwalder, now a missionary at Suakin, came to Cairo as soon as he could to see him. The Khedive made him a pasha and he was promoted to the rank of colonel.

His first duty was to set down an account of the Mahdist government in the Sudan for Major Wingate and the Egyptian Intelligence Department. It was at this time that he wrote:

The contrast between my past and present life, the influence of fresh impressions, the many changes I see around me, sometimes make my head feel heavy – heavy, as though I had just woke up from an evil dream – twelve years' captivity, a long dream indeed.

It was long before my excitement subsided, but gradually I began to settle down and collect my thoughts. Now again in the midst of civilized society, once more a man among men, my thoughts often turn back to the fanatical barbarians with whom I had to live so long, to my perils and sufferings amongst them, to my unfortunate companions still in captivity, and to the enslaved nations of those remote territories. My thanks are due to God, whose protecting hand has led me safely through all the dangers behind me.

How long his servant Ahmed waited with the mule on the edge of Omdurman or what became of his wives and other servants is not known, but at least six Sudanese suspected of helping him were executed.

Charles Neufeld: Gum and Guns

Slatin and Ohrwalder had fled, but there was still one important European prisoner left in Omdurman. Not much is known about the early life of Karl Neufeld (or Charles, as he called himself in Egypt). He was a Prussian, born about 1856 near what is today the Polish town of Bydgoszcz. In 1880 he married an English woman, daughter of a Northwich tailor. It is not known when he came to Egypt, but by the time of the Gordon relief expedition he already spoke excellent English and Arabic and had accompanied the expedition as an interpreter. He was within a few yards of General William Earle when the latter was killed at the battle of Kirbekan in February 1885, returning from a punitive expedition against the tribe that murdered Colonel Stewart and Frank Power. Although Neufeld spent six years in close connection with the British army, his normal occupation in Egypt was as a merchant.

Early in the year 1887 Hogal Dafa'allah, a brother of Elias Pasha, the former Governor of Kordofan, came to Neufeld at Aswan and suggested that Neufeld join him in trying to bring out a large quantity of gum from the Sudan. It could be bought cheap and sold for high prices in Egypt. Only courage and enterprise were needed to make a fortune. The object of the expedition would not be to bring the gum out themselves, but to organize a series of caravans among the tribes of northern Kordofan, principally the Kababish, with money paid on delivery to Wadi Halfa. Neufeld said, 'I being looked upon as an Englishman, and an Englishman's word being then considered as good as his bond, Hogal was sure of a successful journey.'

Hogal and Neufeld went to Cairo and called on General Sir Frederick Stephenson, commander of the Frontier Field Force, and Colonel John Ardagh, requesting permission to go into the Sudan. Both officers did their best to dissuade them from attempting what they regarded as a most risky enterprise. Finding that Neufeld was determined to go, General Stephenson made the best of it by asking if he would carry some letters and a verbal message to Sheikh Saleh of the Kababish, an anti-Mahdist tribe friendly to the government. Neufeld readily agreed. He was asked to tell Sheikh Saleh that his request for arms and ammunition had been granted and that he should send men and camels to Wadi Halfa to pick them up. Stephenson also asked Neufeld to report back to him on his return and give him as much information as he could about conditions in Kordofan.

Their expedition blessed with official permission, Neufeld went on to Wadi Halfa to make all the arrangements while Hogal went off to buy camels. Two guides were hired: Hassib el Gabou and Ali el Amin; Gabou was of the Kababish tribe and was employed as a spy by the Egyptian government. In addition, they intended to take Neufeld's Arabic clerk, his female servant Hasseena, and four men hired by Hogal. They planned to carry with them only essentials: food, water, rifles, ammunition, 300 Turkish dollars in cash and presents for the sheikhs they would meet.

Neufeld reached Wadi Halfa on 23 March and the next day he heard that forty of Sheikh Saleh's Kababish had arrived to pick up arms and ammunition. Gabou came to him and suggested that the best plan would be to join this band when they returned. Neufeld said no, but the guide made the arrangements with them anyway. When Neufeld remonstrated with him for this, Gabou blandly explained that he had taken this step because there were Dervish bands on the road they planned to take. Why had he not told him this before? Neufeld demanded. Gabou said he had forgotten!

Neufeld decided to accept Gabou's advice and go with the Kababish arms caravan, but Hogal and the camels had not yet arrived, although they were due at any time. Neufeld, at Gabou's suggestion, decided he would leave with his clerk, Hasseena and the other guide, and that Gabou would wait for Hogal and catch up with them. As Hogal's fresh camels would not be loaded with baggage, it would not be difficult for him to overtake the slower Kababish caravan.

A few days before they were ready to leave, an Arab, a friend of Neufeld, came to him and warned him against Hassib el Gabou. Gabou was acting as a double agent, he said, and was receiving money from both the English and the Dervishes. Neufeld laughed at his friend's fears, and said he trusted no one. He and Hogal were in charge of the expedition; he was sure they were able to take care of themselves. Besides, if they were successful, he would make a small fortune, and he could gain honour as well if he brought back valuable military information.

About twenty Arabs of different tribes had also joined the Kababish at Wadi Halfa so that with Neufeld's small party the total caravan now consisted of about sixty-five men and 160 camels. On the morning of All Fools' Day, 1887, Neufeld set out on the most foolhardy of adventures.

When they had been on the march for two days and there was still no sign of Hogal and the camels, Neufeld grew uneasy. His anxiety turned into alarm when day after day passed and still they did not come. On the night of 7 April they judged they must be close to the Selima Wells. Scouts were sent out and the wells were located, the scouts reporting the comforting information that it did not appear that anyone had been there for some time past. The next day they reached the wells and began to water the camels and prepare food. About noon they heard a shot. Shortly after a scout came hurrying into camp saying that he had been seen by twenty camelmen who had fired at him and then galloped off to the south.

A conference was held, and it was the general opinion that the camelmen had been the advance guard of a larger party of Dervishes. Ismail, the leader of the Kababish, decided they should push on at once. There was not much time for Neufeld to consider what to do. He had little choice. To return to Wadi Halfa with his own people was out of the question; the Kababish could not spare him a bodyguard. There seemed no alternative: he had to go on with the caravan.

There were five caravan routes running from Selima Wells. By the time they had been on the march a few hours, Neufeld was sure they were on the wrong one. He called a halt and taking out his map he tried to show Ismail and the guides that they had gone astray. An argument ensued in which the guide, a man named Hassan who had been supplied by Gabou, regarded the map scornfully and said, 'I never walked on paper. I have always walked on the desert. I am the guide and I am responsible.' So they took the wrong route.

They pushed on, led by Hassan, but there was continual argument and a demoralizing feeling of uncertainty spread through the caravan. Four days from Selima, they halted in the desert and scouts were sent out. They were gone all day, returning only at night with the report that the 'paper' had been right: they were now too close to the river and in the heart of enemy country. There was a fresh argument as to whether they should go east, west or south. At last it was decided that Ismail, Hassan and a few men would ride in a south-easterly direction while the rest of the caravan rode south for five hours and then halted.

Neufeld and the bulk of the caravan halted between three and four in the afternoon. Almost immediately they were struck by a violent sandstorm. The air was like a yellow fog and the men covered their own and the camels heads with blankets to keep from being suffocated. The storm lasted until sunset, covering their tracks so that the scouting party could not trace them. They fired their rifles and broke up wooden camel saddles to make fires. It was past midnight before answering shots were heard and Ismail with the scouting party found them.

Ismail at once ordered the fires to be put out and the rifles cleaned of sand and prepared for action. He then went around and carefully inspected each rifle. Neufeld took him aside and asked what he had discovered, but he whispered only one word: 'Treachery.'

Ignoring Hassan completely, Ismail ordered the march to be resumed at once and they set out on a zigzag course in a westerly direction. In the hasty departure from Selima, many of the water-bags had gone unfilled. Now they were suffering from thirst and were lost in the desert. At last, six days out of Selima, they found a caravan track, but no one knew where it led. They had no choice but to follow it. Two days later Ismail sent a scout to the west, and they lost a day waiting for him to return. The following day they started without him and soon found familiar landmarks: They now knew that they were but a few hours distant from the wells of Wadi el Kab. They halted, unloaded the camels and, leaving four men to guard the baggage, set off for the wells, expecting to return that night.

Three men were riding ahead as scouts when, about three o'clock in the afternoon, just as they reached the broken ground on the edge of the wadi, they heard a shot. At first they thought it was a signal from the scouts that they had found water, and they pressed on. But there were more shots, and Neufeld, who was riding somewhat in advance, heard bullets whistling around him. As he was mounted on a large white camel and had a brightly coloured scarf wrapped around his head, he was a prime target.

Neufeld and his party dismounted. They were being fired upon by a group of about fifty Dervishes in position on a hillock. Neufeld saw three of their own men fall, including the guide Hassan, and about eight of the enemy. As they advanced up the hillock, the Dervishes retreated, carrying away their dead and wounded and leaving behind two camels. The first man to reach the camels found them loaded with filled waterskins and called out, 'Water for the thirsty! Allah is generous!' The thirsty men made a wild rush for the camels. Rifles were thrown down and the men crowded around, struggling to get to the skins.

It was Hasseena who first saw beyond the struggling men the jibbas of the Dervishes. She ran up to Neufeld crying and pointing. Following her finger, he saw that the Dervishes had returned and that there were more of them. About 150 jibba-clad men were rushing towards them. He tried to give the alarm, but few heard him in the shouting around the two camels. A few looked up in time to fire, but it was too late. The Dervishes were among them, friend and foe confused in one huge struggling mass. Neufeld ran with Hasseena and his Arab clerk towards a hillock, but the clerk, who was a short distance behind, was captured. The Dervishes who were pursuing them stopped to examine the clerk's bag – containing Neufeld's money and his most valuable presents. The delay gave Neufeld and Hasseena time to reach the hillock. Neufeld quickly reloaded his revolvers and pushed up some stones to make a little barricade. Ismail, who had managed to get clear of the mass, jumped on Neufeld's camel, and as he dashed off, he called to Neufeld to find another camel and flee. Neufeld, working valiantly on his diminutive zariba, ignored him, but Hasseena heard and slipped off to look for camels.

The Kababish, most of them still without their rifles, were soon captured and then bound. Hasseena, too, was caught, and with a Dervish guard behind her Neufeld saw her advancing towards him. She called out to him to surrender as he had been given quarter. This he at first refused to do. The Dervishes had orders not to harm him, Hasseena shouted, and, as proof, the Dervishes with her fired their guns in the air and laid them on the sand. Neufeld looked around him. All the others had been captured except for the few who had managed to flee. He was alone, and he saw that resistance was hopeless. He slowly stood up and then walked down the hillock towards the Dervishes.

There were cries of, 'The Unbeliever!' as he came up to surrender, and one man raised his sword as though to cut off his head. Although trembling from all the excitement, Neufeld put up a brave front. Turning to the man and looking him in the eye, he said loudly enough for all to hear, 'Is this the word of honour of your Prophet and master? You liar! You son of a dog! Strike, unclean thing!'

As the man hesitated, a companion pulled at him, 'What are you doing? Have you forgotten our master's orders?'

They hustled him off to their emir, who interrogated him briefly regarding his name and what he was doing in their country. Then he turned to his followers and announced that this was the pasha that Wad Nejumi had sent them to capture. 'Thanks be to Allah we have taken him unhurt!'

The emir then took him to one side and said considerately, 'I see you are thirsty,' and had one of his men pour water over some hard dry bread. Handing this to Neufeld, he smiled and said, 'Eat. It is not good for you to drink.'

Charles Neufeld knew what he meant. Had they not made a rush for the waterskins on the camels, they might have been able to beat off the attack. Later he often wondered if the history of the Sudan might not have changed had he been able to reach Sheikh Saleh and open communication with him. One thing was certain: his capture changed the history of his own life for the next twelve years.

The Dervishes questioned each of their prisoners separately and asked them where the arms were. Neufeld and the Kababish denied all knowledge of any arms except their personal weapons, but two Alighat Arab merchants, under promises and threats, finally agreed to lead the Dervishes back to the spot where they had left the baggage. The entire party, Dervishes and prisoners, then started back along the route Neufeld's party had come. Neufeld was given a camel, but all of the Kababish, even the wounded, were made to walk. They were unable to cover the whole distance that day, but halted for the night, starting out again the next morning. Twenty-five well-mounted, armed men raced ahead and captured the four men who had been left to guard the baggage.

When the main body caught up, the looting began. Boxes were broken open, bales were slashed, and ammunition, sugar and clothing were scattered over the ground. While the Dervishes were looting, the prisoners stood forgotten. Neufeld, who still had his hunting knife, furtively ran to cut the cords binding the other prisoners. But the guards saw him, caught him and took him to the emir. Neufeld said that as he knew something of medicine he was going to help the wounded. The emir complimented him on his thoughtfulness and consideration for others and appropriated the knife. He then warned him not even to speak to the other prisoners.

When the excitement over the loot had died down, a camel was killed and Hasseena was ordered to prepare food for them. Neufeld ate with the emir. The first dish was raw camel's liver covered with salt and red pepper – then, as today, a Sudanese delicacy. Neufeld had seen this dish eaten, but had never tried it himself. He ate it now, not only because he was hungry but because he knew that lack of appetite was considered by Arabs as a sure sign of fear and he wanted to show his captors that he was not afraid.

After dinner, his clothes were taken from him and he was questioned. Neufeld's wallet was given to the emir, who looked through it and asked about the papers it contained. Neufeld said they were only business papers and offered to translate each one for him. The emir seemed satisfied with this, but kept the wallet.

After two days' march, they camped with other Dervishes near some wells and Neufeld was taken before another emir. From the deference shown to him by the others, he could see that this was a man of some importance. Neufeld was questioned closely and finally was accused of being a government spy. Neufeld, an impatient man, was exasperated. 'I have told you the truth,' he declared. 'What do you want me to do now? Tell you a lie and say I *am* a spy? If I do so you will kill me for saying I am one, and if I say again that I am not, you will not believe me and will kill me just the same. I am not afraid of you. Do as you please. I refuse to answer any more questions.'

The emir and those around him were astonished by his brashness. A young Dervish was called in and told to take him to a spot removed from the other prisoners. As they walked along, the young Dervish began to abuse him: 'Allah is just. Allah is bounteous. Please Allah, tomorrow our eyes will be gladdened by seeing a white unbeliever yoked with a shebba to a black one.'

Stung by these words and picturing himself yoked with the terrible shebba, Neufeld, who was a powerfully built man, hit the young man a blow on the head that knocked him senseless. Then, picking up the man's rifle, he strode back into the emir's tent, his eyes blazing with anger. He had no idea of what he was going to do, only the notion that he could either fire the one shot and then start clubbing until he was cut down or that he could shoot himself. One of the emirs, Mohammed Hamza of the Jaalin tribe, immediately stood up and said, 'Wait!'

Neufeld told what he had done, and the emir at once said, 'No, no, no. There must be some mistake. You are not to be put in a shebba. Our orders are to deliver you alive and well to Wad Nejumi.' Turning to the others, he continued, 'Hand this man over to me. I shall deliver him alive and well to Wad Nejumi. I hold myself responsible for him.'

There was some objection to this on the part of his captors, but Neufeld placed the muzzle of the gun under his chin and threatened to pull the trigger unless he was placed in this man's charge. Mohammed Hamza then said, 'If you do not agree and this man does any harm to himself, I declare myself free of blame and responsibility. I have heard of him. He will do as he says.'

At this the others agreed, and Neufeld was turned over to Mohammed Hamza, who told him that Wad Nejumi knew of his journey and had sent out the band that had intercepted him. Orders had been given for him to be taken alive, treated well and brought to Dongola. He did not guarantee that Wad Nejumi would not kill him when he arrived there, but he himself promised to treat him well and keep him alive if he would promise not to try to escape. Neufeld readily gave his word and handed over the rifle; Mohammed Hamza then led him by the hand out of the tent and over to the section of the camp where his own people were camped. On the way he whispered that he was loyal to the government and that Neufeld should trust him. Once in his own camp, he sent for Hasseena and gave her clothes; seeing how the sun had burned the skin from Neufeld's back, Mohammed Hamza also provided clothing for him.

There was some delay in leaving the wells. It was discovered that several of the Dervishes had concealed loot from the Kababish caravan and they were flogged. There was also a determined interrogation of the prisoners in an effort to learn if Neufeld was really a spy. When Hasseena's turn came, she was stripped naked and threatened with the curbash, but she stubbornly maintained that Neufeld was only a merchant and not a government official.

At last the march got under way and by mid-afternoon they were opposite Dongola where they halted. There, just outside the town, a great parade of Dervish troops was staged. There was even a band, made up of former Egyptian soldiers, and in the medley they played Neufeld heard a snatch of the Khedival hymn. The prisoners were now arranged to make an effective exhibit, with Neufeld, as the chief prisoner, placed among the emirs. After the usual display of horsemanship – charging up to a line of bystanders, pulling the horses up short and waving spears over their heads – the captives were brought into the town where Neufeld was taken under guard to the house of Wad Nejumi. He and his guards were kept waiting for some time before the entrance, and while they waited the crowd that had followed them amused itself by shouting insults at Neufeld and prodding him with spears and swords; his guards had difficulty protecting him. Neufeld seems to have been particularly sensitive to their insults, which exasperated and infuriated him even more than the swords and spears.

At last he was led into an enclosure and then taken to a small room where three men were seated on the floor. One of them, a dark, thin man, rose as he entered and said, 'Thanks be to Allah for your safety,' and invited him to sit down. This was the redoubtable Abderrahman Wad Nejumi – stern, ascetic, cunning, and one of the Khalifa's best generals. The three men looked at him for some moments. Neufeld stared back, determined not to be the first to break the silence. Presently food was brought in and Neufeld was invited to eat. This he did, eating stolidly with an air of complete indifference and he made a point of eating on after the others had finished, appearing to take no notice of what was said around him. When he had finished, Wad Nejumi said, 'Do not be afraid. I hope it will be my pleasure to receive you into the true religion and that we shall be good friends.'

He then asked him a few simple questions and assured him that he knew he was not a 'government man'; therefore, his life would be saved, but that all his property must be given to the Beit el Mal. When the interview was over, Neufeld was turned over to the chief of the Dongola Beit el Mal and Hasseena was sent into the harem of the same house.

Early the next morning he was again sent for. In the enclosure of Wad Nejumi's house, Neufeld saw that a number of the Kababish were being questioned. By the time he was called in, Wad Nejumi had already learned that Neufeld had served with the British army on the Gordon relief expedition and he began his interrogation by holding Neufeld's wallet in his hands and asking, 'Which are the government papers?' When Neufeld declared that there were none, Wad Nejumi insisted, 'Are there no papers from the friends of the government?'

'There may be,' Neufeld replied. 'I am a merchant. I buy gum, hides – anything from the Sudan – and sell them again to anyone who will buy them from me. It is all the same to me who the people are – friends or enemies of the government – provided they pay me. I gave good money for what I bought, and wanted good money for what I sold.'

Wad Nejumi then said that the letters had been translated by a girl educated in the Khartoum mission and according to her the letter from General Stephenson was a firman appointing Neufeld as pasha of the western Sudan, with orders to fight the Dervishes.

Neufeld was at first dumbfounded. Then, in spite of his serious position, he laughed. 'If the letter is a firman,' he said, 'it should be written in Arabic, as the Sudanese do not read or understand English.'

Wad Nejumi agreed and added that he himself did not believe the translation as it was different from the information he had received from Hassib el Gabou. Neufeld now knew for certain that he had been betrayed by his chief guide. During the course of the long interrogation, Neufeld admitted that General Stephenson's letter asked him to tell Sheikh Saleh that arms and ammunition were waiting for him at Wadi Halfa, but he denied, and continued to deny, that he himself had anything to do with the shipment.

The next morning, a light ring and chain were fastened to his neck and another light chain fastened to his ankles. He was taken again to Wad Nejumi's house, where he found the kadi and Wad Nejumi at work trying to convert a dozen Kababish and their leader, Darb es Safai, to Mahdism. They were having no success. The Kababish were not to be converted, and shouted abuse at the kadi and Wad Nejumi. Darb es Safai, speaking for them all, said: 'We have ridden behind our master, Sheikh Saleh, and we refuse to follow you on foot as slaves. We have come here to die – let us die.'

Neufeld was taken off to wait in a small mud hut where crowds of people gathered around him and amused themselves by showering him with insults. Darb es Safai and his men were marched a short distance away and set to work digging a shallow trench. When this was finished, their hands were tied behind them, a sure sign that they were about to die, and they were told to kneel at the edge of the trench. When the executioner approached with his sword, Darb es Safai asked to be beheaded last. He wished to see how his men would die, he said. When a few heads had been sliced off and sent rolling into the trench, one of the men jumped to his feet, and Darb es Safai called out sternly, 'Kneel down! Do you not see these cowards are looking at us?'

When the executions were over, the chains were removed from Neufeld and he was again taken before Wad Nejumi for questioning. He was asked what property he had in the caravan and whether he had any slaves. Neufeld said that he had no slaves, only two servants: his Arab clerk and Hasseena, a former slave who had been freed. Hasseena was brought in and questioned. She said that she was Neufeld's slave, but that as slaves were forbidden by the government she had been given a paper that said she was free. Wad Nejumi ended the interview by making a gift of her to one of the

men present. At this, Hasseena squatted on the ground and refused
to budge. She screamed at Wad Nejumi that he could marry her to
whomever he liked, but that her husband would die the same night
as she knew how to poison people secretly. Wad Nejumi changed
his mind. He would send her to the Khalifa instead. For the present
she could return to the Beit el Mal.

Wad Nejumi now called in a number of emirs to discuss the fate
of Neufeld. Wad Nejumi was for keeping Neufeld with him, thinking he might be useful, but most of the others were for killing him at
once. One suggested that his head be cut off and sent to Wadi Halfa
with the 'firman'. Neufeld found it an ordeal to sit by and listen to
his fate being discussed in this fashion. He made up his mind that if
he were condemned to die he would leap at the nearest emir and
sink his finger-nails into his neck. Finally, the decision was reached
that he should be sent to the Khalifa in Omdurman. Wad Nejumi
was kind: he gave Neufeld a jibba and even 100 of the 300 dollars
that had been taken from him.

That evening – it was 27 April, nearly four weeks since he had left
Wadi Halfa – the chief of the Dongola Beit el Mal told him to
prepare for his journey to Omdurman. There was little preparation
he could make, except to beg some sesame oil to rub over his
blistered face, shoulders, back and feet. He had a final session with
Wad Nejumi, during which the Mahdist emir asked him many
questions concerning the Egyptian government, the fortifications
of a number of Egyptian cities, including Cairo, and about the
British army. The slow pace of the Gordon relief expedition had
given Wad Nejumi a poor opinion of the speed with which the
British could move troops. When Neufeld told him of the distance
between Alexandria and London and said that the British could
move an army from England to Egypt in a week by steamer, Wad
Nejumi smiled and said, 'I am not a child that you should tell me a
tale like that.'

Late that night, Hasseena and Neufeld were taken to the out-
skirts of Dongola, where camels and guards were waiting for them,
and they set off at once for Omdurman. The journey was without
incident until their last night's camp. They stopped in a village and
Neufeld was put into a room in what appeared to be a deserted
house. During the night an old woman crept into his room and
began a peculiar wailing. Her sons and all of her family had been
killed by order of the Khalifa. She was the only one left in her family.
Her wailing brought the guards into the room, but she cursed the
Mahdi to their faces. To Neufeld she looked like a spectre as she

stood in the light of the dying fire with her pinched, sunken cheeks, and glistening eyes, gesturing with skinny, hooked fingers. Staring at Neufeld, she prophesied his death. Of all nights, this was one in which Neufeld most needed sleep, but the old woman unnerved him. Shortly after she was dragged screaming from the room by the guards, Neufeld heard the sound of dull thuds, a shriek, a moan and then silence.

With a very uncertain fate awaiting him in Omdurman the next day and the wail of the old woman still ringing in his ears, Neufeld tried unsuccessfully to sleep. Years later, he could still remember the horror of that night: 'The night was one long, horrible, wakening nightmare, but all was real and not a fantasy of the brain. How I longed for the dawn! and how impatiently I waited for it! For the first time I had fears for my reason. The sensation I felt was as if a cord had been slipped round my brain, and was gradually being tightened.'

It was with difficulty that Neufeld, not yet accustomed to wearing chains, shuffled his way to his camel the next morning. The final stage of the journey passed quickly enough, and they reached Omdurman about noon that day, 5 May. They passed through the town almost unnoticed until they reached the market-place. Then the news of their arrival spread quickly and they were surrounded by thousands of curious people. His guards struggled through the mass to get Neufeld into a straw building, called a rekuba, located between the Khalifa's house and the wall of the mosque, near the burial place of the Mahdi. (The tomb of the Mahdi had not yet been built.) Two of his guards went off at once to deliver Wad Nejumi's dispatches and announce the arrival of the prisoner.

Rumour had preceded Neufeld's arrival in Omdurman; Slatin had heard that a European, said to be the pasha of Wadi Halfa, had been captured and was being sent to the Khalifa. He saw Neufeld arrive, surrounded by a crowd of people, but fearing the Khalifa's spies, he was careful not to appear to take any unusual interest in the event.

The Khalifa summoned a council to decide what should be done with the prisoner. Invited were: the other two khalifas, the principal kadis, the ubiquitous Yakub and Nur Angara, one of Abu Anga's officers who had recently arrived from Kordofan. Nur Angara had formerly been a government official in western Darfur and Slatin knew him well. As he was entering the Khalifa's house, Slatin whispered, 'Do your best to save the man.' Then Slatin himself was called in and took his place with the other advisers.

The Khalifa began with the assumption that Neufeld was an English spy and should first be questioned. He delegated Nur Angara and Sheikh Mohammed Taher el Magzub, the chief kadi, to do the interrogation; Slatin, on suggesting that he might question the man in his native tongue, was also included. When they entered the rekuba, Neufeld, to Slatin's horror, greeted him warmly and shook his hand with delight.

Slatin, speaking quickly in German, told him to address himself to Sheikh Taher and to be as submissive as possible: 'Be polite. Tell them you have come to join the Mahdiya and embrace the Mahdi's faith. Do not address me.'

Neufeld was offended by this lack of cordiality from a fellow European and he was angered by the warning to 'be polite'. He was not.

Nur Angara asked most of the questions, his first being, 'Why have you come to Omdurman?'

'Because I could not help myself,' Neufeld replied tartly. 'When I left Wadi Halfa it was to go and trade, not fight.'

Slatin moved behind the others and made signs to Neufeld to adopt a different tone, but Neufeld ignored him. Most of the questions were about military matters. Neufeld, who spoke excellent Arabic, readily replied, but he gave little information of value. Years later, Slatin said, 'His extreme readiness to talk made a bad impression on those present.' Still later, Neufeld, when shown Slatin's comment, said:

> Other captives had grovelled at the feet of their captors; I did not, hence probably the 'bad impression' created; and while the world may blame me for being so injudicious as to treat my powerful captors with such scant courtesy, it can hardly be expected that I, even had I not passed six years in close connection with the British Army on the field of battle, and in times of comparative peace, should in a moment forget and lose my manhood, and cover with servile kisses the hands of a savage black – and one of the murderers of Gordon to boot. I thank God ... that my first impression as the Khaleefa's captive 'made a bad impression'.

After the questioning, Nur Angara, Sheikh Taher and Slatin returned to the Khalifa. It was Sheikh Taher's opinion that Neufeld was a spy and should be killed. The Khalifa turned to Slatin and asked, 'And what is your opinion?'

'All I know,' Slatin replied, 'is that he is a German, and thus belongs to a nation which takes no interest in Egypt.'

Slatin could see that the Khalifa was watching him closely as he handed him some papers and asked him what they said. The papers included a list of medicines in German, a business letter in English and a long letter from General Stephenson in which, among other things, he asked Neufeld to gather as much information as possible about conditions in the Sudan. Slatin translated the papers, but omitted all damaging material. The Khalifa looked at him suspiciously, then told all the advisers to leave him.

When Slatin, Sheikh Taher and Nur Angara left the rekuba, Neufeld was stripped of the jibba Wad Nejumi had given him and in its place he was given a soldier's old jersey and a pair of cotton drawers. Then his feet were fettered and a ring with a long heavy chain was fastened around his neck. An immense crowd of people had gathered to stare and jeer at him, and an ombeÿa was blown repeatedly in his ear. Seeing Hasseena a few yards away sobbing violently, he called her to him. She told him the ombeÿa was summoning the people to see his execution. One of the guards confirmed this. A woman began to walk up and down in front of him, singing and gesticulating, describing in rude rhyme his death agonies and the tortures that would await him in the hell he would surely go to after death.

Slatin climbed up on a pile of bricks to watch Neufeld. Knowing that sentence had not yet been passed, he tried to signal to him, but he was not seen. Then Slatin, Nur Angara and Sheikh Taher were again called in to the Khalifa, who asked each of them in turn for his opinion.

'Then you are for having the man killed?' he said to Sheikh Taher when he had given his opinion.

'And you?' he asked Nur Angara. Nur Angara mentioned Neufeld's bravery and asked that his life be spared.

'And now, Abdel Kader, what have you to say?'

'Sidi, the man deserves to be killed,' Slatin began, 'and any other ruler but yourself would have him killed. But out of your magnanimity and mercy, you will spare him, for he says he has turned Muslim, and your mercy will strengthen his faith.'

Slatin was lying to save Neufeld's life, but he probably did not doubt but that Neufeld would pretend to be converted.

The Khalifa did indeed decide to spare him, but he wanted to play with him, as a cat plays with a mouse. He told the kadi to frighten the prisoner and then put him in prison until further orders. Then he turned to Slatin and said, 'As for you, you will have no more intercourse with him.'

The Khalifa's ordered were obeyed. Neufeld was not killed that day, but all night long the ombeÿa boomed. At dawn the next morning a Dervish came with ropes made of palm fibres. Neufeld was made to cross his right hand over his left, palms downward, and his hands were tied at the wrist. A piece of wood was used as a tourniquet to tighten the ropes until they were drawn deep into his flesh. Then water was poured over the ropes to make them swell. The agony he felt as the ropes swelled and bit into his flesh was excruciating. Pain caused sweat to pour from his body and he was no longer able to conceal his suffering. In this condition he was led out to be the sport of the waiting mob. His bare feet in the dust, his head exposed to the sun, he stood in his pain and despair in the midst of thousands of his enemies. A man with a sword approached him. Thinking he would soon be decapitated, he knelt to say a short prayer, but he was at once prodded to his feet with spears and swords. Two men with ombeÿas came up on either side of him and, placing the instruments against his ears, blew loud blasts. One large man with a spear made several feints as though to run him through. Hoping to end his misery as soon as possible, Neufeld tried to meet the thrust, but each time he was jerked back by the chain attached to the ring around his neck. Everyone laughed.

The tightening ropes around his wrists had now done their work: the swollen skin gave way and the rope sank into his bloody flesh. The ropes left scars that lasted the rest of his life, but now the terrible tension was relieved and Neufeld felt an indifference to the pain. A messenger from the Khalifa came up to ask if he had heard the ombeÿas. Neufeld nodded. 'The Khalifa has sent me to tell you that he has decided to behead you.'

'Go back to your Khalifa and tell him that neither he nor fifty khalifas may so much as remove a hair from my head without God's permission. If God's will it is, then my head shall be cut off, but it will not be because the Khalifa wills it.'

The messenger left, but returned shortly with the message that 'The Khalifa has changed his mind. Your head is not to be cut off. You are to be crucified as was your Jesus the Prophet.'

He was now taken to a rekuba: his head seemed about to split open from the ombeÿa blasts; scores of small, stinging flies were attacking the raw flesh on his wrists; the burning sun beating down on his exposed head made him faint. He waited in the rekuba about an hour before being led out and mounted on a donkey to be taken, as he thought, to the place of crucifixion. Two men walked on either side to steady him and keep him from falling off the animal. When they stopped, Neufeld saw a set of gallows instead of a cross.

He was lifted off the donkey and made to stand on an angareb; a noose dangled just over his head. Then the chief kadi came up to him and laid his hand on his arm. 'The Khalifa is gratified by your courage,' he said. 'He offers you a choice in the manner of your death.'

'Go back to your Khalifa and tell him that he may please himself as to the form of my death,' Neufeld replied. 'But if he wants to do me a favour, be quick about it. The sun burns my brains.'

'You will be dead in a few minutes,' the kadi assured him. 'Will you die as a Muslim or as an unbeliever?' Neufeld, exasperated by this profitless conversation, exploded, 'Religion is not a dress to be put on today and thrown off tomorrow.'

A man on horseback had made his way through the crowd and now came up to the gallows and spoke to the kadi. Neufeld could not hear what he said, but the kadi turned and said, 'Be happy! The Khalifa, in his great mercy, has pardoned you.'

Neufeld, who did not for a moment believe this, cried scornfully, 'Why? Have I asked for his pardon?' However, he was once more hustled on to the donkey and to his surprise returned to the rekuba. There the ropes were cut from his wrists and he was given great plates of food. It was impossible to eat it all and he offered some to the ombeya players, but their lips were so swollen from blowing their horns in his ears that they could hardly eat.

The next day, Neufeld was again taken before the Khalifa, who asked if he would like to send any messages to his family. Neufeld said that he would, and pen and paper were given to him. He began a letter in German to his manager at Aswan, but he had written only a few lines when the Khalifa stopped him and said the letter had better be written in Arabic. This presented a difficulty, for although Neufeld spoke Arabic fluently, he could not write it. Finally, the letter was written for him and given to him to sign. It began:

In the name of the most merciful Allah, and prayers be unto the Lord Mohammed and his submissive adherents, from the servant of his lord Abdallah el Muslimani the Prussian whose former name was Charles Neufeld, to my manager Möller, the Prussian in the Railway, Aswan: I inform you that after departing from you I have come to the Sudan with the men of Saleh Fadlallah Salem el Kababishi, who were carrying with them the arms and ammunition and other articles sent to Saleh by the government. . . .

The letter then went on at length, describing the capture of the caravan, saying that it was done by only six men; it told how he had been sentenced to death, but had been spared by the mercy of the Khalifa; it then said that he had adopted Islam and had taken the name Abdallah. The Khalifa, it said, 'pardoned me because he is gracious, and for the sake of the religion of Mohammed, to which I now adhere'. With only the vaguest notion of what was in the letter, Neufeld signed it. Three months later it was published in the *Egyptian Gazette*.

After signing the letter, he was taken back to the rekuba where, about sunset, a man arrived with orders to remove his chains. While Neufeld was watching, with relief, the chains being prised off his ankles, the chief kadi came into the rekuba and ordered the chains put back on again and the ends cold-welded shut.

The next morning Neufeld was carried off to prison. Here he was taken to an anvil sunk in the ground so that the striking surface was almost level with it. More fetters and chains were hammered on so that in all he had three sets of shackles and a ring with a chain around his neck. Staggering under these irons, he was led to a building about thirty feet square and assigned a place by the wall furthest from the door. The stench in the room was overpowering – sickening. He was placed between two chained men who were dying of smallpox. There were about thirty other prisoners in the room, many of whom were ill and had obviously been unattended for days: excrement, urine and vomit covered the floor. Neufeld fainted.

He did not know how long he remained unconscious or semi-conscious. He was roused at sunset, however, by streams of prisoners coming through the door. About 100 men were jammed into the room and the door was bolted shut. The prisoners fought and cursed as they struggled for places by a wall or a pillar, against which they could rest their backs. Above the cursing and the clanking of chains were the moans of the sick and half-uttered prayers to Allah to relieve them of their suffering. Sleep was out of the question, and for Neufeld this first night in prison was a confused nightmare

When the door was at last swung open in the morning, fresh air rushed in and the prisoners stumbled out. Neufeld again fainted and had to be carried out; when he revived he was carried back in again – 'to get accustomed to the place'.

He passed most of his first three days in prison with fever and in delirium; his legs swelled from the irons clamped on them. On the fourth day, Hasseena was allowed to come and nurse him: she brought him food and bathed his shackled legs. When Neufeld was sent to prison, she was taken into the Khalifa's harem, but she told the wives and eunuchs that she was with child, and, as she had hoped, they turned her out. When she first entered the prison enclosure, Idris es Saier, the head gaoler, shackled her with a light chain and attached her to his harem, but she was permitted to tend her former master. Neufeld was allowed to sit outside now during the day and, for the first time, permitted to talk with the other prisoners, many of whom were old soldiers from the Egyptian army and eager for news of the outside world.

One morning he was lying in the shade amid the filth and flies of the prison enclosure when two camelmen rode in. They had orders from the Khalifa to bring Neufeld to him, they could not say why. It was generally known that there was to be a large parade that day, and it was assumed by most of the prisoners that Neufeld was to be executed. Some of his fellow prisoners tried to be encouraging: one told him to be brave, as 'when they tried to burst your head with the ombeÿas'. Neufeld was hoisted on to one of the kneeling camels and taken off to the parade ground just outside the town.

The swinging strides of the camel rubbed his shackles into his now festering legs. Some of the ulcers broke open and the blood and pus ran down the camel's side. Neufeld was in agony, and by the time they reached the Khalifa on the parade ground he was near fainting. The Khalifa noticed his condition and ordered the chains to be removed that night and lighter ones put on him. In the meantime, Neufeld looked out on a plain covered with cavalry, camelmen and foot soldiers. It had apparently been the Khalifa's intention to display his entire army to him, but seeing that in his present condition he was unable to pay attention, he turned to one of his emirs and said, 'Tell Abdallah (Neufeld) that he has seen only a quarter of the army, and let him be brought for the parade tomorrow.'

His fellow prisoners were astonished to see him return alive that evening; they were even more surprised to hear Idris es Saier ordered to remove his chains and put on a lighter set. The gaolers tried to carry out the Khalifa's orders, but the rings around his ankles were now so buried in the swollen flesh that they could not be brought near enough to the anvil's face to be struck. Therefore, he was brought to the parade ground the next morning in the same wretched condition as the day before. The Khalifa was furious when he saw this and sent for the gaoler to demand why his orders had not been obeyed. Idris es Saier replied that he had no lighter chains and that Neufeld's legs were too swollen. The Khalifa refused to take this as an excuse and ordered that the irons be removed that evening. And so they were, but it was a terrible ordeal for Neufeld.

During the parade Neufeld saw Slatin and tried to get near enough to speak to him, but he found it impossible. He did not know that Slatin dared not disobey his orders not to talk with him. One of the emirs asked Neufeld for his impression of the great Dervish army. Neufeld answered shortly, 'You have numbers, but not training.'

The proud Khalifa heard the remark. He was not pleased. Neufeld was sent back to prison – for four years.

14

Neufeld: Life in Chains

In 1887 the prison in Omdurman consisted of a large zariba of thorn trees and branches about six feet high located near the banks of the Nile. Inside was the one common cell – the 'Umm Hagar', House of Stone – where the prisoners were locked up at night. About thirty gaolers kept order with the aid of their curbashes. There were no sanitary arrangements whatsoever; not even a ditch for a latrine; the Umm Hagar and the prison yard swarmed with scorpions and vermin. Prisoners were fed by friends or relations; if they had neither, they starved.

Of all the people appointed by the Mahdi to posts of importance in his government, only two managed to retain their positions until the end of the Mahdiya. One was the head of the arsenal and the other was Idris es Saier, the chief gaoler. A shrewd man was Idris, and he acquired considerable fame in his profession. In fact, his name became synonymous with prisons. Not only the prison in Omdurman, but all the prisons in the Sudan were called Beit es Saier – House of Saier – or simply the saier, and all the head gaolers were also called saier, as though it were a title. He was a tall, well-built Black who had once enjoyed a different kind of fame as a thief. He liked to tell stories of his exploits, always ending them by pointing out how, thanks to his conversion to Mahdism, he had risen in the world and was now the trusted guardian of all thieves – as well as murderers, traitors, unbelievers and run-away slaves. It was true that Idris es Saier no longer stole now that he was a Mahdist. He had no need to. He had learned to be a clever extortionist, milking his prisoners of their money with simple but effective guile. Almost daily he harangued his charges, telling them how he had once been a robber, but now was an honest man; how grateful he was to the Mahdi for his conversion; and how all the prisoners should also be grateful to the Mahdi and the Khalifa for leading them into the true faith. He then vowed that because he had given all his money to the poor, he now had no money to feed his wives and children. 'I am going to see my starving children now,' he would say near the end of his speech, 'and then I will pray to Allah, asking him to release you if you repent and turn the Khalifa's heart to you.'

To win favour, some of the prisoners gave Idris various sums of oney according to their means. Sometimes he would apply a little pressure. He would tell them mournfully that someone must have done something wrong as he had been ordered to put more chains on the principal prisoners, i.e. those with money. This was the signal for the prisoners to collect enough money to make a donation to the gaoler's wives and children; then the 'Khalifa' would learn of their kindness and generosity and the chains would be struck off.

The hundred dollars Wad Nejumi had returned to Neufeld had been given to Hasseena to hold for him, but Idris es Saier took the money from her 'for safe keeping'. Gradually, under one pretext or another, Neufeld was forced to give it all to Idris.

Idris was an extremely superstitious man, and although the Mahdi had forbidden fortune-telling and the writing of talismans, much of his money went to fortune-tellers. He had also about twenty-five or thirty boards of hard wood, twenty inches square, which he used as tablets. Every day he had someone write suras (chapters) from the Koran on the tablets with ink made from soot, gum arabic, water and some perfume. As soon as it was written he would wash his hands and then very carefully wash off the ink, collecting every drop in a cup. If a drop spilled, the writing would have to be done over again. When he had the sacred words in solution, so to speak, he would then drink it, and his soul felt fortified.

Daily life in the prison when Neufeld first entered began with the opening of the door to the Umm Hagar at sunrise. The prisoners were allowed to shuffle down to the bank of the Nile to wash and to relieve themselves. Then all were assembled for the first prayer of the day. This was followed by the reading or recitation of the Mahdi's ratib (book of sayings), which took about three-quarters of an hour. Each prisoner had to purchase or copy out these sayings of the Mahdi and then memorize them. Although copies had been printed on the old Egyptian government press, it was considered more meritorious to write out a copy by hand. It was usually carried in a small leather case suspended from a cord around the neck, and it was generally considered as a talisman.

At noon, the second prayer was said, and between noon and sunset the third prayer, followed by another recitation of the ratib. The fourth prayer was said at sunset and then everyone was driven into the Umm Hagar. The good Muslim prisoner should have said his evening prayer in the Umm Hagar, but the nightmare inside made this impossible. Filthiness prevailed. Excrement was thrown about the crowded room; parasites made sleep an impossibility. As the night slowly wore on, the heat grew more and more oppressive and the stench from the sweating bodies became overpowering; men clawed and bit and kicked each other with their fetters; anyone who fell to the floor was trampled, and was seldom able to rise again. Sometimes more than 250 men were jammed into the small room. When the pandemonium became too great, the guards would come and lash at those nearest the door with their curbashes, and more men would be trampled. Neufeld fought and kicked and bit with the others to save his life. When the door was opened in the morning, there would frequently be trampled corpses on the floor, sometimes as many as five or six. This went on for night after night, week after week, month after month, for years.

The prisoners worked for a while at making bricks for a wall around the prison to replace the thorn zariba, and digging a well for infiltration water. To lighten the load of chains and bars on their legs, the prisoners attached a cord to them; by lifting up on the cord, they were able to walk, or at least shuffle about. Until the wall and well were completed, Neufeld described life in the prison as 'I might say endurable'. The prisoners were allowed to go down to the river to wash and drink, and this gave them an opportunity to exchange news and gossip with the townspeople. It also afforded a number of prisoners an opportunity to escape. These were usually Blacks. As most of the slaves in town wore chains, the Black prisoners were able to pass for ordinary slaves in spite of their chains. Besides, any blacksmith would remove the chains free for the sake of the valuable iron. This means of escape was not practical for Neufeld, he knew, for he would be quickly recaptured if he remained in Omdurman, but he was not without hope of escaping in some manner. Most of the gaolers kept large establishments with many wives and concubines and the prisoners were often put to work making additions to their houses or doing household tasks. The household tasks were the least distasteful chores and they frequently offered an opportunity to escape. In such large households it was rare that there was not at least one wife or concubine who felt herself neglected or unjustly treated. If a prisoner could win the affections of one of the gaoler's women, he was often able, through her help, to make his escape. The usual procedure was for the woman to report a goat or sheep missing just at sunset. She would take her prisoner-lover with her to find the missing beast, and they would simply not return.

Each month, Idris es Saier had to report on the prisoners and give an account of their 'education'. When a prisoner was missing, he would be reported as having completely repented and reformed and was therefore recommended for mercy. If the Khalifa approved, the prisoner was officially free and the gaoler escaped the charge of having allowed a prisoner to escape; he was only minus a wife or a concubine.

Neufeld had once studied physiology and medicine at the universities of Königsberg and Leipzig. In Upper Egypt he had had a reputation as a doctor and, as he did not charge for his services, his practice had been large. His reputation accompanied him to Omdurman, where he was frequently called upon to administer to the gaolers or their wives. In the course of his 'professional' visits to the harems, he made dozens of proposals of marriage, but he never succeeded in arranging an escape.

One day there entered the prison yard a man he knew: Ahmed Nur ed Din of the Kababish. Neufeld had worked with him when he was in the caravan trade and when he was with the British army. Before he could speak to him, Ahmed made a sign for him to be silent and walked off in another direction. That evening, when they were being driven into the Umm Hagar, Ahmed whispered, 'I have come for you. Be careful. Keep your eyes open. Try to obtain permission to sleep outside the Umm Hagar.'

It was two weeks before they had another opportunity to exchange a few words. Ahmed spent them ingratiating himself with the prisoners who associated with Neufeld so that he was gradually introduced into the circle of prisoners with whom he talked. Ahmed Nur ed Din had an interesting story: he was engaged in a bitter feud with Gabou, the guide who had betrayed Neufeld and the Kababish caravan, and he reasoned that if he could bring Neufeld out of the Sudan his enemy would soon be swinging from the gallows. He had therefore made his way to Omdurman for the express purpose of rescuing Neufeld. At first he had waited in the hope that Neufeld would be released from prison. Finding that this was unlikely, he had arranged a quarrel with a friend in the market-place in order to get himself put into prison.

Ahmed Nur ed Din had friends outside the prison and he had arranged with them to procure camels and provisions for the flight. He had also arranged that when he gave the signal through the boy who brought him his food, his friends were to make a hole in the prison wall through which they would escape. Instructions were also sent out to obtain pistols and ammunition. Finally, all was nearly ready, but only seventeen cartridges could be found. Ahmed decided to wait a few days more in the hope that additional ammunition could be procured. Just at this time, however, he became feverish and Neufeld soon saw that he had all the symptoms of typhus. Ahmed urged Neufeld to make his escape without him, but he refused to consider it. Neufeld and Hasseena nursed the sick Kababish, but he weakened every day and died one night in the hell of the Umm Hagar. Two days later, Neufeld himself fell sick.

Hasseena nursed him carefully and enlisted the help of two boys to carry him from shade to shade as the sun travelled across the sky. Often, in moving him, they tripped on his neck chain and they all fell to the ground. Idris es Saier, who was not deliberately cruel, had the chain removed. Hasseena had her own cure for typhus: vegetable marrow soaked in salt water; the water was drunk and, when the patient was able, the marrow was eaten. This was followed by cramming the mouth with butter. The next operation was to rub the whole body briskly and cover it with oil or butter. Neufeld had nothing to say about his treatment. He was helpless. The vegetable marrow acted as a purgative, the butter felt like boiling oil in his throat and, by the time he had arrived at the final stage of the cure, when he was wrapped in old camel-cloths and sweated, he was too weak to protest. After thirteen days he recovered, in spite of the treatment, but he was terribly weak and thin. By the time he was strong enough to get about, the men Ahmed Nur ed Din had organized for his escape had lost heart and gone away. He was often to regret that he had not steeled himself to leave the dying Kababish and fled while he had the chance.

During his convalescence, the Khalifa sent religious teachers to convert him. One was an old kadi who had served under Slatin. He urged that it would be more politic if he would pretend to be converted and submit, as had Slatin, who now lived in his own house with his own slaves, horses and cultivated land outside the city. Neufeld refused. The kadi pointed to Neufeld's chains, then weighing about forty pounds, and said the Khalifa would surely torture him with them until he submitted. Neufeld knew better than the kadi what those chains meant, but he would not accept nor pretend to accept Islam. The reasons he gave for his refusal, curiously, were not religious ones. He once said that he refused to turn Mahdist because he did not want to be found dead in a jibba, killed by an English bullet. Yet, at the time of his capture and for years after there was little or no fighting between the British and the Dervishes except around Suakin. At another time he said he refused to become converted because the Khalifa would make him proclaim his conversion publicly and then would behead him to prevent him from slipping back into Christianity. Yet, he knew that neither the Mahdi nor the Khalifa had ever executed a single European captive and he had no reason to believe he would be an exception. A stubborn Christian was Charles Neufeld.

For the prisoners in the saier, the most trying time of all was during the great famine of 1888–9. As no food was provided by the prison authorities, many whose friends and relatives could not even provide for themselves starved to death. At the height of the famine, dozens died each day, yet the prison population did not grow smaller, for it was increased daily by those arrested in the market-place trying to steal food. These wretches were dragged to the anvil where they watched while the chains were struck off the corpses of men who had starved to death and then fastened on to themselves.

A portion of all the food brought to the prison by relatives and friends was regularly taken by the guards. Once inside, those bringing food had to fight with the starving prisoners, many almost living skeletons, who ran to the end of their chains or struggled to run in their fetters to grab a mouthful of food. Neufeld was fortunate in having his faithful servant Hasseena, as well as friends such as Father Ohrwalder and Sister Catarine Chincharini who managed to get food to him. Slatin, too, secretly contributed to his support. Hasseena, after being knocked down and robbed several times by starving prisoners, hit upon an ingenious device. She obtained a gazelle skin and made it into a bag which she filled with food and hid between her legs under her dress. She carried a few scraps of food with her, but waited until she reached her master before dropping the bag beside him. Thanks to such charitable and ingenious friends, Neufeld survived the famine.

Of all the tasks given the prisoners, the hardest was unloading Nile boats. Shortly after the death of Ahmed Nur ed Din, when Neufeld was recovering from his own bout of typhus, one of the young gaolers, who had been pestering him unsuccessfully for money, ordered him to go to work unloading boats. Neufeld refused and sat down on the ground. When the gaoler seized him and began dragging him towards the gate of the prison, Neufeld, struggling, managed to kick loose, scramble to his feet and knock him down. The young gaoler jumped up and made off to tell his story to Idris es Saier, who, when he heard it ordered Neufeld to obey. He still refused, complaining to Idris that the young gaoler had tried to extort money from him. Idris answered by hitting him on the head with a large flat stick he had with him, breaking the stick in the process. He then ordered that Neufeld be given 500 lashes with the curbash. Neufeld was so stunned by the blow on his head that he was only half conscious when his flogging began. After sixty or seventy lashes, he lost consciousness altogether. Idris, fearing that he was dead or about to die, stopped the flogging. As Neufeld was considered one of the more important prisoners, the Khalifa would not have been pleased to learn that his gaoler had killed him. Neufeld was carried into the shade and Idris turned on the young gaoler, abusing him for starting the affair; he knew that Neufeld had been telling the truth when he said the gaoler was trying to get money from him. Idris was not adverse to bribes, but he insisted they be paid to him, not his underlings.

Often the gaolers were bribed to allow prisoners to sleep outside the Umm Hagar. Neufeld paid Idris himself for this privilege and further bribed one of the guards to allow him to sleep in a small mud hut in the prison enclosure. One evening when an unusually large number of prisoners had bribed gaolers to allow them to sleep outside, Idris made his appearance and, seeing so many men outside the Umm Hagar, demanded to know the reason. The guards, pretending that they had had difficulty in getting the prisoners into the Umm Hagar, began laying about them with their curbashes and driving the prisoners into the cell. The young guard with whom Neufeld had had trouble, not knowing that the privilege had been purchased from Idris, took this opportunity to single him out with his lash and drive him towards the Umm Hagar, about fifty yards away. Idris saw it and the young gaoler paid dearly. He was dismissed from his post, given 200 lashes, and put in prison himself. Neufeld had the satisfaction of seeing the beating and watching the former guard work at unloading the Nile boats. He thought this the only piece of real justice he ever saw during his entire stay in the Sudan.

Flogging was common in the prison, but there were certain rules that were always followed. One thousand lashes was the maximum number ever awarded and the prisoner was always allowed to keep his clothes on. Five hundred lashes was a common punishment and it was always given in the same way; the first two hundred were given on the buttocks, the next two hundred on the shoulders, and the final hundred on the breast. One thousand was usually ordered to extort a confession, and these were always given on the buttocks. Clothes offered some protection, of course, but after the first seventy or eighty blows they were in shreds and soaked with blood.

Neufeld received his worst beating one night when Idris es Saier again came into the prison enclosure to find an unusual number sleeping outside the Umm Hagar. Although Neufeld had bribed Idris well, the latter was so furious at the money being paid to his guards instead of to himself and his 'starving children' that he ordered all the prisoners without exception to be given 150 lashes. Most set up such a clamour, begging for forgiveness and swearing repentance, that they escaped with twenty or thirty lashes at the most, but Neufeld refused to beg for mercy. As the lash cut into him, he clenched his teeth and bit his lips, resolved that not a sound of pain would escape him. 'Will you not cry out?' demanded the gaolers who were beating him. 'Are your head and heart still like black iron?'

Years later, writing about the flogging, he remembered most keenly the humiliation of it:

> There was I, a European, a Prussian, a man who had fought with the British troops . . . now in the clutches of the tyrant and his myrmidons, whom we had hoped to rescue Gordon from; a white and a Christian – and the only professing Christian – chained and helpless, being flogged by a black, as much a captive as I was, and yet my superior and master. It is impossible for anyone not having undergone a similar experience to appreciate the mental agonies I endured.

In May 1887 Hasseena had escaped the Khalifa's harem by maintaining that she was pregnant, which she was not; in November 1888 she was indeed pregnant, and this presented a difficult situation for both Hasseena and for Neufeld. Hasseena could be stoned to death if it could be proved that she had had sexual relations with anyone other than her master. If Neufeld claimed the child, Idris es Saier would be in trouble for allowing Neufeld so much freedom; and for a prisoner to get Idris es Saier in trouble was to get into serious trouble himself. The matter was complicated by the fact that Idris wanted Hasseena for himself. As for Hasseena, she had no idea who the father of her unborn child might be. She had turned to prostitution and thievery to obtain food for herself and Neufeld during the famine; she had not changed her ways since.

Neufeld consulted his friends among the other prisoners and was advised to claim paternity, even if it did mean trouble for Idris. The Khalifa, they thought, might then release him, for a wife and child represented hostages as it was obviously impossible to escape with them. Neufeld followed their advice and claimed the child, and Idris was indeed unhappy: he was deprived of a chance to obtain Hasseena for himself and he was in danger of suffering the Khalifa's wrath. Fearing the Khalifa's displeasure, Idris worked out a unique solution to his problem: he empanelled a jury of women to decide whether Neufeld could indeed be the father of the child about to be born. The jury examined the matter at length and, either because of Idris es Saier's bribe or to protect their own future activities, came to a most remarkable conclusion: Hasseena was indeed with child by Neufeld but the conception had not taken place in the prison, but nineteen months earlier! Some of the women even maintained that it was possible for gestation to take years.

The child was born in January 1889 and was named Makkieh, meaning 'shackles'. When the Khalifa heard the verdict of the women jury and of the name of the child, he was much amused. He sent Neufeld his congratulations and offered him his freedom if he would promise to make gunpowder for him. Neufeld replied that he did not understand the manufacture of gunpowder, and so remained in prison.

Every prison has its prison aristocracy, and the Khalifa's prison in Omdurman was no exception. Here it was often composed of sheikhs and emirs who had formerly occupied important positions in the Mahdist government, and Neufeld had an opportunity to meet and talk with many of them. Of them all, the man who impressed him most was that remarkable and able man, Ibrahim Wad Adlan, sometime chief of the Beit el Mal. Before the Mahdiya, he had been one of the principal merchants in Kordofan, and rich. He had travelled to Cairo and other parts of Egypt a number of times; he could read and write Arabic, and possessed a brilliant mind. When he succeeded Ahmed Wad Suliman as head of the Beit el Mal in 1889 he completely reorganized the treasury and introduced an intelligible system of accounting, employing experienced Egyptian clerks and accountants. He was a friend of both Slatin and Neufeld, and Neufeld said of him: 'He was a man himself, acted as one, and despised heartily those who, in his opinion, were carrying their obedience to the confines of servility.' Neufeld, like Slatin, confided to Adlan his longing to escape, and Adlan offered to do all in his power to help. But first it was necessary for both of them to be out of prison.

Adlan did not believe he himself would be kept long in prison; affairs at the Beit el Mal were going badly without him and the worse they became, the higher were his hopes of returning to the Khalifa's good graces. Getting Neufeld out was more difficult. Adlan urged him to pretend to be converted, saying that otherwise he would never be allowed out of prison. The old argument was persuasive coming from the one man Neufeld was able to respect, and he finally agreed, sending word through Idris es Saier of his conversion. When the matter was reported to the chief kadi however, he said, 'What! Abdallah Noful a Muslim? No, his heart is the old black one. He is not with us. He is deceiving. He is still headstrong. He is a deceiver. Tell him so from me.'

Neufeld failed to win his release by his unconvincing conversion, but Adlan, as he had predicted, was shortly released and reinstated in his old position as head of the Beit el Mal. Adlan now did his best to obtain Neufeld's release from prison. It was about this time that the Khalifa was searching for someone to design the Mahdi's tomb, and Adlan suggested that Neufeld be supplied with drawing materials and told to submit a design. He accordingly drew up a rough sketch of a proposed tomb based upon tombs of Egyptian rulers he had seen in Egypt. He was then told to make a clay model of the tomb, which he did. A great number of people came to see the model until one day a fanatic kicked it to pieces, saying that the Mahdi's tomb should not be designed by a dog of an unbeliever. Nevertheless, the finished tomb was almost a copy of Neufeld's design except for its distinctive conical roof. Now Adlan sent word to Neufeld to draw up a design for the interior of the tomb. The object of all these efforts was, of course, the hope that if the design was approved, Neufeld would be released from prison to take charge of the work. Adlan recommended Neufeld's designs for the tomb's interior to the Khalifa, adding that it would cost nothing as there was sufficient paint in the Beit el Mal.

It was some time before the Khalifa finally approved the project, but one day Neufeld was led out of the prison and taken to the Mahdi's tomb to inspect it. Adlan met him there and confidently assured him that this would be his last day in chains. And so it might have been if just at this time a European had not escaped from Omdurman. A half-witted Bohemian minstrel who had wandered by accident into the Sudan and had been captured, now as casually wandered out of Omdurman. He never reached safety, for he was murdered not far from the town. Nevertheless, his escape so infuriated the Khalifa that Neufeld, all hope of freedom now dashed, was not only kept in prison, but an extra bar of iron was added to his fetters.

Not long after this Neufeld was astonished and dismayed to see Adlan brought back into the prison and heavily weighted with chains. Neufeld was anxious to speak with him, but everyone was strictly forbidden to go near him and he was put into a small hut some distance from the others in the prison yard. Nothing was possible during the day, but that night Neufeld shuffled towards the hut. When he was a few yards away, he lay on the ground and wriggled close, keeping his chains spread as taut as possible to prevent their rattling. In a whisper he asked, 'What has happened?'

Adlan was startled but whispered back, 'Go away! Go away! Do not speak to me. A big dog has me by the leg this time. Go away, or he will get your leg.'

Neufeld was insistent and asked again what had happened, but Adlan ignored the question and simply begged him to go away. Neufeld reluctantly wriggled back and regained his own hut without being detected, but he knew no more than before. The next day, Adlan's slave boy passed Neufeld and said, 'Do not speak to my master. If you do, you will hear the ombeÿa.'

When asked what he was doing, the boy replied, 'Burning papers. Do not speak to my master.'

A few days later, Adlan was taken out of his hut and led to the anvil to have his chains struck off. All knew what this meant: his execution. Neufeld and the other prisoners were not allowed to go near him, but Adlan called out to them, 'This is my day! Have no fear, any of you. I am a man, I shall say and do nothing a man need be ashamed of. Farewell!'

While still more chains were being fitted to Neufeld's ankles, he heard the sounds of the ombeÿa announcing the death of Ibrahim Wad Adlan. He had run foul of Yakub.

With the execution of Adlan, Neufeld fell into a state of abject despair. All hope was gone. He had, when supplied with drawing material to sketch the Mahdi's tomb, succeeded in writing letters to his agent and friends in Egypt – not, curiously enough, to his wife. He had even found means of getting the letters into the hands of men who would take them to Egypt. Nothing came of his efforts; no answer had come back.

One day an Egyptian doctor, Hassan Zecki, who had married Frank Lupton's widow and was now in charge of the medical stores at the Beit el Mal, came to the prison and talked with Neufeld about the manufacture of saltpetre. Neufeld had seen crystals made in a laboratory while at the university, but he had no experience in bulk production. Nevertheless, Hassan Zecki was interested and said that his assistant was trying to extract saltpetre in and around Khartoum.

Three days later Neufeld was summoned by Yakub to explain the making of saltpetre. On the way from the prison to Yakub's house, Neufeld considered what attitude he should adopt. He knew that if he confessed he did not know anything about bulk manufacture of the chemical, he would not be believed and would probably be flogged; if he pretended to know, he would probably be let out of prison for a while. He therefore assured Yakub that he could make saltpetre, but that he would require the construction of three large tanks about six feet long and four feet wide in which arable soil could be mixed with water and the solution drawn off and allowed to evaporate.

The following morning, Neufeld was taken to the anvil; his iron bars were struck off and his heavy ankle chain was replaced by a piece of light awning chain taken from one of Gordon's old steamers. It was a tremendous relief to have the dead weight of fifteen to twenty pounds removed from his feet. He was then led to the river where Yakub and some emirs, with about thirty workmen were waiting for him beside a Nile boat. A two-hour sail downriver brought them to Halfaya. After nearly four years in prison, this sail on the Nile was a delight Neufeld never forgot. They were met at Halfaya by a Fellata called El Fiki Amin. 'Fellata' is the name used in the Sudan for the West Africans who for centuries have passed through the Sudan on their way to and from Mecca. The trip usually took years, the pilgrims being poor and the journey long and hard. Like a very sluggish stream, the Fellata moved, and still move, across the Sudan, creating an enduring aspect of Sudanese life without its individuals ever becoming part of it. As the Mahdi had forbidden pilgrimages to Mecca, the stream was broken during the Mahdiya, but it is doubtful if even then it was completely dammed.

The Fellata held the secret of making saltpetre and had a virtual monopoly on its production, but most was made in Darfur and had to be transported hundreds of miles by camel to reach Omdurman. Here, however, El Fiki Amin was engaged in producing by very primitive methods small quantities of very good saltpetre, and he did not look kindly on the intervention of a potential competitor.

Yakub ordered Neufeld to search for deposits of earth that might be rich in potassium nitrate. He looked around. Coming upon a dark, damp patch of earth he took some and mixed it with water, pouring off the solution and boiling it in a small coffee pot. He added more solution as the water boiled away, and after two hours he obtained a small deposit of a thin syrupy consistency; this he poured on to a porous brick. When the moisture was absorbed, crystals remained; these burned away when placed on hot charcoal. He then dried some of the earth, rubbed it fine and allowed it to fall in a thin stream on to the fire. The hissing noise it made, combined with an occasional coloured spark, convinced those present that a new deposit had been found. One of the emirs was sent back to Omdurman to tell the good news to the Khalifa.

After he had gone, the Fellata told Yakub that burning the crystals did not prove the substance was saltpetre. Yakub, not knowing whom to believe, ordered Neufeld to make more and send it to Hassan Zecki. This he did, and Hassan Zecki sent back a secret message to Neufeld saying that the crystals were not very good, but that he knew Neufeld would be sent back to prison if he said so; therefore, he would give his approval of the crystals if Neufeld would try to produce them in the form of needles instead of grains. Hassan Zecki then made a favourable report to the Khalifa and asked that Neufeld be sent some large pans. Shortly after this, Neufeld received several copper kettles and an officer's camp bath-tub, probably taken from Khartoum or from the baggage of one of Hicks Pasha's officers.

Neufeld now began to make saltpetre, but the Fellata so resented the competition that it was decided Neufeld should look elsewhere. Neufeld, with an eye to escape, suggested that he search for new deposits further north, but Yakub would not permit it. About this time, Hasseena's child died and the Khalifa thought it would be safer if Neufeld stayed closer to Omdurman. So after about two weeks in Halfaya Neufeld was removed to Khartoum. There he was put in the old Catholic mission, occupying one of the priests' rooms. The mission was in ruins: windows, doors, and all metal and wood had been removed; only the garden, with its fruit trees and vegetables was still maintained. In the chapel, cocks crowed, and hens laid their eggs where the altar had been.

For six months Neufeld worked with fifty slaves constructing large tanks to produce saltpetre in bulk, while at the same time carrying on limited production of four or five pounds a day in the copper kettles and bath-tub. The results of their work were sent over to the arsenal in Omdurman and turned over to Joseph Pertekachi, the Khalifa's maker of gunpowder. As the quality of Neufeld's saltpetre was not good enough to make gunpowder, Pertekachi mixed the gunpowder made from it half and half with good powder from old government stocks when he tested it. As good powder came in from Darfur, Pertekachi simply stored away Neufeld's saltpetre and the deception went unnoticed.

Father Ohrwalder came to visit Neufeld several times while he was at Khartoum. They talked about the past and commiserated with each other, but they never discussed plans for escape, although escape was uppermost in the minds of both men. Father Ohrwalder never tried to explain why he did not try to work a concerted escape plan with Neufeld or other prisoners, but many years later Neufeld wrote:

> That we did not openly discuss such plans now appears to me strange – and yet it is not strange. Where all led for years a life of falsehood, in which deception of self had a no less part than that of others, suspicious of everyone around us, trusting no one, what wonder that deceit became a second nature, and that truth, honour and morality – that is to say, morality as preached in Europe – should have retired to vanishing point!

Although the European prisoners did what little they could to help each other, they trusted no one. In January 1888 a spy-messenger sent to the Sudan by the Anglo-Egyptian army in Egypt with letters for Slatin and Lupton reported back that they had refused to accept the letters in the presence of each other 'owing to mutual mistrust'. Slatin never mentioned this incident.

Among the letters Neufeld had managed to smuggle out was one to an old friend, Mankarious Rizk, the Greek station-master at Aswan. Mankarious had tried to help. He had found a reliable Ababdeh Nubian who was willing to go to Omdurman and give Neufeld 100 dollars and to try to arrange an escape. He arrived in Omdurman while Neufeld was still in prison, so he turned over the money to a Greek to keep. Concluding that it was impossible for Neufeld to escape from prison, he returned to Aswan. The news of Neufeld's position put an end, for a time, to his friends' efforts to free him.

When Neufeld heard of Father Ohrwalder's escape, he cursed him, for he thought he had gone off with some guides with whom he himself had plotted. When Mankarious learned of Father Ohrwalder's escape, he tried again to get in touch with Neufeld. It took him some months to find someone willing to make the trip, but at last he found an old but wiry Arab named Ahmed Abou Hawanein who agreed to go.

With two camels, some money and goods with which to trade, Ahmed set off to make his way up the Nile. In the summer of 1894 he reached Omdurman and found Neufeld in the garden of the mission house in Khartoum. He brought no letters and Neufeld was at first suspicious, but after questioning him thoroughly he became convinced that the man had indeed been sent by his friend and he was soon talking enthusiastically of escape. Unfortunately, Ahmed Abou Hawanein did not think the camels he had were good enough for a rapid flight; he suggested that he return to Aswan to buy two good trotting camels and the two revolvers which Neufeld thought necessary.

Not long after Ahmed Abou Hawanein had left, Neufeld was asked to visit a sick man in the house of a friend of his and he received permission to go. The 'patient' turned out to be a perfectly healthy Arab named Abdallah who gave him a piece of paper on which Neufeld could make out only faint marks. Abdallah told him the writing would emerge when heat was applied to the paper. As cauterization was a common remedy, Neufeld called for some hot coals to be brought to him. With the aid of the coals the writing stood out and Neufeld read that Abdallah had been sent by the War Office in Cairo. In the course of several meetings, an elaborate escape plan was worked out. It was to be put into effect as soon as Abdallah returned to Berber and collected the camels and rifle he had left there. He left and Neufeld never saw him again in the Sudan.

Abdallah's story was a curious one. In Cairo he had been given as his primary mission the task of bringing out Neufeld, being promised £300 if he succeeded; he was also promised £100 if he brought out any of the other captives. This last clause was Neufeld's undoing. Seeing the difficulties of trying to carry off a man who was in chains and closely guarded, Abdallah decided to forget the £300 and to assure himself of the smaller but safer sum by taking one of the other captives. He therefore contacted Father Rossignoli and arranged an escape plan for him. He and Father Rossignoli went as far as Berber on donkeys. When they reached Berber, Father Rossignoli threw himself on the ground and refused to go any further; he demanded that he be taken back to Omdurman. Abdallah was startled and frightened: to return to Omdurman now would be suicide. Father Rossignoli then started wandering about the town; he even told several people that he was being taken by Abdallah to Cairo against his will.

Abdallah knew that he would never collect his £100 if he left Father Rossignoli in Berber. He had procured a camel, and in desperation and exasperation he broke off a branch of a tree and flogged the priest until he climbed upon it. He then mounted in front of him and forced him to escape. Once back in Egypt, he decided he would never again run such a risk. But he had created false hope and left Charles Neufeld bitterly disappointed again.

After Pertekachi blew himself up, there were closer examinations of the saltpetre Neufeld supplied and he was given several warnings about the quality. Fortunately, it was about this time that he obtained a new job working in the mint. Neufeld suggested that they try to make coins with a punch press. He and his companions experimented until they had spoiled several sheets of copper, a number of dies and finally the press itself.

Although still wearing light chains and still closely guarded, Neufeld's life was considerably more bearable than it had been in the prison. However, he had domestic troubles. Hasseena's morals had never been of the best, but she had been loyal to him and undoubtedly had saved his life when he had first been thrown into prison. He owed her much. But now she had become a nuisance and a danger to him. During the famine, she had risked the punishment of a caught thief to provide him with food; now she continued to steal for herself, taking advantage of her position as the wife of a European to steal from the other Europeans, knowing they would not report her. Neufeld's friends strongly urged him to get rid of her before he became involved as an accomplice. He at last decided reluctantly to do it, but as she had been given to him by the Khalifa, he felt that he must have his permission to divorce her.

When Hasseena came to see him, he quarrelled with her openly so that it could be seen they no longer got along well together. Then he asked through his superior if the Khalifa would consent to a divorce. The Khalifa agreed, but said that he would select another wife for him. When Neufeld learned that the woman the Khalifa had in mind was a half-breed French subject, he was horrified. An Islamic marriage was, in his eyes, simply a liaison, but marriage to another European was bigamy. He appealed to his European friends to find him a Muslim wife, and quickly. Casting about for an eligible woman, they found Umm es Shole, an Abyssinian who had been raised in the household of a Greek family in Khartoum and had married one of the sons. On the fall of Khartoum, her husband had been killed and she became the property of the Beit el Mal, eventually being turned over to an emir as one of his concubines. As she refused to lie with the emir, he retaliated by torturing her children to death. Abdel Kader, the Mahdi's uncle, heard of her case and gave her a document declaring her to be a free woman.

When the Khalifa gave his order for all women and girls to marry, Umm es Shole married an old and ailing Jew, whom she nursed until he died two years later.

The Khalifa gave his consent to the marriage, but Umm es Shole objected; she did not want to marry again. Only when told that Neufeld was ill (which he was just then) and would surely die unless cared for did she give her consent. Neufeld was married by proxy and only after the wedding did Umm es Shole see her new husband. She at once set about nursing him and establishing her small household.

The new marriage seemed to be satisfactorily arranged, but the divorce from Hasseena proved somewhat more difficult. Normally, divorce (for a man, but not for a woman) is a simple and private matter in Islam: a man need only say three times, 'I divorce you.' Neufeld followed the prescribed rules, but Hasseena promptly countered by declaring that she was pregnant. The Islamic divorce rules as practised in the Sudan required a husband to keep his pregnant wife until the child was born, and if the child was a son the divorce was null and void. Neufeld decided to send her off anyway, but she returned about eleven months later with a baby boy. Neufeld then kept her for two years more.

Originally, Hasseena had figured in Neufeld's escape plans, and he had intended to take her with him when he fled. Now she was replaced in these plans by Umm es Shole. Abdallah had not returned, but there was still the plan he had worked out with Ahmed Abou Hawanein.

On 28 February 1895 Neufeld was seized without warning, loaded with chains and placed under a double guard at the house of the Governor of Khartoum. Four weeks later he was returned to the saier in Omdurman. As he passed through the prison gate, he saw another prisoner being brought in: it was Ahmed Abou Hawanein.

15

Neufeld: Hell's End

Knowing that all hopes for escape were now crushed, and being once more in the hated saier, Neufeld was in a state of absolute despair close to insanity. For days he shuffled about the prison yard, dragging his chains and irons, refusing to speak to anyone, his eyes on the ground. It is difficult indeed to live without hope, and he would have been a most unrealistic optimist to have seen any reason to support hope in his present position.

Neufeld's sudden return to heavy chains and the saier was the direct result of the escape of Slatin. Ahmed Abou Hawanein was in prison for the same reason. When he returned to Omdurman, he was at once seized and accused of having helped Slatin to escape and of returning to help Neufeld. He was flogged to make him confess, but he refused. Another flogging was ordered, but some of his own people interceded on his behalf and he was finally released. He at once returned to Aswan, where he showed his torn back and festering wounds. This cooled all enthusiasm among the Arabs for further attempts to assist Europeans in Omdurman.

One day Neufeld was near the prison anvil when he heard a man crying. Looking up, he saw a man being shackled and recognized him as Ibrahim Pasha Fauzi, an Egyptian officer whom Gordon had found as a subaltern when he first came to the Sudan, but whom he had continually promoted until he became Governor of Khartoum and Commandant of Troops. Neufeld was shocked to see such a man crying. It was disgraceful. A man of his standing should not act like a child, and Neufeld told him so. Suddenly a change came over Neufeld. Confronted with the wreck of a man that Fauzi was, he felt a responsibility thrust upon him. His own despair lifted and he became the protector of the former governor: as a disappointed child finds comfort and distraction in lavishing affection on a doll, so Neufeld now saw Fauzi: someone who needed him, someone to be comforted.

As Neufeld was in prison only to prevent his escape from Omdurman and not because of any misdeed, Idris es Saier had been instructed to treat him well, and Umm es Shole and her child were allowed to come and visit him at any time. But he was never to be permitted to sleep in the open and was forced to spend all his nights in the Umm Hagar. On the evening of Fauzi's first day in prison, he was placed in the corner furthest from the door with his back against the wall. At first he had enough room to stretch out his legs on the foul floor. When the second batch of prisoners was driven in about an hour and a half later, there was only room for the prisoners to squat. Fauzi, heavily chained and unable to get to his feet, remained with his legs outstretched while four other prisoners sat on him. Neufeld was driven in with the third batch of prisoners, and when all were inside, there was only room to stand. Fauzi, still on the floor, begged those around him not to stand on him.

Neufeld heard him and, fearing that he would be trampled to death, he began to fight his way towards him, lashing about in all directions at friend and foe alike. As the men could see little in the dark and could not tell exactly who had hit them, they struck back indiscriminately at those around them. The Umm Hagar was soon a mass of brawling humanity. Neufeld continued to fight his way towards Fauzi, calling on friends to help him. The guards, hearing the uproar, threw open the doors and laid about with their whips and sticks.

In the confusion Neufeld and a few of his friends managed to fight their way through the swaying, sweating, yelling mass to Fauzi. They pushed men off him and made a human barricade around him. Fauzi himself, who could not tell whether an attempt was being made to save or murder him, fainted.

About midnight, the doors of the Umm Hagar were again thrown open and the guards tried to push in twenty men, each wearing a shebba. There was no room for them, but the guards were determined. They set fire to handfuls of straw and grass and threw them into the cell, at the same time laying about them with their curbashes. Fauzi, still dazed and seeing the fire falling on the heads of the men, thought he was surely in hell. The men bound with shebbas were somehow driven into the Umm Hagar, the doors were pushed shut, and so they were left until sunrise.

Among those in the Umm Hagar that night were Zeki Belal, the brave guide who had helped Slatin to escape. Zeki had been forced to confess that he had helped a man with 'cat's eyes' to leave Omdurman, but swore he did not know who the man was.

During the first few weeks after Neufeld was back in prison, Umm es Shole had little difficulty in begging small quantities of grain and borrowing an occasional dollar to keep him supplied with food. After a time, however, people grew afraid of assisting him and he began to feel the agony of starvation. Then, in September 1895, an Abyssinian woman came to the prison to see him under the pretence that she wanted medical treatment. She slipped him a small packet of letters and whispered that it had been given to her by a man outside the prison who said that he also had money for him and asked to whom he should pay it.

It was three days before he found an opportunity of being alone and opening the packet. In it was a letter from his sister written four years earlier, a letter from Father Ohrwalder and a note from Major Wingate: all told him not to lose hope for attempts were being made to assist him. At irregular intervals over a three-month period, he was visited by the Abyssinian woman and through her he obtained money, plotted for escape and himself managed to write letters for the man to carry back to Egypt. The man was Onoor Issa, and one of the letters he carried out was to Father Ohrwalder. In it Neufeld gave news of mutual friends in the Sudan, asked about his business in Aswan and begged Father Ohrwalder to send him instructions and materials for making coins that would look like silver.

Neufeld's desire to make coins was based on his belief that if he could do work of this sort he would be transferred from the prison to work at the Beit el Mal. However, he was fortunate enough to make this transfer without knowing how to make coins. Awad el Mardi, the head of the Beit el Mal, became interested in trying to extract gold and silver out of certain stones found in the neighbourhood of Omdurman. Neufeld was detailed to assist in this enterprise. His iron bars and heavy chains were replaced by a single pair of ankle rings connected with a light chain, and he was transferred to the government workshops in Khartoum. Here he enjoyed the easiest life he had experienced since his captivity. Awad el Mardi told him: 'I am your friend. Do not be afraid. If you cannot find gold and silver, tell me of anything else you can do, and I will see that work is given to you so that you may not be sent back to the saier.' He was housed in one of the best buildings still standing in the town, sharing the lower floor with an Egyptian who had formerly been the telegraph clerk in Berber. A number of Beit el Mal slaves were put there to guard him, but they were told that his chains were only to prevent his being carried off by the Egyptians. Thus, in effect, his guardians became his servants.

In April 1896 rumours reached Omdurman that British and

Egyptian troops were advancing. Then came news that Dongola had been taken. At first Neufeld could not understand what was meant when he heard that the British were crossing the desert in 'iron devils'; then he understood that a railroad was being built, but this seemed almost equally improbable. It was about this time that Onoor Issa sent him a message that he had been detained in Berber by the emir there, but that he hoped to get away soon and arrange his escape. Neufeld's hopes soared.

With the advance of the Anglo-Egyptian troops into the Sudan, the Khalifa became concerned about his supplies of ammunition. An inspection of the stores and arsenals revealed that large quantities of powder had caked with moisture. The Khalifa threatened to cut off a hand and a foot of the arsenal chief if he did not make the powder into a good explosive. Neufeld was ordered to help, and he set to work with some carpenters to produce a wooden model of a powder machine. He knew that materials for a full-sized machine were not available and he built into the design some serious defects that would make the machine break down if it were ever built, but it looked real enough. When it was shown to the Khalifa, he was so delighted with it that he ordered all Neufeld's chains to be removed.

For ten years Neufeld had been in chains, and for most of the time he also had the additional weight of irons. He had learned to shuffle about, his step limited to the ten or twelve inches of chain and the irons making each step an effort by their weight. When at last he stood freed of chains and irons, he could not contain himself. All that day he ran and jumped about, stretching his legs for the sheer joy of it; intoxicated with his new-found lightness. The next morning, his legs were swollen from his hips to his ankles and his muscles ached so excruciatingly that he was unable to walk. He was still laid up when, thirteen days later, the Khalifa changed his mind and put him once again in chains.

The Khalifa also ordered Neufeld to make a cartridge machine for him. He set to work and designed a model, but Berber had been taken by the time it was ready to show to the Khalifa, who only looked at it and said sourly, 'I want cartridges, not models!' He ordered that Neufeld be removed from his house, kept at work all day in the arsenal and that he spend his nights locked up with other prisoners in the arsenal prison with the convict labourers. The Khalifa's half-brother Yakub was, of course, consulted about the machines Neufeld made. He did not understand them any better than the Khalifa, but he is reported to have said that 'there must be something in the head of the man who invented them, and he was better employed in the arsenal than idling his time in the saier'. Yakub gave orders that Neufeld was to be given whatever materials he needed for his work.

Neufeld now began gleefully to destroy everything he could lay his hands on. He demanded the paddle axle of one of the steamers and cut it into discs, then he turned his attention to destroying as much brass and copper as he could obtain.

In August 1897 Onoor Issa returned to Omdurman and sent a message to Neufeld through Umm es Shole. Neufeld was able to get a letter written and passed to Onoor Issa with instructions for him to give it to the first officer he saw. In it, he gave such information as he knew concerning the forts around Omdurman and asked that Onoor Issa be given a list of medicines, as 'practising medicine facilitates my communication with the outer world'. Onoor Issa took the letter but he was not able to leave Omdurman until the end of December and it was six months before he returned with money and a noncommittal letter from the commandant at Suakin. Meanwhile, towards the end of November, the arsenal was removed from Khartoum to Omdurman and Neufeld was returned to the prison.

The Anglo-Egyptian army under its Sirdar, General Horatio Herbert Kitchener was steadily making its way up the Nile, and the Khalifa and his followers grew more and more apprehensive. Their greatest fear seems to have been of the Sirdar's gunboats, which might appear at any time to bombard Omdurman. It was suggested to the Khalifa that mines placed in the river would stop the gunboats. One mine was made and tested. It worked so successfully that the Khalifa ordered more. When they were completed and being placed in the river they unaccountably exploded, blowing up the *Ismailia*, one of Gordon's old steamers, and killing more than thirty men.

As General Kitchener's army drew closer and closer to Omdurman, the prison boiled with rumours. There were many who had reason to dread the coming of the English, and there were those such as Neufeld who, for years, had dreamed of a British advance, so that almost any rumour dropped on fertile ground and flourished. The prisoners were afraid that they might all be killed by the Dervishes before the army arrived, or that they might be thought Mahdists and shot by the British when they marched in. Many decided that it would be a wise precaution to establish their sympathy with the British cause and they came to Neufeld to give him information or otherwise to prove their loyalty. Neufeld sent out a number of messages to the advancing army through Onoor Issa, giving what he hoped would be useful military information. Idris es Saier turned particularly kind to Neufeld and nervously asked what he should do in case the English won the coming battle; treat him well, Neufeld advised him, and he would speak 'good words' for him.

There was an old prophecy that the final great battle with the infidels would take place in the plains of Kerreri. Accordingly, the Khalifa moved his mighty army, numbering about 80,000 men and including every male inhabitant of Omdurman, to the plains north of Khartoum.

On 1 September 1898 the cry flew through the prison that the gunboats were coming up the river. Next, the prisoners heard a distant booming of guns that grew nearer and nearer. A boy stationed on the roof of a gaoler's house came tumbling down with the news that the gunboats were in sight and had passed Halfaya. A few moments later, the prisoners were covered with a shower of dust and stones as a shell hit the top of the prison wall and ricocheted off without exploding. Everyone ran to the shelter of the north wall and squatted there, thinking this the safest place. More shells went screeching overhead.

Charles Neufeld went mad. He stumbled out into the open prison yard, shouting, laughing, crying, trying to dance in his shackles, kissing his hands to each shell that raced overhead. The Baggara prisoners tried to kill him. Idris es Saier saved him and locked up all the prisoners except Neufeld, Fauzi and the other government sympathizers in the Umm Hagar.

Suddenly, the shelling stopped and the guns fell silent. In the prison yard they waited tensely and expectantly for the next phase of the battle. Nothing happened. Some said that two of the gunboats had been sunk and that the remainder had fled down the river. Neufeld and Fauzi sat in a daze in the prison yard; mad joy gave way to despair. Neufeld broke down and cried.

That night he could hear the Baggara in the Umm Hagar shouting what they would do to that 'son of a dog, Abdallah Nofel', promising themselves that they would drink his blood the moment his brothers reached Omdurman. All night long he could hear the pat-pat-pat of running feet outside the prison walls. No one knew what it meant. It was only later they learned that it was the sound of men running back to Omdurman from the plains of Kerreri.

The next morning at sunrise, the boom of cannon was heard

again in the prison. Later they heard the sound of musketry as well, and among themselves, in complete ignorance, they tried to guess the probable course of the fight. To calm his nerves, Neufeld began to illuminate a ratib with red and black designs. About noon he left this work to attend to the wounds of two young men who had been attached to the prison but had gone off to fight. One had a bullet over the left temple and the other a bullet in his left arm. Neufeld cut out the bullets with a penknife and dabbed the wounds with a bit of carbolic acid. When he questioned them about the battle, they told him that Yakub had been killed and that the Khalifa Abdullahi was retreating.

In the afternoon, the prisoners heard the braying ombeÿas and the beating drums that called the faithful to gather, but did not know what they meant. Idris es Saier came to Neufeld and asked him what he should do. Neufeld told him to shut the gates of the prison and use his rifles on any Baggara that might try to get in; he could then wait and see who would ask for the keys, the Khalifa or Kitchener. Idris took this advice and then linked all the prisoners into gangs connected with chains. This work had just been completed when Idris came to Neufeld in great excitement and told him that the place was filled with his 'English brothers' and that a big, tall man was asking for him.

The chain connecting him to the other prisoners was cut off, and he was led by Idris to the gate of the prison. Neufeld was so filled with emotion that he could only make out a blurred group of officers standing before him. Then he heard the first words of a European language he had heard in seven years: 'Are you Neufeld? Are you well?'

A tall figure approached him and shook his hand. It was the Sirdar, General Kitchener. Neufeld stammered something, shook hands with someone, and felt a friendly slap on the shoulder. The Sirdar looked at his three sets of heavy leg irons and said, 'Can these be taken off now? I am going on.'

A British officer stayed with him and tried to find Idris or one of his gaolers to remove Neufeld's chains, but all had fled. So instead the officer gave him his horse and helped him to mount side-saddle, chains and all, and walked beside him as he led the way to the officers' mess of the headquarters staff in the desert just north of town. It was not imposing. It was dark by the time they arrived, and tired, hungry and thirsty officers and men worked on orders and dispatches by the light of guttering candles. They celebrated their victory that night with a supper of biscuits, water and some of

Neufeld's prison bread. Ernest Bennett of the *Westminster Gazette* saw Neufeld and thought 'he looked very little the worse for his stay in Omdurman'. Shortly after arriving at the mess, Neufeld heard someone calling, 'Where's Neufeld?' The inquirer was Bennet Burleigh, correspondent for the *Daily Telegraph*. Finding Neufeld still in chains, he rushed off to get farriers. With strong language and strong blows, the chain was cut, but the iron anklets remained until the next day when they were removed on board the gunboat *Sheik* with the aid of a vice and a cold chisel.

When Neufeld boarded the steamer that was to take him down the Nile to civilization, he was a man secure in his honour. Throughout his twelve years of captivity, he had maintained his manhood and his faith; he felt proud, too, that he had been able to be of some help to the conquering army by the information he had smuggled out to the Sirdar. The nightmare was over now. He stood on the deck of the steamer, a free man looking forward eagerly to resuming the broken path of his life. He did not yet know of his reputation in the civilized world. He was soon to learn.

Part 3

The Sudan Reconquered

16

Kitchener and the War the Railroad Won

At the end of the last century, the old, poverty-stricken, rotten Ottoman Empire was a ramshackle affair, propped up and preyed upon by a number of European powers. The vibrations caused by the fall of the Sudan reached back to Constantinople and caused the tottering structure to lean even more precariously towards the brink. It still pretended to rule Egypt, but the real pharaoh was the cool, efficient Evelyn Baring. It also pretended to rule, directly or through Egypt, a considerable stretch of the African coastline running all the way along the Red Sea, around Cape Guardafui and the horn of Somalia, down to where the Sultan of Zanzibar vaguely claimed, without effectively controlling, his stretch of African coastline. With the fall of the Sudan, there was a good deal of what Baring called 'Egyptian debris' left over which European powers began to sweep up into their own hands.

British forces occupied Berbera and Zeila, establishing what became British Somaliland. The French seized the area just north of Zeila and began to construct French Somaliland. The Italians, after asking the British if they would mind, grabbed the land around Massawa and formed Eritrea; then Cape Guardafui itself and the south-running coastline to below the equator to create Italian Somaliland. The British garrisoned Suakin, but did not claim it.

Abyssinia, too, came in for her share of Egyptian debris. In 1884, by treaty with Britain, chunks of Sudanese land were given to Abyssinia in exchange for allowing the Egyptian garrisons along the Abyssinian border to withdraw to Massawa. The British also helped the Egyptian garrisons to withdraw from Harar, and Abyssinia occupied – or rather reoccupied – this territory.

In Darfur, the country was so torn and bloodied by revolt, and so reduced by famine and migration, that the Khalifa no longer bothered to keep an army there. In the south, Emin Pasha, the last of Gordon's provincial governors, remained until 1888 when Henry M. Stanley, after near incredible hardships, reached him and carried him, reluctantly, out of the country to the eastern sea-coast. Events in Equatoria have an even vaguer, more unreal quality about them than events in the rest of the Sudan. The Khalifa started to conquer it, recalled his forces for other purposes, and then apparently forgot about it. Emin did not control the entire province and it is doubtful if he actually was capable of governing any of it. When he left, Equatoria drifted into anarchy.

In Egypt, after Wolseley's forces withdrew from the Sudan, steps had to be taken to prevent the Dervishes from coming down the valley of the Nile into Egypt proper. A line was drawn, which remains almost the same to this day, between the Sudan and Egypt, at Wadi Halfa. The border was guarded by British, Egyptian and Sudanese soldiers – all led by British officers – collectively known as the Frontier Field Force. From such information as this force could gather from refugees, deserters, merchants, spies and patrols was pieced together nearly all that was known to the outside world of events in the Sudan. The weekly intelligence reports make interesting reading, not only because of their stories of camel and cavalry patrols and interrogations of people coming out of the Sudan, but because the writers included a human element missing from most modern military reports. Doubtless the officers were bored by the routine. Colonel Josceline Wodehouse wrote on 4 October 1891: 'I understand that the statements of the refugees and others are required in full, more or less. Their information is usually so inaccurate and improbable that it seems hardly worth noting.' When Zubair Pasha's son deserted to the Dervishes, General Grenfell noted that he was a 'lazy, drunken man, who had quarrelled with his father'.

In the eastern Sudan there was some action. In February 1891 Colonel Holled Smith set out from Suakin with a force of 2,000 men and defeated the forces of Osman Digna near the town of Tokar, which he occupied. This was the first attempt to reoccupy any of the Sudan. In England there was considerable agitation to reoccupy more of it. Politicians pointed out that it was dangerous for Egypt to have such a barbarous neighbour, but after the battle of Toski in 1889 no further attempt was made by the Dervishes to invade Egypt and it was quite obvious that no real threat to Egypt existed.

In 1895 there was a change in government in England, bringing into power a Conservative and Unionist administration that was strongly opposed to the Egyptian policy of Gladstone. Governments in democracies generally tend to reflect popular opinion, and popular opinion favoured the reconquest of the Sudan. Queen

Victoria favoured it too, writing that these 'wild Arabs . . . would not stand against regular good Troops at all'. Since the fall of Khartoum and the death of Gordon there had been a strong feeling in England that Gordon ought to be avenged; Britain felt guilty about the loss of the Sudan, although it was believed, certainly in official circles, that she was in no way responsible for it. Writing ten years after the event, Lord Cromer (Evelyn Baring) said: 'Indeed, one of the principal arguments in favour of recapturing Khartoum was that the British public had evidently made up its mind that, sooner or later, Khartoum had to be recaptured.' The escapes of Father Ohrwalder and Slatin, and the accounts of their experiences given to the English-speaking world by Wingate, tended to increase the feeling that something ought to be done; the victories at Toski and Tokar convinced most that it could be, for they had proved that well-disciplined troops, even Egyptian troops, could defeat the much-dreaded Dervishes.

Of course, men always go to war for the sake of high ideals, and suitably noble ones were easily found and eloquently expressed by young Winston Churchill in *The River War*:

> What enterprise that an enlightened community may attempt is more noble and more profitable than the reclamation from barbarism of fertile regions and large populations? To give peace to warring tribes, to administer justice where all was violence, to strike the chains off the slave, to draw the richness from the soil, to plant the earliest seeds of commerce and learning, to increase in whole peoples their capacities for pleasure and diminish their chances of pain – what more beautiful ideal or more valuable reward can inspire human effort? The act is virtuous, the exercise invigorating, and the result often extremely profitable.

Beyond the ideals and the mere desire to reconquer the Sudan, probably the most potent argument for transforming desire into action was the possession of the weapon to do so: the new, British-trained Egyptian army. Of course, somewhat different reasons were given for taking the first belligerent steps. On 1 March 1896 an Italian army was defeated by the Abyssinians at Adowa. The British supposed that the Dervishes were in league with the Abyssinians – a curious supposition as, far from being allied with the Abyssinians, the Dervishes had been fighting them. It was thought that the Dervishes, encouraged by the success of the Abyssinians, might attack the Italians at Kassala, endangering European prestige, then regarded as a valuable, if intangible, asset. Actually the Italian disaster at Adowa tended more to solidify British desire to reconquer the Sudan than to create any real alarm. Nevertheless, it was decided that a British demonstration on the Egyptian–Sudanese border might deter the Mahdists from initiating any aggressive plans they might have, and on the night of 12 March 1896 the Sirdar of the Egyptian army received orders from Evelyn Baring to advance south of Wadi Halfa towards Dongola. Three weeks later, Baring wired Kitchener: 'There is at present no question of a general reconquest of the Sudan. Pray bear this carefully in mind.' But the first step, once taken, could not be withdrawn and the next steps followed each other with a stately cadence: the war of reconquest had begun.

The order to advance into the Sudan meant many things to many people, but to the almost unknown forty-six-year-old Sirdar with the improbable name of Horatio Herbert Kitchener it was a ticket to fame and honour. Born in Ireland, the eldest son of a Lieutenant-Colonel, he did not attend school until he entered the Royal Military Academy at Woolwich. In many ways he was like the man he was now to avenge: both Gordon and Kitchener were sons of army officers, both served in the Royal Engineers, both were extremely religious, both spent time in Palestine studying the archaeological remains of early Christianity, both taught themselves to speak Arabic, and both had served as provincial governors in the Sudan before becoming eventually governors-general. In other ways, however, the two men were quite different. Where Gordon had been exotic and quixotic, Kitchener was methodical and careful. Gordon was flamboyant and colourful; Kitchener was cold and dull.

As a young man, Kitchener was not considered promising. His instructors and fellow students at Woolwich characterized him as 'in no way remarkable', 'quite an ordinary youth' and 'rather slow in learning'. He was considered somewhat below the average standard of a Royal Engineer officer when he passed out of Woolwich in December 1870. Shortly after this he went over to France to offer his services to the French army in their brief struggle with Prussia. This seems to have been a quixotic act contrary to his general character, until it is remembered – as it generally is not – that his father took him there. He caught a chill going up in a balloon with a French officer and fell ill. His father took him home.

His next attempt to see action came twelve years later and ended almost as badly. He was making maps in Cyprus when Arabi's rebellion broke out in Egypt. He asked to be transferred there, but the request was refused. He then took sick leave and went to Alexandria, arriving just in time to be evacuated by the British ships. He witnessed the naval bombardment, but was refused permission to accompany the party that went in to spike the guns of the shore batteries. He did have his first chance to do some intelligence work: with another officer, he went ashore in disguise and made some sketches at Zigazag. When he returned to Cyprus, however, he found himself in trouble for leaving the island without permission and over-extending his leave.

Late in the year 1882 Sir Evelyn Wood was trying to persuade British officers to join the Egyptian army and create it anew in their own image. Posts in the Egyptian army were not considered to be stepping stones for advancement in the regular establishment, but each officer was immediately given an Egyptian rank two steps above the rank he held in the British army and the pay was good. Sir Evelyn Wood found Lieutenant Kitchener and twenty-four other young officers who could not afford to live in good regiments in England. They were good men and service in the Egyptian army gave them an opportunity to prove it: twelve of them became generals.

The young officers, together with a set of excellent drill sergeants, set about the task of remaking the Egyptian army. Kitchener, then thirty-three years old, was given the post of second-in-command of the cavalry and the rank of bimbashi, or major. One of his fellow officers wrote in his diary: 'We all hated the sight of him, for two reasons – (1) because he was a "Sapper", and (2) because he designed a light blue uniform for his cavalry much finer than anything we had!' In general, his associates in Cairo thought him gauche, shy and unclubbable.

Kitchener did not spend much time on cavalry duties. He was soon given a two-month assignment surveying in the Sinai desert, from which he was recalled on the news of the disaster of the Hicks Pasha expedition. Then he was sent to the Sudan border to report on road conditions. From April to June 1884, he was in Aswan organizing a small force of Ababdeh irregulars. On board a Nile steamer near here he wrote to his friend Walter Besant in England on 3 May:

> I am now having an exciting time in Upper Egypt. I have got 1,000 Bedawin under my command and expect 1,000 more, all mounted on dromedaries. I hope to advance soon on Abu Hamed. I am just going back to Cairo to explain matters to the authorities. Excuse scrawl, as this d—d boat is very unsteady.

In June he moved to Korosko and then to Dongola, gathering

information, bribing tribes to be loyal and, from Dongola, sending messengers to Gordon in Khartoum. He was now working for Colonel Sir Charles Wilson, head of intelligence for the Egyptian army, and for the first time he was beginning to make something of a name for himself.

In his dealings with the Sudanese Arabs, Kitchener appears to have been somewhat naïve, giving them more credit for good intentions than they deserved, although he was close enough to the Mahdist movement to form a higher opinion of Dervish character than was generally held by those in Europe. To his friend Besant he wrote: 'Unless an English expedition comes, I do not think we shall be able to hold this frontier, as the rebels mean coming on, and are much more disciplined and fanatical than people give them credit for.'

In September 1884 Lord Wolseley arrived in Egypt to take charge of the relief expedition. In a letter to his wife Wolseley announced his intention of taking '1,000 or 1,500 men on camels into Khartoum, *capture* Gordon, and bring him back with me'. Lord Wolseley appears to have understood Gordon's character better than Kitchener and his immediate superiors, who were then offering £10,000 to the Kababish if they could rescue Gordon. When Lord Wolseley took command, Kitchener came under him and was appointed to the Intelligence Department with the additional duties of Deputy Assistant Adjutant-General and Quartermaster-General at Dongola.

As the relief expedition advanced slowly up the Nile, Kitchener was again engaged in intelligence work, principally in trying to maintain contact with Gordon. He worked hard, but Gordon was contemptuous of his efforts. In his journal (24 September 1884) Gordon wrote:

It is the most extraordinary thing, quite incomprehensible, that with only one exception . . . not one single messenger has entered this place on the proper initiative of outsiders. It has been invariably *my* messengers, who were sent out by me, from Khartoum, who did bring me any news. . . . Either these officers outside do not care to spend a sou in spies to give me information, or else they think it is a matter of supreme indifference whether I know what is going on or not. . . . There is a lot of 'I hope you are well', etc.; men like Kitchener . . . might be expected to have more brains than that. . . . I never saw such a feeble lot in my life! One has only to compare the telegrams &c, we send down, with the *rubbish* sent in by *our own messengers*. . . . Kitchener's note to Stewart on the same paper – it perfectly exasperates one. Kitchener asks

Stewart 'what he can do for him' – nothing of what has gone on with respect to the Sudan . . .

Meanwhile, Kitchener, who was doing his best to get messages to Gordon, complained that he heard little news from him. Although he did not please Gordon, he pleased his superiors in the field and in Cairo. But with the fall of Khartoum and the death of Gordon, the relief expedition was deemed superfluous and was abandoned. Kitchener went on leave to England for two months, studied Ottoman law in London and then was appointed to a commission in Zanzibar. When at Suez on his way home, he received a telegram appointing him 'Governor-General of the Eastern Sudan and the Red Sea Littoral'. The title was bigger than the territory. Osman Digna's Dervishes held all this land except for the squalid town of Suakin.

On his arrival at Suakin, Kitchener embarked upon a policy of making friends with the local tribes, regardless of their conduct in the past, and he had written over the gate to the town: 'Peace to those who enter and who leave this place.' In January 1888 he felt that he had become strong enough to attempt an attack on Osman Digna, then encamped at Handub, only fifteen miles from Suakin. Kitchener's force consisted of only about 450 men, most of whom were 'friendlies'. Permission to make the attack was given to Kitchener only if he did not use regular troops, but he took along some Blacks from the 10th Sudanese Battalion. It was the first time he had ever actually planned and directed a battle.

He set out from Suakin just before dawn on 17 January, and after a three-hour march he halted and directed his infantry and the friendlies to advance and attack the camp. He made a strange error for an engineer officer: he thought the enemy camp was near by when it was actually three miles from his halting place. After waiting for some time without receiving any news, he advanced himself with his cavalry at a fast trot. The Blacks and friendly tribesmen had apparently taken the Dervishes by surprise when they charged into the village, but Osman Digna quickly gathered his force together and attacked the attackers from the rear. Kitchener's friendlies bolted, leaving the regulars of the 10th Sudanese to extricate themselves as best they could. As usual, the Blacks fought bravely and were holding off an attack from two sides when Kitchener arrived on the scene.

Kitchener dismounted his men and poured several volleys into the Dervishes. With difficulty, he managed to disengage the Blacks and make an orderly retreat, but the Dervishes continued a murderous fire and Kitchener was wounded so severely in the lower jaw that his second-in-command had to take charge of the retreat to Suakin.

For this effort, Kitchener was rewarded by being made a brevet colonel. After leave in England to recover from his wound, he went back to Cairo. He commanded the cavalry at the battle of Toski and then spent a year as head of the Egyptian constabulary before becoming adjutant-general in the summer of 1891. In April of the following year, Sir Francis Grenfell resigned the Sirdarship of the Egyptian army. Kitchener was not the most popular choice to succeed him, but he had the most powerful supporter: Sir Evelyn Baring. As the man most responsible for the finances of the Egyptian government, Baring favoured a sirdar who knew how to save money as well as spend it. Kitchener was his man, for, as Lord Salisbury once said, he was the only soldier he ever knew who understood and practiced economy. Baring had his way and Kitchener was appointed Sirdar of the Egyptian army.

The army Kitchener commanded consisted of 18,000 men organized into fourteen battalions of infantry (eight of Egyptian fellahin and six of Sudanese Blacks), four squadrons of cavalry and three batteries of artillery; there was a small cadre of supply and transport troops, but no engineers – they would be too expensive. Nothing was wasted or thrown away until it fell apart. Old leather and badly worn uniforms were reworked in army workshops; cheaper cloth was used for clothing; men were put in the reserve two years ahead of their time. The parsimonious Kitchener was not popular with his officers, but Baring liked him.

The Egyptian army under Kitchener was a far different organization than it had been in the days before Arabi's rebellion. In spite of their ragged appearance, the soldiers were drilled and trained by honest and conscientious British officers and non-commissioned officers. They were also paid regularly and were not maltreated. Egyptian officers were expected to learn their trade and soldier in the British manner, although none held rank higher than kaimakam, or lieutenant-colonel. Unlike the Egyptian units, the Sudanese battalions were composed entirely of volunteers, many of whom were former bazingers or deserters from the Dervish army. They were Blacks from the forest and swamps of the southern Sudan – Shilluks, Dinkas and Gallas mostly. Each battalion contained 759 men divided into six companies, each with four British officers.

While training his battalions and husbanding his resources, Kitchener was also gathering all the information possible about the

Sudan. He was fortunate in having as the head of his intelligence department a most remarkable officer: Colonel Francis Reginald Wingate. He was born on 25 June 1861, the seventh son of a Scottish merchant who died a year later. He was educated at St James Collegiate School and at the Royal Military Academy at Woolwich and was gazetted as a second lieutenant in the Royal Artillery in July 1880. After service in India, where he learned Hindustani and was bitten by a panther, and in Aden, where he studied Arabic and Freemasonry, he was appointed to the new Egyptian army in 1883 and posted to the 4th Infantry Battalion. His first major assignment was to set up a hospital during the cholera epidemic. Three months later he had won the Order of Osmanieh (4th class) and was himself taken ill and invalided back to England.

Three months later he was back in Cairo as aide-de-camp for the Sirdar, General Sir Evelyn Wood. Word had just been received of the defeat of Hicks Pasha and the twenty-three-year-old Wingate found himself in an interesting and exciting position at headquarters, where he could see and be seen during the rapid development of events in the Sudan: the defeat of General Baker and the fighting around Suakin, Gordon cut off in Khartoum, the disaster to Colonel Stewart and his party, the organization of the relief expedition under Lord Wolseley, the tragic news of the fall of Khartoum, and the retreat of the desert column of the relief expedition. For his staff work, Wingate was given the Queen's Medal, the Khedive's Star, and the Order of Mejidieh (4th class). It had been an interesting and exciting two years, but when Sir Evelyn Wood resigned his Sirdarship and it became evident that the Sudan was not to be reconquered, Wingate also resigned from the Egyptian army and returned to the 'Regular Establishment', still as A.D.C. to General Wood but in England.

He was in England for less than a year, but it was time enough to pass the examination for his captaincy and to become engaged to Miss Kitty Rundle. Not having enough money to marry and live in England, he returned to the Egyptian army and was assigned as Assistant Military Secretary to the new Sirdar, Sir Francis Grenfell. One of his colleagues was Leslie Rundle, his fox-hunting future brother-in-law, who amused himself by teaching English to the natives with some success. Sir Francis, while on a tour of inspection, was once surprised to find himself greeted on entering a village by cries of 'Tally-ho!' and on leaving with 'Gone away!'

In 1887 Wingate was doing recruiting and some intelligence work; two years later he was devoting himself exclusively to

intelligence. His work involved collecting not only military information on the strength and disposition of the Khalifa's forces but also
political and economic information on conditions in the Sudan. In
addition to this, but related to it, was the task of attempting to effect
the escape of the European prisoners of the Khalifa. Wingate
finally collected so much information about the Sudan that he
decided to write a book about it, and *Mahdiism and the Egyptian
Sudan* was published in October 1891. The original manuscript
contained a good deal of political comment regarding the British
government's relations with Egypt and the Sudan, but on Baring's
advice most of this was eliminated. However, he could not resist
saying: 'That a new and better Soudan will be raised over the ashes
of Gordon, and all those brave officers and men who have perished
in the loyal performance of their duty, is the present hope of every
well-wisher for the prosperity of Egypt.'

Two months after the publication of this book, Father Ohrwalder
and the two nuns made their dramatic escape with the help of
Wingate. An account of Father Ohrwalder's life in captivity and his
flight from Omdurman was published by Wingate shortly after.
The book created something of a sensation and undoubtedly
stimulated interest in the reconquest of the Sudan. In 1892, when
Kitchener became Sirdar, Wingate's network of spies and in-
formers was given an official status with the creation of a formal
Intelligence Department, with Wingate as its chief. In 1894 he
helped Father Rossignoli to escape. Then, in 1895, he was primarily
responsible for the escape of Rudolf Slatin. This was rightly considered a great coup, and Wingate was rewarded with the Iron
Crown of Austria, bestowed on him by the Emperor Franz Josef,
while Queen Victoria made him a Companion of the Bath, a rare
honour for a thirty-four-year-old major of artillery. The news of
Slatin's escape and Wingate's translation of Slatin's account of his
experiences, published under the romantic title of *Fire and Sword
in the Sudan*, maintained British interest in the Sudan and height-
ened a desire to subdue the Khalifa and reconquer the country.
Thus Wingate became not only the chief source for gathering news
about the Sudan, but also the chief propagandist for its reconquest.

The Sirdar found Wingate a very useful staff officer. Although it
has never been admitted, there is a suspicion that Wingate's spies
were not all in the Sudan; some, perhaps, were in the household
and government of Abbas Hilmi II, the new twenty-year-old
Khedive of Egypt, who succeeded his father, Tewfik, in 1892. A
private document came into the Sirdar's hands just before the first

inspection by the Khedive of the Egyptian army; in it, the Khedive expressed his intention of discrediting the British officers who were running his army. The document seemed so incredible that at first it was believed to be a forgery, but the young Khedive's conduct followed the plan.

As the Khedive and his retinue, with Kitchener and his staff, proceeded from north to south up the Nile in the khedival yacht inspecting the troops, the Khedive's comments on the efforts of the British officers became more and more acid. At the final review at Wadi Halfa he was particularly cutting. Every British-led battalion was censured and every Egyptian-led battalion was praised. Finally the Khedive turned to his Sirdar and said, 'To tell you the truth, Kitchener Pasha, I consider it disgraceful for Egypt to be served by such an army'.

Kitchener testily replied: 'As Your Highness is evidently displeased with the efforts of myself and the British officers in training your army, nothing remains for me but to place my own resignation and that of all the British officers in your hands.'

The Khedive, realizing that he had gone too far, tried to be conciliatory, but Kitchener was adamant. Wingate drew up a report on the Khedive's inspection tour that was quickly dispatched to Baring, who passed it on to London. Baring supported Kitchener and the British government supported Baring. The result was that the Khedive was forced to issue an official statement to the effect that he was completely satisfied with the work of Kitchener and the British officers and the British government expressed its support of the Sirdar by creating him K.C.M.G.

If it was not clear before, there could be no doubt after this incident that Britain ruled Egypt and Baring was her viceroy; Baring controlled the Egyptian army and Kitchener was his commander-in-chief. Although the Khedive was 'brought to his bearings', he never forgave Kitchener nor Britain, and when World War I began he defected (according to British views) by maintaining his allegiance to the Sultan of Turkey, whose khedive he was supposed to be. There was never the enthusiasm in Egypt for the reconquest of the Sudan that prevailed in England. Although the war against the Khalifa was fought primarily with Egyptian and Sudanese troops of the Egyptian army, *en principe* for Egypt, it was Britain's war, not Egypt's.

It was only the morning after Kitchener had received his marching orders that anyone thought to tell the Egyptian government what their army was going to do; Baring quickly convened the Egyptian cabinet for it to give its approval and vote a decree. The following day the reserves were called up and the next day, after a review by the Khedive of the troops of the Cairo garrison, Kitchener informed the Khedive that the first troops would move south that night. He did not bother to tell him that already, that very day, troops of the Egyptian army had started their march south from Wadi Halfa across that invisible line between Mahdism and the rest of the world. The 11th and 12th Sudanese battalions seized Akasha, about forty miles south of Wadi Halfa, without a fight on 22 March 1896. This first advance into the Sudan was led by an exceptionally capable officer named Hector Archibald Mac-Donald, who shortly rose to command a brigade of Sudanese.

MacDonald was the youngest of five sons of a Scottish crofter. At eighteen he enlisted as a common soldier in the Gordon High-landers and served nearly ten years in the ranks, rising to the rank of colour-sergeant. He so distinguished himself by repeated acts of bravery and exceptional leadership during the Afghan wars that Lord Roberts gave him a commission. After active service in Natal, where he again displayed his exceptional courage at the battle of Majuba, he came to Egypt to accept an appointment in Valentine Baker Pasha's constabulary in 1883. He was aptly called 'Fighting Mac' for he always seemed to be on hand when there was fighting to be done.

In the next few weeks following MacDonald's advance, Akasha was made into a strong camp while the bulk of the Egyptian army was carried by Nile steamer and railroad to the frontier. Some cavalry skirmishes took place south of Wadi Halfa in May, but it was June before the next major advance was made. By this time Kitchener had assembled about 9,000 men within striking distance of Firket, the closest Dervish stronghold, only ten miles from Akasha. The army was composed of an infantry division of five Egyptian and five Sudanese battalions, seven squadrons of Egyptian cavalry, a camel corps of eight companies, three batteries of artillery and one battery of four Maxim guns. On 7 June this force attacked and captured Firket. Although the bulk of the fighting was done by the Sudanese under Major MacDonald, the Egyptian troops behaved very well; the British officers who had trained them had done their job well. Two days after the battle of Firket, Mac-Donald's brigade occupied Suarda, about twenty-five miles further south, and this became the most advanced post of the conquering army.

Supply was the biggest problem. Most of the river transport on the lower Nile was handled by the enterprising firm of Thomas Cook and Son, but above the first cataract land transport was needed. There had once been a railroad running south from Wadi Halfa to Firket. The road-bed was now in ruins and the sleepers gone, but most of the rails were still around – some had been used by the Dervishes at Firket to construct a gallows. This railroad was now repaired and extended as far as Kosheh, a little village of mud huts ten miles south of Firket. It was used to bring up supplies, reinforcements and even gunboats in sections to be assembled on the banks of the Nile and floated above the second cataract.

The next Dervish position was at Kerma, at the third cataract, 127 miles by river and eighty-six miles by land from Kosheh. The force at the Sirdar's disposal at this time consisted of an additional two battalions of Egyptian troops, a battalion of British troops (the North Staffordshire Regiment) and a flotilla of five gunboats and three armed steamers, a total of 15,000 men. Nearly the entire Egyptian army – thirteen out of the sixteen battalions – was at the front. The advance on Kerma began on 23 August, again led by MacDonald's brigade consisting of the 11th, 12th and 13th Sudanese battalions. The army reached Kerma on 19 September and found that the Dervishes had moved over to the opposite side of the Nile. The action was primarily between the gunboats and the entrenched Dervishes. After a two-hour duel at long range, the Dervishes retreated. The army marched on, and Dongola, thirty miles further on, was taken without difficulty, ending the 'Campaign of 1896'. As such matters are reckoned in war, the cost had been small: forty-three men were killed and 139 wounded in action, while another 130 men had died of cholera and other diseases.

A year passed before there was any further action. The delay was caused by the difficult question of supply. As Winston Churchill said in his colourful prose: 'Victory is the beautiful, bright-coloured flower. Transport is the stem without which it could never have blossomed.' Although the Nile had been the main road for supplies during the Campaign of 1896, the repair of the railroad to Kosheh had been an invaluable asset. To build and run the railroad, a railroad battalion was formed: a motley crew of Egyptians, Blacks and captured Dervishes, many of whom had never before seen a railroad track or a train. There were only eight locomotives and these were so decrepit that at times only three of them were operational. Nevertheless, a handful of young engineer officers managed to keep the railroad running. The Sirdar now considered extending it across the desert to Abu Hamed. After seeking the advice of experienced British railway engineers and of other military men who had built and operated railroads – all of whom agreed that it was impossible – the Sirdar decided to build it. He turned over the entire project to a young Royal Engineers officer of French Canadian ancestry named Lieutenant Edouard Girouard.

Fifteen new engines and 200 cars were purchased in England, 1,500 additional men were recruited for the railway battalion, and workshops were constructed at Wadi Halfa. Eventually, forty engines of ten different makes and of various ages were put into service. The task of extending the railroad into the desert was a formidable one. Added to the difficulties was the fact that nearly every man had to be trained for his job: almost every engineer, switchman and clerk had to be taught his trade; even men who could not read and write were made at least semi-literate in classes under palm trees.

The desert into which the railroad moved was believed to be waterless. Two successful wells were eventually sunk, but in the main the water for the engines and for the men had to be carried out to them on the trains, in addition to food and supplies. The further away they moved from Wadi Halfa, the more difficult it was to supply the graders and track layers. It also became more dangerous, so that in addition to the men working on the railroad itself, soldiers had to be provided to guard the workers and the laid track. Yet, off into the desert the line of track moved, headed for Abu Hamed – which had not yet been captured.

Abu Hamed is 210 miles in a straight line from Wadi Halfa. The railroad had been pushed out 130 miles when it paused to wait for the capture of Abu Hamed. To secure this important position, a flying column was organized under the command of Major-General Archibald Hunter, a brave, experienced, and very popular officer – it was Hunter, not Kitchener, who was the most respected man in the Egyptian army. The flying column consisted of MacDonald's brigade, now composed of the 9th, 10th and 11th Sudanese battalions, plus a troop of cavalry and a battery of field artillery – about 3,600 men. Starting from a little village near Merawi on 29 June, the column had to cross 146 miles of desert. The troops suffered from the heat and from struggling through the soft, deep sand. Three men died on the march. When they reached Abu Hamed early on the morning of 7 July they were nearly exhausted, but Hunter pushed them forward to the attack, for he had heard that Dervish reinforcements were on their way. Although the place was stoutly defended, MacDonald's Sudanese battalions carried the town. Two British officers and twenty-one men were killed and sixty-one were wounded, but now the railroad could continue.

Kitchener had intended to bring his army up to Abu Hamed and carefully build up his supplies for the next big jump to Berber, but an unexpected development caused him to move faster than he had planned. Towards the end of August, a group of forty Ababdeh tribesmen loyal to the government were sent out to reconnoitre in the direction of Berber. They went on, meeting no resistance, until they actually entered Berber; finding that the Dervishes had retreated, they occupied the town and sent word of its capture back to Abu Hamed. Two days later, when the Sirdar heard of it, he had to decide whether to recall the audacious tribesmen and be safe, or move in troops to occupy Berber. He decided to be daring and send his troops ahead; Hunter was dispatched with the 9th Sudanese in four gunboats to Berber, which he occupied on 10 September.

The occupation of Berber had the desired effect on the tribes in the Red Sea littoral and soon the route between Suakin and Berber was opened again by a camel corps patrol and a group of war correspondents, who boasted that they were the first Europeans to use the route in thirteen years.

In October a flotilla of gunboats steamed up the Nile and spent two days destroying the forts at El Metemma. By the end of the year, the army had reached the junction of the Atbara river with the Nile and built a strong camp there. Spies reported that the great Dervish army at Omdurman was about to advance, so Kitchener requested and obtained a brigade of British troops. The brigade consisted of one battalion each of the Cameron Highlanders, the Royal Warwickshire Regiment, the Lincoln Regiment and the Seaforth Highlanders, all under the command of General William Gatacre. The essential railroad pushed further and further south, past Berber and El Metemma to the camp on the Atbara.

In March 1898 a Dervish force of about 16,000 men under the command of Mahmud Wad Ahmed and Osman Digna tried to go around the east end of the Atbara camp and attack Berber. Kitchener countered this by moving the bulk of his army, 14,000 men, up the Atbara to intercept them. For a week both sides sat in their zaribas, seven miles apart, each waiting for the other to attack. Finally, the Sirdar decided to make the first aggressive move. On the morning of 8 April, Highlanders, Egyptians and the Sudanese battalions marched through the sand and heat to the skirl of bagpipes towards the zariba of the Dervishes 'in all the majesty of war', as Churchill said, 'an avalanche of men, stern, unflinching, utterly irresistible'. The Dervish army was defeated, Mahmud Wad Ahmed was captured and the wily Osman Digna fled. On the Anglo-Egyptian side, eighty-two were killed, mostly Blacks from the brave Sudanese battalions; the Dervishes lost about 3,000 men.

Thanks to the railroad, Kitchener had now transported his army to less than 200 miles from the Khalifa's capital. All knew that the next battle would be the biggest one, and decisive. Kitchener put his troops in summer camp and prepared for the struggle ahead. More men and equipment were ordered: another brigade of British infantry, a battery of heavy howitzers, a battery of Maxim machine guns, three new screw steamers and the 21st Lancers. By the middle of August 1898, Kitchener had assembled a force of 17,600 Egyptian and Sudanese troops and 8,200 British troops; counting the weapons on the steamers, there were eighty cannon and forty-four Maxims; there was a flotilla of ten steamers, and on land 3,524 camels, 2,469 horses, 892 mules and 229 donkeys. With this force the Sirdar began his march on Omdurman, where an estimated 50,000 Dervishes were waiting to destroy him.

On 1 September 1898 Kitchener's army was within a few miles of Omdurman. Early that morning the 21st Lancers were sent out to find the enemy, even if they had to go to the gates of Omdurman itself. In command of one of the troops was a young subaltern named Lieutenant Winston Churchill (or Winston Spencer-Churchill as he then called himself). As the squadrons rounded the shoulder of the Kerreri Hills, he saw in the distance a pointed dome rising above the horizon: the tomb of the Mahdi in Omdurman.

The Battle of Omdurman

All through the summer of 1898 when Kitchener was bringing up his army, weapons and supplies, the Khalifa was gathering in the tribesmen for his last great effort. Proclamations were sent in all directions summoning the faithful to the jihad, and 50,000 fighting men answered his call. He built seventeen forts to command the river approaches and tried to devise mines and string chains across the river to stop the gunboats. He possessed sixty-three guns, but most of these were in the forts along the river and only five were taken with him on 31 August when he led his army out of Omdurman, north towards the Kerreri Hills to meet the invaders.

The Khalifa arranged his army in battle formation on the plains of Kerreri. In the centre were 12,000 Black riflemen (the jihadia) and 13,000 spearmen with a strong detachment of mulazemin thrown out in front. The Khalifa himself was in the centre of the line with 2,000 of his bodyguard. Behind him was the rearguard of 13,000 spearmen under the command of Yakub. The right wing was commanded by the Khalifa Sherif and was composed of 2,000 Donagla tribesmen plus 1,700 Hadendowa under the command of the wily Osman Digna on the extreme right nearest Omdurman. Khalifa Ali Wad Helu was on the left with 5,000 warriors extending into the desert.

What they lacked in discipline, they made up in fighting experience and in fanatic loyalty to the Mahdist cause. Unfortunately for the Khalifa, he did not have modern weapons. He had fewer rifles than his enemy and those he had were old with faulty ammunition; his cannon were also obsolete and his powder was not the best. But most unfortunate of all was the lack of good generals. The great Abu Anga, brave Wad Nejumi and the stout Zeki Tamal were all dead. The Khalifa himself had little experience in commanding armies, nor had the other khalifas; most of the rifles were under the command of the Khalifa's son Osman, who had no experience at all.

When the 21st Lancers joined the Egyptian cavalry on a ridge they looked down with astonishment on this mighty army, its huge banners flying, drums beating and spears flashing. It must have been a striking spectacle. Those who saw it were the last ever to see such a sight, for never since has such a huge barbaric army been displayed in all its wild splendour. Most impressive of all to young Lieutenant Winston Churchill was the deep murmur of the tens of thousands of voices that came rolling up towards them.

Except for a bit of cavalry skirmishing, the first major action was the fight between the gunboats and the Khalifa's forts along the river. It was an uneven contest. The mud forts with their outdated cannon were no match for the well-armed steamers: the shells from the gunboats blew the mud walls to pieces and the Maxim guns mounted on the decks swept the trenches. The steamers then made their way upstream and bombarded the city itself, killing a number of women and children.

The howitzers were landed and they, too, began to shell the city. In all, 410 high explosive shells were thrown into the mud walls of Omdurman. The dome of the Mahdi's tomb was their aiming point, and they made several direct hits on it. Although the Anglo-Egyptian force did not know it, none of this shelling of Omdurman had the slightest effect on the battle, for, excepting a small percentage of deserters, every man able to hold a spear was with the Khalifa Abdullahi on the plains of Kerreri.

The Sirdar's army expected the Dervishes to attack at once and stood ready to meet it. On 1 September Lieutenant Churchill had lunch with Colonel Wingate and asked him if there was really going to be a battle. 'Certainly, rather,' he replied.

'When? Tomorrow?'

'No. Here, now, in an hour or two,' said Wingate.

But he was wrong. By mid-afternoon it was apparent that there would be no fight that day. As there was some fear of a night attack, the Anglo-Egyptian army did not make a regular camp but slept on the ground in battle positions.

The following morning, 2 September 1898, bugles sounded throughout the camp by the river at four-thirty. There was not the slightest doubt in anyone's mind that this was the day of the great battle. The Anglo-Egyptian forces were arranged in a half-circle with their backs to the river around the little village of Egaiga. The gunboats protected their flanks and the Egyptian cavalry and camel corps occupied the high ground in the Kerreri Hills to the north-west. Shortly after dawn, the invaders saw before them the host of the Khalifa, stretched out for five miles on the open plain. To turn his superiority of numbers to advantage and minimize his defects in equipment, the Khalifa ought to have attacked by night. This was urged on him, but he rejected the suggestion. Perhaps he feared that his warriors would not be brave enough unless under his watching eyes. So it was bright morning as his men charged across an open plain into the mouths of modern rifles, machine guns and artillery.

Six thousand Dervishes poured over the ridge of Surgham and bore down on the left flank of the Anglo-Egyptian army. Then Osman with 8,000 men attacked the centre. Ernest Bennet, an Oxford don who was serving as war correspondent for the *Westminster Gazette*, described this first Dervish charge: 'In the clear morning air the pageant was truly magnificent, a splendid panorama of some forty thousand [*sic*] barbarians moving forward all undismayed to do battle with the largest army which Great Britain had placed in the field for forty years.' The Anglo-Egyptian artillery opened fire at 2,800 yards; the rifles of the infantry at 1,200 yards. The Dervishes were shot down by the score. And when a Dervish was hit by a British bullet he fell, for the British troops were using dumdums: hollowed out, soft-nosed bullets that spread when they hit, creating horrible wounds; called 'man-stoppers', these cruel missiles have since been outlawed by international agreement.

Some of the Maxims ran out of water to cool their barrels; they were filled from the canteens of the Cameron Highlanders. Few Dervishes came as close as 500 yards from the front rank of the Anglo-Egyptian infantry, and none came within striking distance. A number found cover in a small depression, but the artillery searched them out and hounded them with shrapnel. This first attack, begun at 6.45 in the morning, was finished by 8.00 a.m. G. W. Steevens, one of the sixteen war correspondents who were there, said, 'It was not a battle, but an execution.' Even after the enemy had retreated, the excited soldiers kept firing at the scattered writhing wounded stretched out before them. Kitchener rode across the front of the 2nd Egyptian Brigade calling 'Cease fire! Cease fire! Cease fire!' and he was heard to exclaim, 'Oh, what a dreadful waste of ammunition!'

Meanwhile, Colonel Broadwood with the Egyptian cavalry and the Camel Corps in the Kerreri Hills received an order to retreat behind the main lines. But Broadwood knew that his force was in a position to divert the Dervish cavalry, which was now coming towards him. He decided to disobey the order to retreat and instead to lure the enemy cavalry away from the main battle. He therefore moved north, drawing the Dervish horsemen after him.

His camel corps, however, found the rocky ground difficult and the Dervish cavalry was gaining on him. He was fortunate enough to reach the river and come under the protection of the guns of a steamer just in time. Thus protected, his camel corps was able to get back to the main lines, while he rode on with the cavalry and drew the Dervish horsemen another three miles north.

On the other end of the Anglo-Egyptian lines, the 21st Lancers were riding south, around the edge of Jebel Surgham, between the ridge and the river. They found the east end of the ridge unoccupied, but they could see groups of Dervishes making their way towards Omdurman. In a khor, or dry watercourse, directly in front of them was a Dervish force of about 700 men. The 21st Lancers prepared to attack, but before they could, and unknown to them, the defenders of the khor, who stood between the lancers and Omdurman, were reinforced by nearly 2,000 Dervishes detached from the main body by the Khalifa as soon as he learned of the advance of the cavalry. The reinforcements had moved up unseen by another khor.

Colonel R. H. Martin, in command of the lancers, had explicit orders only to reconnoitre and harass the enemy, but he could not resist the temptation, seemingly so strong in cavalry officers, to charge. He ordered his bugler to sound 'Right wheel into line!' and the regiment, 320 officers and troopers, trotted off towards an enemy of unknown strength. The ground in front of them appeared smooth, but they came unexpectedly upon a small khor filled with Dervishes who sprang up to attack the attackers. Each trooper crouched over his lance and dug his heels into his horse in an effort to gain enough momentum to carry him through the dense mob before him. In the brief hand-to-hand fighting that followed, the smart line of lancers was broken by the Dervishes, who pressed the muzzles of their rifles against the flanks of the horses or swung their heavy swords at the cavalrymen. They did not panic under the impact of the charge as undisciplined savages were supposed to do. These men were familiar with this type of warfare and their conduct in the fight was superb.

Lieutenant R. F. Molyneux fell from his horse in the khor amid the Dervishes. Unhurt, he leaped to his feet, pistol in hand. While he fired at one man, his right hand was slashed by another. He jumped out of the khor and ran in the direction taken by his regiment, pursued by four or five of the enemy. Seeing a trooper riding across his path, he called to him for help. With a cheerful, 'All right, sir!' the trooper wheeled and charged Molyneux's pursuers, waving his sword. He was wounded in his chest by a Dervish spear, but his action allowed the young lieutenant to escape. The trooper himself fought his way clear.

Lieutenant Churchill's troop was riding on the right wing of the charging lancers and hit only the edge of the massed Dervishes. Churchill saw two jibba-clad men standing before him in front of the khor. He rode between them. They shot at the future prime minister, but missed him; the trooper immediately behind him was killed. Then his horse dropped into the sandy khor and he found the enemy all around him, though not as thick as on his left, where some troopers were stopped in their tracks, unable to force their way through the densely packed Dervishes. Churchill rode straight through and up the opposite bank of the khor, his horse again trotting on the hard, crisp desert soil. In the excitement, he had no sense of danger or disaster but trotted about, shooting at stray Arabs, until he realized that he was alone and ought to be with his troop. He spurred his horse into a gallop and soon found his men re-forming and facing about. A Dervish jumped up among them, and there was some confusion as several troopers jabbed at him with their lances. Churchill shot him.

Finding that he had fired the entire clip from his Mauser pistol, he reloaded and while he did so he asked one of his sergeants if he had enjoyed himself. The man replied honestly: 'Well, I don't exactly say I enjoyed it, sir, but I think I'll get more used to it next time.'

Most of the lancers managed to fight their way through and passed on about 200 yards beyond the khor before pausing to reform and turn back to face the enemy again. This was a separate battle, a private war. Without Maxims or artillery, it was primarily lance and sword against spear and sword. But the romance of the cavalry charge no longer seemed so alluring. In the two minutes it had taken the regiment to pass through the Dervishes in the khor five officers and sixty-five men had been killed or wounded, and out of 320 horses, 119 were dead or wounded. The 21st Lancers had lost a quarter of its strength in less than ten minutes time. The pocket watch of Lieutenant R. Grenfell, who was killed in the charge, was pierced by a Dervish spear; it had stopped at 8.40 a.m.

Colonel Martin, who had bravely and stupidly ridden through the Dervish-filled khor without drawing sword or pistol, finally came to his senses, and instead of charging back into the khor, sounded the order to gather his men together and led them around to the flank of the enemy where he could enfilade them with carbine fire. The Dervishes were routed and, twenty minutes after starting their reckless charge, the remains of the 21st Lancers were taking breakfast in the khor. Near by were about thirty or forty dead Dervishes and the hacked and mutilated bodies of more than twenty lancers. Three Victoria Crosses were awarded for bravery in this action, including one for the trooper who saved the life of Lieutenant Molyneux; Colonel Martin was commended for 'excellent services performed' in Kitchener's official report of the battle. Not for the first time, a blunder by British cavalry was made an example of military glory.

The charge of the 21st Lancers was a minor action; the main event was still taking place behind them on the Kerreri plains. Kitchener, apparently thinking the battle won and anxious to occupy Omdurman before the Dervishes could fall back upon it, ordered his infantry to re-form in marching order and swing south. The brigades of British and Egyptian infantry began their cumbersome movements. Although G. Gorringe, a young lieutenant at the time (he later became a lieutenant-general), said afterwards that Kitchener knew what he was doing, it seems highly unlikely that he was aware of the fact that he was marching his army across the front of the main body of the Dervish army, leaving a strong, undefeated enemy on his flank. The two British brigades, which had been on the left of the arc around Egaiga, were the furthest south and they moved to occupy the east end of the Jebel Surgham ridge. The Egyptian brigades started to follow, but MacDonald's brigade of the 9th, 10th and 11th Sudanese battalions and the 2nd Egyptians, in all about 3,000 men, found Dervishes firing at them from the front (west) and they turned to meet them.

It soon became apparent to the experienced MacDonald that he was being attacked in great force, as indeed he was: this was the Dervish main force under Yakub, nearly 20,000 men. MacDonald's brigade was at this time about a mile from the nearest brigade on his left. He received an order to retreat, but he is reported to have said, 'I'll no do it. I'll see them damned first. We maun just fight.' And fight he did.

Although the Dervishes pressed home their attack with great bravery, they were cut down by superior fire-power, steadily and capably directed. The attack of Yakub's warriors was supposed to have been co-ordinated with those of the troops under the Khalifa's son Osman coming from the Kerreri Hills. Unfortunately for the Khalifa and his cause, MacDonald's men were able to blunt the charge of Yakub's men before those of Osman came on the scene.

MacDonald coolly and skilfully swung his troops by half-battalions in an arc to meet the attack on his flank, his Blacks executing each movement with parade-ground precision. Bennet Burleigh, who saw MacDonald's performance from a distance, said: 'Had the brilliant, the splendid deed of arms wrought by MacDonald been done under the eyes of the sovereign, or in some other armies, he would have been created a general on the spot.' But it was performed under the eyes of Kitchener. Had the attack on Mac-Donald been well co-ordinated, it appears most likely that he would have been overwhelmed by superior numbers and the Dervishes would then have been able to fall on the flank of the Anglo-Egyptian army while they were in motion. Even so, had Mac-Donald's Sudanese battalions not stood firm and the ammunition not held out, or had MacDonald not handled his battalions so skilfully, the results might have been tragic indeed for Great Britain. How close the Anglo-Egyptian army came to disaster can be judged by the fact that when the battle was over and the ammunition counted in MacDonald's battalions it was found to average only two rounds per man.

While MacDonald's brigade fought, Kitchener flew about the field shouting orders in an effort to bring his troops about to face the new menace. He worked neither through his staff nor through the chain of command, but even gave orders to battalion commanders, tossing brigades and battalions about the field. The army swung round clumsily and the other brigades moved ponderously up to MacDonald's support. But MacDonald had handled the situation without the aid of the rest of the army. He had saved the day. His accomplishment was later used as an example of the proper handling of troops in battles of this sort at the Staff College.

The bravery of the Dervishes astonished the British. War correspondent G. W. Steevens wrote:

> Our men were perfect, but the Dervishes were superb – beyond perfection. It was their largest, best and bravest army that ever fought against us for Mahdism, and it died worthily of the huge empire Mahdism won and kept so long. Their riflemen, mangled by every kind of death and torment that man can devise, clung round the black flag and the green, emptying their poor, rotten, home-made cartridges dauntlessly. Their spearmen charged death at every minute hopelessly. . . . A dusky line got up and stormed forward: it bent, broke up, fell apart, and disappeared. Before the smoke had cleared, another line was bending and storming forward in the same track.

The bravery of the Dervishes was indeed magnificent – and useless.

When Kitchener had all his troops in line facing west again, they drove the remnants of the great Dervish army into the desert. By noon the battle was over. So was the campaign. The Khalifa had fled. Yakub was dead. So were 10,800 other Dervishes. On the Anglo-Egyptian side, only forty-eight men were killed (of whom nearly half were 21st Lancers) and 382 wounded. Kitchener's generalship had not been very good, but it had not needed to be. The Khalifa had proved a worse general and victory had gone to the best drilled battalions with the best weapons; cool efficiency had triumphed over hot religious fanaticism.

The battle now definitely won, Kitchener, guided by Slatin, proceeded with his army to Omdurman. With a Sudanese battalion and four guns, he approached the town, entering it through the main gate, and followed the straight road that ran to the Khalifa's house and the Mahdi's tomb. Steevens, one of the first newspaper correspondents to enter the town described its appearance in un-flattering terms:

> Omdurman was just a planless confusion of blind walls and gaping holes, shiftless stupidity, concentrated filth and beastliness. . . . Oppression, stagnation, degradation were stamped deep on every yard of miserable Omdurman. . . . Everything was wretched. And foul. They dropped their dung where they listed; they drew their water from beside green sewers; they had filled the streets and khors with dead donkeys; they left their brothers to rot and puff up hideously in the sun. The stench of the place was in your nostrils, in your throat, in your stomach.

Of the area around the Khalifa's house Steevens wrote:

> Tiny round straw tukls, mats propped up a foot from the earth with crooked sticks, dome-topped mud kennels that a man could just crowd into. . . . On every side, of every type, they jumbled and jostled and crushed; and they sweated and stank with people.

There were still a few small pockets of resistance in the town and the gunboats continued to lob shells into the centre of town until one nearly killed Kitchener. Herbert Howard, a former officer who had served in Matabeleland and was here acting as correspondent for *The Times* and the *New York Herald*, had charged with the 21st Lancers that morning and had been actively covering the fighting all day. Now he had entered Omdurman with the Sirdar. 'This is the best day of my life,' he said to a companion. Then he went into the courtyard of the Khalifa's house to take a photograph and there, ten minutes later, he was killed by one of the last shells thrown into Omdurman. Today, a plaque marks the spot where he fell.

When the battle began, many of the inhabitants of the town had sought sanctuary in and around the Mahdi's tomb. More than a hundred were killed there by the high explosive shells from the gunboats and howitzers. When Kitchener arrived on the scene, he found the area of the tomb covered with blood and corpses. After posting guards over the main buildings, he made his way to the prison, where he released Neufeld and other political prisoners. That night most of the Anglo-Egyptian army slept within the walls of the captured capital.

Rudolf Slatin, who had accompanied the Anglo-Egyptian army as Wingate's assistant, was disappointed that the Khalifa had escaped. Now he rode with the Egyptian cavalry and the camel corps to pursue him. They went about thirty miles south, and the gunboats steamed on a further sixty miles, but the Khalifa, with a few thousand faithful followers, made good his escape, going first south and then west into Kordofan, to his own country which he had left so many years ago to become the leading follower of the Mahdi.

Two days after the battle of Omdurman, Kitchener ordered a memorial service to be held for Gordon at the ruins of his former palace in Khartoum. Representative detachments of officers and men from the British and Egyptian battalions were ferried across the river and amid the weeds and broken walls the band played the Dead March from *Saul* and Gordon's favourite hymn, 'Abide with me'; the Union Jack and the Crescent and Star were again hoisted over the walls; the troops gave three cheers for the Queen. Kitchener was much affected by the ceremony he had created. He burst into tears, and had to ask another officer to dismiss the parade.

On 5 September Kitchener wrote to Queen Victoria, reporting on how he had carefully loaded the wounded on barges to be taken down the Nile and describing the memorial service for Gordon. The Queen was much moved by his letter. Of Gordon she wrote in her journal: 'Surely, he is avenged!'

Most of the British soldiers probably knew about Gordon, and the task of avenging him was doubtless a suitable enough explanation as to why they had come to this remote land to shoot Sudanese with their dumdum bullets and machine guns, but few were aware of the larger political issues involved. Possibly more than one Tommy did not know the difference between the Khedive and the Khalifa. Two days after the battle of Omdurman some prisoners were brought in and it was rumoured that the Khalifa had been captured. As the soldiers in camp ran out to see, one British soldier was heard to call out, ''urry up, Bill, come along. They've cotched the bloody Khee-dive!'

Kitchener now had other work before him, which shifted his attention from Dervishes to Frenchmen. A month before the battle of Omdurman he had received sealed orders which he was instructed to open after the capture of Khartoum. The day after the battle he opened them and found himself ordered to take personal command of an expedition south in order to end French pretentions on the upper Nile.

Just as many Britons dreamed of British territory extending from the Cape to Cairo, so many Frenchmen dreamed of French colonies stretching east and west across Africa from coast to coast. These two ambitions were bound to clash and the result was what has gone down in history as the Fashoda Incident. In an effort to grab the southern Sudan for herself, France had, two years earlier, dispatched an expedition under the command of Major Jean Baptiste Marchand to central Africa. After enduring terrible hardships and overcoming fearful obstacles, Marchand reached the Bahr el Ghazal and on 10 July 1898 raised the tricolour at Fashoda, a village on the White Nile sixty miles north of the junction of the White Nile and the Sobat river. The expedition had beaten off one Dervish attack and was awaiting another when Kitchener, accompanied by Wingate and Slatin, arrived on the scene with a battalion of Sudanese infantry and a battery of artillery.

Sir Geoffrey Archer has said: 'I suppose that in the history of the "Scramble for Africa" no episode was so serious or so menacing.' Fortunately, both Marchand and Kitchener, representatives of the bold imperialist policies of their respective governments, realized the seriousness of the situation. Marchand claimed the entire Bahr el Ghazal and said he would have to fight if Kitchener tried to make him lower his flag. Kitchener, who had donned the uniform of an Egyptian general, complete with tarboush, said he was ordered to raise the Egyptian flag and to protest against the raising of the French flag. After a friendly talk over lunch on a gunboat, they agreed that there was nothing to prevent both flags from being raised and referring the entire matter to Paris and London. Kitchener landed his Sudanese battalion, raised the Egyptian flag and steamed away, leaving the two garrisons to stare uneasily at each other and to try to keep out of each other's way until the affair could be decided by the politicians in Europe.

Kitchener's duties in the Sudan were now ended for the time being and he returned to England to receive the honours and hero's welcome that awaited him. W. T. Stead wrote in his *Review of Reviews* that 'not Wellington returning from the Battle of Waterloo could have been accorded more triumphal honours'. He was given the freedom of a number of cities, Cambridge gave him an honorary LL.D., parliament voted him £30,000, and he was elevated to the peerage, becoming Lord Kitchener of Khartoum. There were, however, some dissenters and fault-finders among those who spoke of Kitchener's glory, for, as Baring once said, the Sirdar had 'not the faculty of making friends'. Some criticism of his conduct after the battle was expressed even before he arrived back in England. There was, for example, the question of the Mahdi's skull.

Four days after the capture of Omdurman Kitchener decided that if Mahdism was to be erased the Mahdi's tomb should be destroyed, and the task was given to Gordon's nephew, Major W. S. Gordon of the Royal Engineers. Assisting Major Gordon were Sergeant J. P. Maynard of the Royal Marines and six Dervish prisoners. It was rather naïvely believed that the Dervish prisoners would spread the word and confirm the desecration of the tomb. It would appear, however, that they wisely kept silent about their part in such an affair. The walls of the tomb were about six feet thick and it was found difficult to destroy them. Only after trying three times to dynamite it was the tomb sufficiently demolished. The remains of the Mahdi were dug up and his bones were thrown in the river. His skull was saved, however, and James Watson, one of Kitchener's A.D.C.s, presented it to his chief, who did not quite know what to do with it. It was suggested that he should mount it in silver and make an inkstand out of it, but Kitchener thought perhaps he would send it to the College of Surgeons in London.

When news of this affair reached England there was a considerable reaction. The desecration of the Mahdi's tomb was condemned by the press, by the army and by members of parliament. The Queen thought it savoured too much of the Middle Ages. Baring advised Kitchener to get rid of the skull as decently as he could, and he had it buried somewhere near Wadi Halfa on his way home.

There was also criticism of Kitchener's handling of the Dervish wounded. Ernest Bennet said: 'It is certain that in many cases wounded Dervishes, unarmed and helpless, were butchered from sheer wantonness and lust of bloodshed. The whole formed a hideous picture, not easy to forget.' On the other hand, Captain

Adolf von Tiedemann of the Prussian General Staff, who accompanied the expedition as an observer, defended the practice: 'As regards the killing of the wounded on the battlefield, that was a necessary measure which was as regrettable as it was indispensable.' The justification was that even the badly wounded Dervishes continued to fight the 'Turk' as long as they had any strength left in their arms.

Still another criticism was that even days after the battle, Kitchener found it impossible to care for the vast number of wounded Sudanese, estimated at 16,000. Some lay on the battlefield in the sun until they died; many dragged themselves to the Nile to relieve their thirst and died along the river banks; thousands made their way to Omdurman. Kitchener's medical department was not equipped to cope with such numbers. Hassan Zecki, the Egyptian medical officer who had married Frank Lupton's widow, set up a makeshift hospital in the centre of town and the army surgeons did what they could, but unknown hundreds must have died of untreated wounds.

Kitchener's critics were in the minority, however, for he had achieved that for which all generals strive: victory. Lord Salisbury, speaking in the House of Lords on 8 June 1899, said admiringly that his victory had been achieved 'with absolute accuracy, like the answer to a scientific calculation'. In a sense, this was true. In spite of the dramatic battle of Omdurman with its romantic charge of the 21st Lancers and the exotic setting of the entire campaign, victory had really been made possible by Lieutenant Girouard's prosaic railroad, which pushed into the desert and brought the soldiers with their arms, ammunition, food and all the cumbersome material of European warfare into the heart of the Sudan. Evelyn Baring, Kitchener's chief, summed up the Sirdar and his war quite succinctly:

I have no wish to disparage the strategical and tactical ability which was displayed in the conduct of the campaign. It is, however, a fact that no occasion arose for the display of any great skill in these branches of military science. When once the British and Egyptian troops were brought face to face with the enemy, there could – unless the conditions under which they fought were altogether extraordinary – be little doubt of the result. The speedy and successful issue of the campaign depended, in fact, almost entirely upon the methods adopted for overcoming the very exceptional difficulties connected with the supply and transport of the troops. The main quality required to meet these difficulties was a good head for business. By one of those fortunate accidents which have been frequent in the history of Anglo-Saxon enterprise, a man was found equal to the occasion. Lord Kitchener of Khartoum won his well-deserved peerage because he was an excellent man of business; he looked carefully after every important detail, and enforced economy.

Kitchener boasted that he had conquered a million square miles and two million inhabitants at a cost of £2 6s. 6d. per square mile and £1 3s. 3d. per head. In spite of all criticism, he was very pleased with himself. The reconquest of the Sudan was acclaimed, at least in Britain, as an achievement of British arms, but although all of the senior officers and, in the final stages, about one-third of the force engaged were British, the bulk of the soldiers were Egyptians. Yet, there were more men killed in the six Sudanese battalions than in all of the rest of the force combined. By chance or design, it was the brave, dependable Blacks who bore the brunt of the fighting.

Although the Khalifa Abdullahi and the slippery Osman Digna had escaped and there were still great numbers of tribesmen loyal to the Dervish cause scattered throughout the vast Sudan, Mahdist rule was ended. It had lasted for more than thirteen years and the great human upheaval of the Mahdiya has left its mark to this day.

18

Epilogue

The Sudan had been reconquered. The question remained: What was to be done with it? There was also the question of who would, or had a right to, do anything with it. In short, who was to rule the Sudan? The British felt that it was they who had conquered the Sudan. They were obviously the masters of the political situation, but they had, after all, only conquered in the name of Egypt; Kitchener, the conquerer, although British, had commanded the victorious troops as Sirdar of the Egyptian army. And it was Egypt that paid two-thirds of the cost of the reconquest.

Legally, Egypt seemed to have the most right to the Sudan. It had belonged to her before the Mahdi's rebellion and it had been reconquered in her name. Yet it seemed intolerable to British minds that so much money and effort should have been spent and British blood spilt simply to return the land to Egyptian misrule. Turkey, too, had her claims, but these could easily be ignored, as could any thoughts of allowing the Sudanese to rule themselves, which was not even considered. For Britain to convert the Sudan into a colony would have been to flout world opinion and insult Egypt. After all, the French had been told to get out of Fashoda on the grounds that it was Egyptian territory. Nevertheless, Britain now demanded control boldly and baldly on the basis of 'right of conquest'.

Yet Britain managed to usurp Egypt's rights without seeming to do so. This trick was achieved by that very clever man, Evelyn Baring. It was Baring who conceived the idea of creating what he himself once described as a 'hybrid form of government, hitherto unknown to international jurisprudence'. It was called a condominium. H. C. Jackson, who spent twenty-four years in the Sudan Civil Service, called the condominium, 'A curious experiment in administration which only the British could have devised, and which none but they would have had the slightest hope of being able to carry through.' It is probably true.

Baring's scheme took the form of an agreement between Britain

and Egypt whereby the two countries would jointly rule the Sudan –
at least there was the appearance of joint rule: both the Egyptian
and British flags would fly in the Sudan, the Governor-General
would be appointed by khedival decree on the recommendation
of the British government and the country would be called the
Anglo-Egyptian Sudan. The laws of the land were to be simply the
proclamations of the Governor-General. Nothing was ever said
concerning the nationality of the Sudan's ruler, but as long as there
were Governors-General they were British. There was to be no
interference from other European powers: no foreign consuls could
reside in the Sudan without the consent of the British government.

The geographical boundaries of the country were kept as vague
as its political status. The northern frontier was fixed at the 22nd
parallel, but the southern and western frontiers were left undefined.
The actual boundaries of the country were not completely fixed
until 1926. Baring was once asked what would happen to Europeans
who were married or buried in the Sudan. He blandly replied that
'any European who considered it essential that his marriage or
burial should be attested by a Consular representative of his
country, would do well to remain in the territory lying north of the
22nd parallel of latitude'.

The Convention that created the condominium was signed on
19 January 1899. When the faint murmured objections of the
Egyptians died away and the European powers recovered from
their shock of amazement, this strange political creature of Britain
was accepted by the world and the British set out with their usual
perseverance and efficiency to tame and control it. The first
Governor-General was Lord Kitchener of Khartoum.

It was doubtless Baring's intention to rule the Sudan through
his own hand-picked man, for Kitchener, as Governor-General,
was to be ruled by Baring. The entire campaign for the reconquest
of the Sudan had been classed as a 'Foreign Office war' and
Kitchener's immediate superior had been Baring throughout. It
was only necessary that this chain of command be continued. But
now that Kitchener was a peer and a hero, he was no longer content
to be Baring's agent. He wanted to rule the Sudan without Baring's
guidance or control. He appeared to feel that it was *his* country. He
had conquered it; now he would rule it. And Kitchener's rule was
a stern one.

The capital of the Sudan was again to be Khartoum, and Lord
Kitchener wanted it to be a suitable one. First of all, the palace was
to be rebuilt. While still in England, before his return, he wrote to

Wingate instructing him to 'loot like blazes. I want any quantity of marble stairs, marble pavings, iron railings, looking-glasses and fittings; doors, windows, furniture of all sorts.' Five thousand men were set to work rebuilding the town: new streets were laid out, 7,000 trees were planted and government buildings were built. He called on Britain for money to build a school and more than £100,000 was subscribed by the British people to build Gordon College (now the University of Khartoum).

Kitchener never consulted Baring; he refused to take his advice; and he even refused to account for any of the money he spent. He ruled the Sudan as though it was a regiment and he resented any criticism, however mild, from Baring. At first, Baring was reluctant to criticize his own man to his superior, Lord Salisbury, but he was obviously disturbed. In January 1899 he wrote that Kitchener's methods were 'a little more masterful and peremptory than is usual in dealing with civil affairs'. When Baring warned Kitchener that land speculators were sending money to the Sudan for Greeks to make purchases, and that Kitchener should take care as they had no legal means for acquiring titles to the land, Kitchener simply snapped back that he could not expel every Greek who bought and sold anything. In April, Baring confessed to Salisbury: 'He is, I fear, terribly bureaucratic.'

Although Kitchener had broken the back of the Mahdiya, the Khalifa and some of his leading emirs, including Osman Digna, and several thousand faithful ansar were still free. Expeditions were sent out from time to time to apprehend them; one was led by Kitchener personally. When famine once again broke out in the Sudan, Kitchener told Baring that this suited his policy admirably as it would deprive the Khalifa and his followers of local support.

In November 1899 spies reported that the Khalifa was making for the Nile about 180 miles south of Khartoum. Wingate was dispatched with a column consisting of 250 camel corps soldiers, the 9th and 13th Sudanese battalions, some light artillery and about 1,000 irregulars. The column left Omdurman on 19 November. Four days later it surprised a large Dervish raiding party and killed 400. Scouts brought in word that the Khalifa himself was camped only a few miles away at a place called Umm Diwaykarat, near present-day Kosti. Wingate made a forced march by night and dawn found him in position on high ground overlooking the Khalifa's camp.

Wingate's force consisted of 3,700 well-armed men; the Khalifa had about 5,000 badly-armed Dervishes. As soon as it was light, the Dervishes attacked. Wingate's men cut them down with rifle and machine-gun fire and then advanced for the kill. It was over in half an hour. The Khalifa Abdullahi along with Khalifa Ali Wad Helu and most of their principal emirs were found dead, the Khalifa lying on his sheepskin rug facing Mecca. Only the wily Osman Digna, that expert in escaping from lost battles, managed to escape again, the last of the great Dervish generals.

It was more than a year later before Osman Digna was finally betrayed. He was found, not with an army but alone with a servant in a cave near Tokar. A British captain, together with the Suakin commandant of police, Mohammed Bey Ahmed, led a small force of Sudanese policemen to surprise him. Although the entrance to the cave was surrounded, he nearly escaped again. He was waiting for his servant to prepare his breakfast when the police appeared. As soon as he saw them, he jumped up and ran back into the cave and out another entrance. He was soon spotted, however, and the police set out after him as he scrambled up a steep hillside. One of the policemen paused to call out to him to stop: 'Your time for running away has now passed!'

'I do not run away,' Osman Digna shouted back, 'but now, as ever, and in accordance with my master's commands, I turn my face away from the unbelievers.'

He was caught nevertheless. He refused to give his name and as none of his captors had ever seen Osman Digna before, they were at first not sure that they had actually captured him. Then Mohammed Bey remembered past battles from which the wily old warrior had escaped but not unscathed. They looked over their captive and found the known scars of old battles: the sword wound in the middle of his head, the bullet wound on his left wrist and the mark of a bayonet on his back. There was no doubt. This was Osman Digna, and they carried him back to Suakin in triumph.

When he was brought to Cairo, Wilfrid Scawen Blunt quoted a newspaper account and recorded his indignation in his diary:

Osman Digna has been captured at last and brought in chains to Cairo. 'A large crowd pressed forward eager to see the dark, long face, brilliant eyes, large mouth, and long grey beard, of a frightened and dignified old man who sat with chains round his sore ankles and swollen, bare feet.' I quote 'Our own correspondent.' This is how the British Empire makes its 'Roman holiday'!

Osman Digna was about sixty-four years old when he was captired on 19 January 1900, but he lived on for another twenty-six years. He was transferred about to several prisons, but as the years went by his prison life became easier and easier. Towards the end, he had a pleasant house at Wadi Halfa and lived the life of a religious recluse, more like an honoured pensioner than a prisoner: the government supplied him with food and a military guard that served more to keep the curious from bothering him than to prevent his escape. In 1924 he was given his complete freedom and made the pilgrimage to Mecca. He died in 1926.

One month after the battle of Umm Diwaykarat and the death of the Khalifa, Kitchener left the Sudan to become second-in-command of the army fighting the Boers in South Africa. Although a hero to countless English schoolboys, he was never popular with his associates. He added to his honours, and his prestige became enormous, but he never mellowed. He organized the British forces to fight the guerrillas in South Africa and then spent seven years as commander-in-chief in India. He was made a field-marshal in 1909, and when World War I began he became Secretary of State for War. This cold, harsh man died in the cold, harsh waters of the North Sea when H.M.S. *Hampshire* struck a mine on the evening of 6 June 1916. He had been on his way to visit the Tsar and the Russian front.

Kitchener was succeeded as Governor-General of the Sudan by Sir Reginald Wingate, the man who had organized and operated so effectively the Military Intelligence Department of the Egyptian army. Wingate ruled wisely and well for seventeen years. They were difficult years, for in spite of the defeat of the Dervish forces and the death of the Khalifa, the Sudan was far from subdued. Wingate faced his first crisis only one month after Kitchener left: a crisis caused not by the Mahdists but by the stern discipline of Kitchener. The 14th Sudanese battalion, led by its Egyptian officers, mutinied in Omdurman.

Wingate was in Cairo when the mutiny occurred, but he hurriedly returned to the Sudan. Refusing the offer of British troops, he listened to the complaints of the Egyptian officers, who were merely dissatisfied with Kitchener's economies, particularly in regard to their field allowances, and made an investigation into the reason why the brave and faithful Blacks had turned on their British masters. It had been rumoured in the officers' messes that the Sudanese battalions would be sent to fight in South Africa. The disgruntled Egyptian officers had made good use of the rumour, telling their ignorant soldiers they were to be sent out of the Sudan to be slaughtered by the Boers. Wingate won back the soldiers by promising them an amnesty and the seven officer ringleaders were drummed out of the service and returned to Cairo under escort.

There were no more mutinies, but there were continual revolts, most of which were of a messianic nature. In 1900 there was trouble among the ansar who expected the coming of the Prophet Jesus. The leaders of this movement were tried by a religious council and sent into exile as heretics. In 1903 a new mahdi sprang up in eastern Kordofan. He was captured and hanged. In 1904 a Prophet Jesus appeared at Sinja on the Blue Nile. Four years later a former Dervish emir raised a fair-sized revolt that had to be crushed by a military expedition. In 1912 there was still another Prophet Jesus in Kordofan who had to be put down. There were also numerous revolts created from other than religious motives. In 1913 there were no less than nine expeditions sent out to stop intertribal wars, halt the arms traffic and uphold the authority of the government. There were a number of military operations over the years in the Nuba Hills to bring the refractory Nuba tribes under the control of the government. The fighting went on intermittently for years. In the first thirty years of the condominium more than 170 military expeditions were sent out.

But perhaps the most serious disturbance to the condominium was created in 1924 by the Egyptians, who wanted complete control again. Zagloul Pasha, one-time Egyptian Prime Minister, declared in a speech that 'The Sudan belongs to Egypt, and we must have it. We will dispose of it as any landlord disposes of his own property.' The Egyptians formed secret societies and created a barrage of anti-British propaganda. Sir Lee Stack, then Governor-General of the Sudan, was shot and killed in the streets of Cairo. The British retaliated by throwing all Egyptian officials out of the country and Egyptian battalions in Khartoum were surrounded by British troops and unceremoniously shipped north. The British remained masters of the Sudan.

After the fall of Omdurman, Darfur became an autonomous state under Sultan Ali Dinar, a descendant of the ancient ruling family. He had an army of slaves whom he equipped with rifles and, although supposedly subordinate to the condominium, he refused to allow officials of the Sudanese government to enter his realm. It was not until 1916, in the middle of World War I, that Darfur was reconquered by a force of between two and three thousand men supported by three aeroplanes. One of the pilots, John Slessor (who was wounded in the leg by an old Remington), later became Marshal of the Royal Air Force.

Darfur remained turbulent, and there was an uprising in

southern Darfur in 1921, when a religious fanatic assured his followers that bullets from government rifles would turn to water when directed against them.

There has never been any common ground for understanding between the Arab of the north and the Black of the south, and hatred has grown through the years. In August of 1955, there was an army revolt in the southern Sudan. The Blacks killed their Arab officers and the revolt spread to the police, game wardens and tribesmen. Northern Sudanese officials were killed or fled and soon all of Equatoria and the Bahr el Ghazal were in revolt and only Malakal remained in government hands in the Upper Nile province. Being without proper leaders, the revolt failed, but to this day there are sporadic uprisings and much discontent among the restless Blacks.

Wingate's greatest service to the Sudan was not in suppressing revolts but in building up a sound government administration. All the senior officials were British; the minor officials were Egyptians who, after about fifteen years, were gradually replaced by Sudanese. Thanks to Wingate, the Sudanese Civil Service (later renamed the Sudan Political Service) developed a reputation for being the best in the British Empire. There was no nonsense about competitive examinations. University graduates were examined by a board in London, and sometimes Wingate himself sat with the examiners. Character was what they were looking for, but as character is difficult to detect in untried young men, the board generally settled for athletes. It used to be said that the Sudan was a country of Blacks and Browns administered by Blues. Considering the climate in the Sudan, its diseases, and its lack of civilized comforts, this was probably not a bad method. In any case, many of the young men thrived, few were dishonest, and most worked hard to make the Sudan civilized.

An interesting aspect of the condominium was that slavery was not abolished. One of the great moral reasons the British had given themselves for interfering in the Sudan had been the need to abolish the slave trade, but when the Sudan was finally conquered they decided that Sudanese life had been disrupted enough by the Mahdiya without attempting to abolish a custom so deeply rooted. Besides, emancipation of the slaves would have been dangerous. The government therefore embarked on a plan of gradual abolition, which began by giving freedom to all children of Arab fathers and slave mothers. Slavery was not completely abolished in the Sudan until 1940.

Wingate's chief assistant in ruling the Sudan was the man he had helped rescue and who became his close friend: Rudolf Slatin. When Wingate was appointed Governor-General, Slatin was made Inspector-General, a title created specially for him. After his escape, he had gone home to Vienna to see his family, then to England, where he was welcomed as a hero and had an interview with Queen Victoria. On 19 August 1895 the Queen wrote in her journal:

Slatin Pasha, who had escaped from his long captivity with the Mahdi, three months ago, and Major Wingate, who had been instrumental in his escape, arrived. After dinner I decorated Major Wingate with the C.B. Had a great deal of conversation with him and Slatin Pasha, which was most interesting. The latter is a charming, modest little man, whom no one could think had gone through such vissicitudes, for he looks so well; but there are lines in his face which betoken mental suffering. . . . What has been a great sorrow to him, is that his mother died before hearing of his escape.

When Slatin's account of his captivity, translated and edited by Wingate, was published in 1896, it was dedicated to the Queen, 'who has ever shown deep solicitude for and gracious sympathy with the European prisoners in the Sudan'. Wilfred Scawen Blunt, the ardent arabist and anti-imperialist, read the account and wrote in his diary:

Slatin is a mean wretch to have published it, and the Mahdi made a mistake in not cutting his head off at once when he surrendered, and sending him straight to paradise. His professions of loyalty to the Khedive and to our gracious Queen are fulsome, and those of disloyalty to the people whose religion he adopted to save his miserable life, disgusting.

After Blunt met Slatin he described him as 'a commonplace little German, quite unworthy of ever having served the Mahdi'.

Blunt's feelings were the exception. For most, Slatin was a hero and a wonder. Baring called him 'a gallant and very capable officer'. Wingate asked if some medal could not be given to him, even though he was not a British subject. Lord Wolseley approved, and in October Slatin was decorated with the Civil C.B. The Khedive had made him a Pasha and other honours followed through the years: He was knighted in 1898 (K.C.M.G.); in 1906, he was made a Baron of the Austrian Empire; and in 1907, he became an honorary Major-General in the British army. From plain Rudolf Slatin he had added to his name the titles of three countries;

he became Major-General Baron Rudolf von Slatin Pasha, K.C.M.G., C.B. He received so many medals, in fact, that according to Sir Geoffrey Archer, Governor-General of the Sudan in 1925–6, King Edward VII is alleged to have said, 'The next time you come here, Slatin, I shall have to pin the decoration on your back-side.'

Slatin, with his intimate knowledge of the language, customs and people of the Sudan, was an invaluable aide to Wingate, but he did not always understand the outlook of the young English athletes from Oxford and Cambridge who came to the Sudan to assist them. He took them in tow and tried to tell them about the country and to teach them their duties in it, but he had little knowledge of sports and once introduced a young man who had won his post in the Sudan Civil Service by his ability to pull an oar as the man who had rowed the fastest in the Oxford boat.

After a short training period in Khartoum, the young men of the civil service were sent out to rule in the remote provinces. Among the pieces of advice given them by Slatin was that they should always try cases and judge disputes with a stick between their teeth. If they did not, he warned, the Sudanese would tell by watching their lips if they were believed.

In the spring of 1914, Slatin returned to Austria on leave. On 21 July of that year, at the age of fifty-seven, he married Alice von Ramberg, a baroness. She was forty-one. Two months later, World War I broke out and Slatin found himself torn between his loyalty to Austria and his loyalty to Britain. When he received his C.B. from Queen Victoria, she had written in her journal that he was a man who was 'ready at any time to shed his blood in my service'. But he was not prepared to fight his own countrymen and he resigned his post. Although offered a military post in the Austrian army, he could not bring himself to fight against the British either. He joined the Austrian Red Cross and was responsible for aid to prisoners of war: a fit post for one who had himself been a prisoner for so long.

The outbreak of war between Britain and Germany found Slatin in possession of a set of cipher books. Wingate received a letter from him through the British Consul in Zürich in which he swore that he had sealed the books and locked them in his safe at home. It did not matter. Slatin did not know it but the ciphers were obsolete as far as the Foreign Office was concerned and had simply been allowed for use in the Sudan. Still, it was a decent gesture.

On 12 November 1916 Alice von Slatin gave birth to a baby girl,

Anne Marie. In June 1918 Wingate's youngest son was killed in action and Slatin wrote a letter of condolence. In the same year, Slatin received one of his last honours when he was elected Honorary Chief Scout, and to this day there is a scout group in a Vienna suburb that bears his name. The war, with its conflict of loyalties, the unaccustomed cold climate of Europe and age combined to erode his vigour and put an end to his career, and he did not return to his post in the Sudan. In 1921 his wife died and he was left a sixty-four-year-old widower with a five-year-old child to raise on a meagre pension.

In the winter of 1927 Slatin returned to the Sudan as a guest of the Sudanese government. There is a story, perhaps apocryphal, that he made a visit to the Khalifa's house as an ordinary tourist. The official guide pointed to the spot where, he said, Slatin used to stand when he was a mulazem at the gate. The visitor spoke up to correct the guide. There was a brief argument which the visitor ended with, 'But I am Slatin.' It was the sort of theatrical gesture Slatin loved. Perhaps it really happened, for his name appears in the visitors' book for 24 November 1927.

Throughout his life, Slatin remained a close personal friend of Wingate, and to Wingate's children he was always 'Uncle Rowdy'; after the war it was Wingate who was instrumental in having his medals restored to him. Almost every summer Slatin went to England with his daughter. Once he was staying with Sir James Currie, a former Director of Education in the Sudan, when a party of Sudanese came to visit. That evening, when the Sudanese slipped outside to say their evening prayers, Slatin quietly went out and prayed with them.

Slatin Pasha died near Vienna on 4 October 1932 at the age of seventy-five and was buried in the cemetery at Ober St Veit, where he was born and where there is still a street named after him: Slatingasse. There was once a street in Omdurman named Shari Salatin, but this has now been changed to Shari Wad al Nejumi.

In 1917 Wingate became British High Commissioner to Egypt. He did not last long. He quarrelled with Lord Curzon and, although not yet fifty-eight years old, he was retired in 1918 on a pension of only £1,300 per annum. He had always been an active Freemason – he had been Grand Master of Egypt and the Sudan – and he now became Grand Warden of England. He lived on to a ripe old age, outliving his wife and all his old friends, and died in London in 1953 at the age of ninety-one.

Even Wingate did not outlive one of the subalterns who had

taken part in the charge of the 21st Lancers at Omdurman and who wrote, if not the best, at least the most dramatic account of the campaign for the reconquest of the Sudan. When the war was over, Lieutenant Winston Churchill paused in Cairo on his way home to collect material for his book, *The River War*. He later returned with a draft, which he showed to Baring, asking for his comments. Baring, now Lord Cromer, slashed up the manuscript of the young officer ruthlessly, but he sent him an encouraging letter, saying: 'One of the very few things which still interest me in life is to see young men get on.' This young man did.

Evelyn Baring, who became Baron Cromer in 1892, a viscount five years later and the Earl of Cromer in 1901, retired in 1907 to devote himself to classical studies and to writing about the Egypt he had known and whose affairs he had directed. In 1916 he presided over the Dardanelles Commission; he died following one of its meetings on 29 January 1917.

Besides Slatin, one other provincial governor escaped from the Sudan – although 'escape' is perhaps not the right word. Edouard Schnitzer, better known by his alias of Emin, was governor of Equatoria, southernmost province of the Sudan. He was never actually in the hands of the Dervishes, but the Khalifa could have had Emin and his province any time he wished. Equatoria was isolated on three sides by savage tribes and unknown country and in the north by the Dervishes. Emin managed to get several letters out to Europe and when it became known that one of 'Gordon's lieutenants' was still alive there was a great cry for something to be done to rescue him.

The man selected to go to the relief of Emin Pasha in his remote province was Henry Morton Stanley, the man who had found Livingstone, who had discovered the course of the Congo river and who had founded the Congo Free State. An expedition was launched via the Congo and eventually, after near incredible hardships that resulted in the loss of 512 men out of 702, Stanley reached Emin. But Emin was not unhappy in his lost province. True, he had had difficulties in controlling his soldiers, but he was really more interested in flora and fauna than in political administration, and Equatoria was a marvellous place in which to study botany and zoology. He was not sure he wanted to leave. Nevertheless, Stanley carried him out.

On 4 December 1889 they reached Bagamoyo, on the shore of the Indian Ocean in Tanganyika. That night the German officers stationed there gave them a banquet. Emin perhaps had too much to drink; he wandered out on a balcony, fell off and cracked open his skull. When he recovered, he turned his back on civilization and went back into the interior of Africa. A few months later, Arab slavers slit his throat.

The colourful and tragic career of Valentine Baker Pasha ended in Egypt when he died of angina pectoris on 17 November 1887, two and a half years after his disastrous defeat at El Teb.

After the reconquest, Father Ohrwalder, like Slatin, returned to the Sudan. H. C. Jackson, one of the athletic young men from Oxford who made his career in the Sudan during the condominium, described meeting Father Ohrwalder in Omdurman. He was 'tall, sad and placid' with lines of suffering etched on his face. He was still handsome with a fine beard, now turning white. While Slatin delighted in describing his experiences as a captive of the Mahdi and Khalifa, Father Ohrwalder was reluctant to speak of this part of his life. When he met him, Jackson assumed that his air of sadness was the result of his sufferings during the Mahdiya. It was not. Father Ohrwalder was forbidden to say mass because of some unknown sin he had committed some time during his years under the Khalifa. He died in the Sudan in 1912.

Sister Elisabetta Venturini, one of the nuns who escaped with Father Ohrwalder, also returned to the Sudan after the reconquest. She served in missions at Khartoum, Omdurman and Atbara before, advanced in age, she died in Khartoum in 1937. Of Sister Chincharini, the other nun who escaped with Ohrwalder, nothing is known. Sister Grigolini, who married the Greek, bore her husband two sons and remained for many years in the Sudan, assisting the Roman Catholic missionaries in re-establishing themselves. She eventually returned to Italy and died in Verona in 1931.

After his escape in 1894, Father Paolo Rossignoli remained for several years in Egypt until called to Rome where he was made a canon. He died in 1919 at the age of sixty-seven.

Father Bonomi, who had been Father Ohrwalder's superior at the Dilling mission station and who escaped from El Obeid shortly after his capture, became a chaplain in the Italian navy in 1888. He was later in Eritrea as chaplain of an Italian military hospital in Asmara, where he died in 1927.

Of all the prisoners of the Khalifa, the stubbornest, stoutest and one of the bravest was Charles Neufeld, yet the reception he received from the civilized world he had longed for and dreamed of was disgraceful. He had thought that perhaps he would be

honoured in some way for the information he had been able to send
out to the advancing Anglo-Egyptian army. He had certainly risked
his neck to do so. Instead of honours, he found his reputation ruined
by slander. What little was known of his life in the Sudan was interpreted in the worst possible manner in Egypt and in Europe. At first
he was reported dead, then it was said that he was alive but that as
he had taken a Negro wife he did not want to leave the Sudan.
Worst of all was the charge that he had made gunpowder for the
Khalifa. No one reported his staunchness or his sufferings, his
defiance of the Khalifa or his faithfulness to his religion. Both the
Austrian and the Anglo-Egyptian governments tried to help
Slatin; government and Church worked to secure Father Ohrwalder's escape; but no such powerful allies made any vigorous
attempt to assist Neufeld.

When his friend Mankarious wrote to the German Consul in
Alexandria about his business affairs, he was told in a letter dated
12 March 1889, that

> Mr Neufeld is no longer a German subject nor *protégé*, because during
> his stay in Egypt Mr Neufeld has never claimed the protection of
> Germany, where he was born. Thus he has lost his nationality. This
> is according to what we learn from the parties interested in Germany.
> Upon this, this Consulate can in no way look into the affairs of Mr
> Neufeld nor protect his rights.

Neufeld's English wife was apparently able to do nothing. In
September 1888 it was reported to her that he had attempted to
escape, but had been recaptured and executed. On 10 March 1890
the Intelligence Department of the Egyptian army informed her
that her husband was alive, but mixed a considerable amount of
wormwood with the sweet news:

> Mohammed Effendi Rafai, late Sub-lieutenant, 4th Battalion, 5th
> Regiment, who left Khartoum three months ago, states he knew
> Neufeld very well, and saw him at Omdurman only a few days before
> he left. Neufeld had been under surveillance until about five months
> prior to this, but was now free. His release was owing to one of the
> Emirs representing to Abdullah Khalifa the great service Neufeld had
> been in enabling arms and ammunition to be taken from the Kabba-
> bish at the time Neufeld was captured. He now was employed as one of
> the Khalifa's mulazimeen, and received a small salary; the Khalifa
> gave him two wives, and treats him well. Neufeld has very little to
> complain of except want of funds, which renders living difficult, good
> food being very dear. He is frequently staying with Ibrahim Bey
> Fauzi, who has opened a small coffee shop. It is untrue that the

Khalifa ever threatened Neufeld's life; he was only threatened with imprisonment unless he turned Mussulman. Does not think it possible that Neufeld can receive any letters, etc., from outside. Neufeld does not occupy himself in business in any way. Has never heard Neufeld express any wish to go away, but does not think he would be able to do so even if he wished it, as everyone knows him.

Neufeld returned to find a story circulating that he had actually been fighting with the Dervishes and had galloped from the battle-field to the prison just in time to be found in chains by Kitchener. In Egypt he found his business ruined. Claims had been filed against him by people he had never heard of, and some of these had even been paid from his assets. At the German consulate he was informed that his citizenship had lapsed because he had been away from his homeland for too long. When he had first been captured, an English newspaper had raised a fund by subscription to try to rescue him; he was now asked to repay the money subscribed. The War Office demanded repayment for £20 that had been given him just before he left for the Sudan. When offered money by a magazine to write his experiences, he was at first told that as he was technically a prisoner of war he was not at liberty to enter into agreements of this sort.

Neufeld was hurt most by the false stories about him that appeared in print. One such story, that appeared in a number of London and provincial newspapers read:

Twice had every preparation been made. The relays of camels to take the exile across the desert were ready. Nothing remained but for Neufeld to pluck up courage and quit Omdurman. Each time he backed out at the last moment. At length he confessed the truth, namely, that he did not care to come away. He had married a black wife. His friends in Germany were dead or had forgotten him. He would stay where he was.

This article was also reproduced in German newspapers and Neufeld found himself socially ostracized by both Englishmen and Germans.

Ernest Bennett wrote a hastily written book, *The Downfall of the Dervishes*, in which he spoke of Neufeld:

The prisoners were released from their fetters on the night of the battle. ... I saw Charles Neufeld, and he looked very little the worse for his stay at Omdurman. A great deal of English sympathy has been wasted on this person. The harrowing stories we have read in the papers of the poor captive languishing in hopeless captivity are sheer nonsense. On two separate occasions Neufeld had the chance of escape, for a clever and courageous Arab named Oman had been dispatched by the Intelligence Department to rescue the captive. Neufeld, however, refused to leave Omdurman unless he was accompanied by a black woman with whom he lived. This was obviously out of the question. So Father Rossignoli was rescued instead, and brought safely to Assouan.

On his way down the Nile to Cairo, Neufeld learned that Hasseena was in Berber. He stopped off there to look for her, and finally found her living in a brothel. He brought her out and made arrangements for her to lead a respectable life again, but shortly after arriving in Cairo, he received a telegram telling him that she had returned to her old way of life. In the international colony in Cairo, however, it was said that he had brought her back with him and that his English wife, after her years of anxiety, was confronted with her husband's 'black wife'. What Neufeld did about Umm es Shole is not known. He did not bring her to Cairo with him, but he had married her. True, it was an Islamic, not a Christian, marriage, but their relationship was more than platonic: Neufeld had a daughter by Umm es Shole called Bakhita.

In a Cairo hotel one day a newspaper friend was showing Neufeld some newspaper articles about him when the Cairo correspondent for Reuters came up and said, 'Hello, how is that book of Neufeld's getting on?'

Neufeld's friend asked if he knew Neufeld. 'Know him!' exclaimed the Reuters man, 'No. Nor do I want to know him, considering the number of English soldiers he has sent to eternity with his gunpowder. I would not even look at the fellow's face.'

'This is Neufeld,' said his friend.

The man from Reuters fled.

Fortunately, Neufeld had some friends left and there were some who did not believe all the stories told against him. Duke Johann Albrecht, the Regent of Mecklenburg, sent him money through the German consulate, but when Neufeld called for it the money was refused him because of the claims against him. It was five months before he was able to obtain it.

Hard pressed for money, he went to see a German friend of his, Hewlett Moxley of the Imperial Ottoman Bank. When he had stated his case, Moxley turned over the papers Neufeld had given him and made some passing remarks to the effect that Neufeld's 'guarantees were not of the highest order' and that his 'credentials were not of a very satisfactory nature'. Neufeld's heart sank, but Moxley was a friend indeed. He gave Neufeld £150 for his immediate needs and opened a credit for a further £250. It was the first helping hand he had seen in Cairo.

The strain of returning to freedom and civilization, the anxiety caused by his reception and the worry caused by his financial plight, proved too much for him. The Khalifa could not break this strong stubborn man, but his fellow Europeans did. Neufeld fell ill. When he heard that Sir George Newnes, the British magazine publisher wanted to see him, he had to climb from his sick bed to talk with him. He had been told that Sir George was an 'ogre', but instead he found in him a sympathetic friend. Sir George encouraged him to write his book and collect every scrap of evidence he could to substantiate his story. Neufeld was much heartened by this interview. Later, Newnes introduced him to Chapman and Hall, who published his book in 1899, and Newnes himself ran the story in *The Wide World*, a weekly.

Very little is known of the subsequent history of this remarkable man. He established a tourist agency at Aswan, but when World War I broke out, he was repatriated to Germany. In 1916 he was the Arabic interpreter for a German military mission that sought to enter Abyssinia and the Sudan by travelling through the Hejaz. It got as far as Yenbo, but shortly after was turned back by hostile Arabs who captured part of their baggage. Colonel Baron Othmar von Stotzinger, head of the unsuccessful mission, spoke highly of Neufeld's fluency in Arabic and mentioned his eighteen-year-old Kurdish wife. Back in Damascus, Neufeld wrote a long report which outlined a method for dealing with the Arab revolt and recommending the establishment of a German intelligence unit in the Middle East. He died in Germany in 1918, just before the end of the war.

When Slatin returned to the Sudan, he made it a point to find Zenuba, the wife of Frank Lupton. She was happily married to Hassan Zecki, by whom she bore three other children in addition to her two daughters, Fatma and Victoria, by Lupton. Slatin later tried to send the eldest girl, whom he called 'Fanny', to Europe to be educated, but both mother and daughter were against this. Fanny later married a Sudanese. A few years after the re-conquest, Frank Lupton's brother Malcolm visited the Sudan, met Zenuba, and arranged to have his brother's grave transferred to the Christian cemetery in Khartoum. Zenuba's descendants by both Frank Lupton and Hassan Zecki are alive in the Sudan today.

To end this account of those whose lives became entangled in Sudanese history by the revolt of Mohammed Ahmed, it remains to say a few words concerning two officers who were primarily responsible for the success of the reconquest of the Sudan: Hector Archibald MacDonald, who led the gallant Sudanese battalions and saved the battle of Omdurman for Kitchener, and Edouard Girouard, who built the railroad. For his services in the Sudan MacDonald was made C.B., a brevet colonel and an extra A.D.C. to Queen Victoria. Some Scots thought the honours given Mac-Donald were too skimpy and a Scottish newspaper, the *North Star*, pointedly asked Britain if she wanted no more Highland recruits. It was also noted that being appointed A.D.C. to the Queen was a fine honour but brought in no extra pay and would even cost the Scottish hero money for a fancy uniform. MacDonald continued his fighting career in India and South Africa, rising to the rank of Major-General; he was created K.C.B. in 1900. He was in command of the troops in Ceylon when there was 'an opprobrious accusation against him' (according to the *Dictionary of National Biography*), and he went to London to defend himself at the War Office. The authorities there ordered a court of inquiry to be held in Ceylon. He started back to Ceylon, but on 25 March 1903 this exceptionally brave and capable officer shot himself in the Regina Hotel in Paris.

Edouard Girouard was only twenty-nine when he became director of the Sudan railways and built Kitchener's lifeline into the Nubian desert. (The railroad was later extended and the first train reached Khartoum on 10 January 1900.) After the Sudan was won, Girouard was appointed President of the Egyptian Railway and Telegraph Administration. This appointment was brief, for he was soon called to South Africa to control the vital railroads needed to defeat the Boers. In 1907 he went to Nigeria and a year later succeeded Frederick Lugard as Governor of Northern Nigeria; there he built the country's first railroad. He resigned in 1912, but returned to government service three years later as director-general of munitions supply. He died in London in 1932.

Kipling had predicted that 'In due time the demand will go up "the Sudan for the Sudanese"', and so it did. The condominium came to an end when the Sudan became independent on 1 January 1956. Sudanese political figures, like other African leaders, delight in throwing verbal spears into the corpse of colonialism; but if one country can ever successfully rule another, the British can be said to have ruled the Sudan well. The Sudan owes much to British rule: it gave her diverse peoples a measure of peace and freedom from famine, enabling the population to increase and to enjoy a prosperity they could not have hoped to achieve under the Egyptians or by themselves. Young, British-educated Sudanese today are not yet wise enough in the ways of the world nor of history to appreciate the foundations on which they were given to build.

When the British left the Sudan to the Sudanese, there was an attempt to form a democratic government, but as in all other African countries, the attempt failed. First there was an election to determine whether the Sudan should be independent or join Egypt. One of the strongest of the political parties was the Umma Party, headed by Sayyid Abdel Rahman el Mahdi, posthumous son of the Mahdi. It favoured independence and this view prevailed. There were the usual political difficulties of a people struggling with democratic methods and institutions for the first time; then the military took over the government in 1958. The military dictatorship of General Ibrahim Abboud provided the country with reasonably stable government until 1964.

One of the sights of Khartoum when the British ruled the Sudan was a large bronze statue of Gordon mounted on a camel that stood near the palace. It has had a curious history. There are two identical statues, the creation of Onslow Ford. One, the original, stands today where it has always stood: at Brompton Barracks, Chatham, Kent. Its double once stood near Trafalgar Square where the statue of Nurse Edith Cavell now stands. Kitchener thought it should be in Khartoum and it was sent there in the early days of the condominium. After independence, the Sudanese, long since bored by England's Christian martyr hero, packed up the statue and shipped it back to England. In 1959 it was presented to the Gordon Boys School at West End, Surrey, near Woking. In Khartoum the statue looked from the palace out over the desert; now it stands in the corner of a green playing field.

Khartoum still has the trees Kitchener planted, and they have now grown tall and beautiful. Today the city contains the offices of the government, the bulk of the European population of the Sudan, and the homes of the wealthier Sudanese, including the residence of Imam El Hadi el Mahdi, grandson of Mohammed Ahmed and religious leader of the ansar, still some three million strong.

Khartoum now has a small but modern airport, built by the British. The first aeroplane to land there, on 21 January 1914, was piloted by Marc Pourpre, a French aviator. As he climbed out of his cockpit, an excited Sudanese woman ran up to him, demanding to know if he was a man or an angel. When M. Pourpre assured her that he was a man, and, in answer to her next question, admitted that he was also a Christian, she was amazed. This was the only fine thing she had ever known a Christian to do, she exclaimed. A few months later, Slatin, to celebrate the nineteenth anniversary of his escape, flew over Omdurman in the second aeroplane ever to visit Khartoum.

A bridge connects Khartoum with the African city of Omdurman, which is not much different now from the days when the Khalifa made it his capital. The streets are narrow and twisting, the houses of mud. The Khalifa's house still stands, now a museum of the Mahdiya, but there is a football stadium on the site of the Beit el Mal. For fifty years the Mahdi's tomb remained in ruins. In 1924 a visitor to the Sudan, Major A. Radclyffe Dugmore, described it:

> The ruined remains of the Mahdi's tomb may still be seen on the eastern side of the town, and this is gradually falling apart in its walled enclosure, which is always kept locked. The native Mohammedan still has a certain respect for it, for on entering the place he always removes his footwear.

The tomb was finally rebuilt in its original shape by the Mahdi's son in 1947. The ansar have chosen to forget Kitchener's act of desecration and it is commonly believed that the Mahdi's remains are still in the grave.

In the early days of the condominium Mahdism was outlawed and it was forbidden to read the sayings or recite the prayers of the Mahdi, but over the years the attitude of the government softened. After the battle of Umm Diwaykarat Wingate had telegraphed his wife: 'Hurrah Mahdism finished.' But Mahdism did not die, it only grew respectable. The man primarily responsible for keeping it alive and for making it respectable was Abdel Rahman el Mahdi. The other nine sons and ten daughters of the Mahdi died at an early age, but Abdel Rahman lived to be seventy-five years old and did not die until 1959. He was knighted by the British and created a pasha by the Egyptians. He made himself one of the richest men in the Sudan, and Abba Island, birthplace of Mahdism, became one of his country estates. On a visit to London, Abdel Rahman called at No. 10 Downing Street while a cabinet meeting was in progress. A cabinet meeting is rarely interrupted, but a private secretary thought Sir Winston should be advised. The Prime Minister, told the private secretary that the Mahdi would have to wait, but added, 'Unless you think he will go off and make another revolt.'

The Nuba Hills, where Father Ohrwalder and his colleagues began their work, has remained one of the more backward areas of the Sudan, although Dilling now boasts a government institute of education. Today a gravel road connects Dilling and El Obeid, but the surface is usually corrugated and it takes a heavy toll of the trucks that use it.

The Fashoda Incident ended in the removal of Captain Marchand's gallant little force. For a time there was talk of war in London and Paris, but as Wingate said in a letter to his wife, 'For England and France to quarrel over a mud fort in a swamp was futile.' Britain, having the most might on the scene, carried the day, but in deference to French sensibilities Fashoda had its name changed to Kadok, and by this name it is still known. Although not shown on any map, there exists a small village about eight miles from Kadok that is called Fashoda. The chief of the Shilluks lives there.

It is doubtless foolhardy to predict the future of such an unpredictable country as the Sudan, but Mahdism has proved durable as both a religious and a political concept. At the time of writing (1967) the Mahdi's Umma party has become the main political force, and today a grandson of the Mahdi rules over the land of his grandfather.

Glossary of Arabic and Sudanese Words

angareb – A low bed consisting of a wooden frame laced with leather thongs.

ardeb – A unit of capacity in many Islamic countries. The amount varies from place to place, however. In the Sudan at this time about 5½ bushels.

ashraf – The name given to the relatives of the Mahdi.

asida – Sorghum (durra) mixed with water and made into a paste over which is poured a strong sauce of spices and peppers. A staple dish in the Sudan, eaten with meat or milk.

Baggara – Cattle-owning Arab tribes living mostly in southern Darfur and southern Kordofan.

bazingers – Armed slaves, usually Blacks from the southern Sudan who were trained to use fire-arms and fight as soldiers. They were the main strength of the slave hunters.

beia – The Mahdi's oath of allegiance.

Beit el Mal – Storehouse and treasury. In the Mahdist government this housed slaves, animals, furniture and anything else of value. There were several of these, located in all the principal towns.

Blacks – Hamiticized Negroes from the southern Sudan. Nilotes.

curbash – A whip, usually made of rhinoceros hide.

Dongolawi (pl. *Donagla*) – A native of Dongola and its vicinity.

durra – A kind of millet (*sorghum vulgare*). It was, and still is, the staple food crop of the Sudan.

emir – A chieftain.

farda – Cotton or woollen shawl.

Fellata – West African pilgrims working their way across the Sudan to Mecca.

gellabas or *jellaba* – Itinerant merchants, traders, usually in slaves. Many kept armed slaves as retainers. Most came from the Nile valley and among the Arabs of the western Sudan the name was synonymous with a Nile valley native.

imam – A Muslim priest or anyone who is considered an authority on theology or Islamic law.

jebel – A hill or mountain.

jibba – A patched, shirt-like garment worn by the Dervishes.

jihad or *jehad* – In Islam, a religious war against unbelievers.

kadi – In the Sudan during the Mahdiya the word meant simply 'judge'.

khor – A dry watercourse.

Mahdiya – The period when the Sudan was ruled by the Mahdi and the Khalifa, 1885–98.

Mudiria – A district, ruled by a mudir. Also, the building or buildings which constituted the headquarters for the district's governor; government house of the district.

muezzin – In Islam, the man who calls the faithful to prayer.

mulazem (pl. *mulazemin*) – A combination servant, bodyguard and courtier serving the Khalifa or the Mahdi.

muslimaniya – Former Christians who have renounced Christianity for Islam.

Nubia – Egyptian Kosh; biblical Cush; Arabic Bilad el Barabra. This is the desert and steppe-land between Khartoum and Aswan, an area of about 22,000 miles. It forms a broad hyphen between Egypt and the Sudan.

ombeÿa – A horn made from an elephant's tusk.

ratib – A small book of sayings of the Mahdi, which largely replaced the Koran itself during the Mahdiya.

rekuba – A light hut consisting of poles supporting a roof of matting and palm leaves.

shebba (*shayba*) – A forked stick which was fastened to the neck of slaves to prevent their escape.

sirdar – Commander-in-chief. Here, the head of the Egyptian army.

Turkiya – The period of Egyptian rule in the Sudan, 1821–85.

ulema – General term for religious leaders.

Umm Hagar – Literally, 'stone house'. This was the name given the house inside the prison zariba at Omdurman that acted as a common cell in which the prisoners were locked up at night.

zariba – Thorn bushes placed for protection around a temporary camp.

Manuscript Sources

Diary of Abbas Bey in the Library of the University of Khartoum.

The War Office Library contains:

FFF 1–106	Dairy of the Frontier Field Force
FFF 107–127 and 166–249	Staff Diary and Intelligence Report of the Frontier Field Force
GMRES (1890) and GMRES (1891)	General Military Report on the Egyptian Sudan. Intelligence Division, War Office, London.

The British Museum possesses a number of letters from Gordon, Slatin, Emin Pasha and Gladstone:

Add. MS 33222
Add. MSS 34474–34479
Add. MS 40665
Add. MS 41340, ff. 6–60b
Add. MS 42181, f. 73
Add. MSS 44147, f. 11, and 44629, ff. 71, 73 and 192
Add. MSS 44768, ff. 15–91 *passim* and 44769, ff. 15–85 *passim*.

The School of Oriental Studies of the University of Durham holds the papers of Sir Reginald Wingate and of Slatin Pasha.

Selected Bibliography

NEWSPAPERS

Fortnightly
Nineteenth Century
Pall Mall Gazette
Punch
Sudan Notes and Records
The Graphic
The Times
Westminster Gazette

BOOKS

ALFORD, H. S. L. and SWORD, W. DENNISTOUN. *The Egyptian Soudan – Its Loss and Recovery*. London, Macmillan, 1898.

ARCHER, SIR GEOFFREY. *Personal and Historical Memoirs of an East African Administrator*. Published for the author by Oliver & Boyd, Edinburgh and London, 1963.

ARCHER, THOMAS. *The War in Egypt and the Sudan*. London, Blackie, 1887.

ARKELL, A. J. *A History of the Sudan to A.D. 1821*. London, Athlone Press, 1955.

ARNOLD, SIR THOMAS and GUILLAUME ALFRED, eds. *The Legacy of Islam*. Oxford University Press, 1931.

ARTHUR, SIR GEORGE, ed. *The Letters of Lord and Lady Wolseley*. New York, Doubleday, Page, 1922.

— *Life of Lord Kitchener*. 3 vols. London, Macmillan, 1920.

ATTERIDGE, A. HILLARD. *Towards Khartoum*. London, A. D. Innes, 1897.

BARBOUR, K. M. *The Republic of the Sudan*. London, Athlone Press, 1961.

BENNETT, E. N. *The Downfall of the Dervishes*. London, Methuen, 1899.

BLUNT, WILFRID SCAWEN. *My Diaries*. Part One (1888–1900). New York, Knopf, 1922.

— *Secret History of the English Occupation of Egypt*. New York, Knopf, 1922.

— *Gordon at Khartoum*. New York, Stephen Swift, 1911.

BRACKENBURY, HENRY. *The River Column*. Edinburgh and London, Blackwood, 1885.

BURLEIGH, BENNET. *Khartoum Campaign 1898; Re-Conquest of the Sudan*. London, Chapman and Hall, 1899.

CALVILE, H. E. *History of the Sudan Campaign.* (Official publication, compiled in the Intelligence Division of the War Office.) 2 vols. H.M. Stationery Office, n.d. (1889 or 1890).

CASATI, GAETANO. *Ten Years in Equatoria.* 2 vols. trans. by J. Randolph Clay and I. Walter Landor. London, Frederick Warne, 1891.

CHURCHILL, WINSTON S. *My Early Life.* London, Cassell, 1930; Fontana Books, 1959.

— *The River War.* London, Eyre & Spottiswoode, 1899; Landsborough Publications, 1960.

COATES, THOMAS F. G. *Hector MacDonald.* London, S. W. Partridge & Co., 1900.

COLBORNE, J. *With Hicks Pasha in the Soudan.* London, Smith, Elder, 1884.

COLLINS, ROBERT O. *The Southern Sudan, 1883–1898.* Yale University Press, 1962.

CRABITÈS, PIERRE. *Gordon, the Sudan and Slavery.* London, George Routledge, 1933.

— *Americans in the Egyptian Army.* London, George Routledge, 1938.

CROMER, EARL OF. *Modern Egypt.* 2 vols. New York, Macmillan Co., 1908.

DARLEY, HENRY. *Slaves and Ivory.* London, Witherby, 1926.

DAVIES, REGINALD. *The Camel's Back.* London, Murray, 1957

Directory of the Republic of the Sudan 1960. London, The Diplomatic Press and Publishing Co., 1960.

DUGMORE, A. RADCLYFFE. *The Vast Sudan.* London, Arrowsmith, 1924.

FARWELL, BYRON. *Burton.* London, Longmans, 1963.

— *The Man Who Presumed.* New York, Henry Holt, 1957

GORDON, C. G. *The Journals of Major-Gen. C. G. Gordon, C.B. at Khartoum.* London, Kegan Paul, 1885.

GRAY, RICHARD. *A History of the Southern Sudan 1838–1889.* Oxford University Press, 1961.

GROGAN, E. S. and SHARP, A. H. *From the Cape to Cairo.* London, Hurst & Blackett, 1900.

GUNTHER, JOHN. *Inside Africa.* New York, Harper, 1953.

HANSON, LAWRENCE and HANSON, ELIZABETH. *Chinese Gordon – The Story of a Hero.* New York, Funk & Wagnalls, 1954.

HENDERSON, K. D. D. *The Making of the Modern Sudan.* London, Faber, 1953.

HILL, RICHARD. *Egypt in the Sudan 1820–1881.* Oxford University Press, 1959.

— *Slatin Pasha.* Oxford University Press, 1965.

— *A Bibliography of the Anglo-Egyptian Sudan from the Earliest Times to 1937.* Oxford, London, 1939.

HITTI, PHILIP K. *History of the Arabs from the Earliest Times to the Present.* London, Macmillan, 1964.

HOLT, P. M. *A Modern History of the Sudan.* New York, Grove Press, 1961.
— *The Mahdist State in the Sudan 1881–1898.* Oxford University Press, 1958.
HYSLOP, JOHN. *Sudan Story.* London, The Naldrett Press, 1952.
ISHAQ, IBN. *The Life of Muhammad,* edited by Michael Edwards. London, The Folio Society, 1964.
JACKSON, H. C. *Behind the Modern Sudan.* London, Macmillan, 1955.
— *The Fighting Sudanese.* London, Macmillan, 1954.
JAMES, F. L. *The Wild Tribes of the Soudan.* New York, Dodd, Mead, 1883.
The Koran, translated by George Sale. London, Frederick Warne, n.d.
KUMM, H. KARL W. *The Sudan.* London, Marshall Bros, n.d.
LONGFORD, ELIZABETH. *Victoria R.I.* London, Weidenfeld & Nicolson, 1964.
MACMICHAEL, SIR HAROLD. *The Anglo-Egyptian Sudan.* London, Faber, 1934.
— *The Tribes of Northern and Central Kordofan.*
MAGNUS, PHILIP. *Kitchener; Portrait of an Imperialist.* London, Murray, 1958.
— *Gladstone.* London, Murray, 1954.
MANDOUR EL-MAHDI. *Short History of the Sudan.* Oxford University Press, 1965.
MANN, ANTHONY. *Where God Laughed.* London, Museum Press, 1954.
MAXWELL, J. LOWRY. *Half a Century of Grace.* London, Sudan United Mission, n.d.
MEEK, C. K. *A Sudanese Kingdom.* London, Kegan Paul, 1931.
MIDDLETON, DOROTHY. *Baker of the Nile.* London, Falcon Press, 1949.
MILNER, ALFRED. *England in Egypt.* London, Edward Arnold, 1892.
MOOREHEAD, ALAN. *The White Nile.* London, Hamish Hamilton, 1960.
NEUFELD, CHARLES. *A Prisoner of the Khaleefa.* New York, Putnam, 1899.
OHRWALDER, FATHER JOSEPH. *Ten Years' Captivity in the Mahdi's Camp 1882–1892,* trans. by F. R. Wingate. London, Sampson Low, 1893.
PETHERICK, JOHN. *Egypt, The Soudan and Central Africa.* Edinburgh and London, Blackwood, 1861.
POPE-HENNESSY, JAMES. *Monckton Milnes; The Flight of Youth.* London, Constable, 1951.
POWER, FRANK. *Letters From Khartoum Written During the Siege.* London, Sampson Low, 1885.
ROBINSON, RONALD and GALLAGHER, JOHN, with DENNY, ALICE. *Africa and the Victorians; The Official Mind of Imperialism.* London, Macmillan, 1961.
ROYLE, CHARLES. *The Egyptian Campaigns 1882–1885,* new and rev. edn, continued to December 1899. London, Hurst and Blackett, 1900.
RUSSELL, HENRY. *The Ruin of the Soudan.* London, Sampson Low, 1892.

SAID, BESHIR MOHAMMED. *The Sudan, Crossroads of Africa*. London, The Bodley Head, 1965.

SCHWEINFURTH, G., RATZEL, F., FELKIN, R. W. and HARTLAUB, G. eds. *Emin Pasha in Central Africa*, trans. by Mrs R. W. Felkin. New York, Dodd, Mead & Co., 1889.

SELIGMAN, C. G. *Races of Africa*. Oxford University Press, 1957.

SHIBEIKA, MEKKI. *British Policy in the Sudan 1882–1902*. Oxford University Press, 1952.

SLATIN, RUDOLF C. *Fire and Sword in the Sudan*, trans. by F. R. Wingate. London, Edward Arnold, 1896.

STEEVENS, G. W. *With Kitchener to Khartoum*. New York, Dodd, Mead & Co., 1899.

STRACHEY, LYTTON. *Eminent Victorians*. London, Chatto and Windus, 1918.

Sudan Almanac. Government Printing Press, Khartoum, 1963.

SYMONS, JULIAN. *England's Pride*. London, Hamish Hamilton, 1965.

TAYLOR, DON. *The British in Africa*. London, Robert Hale, 1962.

THEOBALD, A. B. *The Mahdiya; A History of the Sudan, 1881–1899*. London, Longmans, 1951.

— *Ali Dinar, Last Sultan of Darfur 1898–1916*. London, Longmans, 1965.

TOYNBEE, ARNOLD, *Between Niger and Nile*. Oxford University Press, 1965.

TRIMINGHAM, J. S. *Islam in the Sudan*. London, Frank Cass, 1965.

WHYTE, FREDERIC. *The Life of W. T. Stead*. 2 vols. New York, Houghton Mifflin, n.d.

WILSON, SIR CHARLES W. *From Korti to Khartum*. Edinburgh and London, Blackwood, 1886.

WINGATE, F. R. *Mahdiism and the Egyptian Sudan*. London, Macmillan, 1891.

WINGATE, SIR RONALD. *Wingate of the Sudan*. London, Murray, 1955.

WOOD, SIR EVELYN. *From Midshipman to Field Marshal*. 2 vols. London, Methuen, 1906.

— *Winnowed Memories*. London, Cassell, 1914.

WRIGHT, H. C. S. *Soudan '96*. London, Horace Cox, 1897.

WYLDE, A. B. *'83 to '87 In the Sudan*. 2 vols. London, Remington, 1888.

ZETLAND, THE MARQUESS OF. *Lord Cromer*. London, Hodder & Stoughton, 1932.

Index

Index

Abba, 4, 7, 9; proclamation of Mahdi at, 11; Mahdi defeats Abu Saud's mission at, 13

Abbas Bey, 39–40, 42

Abbas, 92, 147

Abbas Hilmi II, 296–7

Abd al-Rahman Wad Nejumi, 90, 181, 248–50, 260

Abdel Kadir Pasha Hilmi, 15, 17, 21–2, 26, 35

Abdel Kerim, 168–9

Abderrahman ben Naga, 135

Abdul Shakour, Emir, 84, 86, 132–3

Abdullah Daffalah, 15

Abdullah Wad Ibrahim, 153

Abdullahi Ibn Sayed Mohammed, 13, 151, 176, 228, 271, 273–4, 274–5, 282, 315; swears allegiance to Mahdi, 9–10; as discoverer of Mahdi, 10–11; appointed khalifa, 17; controls central Sudan, 100; meeting with Slatin, 133–5; takes Slatin as his mulazem, 137; and Oliver Pain, 139–45; asks Slatin to decipher Gordon's note, 154–5; visits Slatin in prison, 159–60; takes Slatin as his slave, 161–4; gives Slatin a slave, 166; succeeds Mahdi, 167; establishes himself in power, 168–9, 172–5; suspicions of Slatin, 171–2, 183–7, 224–6; deals with revolts, 180–1; abortive attempt to invade Egypt, 181–2; orders death of Ibrahim Adlam, 182–3; quells Ashraf revolt, 185–7; sees Dilling missionaries, 189–91; attempts to convert missionaries, 196; qualities as ruler, 219; state of Sudan under, 220–4; writes to Queen Victoria, Khedive of Egypt and Sultan of Turkey, 219–20; and rivals, 224; interrogation of Neufeld, 252–3; and Neufeld, 255, 257–8; attempts to convert Neufeld, 263–4; asks Neufeld to make gunpowder, 267; orders his forces for battle of Omdurman, 303–4; death of, 318–19

Abu Anga, 45, 149–50, 151–3, 173, 174–5

Abu Girga, 43

Abu Hamed, 299; capture by Hunter, 300–1

Abu Klea, battle of, 95

Abu Saud, 66

Abyssinia, 68, 69–70, 74, 287

Abyssinian Expedition, 65

Afifi Wad Ahmed, Sheikh, 114, 122

Ahmed Abou Hawanein, 231, 272–3, 275, 276

Ahmed Arabi, 26

Ahmed Hassan, 207, 210–18

Ahmed Nur ed Din, 262–3

Ahmed Wad Ali, 135

Ahmed Wad Suleiman, 135, 166, 168, 267

Akasha, 298

Akila, 40–1

Al-Marabi, 33

Al-Senussi al Mahdi, 18, 22–3

Al Qurashi, *see* El Korashi

Ala al-Din Pasha Siddik, 35, 38, 39, 43

Alexandria, British bombardment, 26

DATE DUE